FROM FOGGY BOTTOM TO CAPITOL HILL

FROM FOGGY BOTTOM TO CAPITOL HILL

Exploits of a GI, Diplomat, and Congressional Aide

JOHN CHAPMAN CHESTER, SR.

Arlington Hall Press
Arlington, Virginia

ARLINGTON HALL PRESS
4000 Arlington Road
Arlington, Virginia 22204-1500

Arlington Hall Press is an imprint of the
Association for Diplomatic Studies and Training,
a nonprofit organization that promotes education
in international relations.

Printed in the United States of America

Cover Photo:
© Architect of the Capitol

Design and Production by
CONCEPT LLC
Irene Petrlik
Judith Giuliani

ISBN 0-9653949-1-3
Library of Congress Catalog Card Number: 99-97238

CONTENTS

Illustrations appear between pages 294 and 295

PREFACE

My maternal grandmother, Laura Chapman Miller, was a "grande dame," a poetess, and a major source of information about the family—not only the Chapman-Miller side but also the Chester side. Her memory was especially attuned to the details of events that occurred prior to the turn of the century. She died in 1960 at the age of 94.

Unhappily, my generation was too preoccupied with immediate problems and concerns to listen carefully and record her vast fund of information—most of which she took with her to the grave. In my own retirement, which began over a decade ago, I determined not to repeat that particular sin with respect to my own reservoir of knowledge (such as it is). For better or worse, what I did, learned, or experienced, at least in my professional life, will be preserved for the benefit of posterity.

This account of what I did in my public career is designed above all to entertain rather than instruct, although the two need not be mutually exclusive. It is not a policy document, an apologia, or an explanation of my impact on major historical events—despite ample substantive context. Mainly, however, this story recounts a professional life in an assortment of roles between 1953 and 1986. I believe that those who have the courage and persistence to read the whole book will agree that I have had the distinct advantage of a *varied* career.

The appendices are documents of my authorship that may be of interest primarily to researchers one or two generations down the road who wish to focus on Africa (Malawi in particular) as it was in 1969–70 and the history of the interparliamentary exchange mechanism. While I am presumptuous enough to believe that this material is of substantive value, I do not require any of my family or friends to feel obliged to wade through it.

No one asked me to undertake this project or contributed to its original preparation. However, without the acceptance and encouragement of Margery Boichel Thompson, publishing coordinator for the Association for Diplomatic Studies and Training, and the detailed guidance of a talented editor, G. Harvey Summ, these recollections might never have made it to publication.

Therefore, this book is dedicated to both of them, as well as to my eventual readers, who have the advantage of bearing no responsibility for its contents.

JOHN CHAPMAN CHESTER, SR.

From Foggy Bottom to Capitol Hill

PART I

INTRODUCTION

CHAPTER 1

Preparing for a Career in Foreign Affairs

As the lion observed
to the beveled giraffe:
My, I am served
By a high-level staff!

But if you have heard
That at times they can bungle,
Please get out the word
From the king of the jungle:

(Who may, it is said,
Be both candid and balky) —
That still you are led
By the man from Milwaukee!

This is my poem and I am from Milwaukee, but I am not this "man from Milwaukee." He was Clement Zablocki, former chairman of the Committee on Foreign Affairs of the U.S. House of Representatives. Zablocki was a mentor of mine on the committee, on whose staff I served for the last fifteen years of my professional career. He was also the second of three Democratic chairmen under whom I served as a Republican protégé of my friend and another mentor, Rep. Peter Frelinghuysen of New Jersey. More personally, Clem

Zablocki was the product of a Polish immigrant, working-class family from the south side of Milwaukee.

I, on the other hand, started my life as a child of privilege. An ancestor, also named John Chester, fought at the Battle of Bunker Hill. Another was the founder of Wisconsin's first department store. But from childhood I began to rebel against my privileged background and was determined to make it on my own. How I triumphed over my background, how in my forties I met Clem Zablocki, and how, as the "poet laureate" of the Foreign Affairs Committee, I came to write this poem and others like it are the principal themes of these memoirs.

EARLY LIFE

I was born in Milwaukee on January 2, 1930, the youngest of four children. I was always a happy, even a happy-go-lucky, perhaps somewhat mischievous child. I always found it easy to make friends. My youth was in all respects a privileged one. As long as I can remember, I wanted to make my own way independently. At the same time, I acknowledge the substantial benefits I derived from my upbringing, particularly the education and travel opportunities they afforded me.

I had two older brothers and a sister. Until I was twelve, we lived—unlike most of Milwaukee's "gentry"—not far from downtown, in an undistinguished but very large and comfortable brown wooden house, in a neighborhood that tended to deteriorate with each passing year. I used to brag to my contemporaries that I lived, during the week at least, in the "slums of Knapp Street." The house was located in an area considered fashionable in the last century, on a street just behind my grandmother's historic mansion overlooking Juneau Park. Frank Lloyd Wright's son once commented that the mansion should be eternally preserved as a prime example of the "excesses of Victorian architecture." Our "town house" was more than adequate for our purposes and had a large backyard with a toboggan slide, which abutted my grandmother's property.

Summers and weekends we spent on our country estate located on an inland lake about thirty miles west of Milwaukee.

In 1942 my parents gave up on downtown living and moved north to posh Shorewood, where we occupied a large five-bedroom stone house above Lake Michigan. It had two maid's rooms. A caretaker—and his wife, who worked in our kitchen—lived in an apartment above the garage. The house had an elevator, which we reactivated after my father's first heart attack. This house could be considered more elegant, but it was no larger or more comfortable than the one on Knapp Street (later a sorority house for the University of Wisconsin's Milwaukee campus).

My father, William Merrill Chester, was a Milwaukee native (as was my mother), the son of the pastor of Immanuel Presbyterian Church, located just a block away from my grandmother's historic mansion. The Chesters all started out in Connecticut but managed to migrate west to Wisconsin at some point. (My grandfather reversed the trend: he must have been the only Presbyterian minister in the midwest who ended up as a stock broker in New York City.) Although he began his career as a lawyer, my father became president of the T. A. Chapman Company, Milwaukee's leading department store, originally founded by my maternal great-grandfather, Timothy Appleton Chapman, in 1857. (In a recurring pattern, by sheer coincidence Chapman sons-in-law rather than sons ran the family business, up to and including my generation.)

My mother, Alice Chapman Miller, was, like her mother, one of Milwaukee's "grande dames." Her scope extended beyond Wisconsin; she was, for example, Vice President of the Girl Scouts of America, and subsequently President of "Our Chalet" in Adelboden, Switzerland (one of four World Centers of the international Girl Scouts/Girl Guides movement). Camp Alice Chester in Wisconsin is named for her. She was also founder of the Junior League of Wisconsin. During the early postwar years, when my siblings were in graduate school or otherwise preoccupied, I often traveled in Europe with my father while my mother attended Girl Scout conventions.

An incident that occurred when I was nine illustrates both my family background and the way I challenged it, sometimes awkwardly. I remember it so well because the date was September 1, 1939, the day Germany invaded Poland, and my family (after a three-week pack trip in eastern Oregon) was having dinner with ex-President and Mrs. Herbert Hoover at their home in California. My mother and Mrs. Hoover were close friends through their work with the Girl Scouts. Mr. Hoover was called to the phone three times, each time to be briefed by President Roosevelt, and each time he returned looking gloomier and ever more depressed. The atmosphere was lugubrious, and hardly anyone spoke except for Mr. Hoover.

I had been seated between my two brothers, who were supposed to keep me from doing anything gauche. They failed. When blueberry pie, a dessert I disliked, was served, I tried to do the courteous thing: I placed my linen napkin firmly on top of the pie, to keep my dislike of it hidden. The maid lifted up the napkin, with pie attached, and it splattered all over the tablecloth. My mother blanched: my family was humiliated, but tensions had reached such a level that a moment of comic relief was welcome. Everyone (except my parents) laughed, including Mr. Hoover, who had not smiled once up to that point. Fortunately, Mrs. Hoover, a lovely and thoughtful lady, saved the day: "It has been a long day for you, my dear," she remarked, putting her hands on my shoulder. "How would you like to go outside and play with the dogs?" (She had a full kennel of Norwegian elkhounds.) My response was in the enthusiastic affirmative!

The family moved in similar circles abroad. In the late 1980s I met Princess Margaret at a reception at the Court of St. James's following dedication of a Girl Scout–Girl Guide hostel in a London suburb. (My mother's name was engraved on a plaque near the main entrance, along with other scouting leaders.) All major contributors to the facility, including my sister, representing our family, were honored and presented with certificates of appreciation by Princess Benedikte of Denmark. To my astonishment, Princess Margaret well remembered details of a story I told her of a similar ceremony in 1950 at Oxford, where she, my mother, and other dignitaries were honored while my father and I stood on a nearby hill.

Education

My primary and secondary education was at the exclusive all-male Milwaukee Country Day School. Our female counterpart was the Milwaukee Downer Seminary, where I often attended black-tie dances. However, on Friday nights, together with my more venturesome Day School classmates, I often picked up girls from the wrong side of the tracks at a dance hall in the basement of a Catholic church which would bring in under one roof all the wayward adolescents who might otherwise be on the street. In my case, it was an exciting exposure to a world I had never known and a clandestine act of rebellion.

Upon graduation from the Milwaukee Country Day School in 1947, I was accepted at Princeton but was considered too young and immature to go to college. Under the course distribution system, I would have had to pass a science requirement at Princeton. The dean of admissions, a close friend of my father's, persuaded him that I was weak in science. (I was not only weak, but had successfully avoided taking any.)

My family arranged for me to go to the Phillips Exeter Academy in New Hampshire for a postgraduate year. It turned out to be the best academic year of my life. When I walked into Exeter in the fall of 1947, I knew not one student, but I soon made lifelong friendships (some of those friends went with me to Princeton). Exeter may be a prep school, but it was run like a college, and the professors were mostly superior to those one is exposed to in the first two years at an Ivy League institution. My only regret was that I only spent one year there. (My two sons compensated for that failure by each spending three years as Exonians.)

My first two years at Princeton, where all male Chesters had gone for several generations, were devoted primarily to social and extracurricular activities. I was on three freshman teams, crew, hockey and lacrosse. I subsequently joined an eating club and became engrossed in a theater group, the Théatre Intime, and eventually the Triangle Club (the musical comedy counterpart of Harvard's Hasty Pudding Club). Incidentally, by the fall of 1948 psychology had been classified as a science, so my year of basic chemistry at Exeter was superfluous.

NASSAU HERALD 1952

JOHN CHAPMAN CHESTER
Chips, Chestie

January 2, 1930   Milwaukee, Wis.

Father: William M. Chester, Princeton '13
Mother: Alice Chapman Miller

Exeter (was also graduated from Milwaukee Country Day School): Football, Hockey, Tennis, Track Mgr., Glee Club, Rifle Club, Student Council.

Princeton Activities: English; Ivy Club; Hockey 1; Triangle Club 4; Theatre Intime 3; Chicago Club 1, 2, 3, 4; Princeton Hunt Club (Pres.); Sons of '13; Club hockey. Roommates senior year: Thomas S. Knight, Douglas L. Goldman, and Chauncey C. Loomis. Plans graduate work in English at Princeton or Columbia; expects to serve in the U. S. Army Field Artillery following graduation. Future is probably in Business or Publication. Presbyterian.

Permanent Address: 3590 North Lake Drive, Milwaukee, Wis.

Only in my junior year at Princeton, when I began my major in English and German literature, did I become seriously involved in academic life. As usual, however, I did just enough work to get by. In those days a C or C+ was considered a "gentleman's grade" and most of us aspired to little else, as a C average was sufficient to get one into graduate school, if desired. (A B was an honors grade and a B+ high honors. I didn't know anyone who received an A with any regularity.) My senior thesis, on the influence of Goethe on the Victorian novelists, was written in three weeks, although it was supposed to have represented an entire year's work. The B- awarded by the German Department (C+ by the English Department) was actually more than the product was worth. On another occasion, I received an A+ on a paper written between Sunday midnight and 3:00 A.M. on the night before it was due. That achievement was somewhat diminished by the intelligence I received some two weeks later that the professor had been taken in a straightjacket, ranting and raving, to a mental institution. In any case, writing under pressure (often self-created) turned out to be a valuable skill in my later professional career, particularly in my work on the Hill.

Even so, on Class Day, just prior to graduation, I got 80 percent of the vote for the honor of "most unconscious" member of the class of 1952 (Dick Kazmeier, Heisman trophy winner that year, got only 60 percent of the vote for best athlete). I may have qualified for this honor in part because I once took a final exam in, got a grade of B- in, and received credit for, the wrong psychology course. Apparently I had done so little work in the course that I did not even recognize I was in the wrong exam room. As it turned out, I managed to guess right on a multiple-choice test. Still, this Class Day distinction was not exactly a harbinger for a successful later career!

ARMY ENLISTED MAN

Given my early background, my entry onto the public payroll via a two-year tour in the army was a transcendent event that helped me, in ways I never could have foreseen, to forge a professional career on my own. My basic training as an enlisted man, a sharp contrast with my sheltered background, gave me an understanding of American life that I never could have acquired as an officer. The rest of my army service, in Germany, proved an apprenticeship for my professional foreign affairs career.

Introduction to the army began in a chow line at Camp Kilmer, New Jersey, at approximately 5:00 A.M. on a cold overcast day, some time in late January 1953. Kilmer was then known as a "repo-depot," or a kind of over-size pen in which to hold large numbers of new recruits pending reassignment to basic training sites. The temporary nature of the quarters made them unusually depressing—even for an army base—and contrasted starkly with the fashionable Weisses Rössl Hotel in Kitzbühel in the Austrian Tyrol, where I had stayed just seven days previously on a skiing vacation. (Among that hotel's special attributes was a local bartender who had been taught by Tyrone Power how to make a "super-American" martini.)

Back to Camp Kilmer. I had just turned twenty-three. Unlike other recruits in the chow line, I held the exalted rank of private first class, having been assigned for two years to an army reserve unit based in Trenton, New Jersey. When the Korean War broke out in 1950, I had completed my sophomore year in college, and it was too late for the ROTC (Reserve Officers Training Corps). Consequently, together with classmates in the same category, I signed up for enlisted reserve duty until graduation—at which time we were told we would all go off to war "together." When graduation arrived, however, the rules had changed, and we were all classified as individually draftable. Hence, to keep my one stripe, I applied for extended active duty for two years (the same period assigned to a draftee). Everything in life, I discovered, is relative. Private first class may not sound like much to the casual reader, but it was considerably preferable to the bottom grades of privates E-1 and E-2.

From Camp Kilmer we were sent to the Indiantown Gap Military Reservation near Harrisburg, Pennsylvania (also near Pennsylvania Dutch country), for four months of infantry (heavy weapons) basic training. As army bases go, the Gap was unusually picturesque: the barracks were all painted white instead of olive drab, and the base was nestled in a valley surrounded by mountainous terrain. The scenery, we discovered, had something to do with our assignment: for the first time during the Korean War, an entire division (the Fifth "Red Diamond" Division)—consisting largely of recruits trained at the Gap—was to be sent directly to the front lines following basic. For that reason, our training turned out to be unusually rigorous—with much night work and climbs up and over a mountain called Old Baldy (named for the original in Korea). As time passed, therefore, some of the mountains began to lose their charm.

We arrived from Kilmer by bus at about 2:00 A.M. one evening in January. It was pitch-dark and bitterly cold, and a sergeant announced that we had exactly two hours to sleep before falling out on the company street. He and his colleagues in the training cadre then ensured this result by dumping all the bodies off the cots onto the floor at 4:00 A.M. Despite my somewhat comatose state at the time, I vaguely recall having been appointed "platoon leader"—primarily because I was just about the only one in the barracks who could speak English. My platoon, I discovered, consisted mainly of Puerto Ricans who had recently left their native island for New York's Harlem district, only to be drafted soon after arrival. Most of them were desperately poor, small of stature, and both physically and mentally unprepared for army life. On the other hand, anyone who was actually *prepared* for basic training was probably a psychopath of one kind or another.

When we fell out on the company street, all of the platoon leaders shouted (into the total darkness): ALL PRESENT AND ACCOUNTED FOR, SIR! So when it came my turn, I said the same thing. It seemed like the right thing to do! Then we turned right-face and went off on a twenty-six mile forced march over to the mountains and back. When the sun finally arose, I discovered that at least half of my platoon were missing, and I was thereupon relieved of my "command."

Despite a somewhat rocky start, things worked out well between me and the Puerto Ricans in my platoon. The biggest problem was the language barrier, which inhibited the learning process. It was particularly difficult to teach them to keep their rifles pointed downrange, instead of at the instructor. And they had a disconcerting habit of throwing bayonets around the barracks indiscriminately, just to see how close they could come to a "buddy" without hitting him!

Aside from the Puerto Ricans, one character stood out from the crowd and remains forever etched on my fading memory. He was a large ungainly young black man from Newark, New Jersey, named (actually) Alexander Graham Bell. There is simply no other way to describe Bell than to say he was a classic "f--k-up"—but with a unique sense of humor and style. On the day we were first ordered to line up in platoon formation on the company street, Bell showed up with bright argyle socks folded over his boots and a loud pink tie with a naked lady as the primary "theme." When he squeezed a rubber plunger in his right-hand pocket, it would light up with the words, "Kiss me in the dark, baby." The first sergeant was livid with rage and his face turned crimson, except for his nose, which displayed purple veins: "GODDAMMIT BELL," he finally managed to blurt, "YOU'RE OUT OF YOUR GODDAM UNIFORM!" "Well, sarge," the private E-1 responded, "I've got *on* my full uniform; only I thought I'd just dress it up a little."

For this sin Bell was assigned KP (kitchen police) for a full month. The frustrating thing about Private Bell, however, was that he liked KP. He may have been deficient in education (he could not learn his general orders—and never even tried), but he liked to ride out on the back of the mess truck at lunchtime and wave to the rest of us, who were on another forced march. He was, in fact, crazy like a fox. One quote of his remained with me throughout my government career. We both happened to be on KP together, although my assignment was temporary, while his was permanent. We were scraping the contents of chow trays into trash buckets outside the mess hall in about fifteen-degree weather. Specifically, we were separating cans from paper and food and placing each in the proper receptacle. To say the least, this was hard on the hands, which began to freeze up. As all soldiers manage to do under such circumstances, I eventually started bitching about the whole deal. "Hold on, Chester," Bell countered. "Just think of it this way: you're learning a useful trade!"

There is a fundamental truth about army life, especially during basic training, namely, "Misery loves company." Nothing is more essential to an individual soldier's morale than the ability and opportunity to complain vociferously into a sympathetic ear. About a week after my arrival at the Gap and following my less-than-successful leadership of the Puerto Ricans, two new recruits, Don Reiss and Dan Perovich, were transferred into my barracks and immediately became my best buddies. Both were eloquent in dissecting, analyzing, and then rejecting every aspect of military life. It made all the rigors of basic that much more bearable. Dan in particular could describe the current condition of his body in such vivid terms, complete with appropriate gestures and grunts, that it immediately touched a sympathetic chord in a listener's sore frame. Don's criticism was somewhat more cerebral (he was to become president and first in his class at NYU Dental School) but less graphic. Their expressions of distaste, however, were highly articulate, effective, and well received by the English-speaking occupants of our barracks.

Dan's apparent inability to adjust to army life amazed me: he was strong, powerfully built, and used to considerable physical exertion. His civilian jobs had included one as a high-tension-wire repairman, who often arose at 5:00 A.M. to undertake his duties. One would have thought basic training would have been a breeze for someone with this background. On the contrary, Dan was most resistant to military discipline. "I don't mind getting up at 4:00 or 5:00 A.M.," he used to say, "but I can't stand being awakened by that dumb f-----g sergeant blowing on that f-----g *whistle*." I think being ordered around by people he considered inferior (they were) bothered him the most. By contrast, Don and I never had any other expectations. Basic training was pretty much what we had anticipated.

Despite the regimentation and discipline, for many recruits in Company L the army also represented an improvement in their standard of living. All soldiers received "three squares and a sack," clothing, and medical and dental care—some apparently for the first time in their young lives. This was particularly true of a small number of white boys from the hill country of Kentucky or Tennessee. (Just how they happened to be assigned to a company almost exclusively composed of New Jersey and New York residents remains a mystery—as it was to the training cadre.)

One young lad (who was only seventeen and had probably lied about his age) had evidently volunteered for service to escape his Dogpatch-like surroundings in the Kentucky mountains. He had clearly never before in his life seen a dentist. His teeth, it turned out, were all black and rotted to the core. The dental officer who examined him decided to *pull* his uppers and lowers *en masse* and start over with two new bridges. For a week or so, of course, he was unintelligible—but that was nothing unusual. When he finally received his new "bridges," I noticed that they seemed to float around in his mouth without being attached to either gum. Finally, one day a full colonel appeared in our barracks—with a large retinue of senior officers. There was much shouting of AT-TEN-SHUN! The colonel asked for Private "Yokum" (not his real name) and explained good-naturedly that there had been a mix-up: the colonel had received the private's teeth and vice versa. After the exchange was made, "Yokum's" mouth, diction, and morale improved enormously.

This small incident also taught me another valuable principle about the military hierarchy: the higher the rank (generally speaking), the easier the guy. For a brief period I became a driver for a major, who could not have been more considerate or generous—even though he rarely had any idea of what was going on below battalion level. In the army, at least, the worst offenders were people who are bucking for first lieutenant or sergeant!

In retrospect, however, I have no doubt that basic training was a valuable experience—a necessary evil, perhaps, but vital preparation for combat. We learned a good deal—not merely how to shoot an M-1 rifle and carbine, a recoilless rifle and mortar, but also how to survive nights on top of Baldy Mountain at below zero temperatures. The trick was how to take *off* your clothes under such conditions and wrap up with another body in a blanket. Once I drew Alexander Graham Bell as a partner. If it is cold enough, sensibilities along this line or tendencies toward bigotry rapidly disappear. The quickest way to freeze up "solid" is to sleep with your fatigues and boots on. In this respect, there is no substitute for personal experience.

When basic ended, I must admit, I was in the best condition of my twenty-three years (or thereafter). I even recall running down a mountain and across a fifteen-mile valley with a rifle and sixty-pound pack on my back without getting winded. Despite their complaints, Dan and Don were in the same shape—and all three of us were *prepared* to take on the "gooks" in Korea (whether inclined to or not).

Although we had long since resigned ourselves to heading for the Korean battlefield as a division, a funny thing happened on the way to the war: the war *ended* (about two weeks before basic training did), and the entire division was broken up and reassigned to other areas of the world. When we boarded the U.S. troopship *SS General Sturgis* in New York harbor, we were still uncertain of our ultimate destination. (A last-minute rumor had it that we were headed for the Pacific via the Panama Canal.) After a day at sea, however, it became evident that we were heading for Germany.

Assignment to Germany

Compared to first-class on the *Queen Elizabeth*, an army troopship leaves much to be desired. That is especially true if one is assigned to the KP compartment. (It was the only time in the military that I volunteered unsuccessfully for latrine duty.) At one point we passed through the outer edge of a hurricane, and the motor was turned way down, if not off. We plunged down and then up for some twenty-four hours, during which period most of the passengers became violently ill. That did not stop them from going to chow, however, so there was no time off for the KPs.

At one point in the voyage, I received a false alarm about a possible assignment that might get me off KP: a friend of mine, Lt. (USAF) John Wilkerson (with whom I had served in the Experiment in International Living in Vienna in 1949) was a fellow passenger. When we met (somewhat surreptitiously because of rules about officer-enlisted fraternization), John told me that the Troop Information and Education (TI&E) officer, an army captain, planned to gather all German-speaking personnel in a specified area at 1:00 P.M. the following day to conduct German classes for the rank and file. The idea was merely to keep everyone occupied aboard ship and out of trouble, not to undertake any grammatical instruction. My friend assumed, quite accurately, that very few people would hear or understand the announcement, and consequently I might be selected for the project.

At the appointed hour I found the room filled with German-speaking GIs, most of whom had just immigrated to the United States and were then drafted. Their problem, by and large, was not German but *English*. Although no one had heard anything on the "bitch box" (the PA system), word had gotten around. Finally the TI&E captain arrived and passed out training manuals. "Well," he said, "I'm glad that so many of you speak the Dutch." "Ja," one private responded, "but Herr Hauptmann (captain), wir sprechen *deutsch*, not *Dutch*. These *Buchen* are in ze *Dutch* language!" The captain blanched. "You mean there is a difference? Well, give me back the books and I'll look into it. They didn't tell me that in New York.

That'll be all, men, for today. I'll let you know what to do in due course."

Thus ended the German instruction program. The captain was so embarrassed about the manuals that he dropped the subject entirely. When John queried him about the "program" during dinner in the officers' mess, the captain was evasive and indicated only that a few "snags" had developed. It goes without saying that I returned to KP. It is perhaps a supreme irony that on my eventual return to the United States aboard the troopship *SS Gen. Harry Taylor*, I had risen to the exalted rank of sergeant. No longer vulnerable for KP duties, I was named "mess sergeant" of the entire ship—a much worse fate. That made me responsible for the whole chow operation and I never had a break between sittings.

Getting Out of the Infantry

The army base at Zweibrücken, where I was sent on arrival in Germany, was essentially the European version of Camp Kilmer, namely, a place for "casuals" to live temporarily until assigned elsewhere. A much more attractive environment than Kilmer, it was located on a hill near the German-French border. Zweibrücken's sole purpose was to provide incoming troops with a so-called "classification and assignment" interview. If one was a private first class (PFC) with a military occupational specialty (MOS) number designating "Infantry—heavy weapons," the interview normally lasted approximately ten seconds. This was called "pipeline," and it was a way of filling up infantry divisions in the field. While I didn't know much in the summer of 1953, I did realize that getting off "pipeline" was a major goal.

My interviewing "specialist" turned out to be another PFC like myself and from the same Princeton class. "What can you do besides shoot an M-1?" he asked in a tone of urgency. "I have a potential primary MOS as a German interpreter," I said, but that was less than useful—a whole shipload of German-Americans had just preceded me, and all of the interpreter positions were filled. "Go into the next room and take a typing test," he suggested. I did, and that is how I switched from the infantry to the military police. Within two days I was headed for Heidelberg with a fistful of orders designating me as a certified "clerk-typist." (In the army you always received about twenty-five copies of orders. The top one or two you used to get to wherever you were assigned; and the other twenty-three copies you threw away.)

Clerk-Typist in the Military Police

To my surprise, Heidelberg was still a relatively quaint, architecturally homogeneous university town, despite the overwhelming and stifling presence of the U.S. Army. The city still maintained a number of comfortable old-fashioned hotels and narrow winding thoroughfares; some historic buildings (including those originally connected with the university); venerable *gasthaüser* (pubs); and a large castle high upon a hill that dominated most postcard scenes of the area. Heidelberg had escaped destruction in two world wars and had last been attacked by the French during the Franco-Prussian War of 1870–71.

The headquarters of the United States Army, Europe (known as USAREUR) had been mercifully constructed some distance out of town. The complex consisted of numerous barracks, bachelor officers' quarters, and noncommissioned officers' and officers' clubs: in other words, what today would be termed "infrastructure." It was a world unto and of itself that could just as easily have been located in the continental United States. But it did serve one useful purpose: it kept the town proper from being overrun at all times by American servicemen (at least during working hours). At first the USAREUR "city" reminded me of that old canard about the fellow who entered the Pentagon as a private and finally became a major by the time he found his way *out*.

Within this cornucopia of modern construction, I found myself assigned to a small Criminal Investigation Detachment (CID), just down the hall from the provost

18

marshal (or chief military policeman) of all Europe. Suddenly Old Baldy seemed far away in terms of both distance and culture.

My typing skills consisted of a hunt-and-peck system, which has not changed much over the years and might be described as "substandard." It was more than adequate for my detachment, however, as speed was not a requirement. Cleanliness rather than productivity, it seems, was the main requirement: early on, I was warned that the provost marshal, a brigadier general, had a "thing" about dirty typewriters; if he found one, he would throw it out the window—and it was up to the clerk-typist to repair the machine. (Given my level of technical expertise, this would have been a disaster for me. Consequently I kept a tidy if slow-operating typewriter on my desk at all times.) The "morning report," a daily strength report showing where everyone in one's unit was on a given day, was my major responsibility, and getting the numbers right and into the right boxes on the form was the major challenge, not typing speed. The fact that I soon developed a reputation for competence and accuracy says something about the clerical demands of that office.

My memories of USAREUR headquarters have dimmed with time and tend to focus on the extracurricular. Perhaps the best-known ballad about Heidelberg is a love song, the first stanza of which goes in part:

> *"Ich hab' mein Herz in Heidelberg verloren*
> *In einer Lauen Sommer Nacht*
> *Ich war verliebt bis über beide Ohren —*
> *Und wie ein Röslein hat ihr Mund gelacht . . ."*

Translation:

> I lost my heart in Heidelberg
> On a tepid summer night
> I was over both ears in love —
> And her mouth laughed like a little rose . . .
> (*Note:* It sounds better in German)

The truth is that I too lost my heart in Heidelberg to a German divorcee who resembled Hedy Lamarr but caused me no end of grief for the remainder of my overseas tour. All that is beyond the confines of this document, however, so I will drop the subject right here.

(I decided at the outset of these memoirs not to include any of the women in my life, with the sole exception of my late wife, Clara, whom I married in 1956 and who was directly involved in my Foreign Service career. Just recording my thirty-one years of government service is enough of a challenge for this author without becoming distracted by romantic fantasy along the way. If I want to complete this document before I die, I had better stay on target. Besides, this is intended as a semi-official record of my career, not a soap opera.)

WAR CRIMES PRISON, LANDSBERG, BAVARIA

In any case, soon I was headed south in a third-class coach toward a new "historical" frontier. The transfer was by direct order of the provost marshal, not, I hasten to add, on account of a dirty typewriter, but because of a second lucky break. A German-speaking soldier with a secret clearance was needed as a censor-interpreter at the War Crimes Prison No. 1 in Landsberg, Bavaria. Apparently the prison director had appealed directly to the general, and the latter ordered someone in personnel to spend a weekend looking over all the service records at MP headquarters. My file must have surfaced at some point, and the orders were issued.

I arrived in Landsberg on the river Lech around the middle of October 1953. I was accompanied by one duffel bag filled with army uniforms and supplies, plus one small suitcase stuffed with civilian clothes, which had been forwarded to me from Milwaukee. Shortly prior to my departure from Heidelberg, the commanding general of USAREUR had authorized the wearing of civilian clothes by off-duty military personnel—a major relaxation of postwar occupation policy. In later (Foreign Service) years, I recalled with some nostalgia how easy it was to travel with only two pieces of luggage! I was met by a large truck—much too wide for the local roads—driven by an overage corporal; one prison inmate sat in the back to handle my "luggage."

Landsberg was a quaint and even picturesque Bavarian town that still bore many outward characteristics of a traditional country village. It had a central market place, with an appropriate Denkmal (monument), which could be approached on one side through a stone archway. The Stadtmitte (center of town) architecture was suitably old-fashioned and decorative, and authentic restaurants and pubs abounded. Landsberg formed a triangle with Munich, exactly thirty miles due east, and Augsburg, twenty-six miles north. Oberammergau, the site of the famous Passion Play, and nearby Garmisch-Partenkirchen, a resort on the Austrian border then dominated by the U.S. military, were an hour and a half's drive away. Obersdorf, an all-German ski resort also on the Austrian border near the Vorarlberg, Austria's westernmost region, was about an hour and a half further. From the standpoint of leave or R&R, Landsberg's geographical location was thus practically ideal. The town was overrun, however, by U.S. airmen from the fully operational U.S. Air Force base just a few miles away. The prison, in contrast, held a detachment of only fifteen enlisted men.

War Crimes Prison No. 1, a venerable structure, was situated on a hill overlooking the Stadtmitte (on the opposite side from the air base) and was quite well laid out. As prisons go, it was not unattractive from the outside—especially the main gate, which was no more than one story high and covered with vines and shrubbery. Once inside, however, the various high-ceilinged buildings looked more imposing and formidable. The complex was Bavarian in construction and architecture and had been left completely intact by a succession of postwar American administrators. It had been the major Bavarian state prison, where Adolf Hitler had been incarcerated in 1923 following the abortive Nazi beer hall putsch and where he wrote much of his infamous *Mein Kampf*.

The American military establishment at the prison was not much to write home about. Most of the officers had battlefield commissions and elected to stay on active duty following World War II. One captain had some "bad time" on his record (translation: time in the stockade). Another ended up in the stockade after completion of his Landsberg tour for dealing illegally in black market (East German) currency. The War Crimes Prison was not a place for ambitious careerists.

The enlisted ranks were hardly more impressive. The detachment was top heavy in rank; most of the sergeants had been in grade for a long time and had backgrounds in military police or stockade guard work. To them, every inmate was the same: a potential troublemaker. The only other college graduates were both PFCs like myself, and both became lifelong friends. Together, they appeared almost comically like "Mutt and Jeff."

Eric Zehnter was a large and good-natured fellow from the Bronx with a German background. He spoke excellent German without an American accent, and was perhaps the only American in the prison who could pass for a German. In fact, Eric usually looked out of place in an American army uniform, especially in a waist-length "Ike" jacket. He was steeped in the local culture and took an especially keen interest in *Fasching* (Carnival) activities. During an inspection, his locker was found to contain nothing but brightly colored *Fasching* costumes. This was *not* "regulation," and he was reprimanded severely. (Eric later made a special effort to attend my wedding and even appeared at the rehearsal dinner in Washington, D.C. Many years later, he and his wife, Rita, an adjunct professor of psychology at St. John's University in Brooklyn, drove all the way to Maine for my oldest son's wedding. I was both startled and touched. Eric once described his own wedding as the "melding of the German and Irish traditions." Eric and Rita had five children and now live in Syosset, Long Island.)

James T. King, by contrast, was quite small of stature but clearly not lacking in brainpower. He had a master's degree from Yale and already had a good knowledge of Wall Street. Born in Shanghai of Chinese parents who subsequently moved to Hong Kong, Jim had spent a great deal of time in the United States and was quite Americanized in his outlook. (He subsequently divided his time between New York and London, where he now lives with his wife and two children. Although he maintained a desk at Oppenheimer & Co. in New York for many years, he spent most of his time in Europe and Hong Kong. Except for a problematic German real estate venture, Jim has been highly successful and now owns and operates his own investment firm in London.)

The War Crimes Prisoners

The Landsberg prison included some of the most famous—or infamous—names from World War II. Many had been hanged, including Hitler's foreign minister, Joachim von Ribbentrop, along with many others whose names I have forgotten. Fortunately, the last hanging had taken place prior to my arrival, so I missed that grim chapter in the prison's history. During my period of service at Landsberg, three of the German officers serving prison terms were of particular interest to me.

The legendary Sepp Dietrich was perhaps the most popular of the generals still alive and serving long, if not life, sentences. He was probably the most popular military man in the prison. A Bavarian, he was virtually unique among the top brass. Among his unusual qualifications was his having been a captain during World War I, commanding the unit to which Corporal Schickelgruber (later known as Hitler) had been assigned.

Hitler evidently remembered Dietrich's charismatic leadership qualities and promoted him to four-star rank after the Nazis came to power. Dietrich was often called the George Patton of the German army, in terms of the high respect in which he was held. He had the reputation of being an inspiring troop leader. A man of unusual courage, he would travel to the front line and "kick butt" if he discovered insufficiently aggressive soldiers. Everyone who had served under him (and many who had not) idolized him as the embodiment of the best features of the German military tradition. When he walked into a room in the prison, he would call the other prisoners by their first names (very unusual for rank-conscious Germans—even Bavarians), and they would automatically defer to him. He was in prison because of his involvement in the notorious "Malmedy" case (discussed below).

Perhaps the most remarkable, versatile and unfathomable character in the entire institution was former Colonel Joachim Peiper, a (nominal) Dietrich subordinate during World War II. A recognized genius and superb tactician, Peiper had conceived and masterminded the Battle of the Bulge. His expertise in the field of tank tactical warfare was so highly regarded, in fact, that American armored specialists sought his professional advice on several occasions—even after he had been imprisoned for eight years.

Despite his military prowess (he was a full colonel at the age of twenty-nine, which was almost unheard of in the seniority-driven German army of that era), Peiper had the spare frame, narrow angular face, and ascetic manner of an intellectual. He had studied at Oxford in his youth and spoke perfect English, with a slightly clipped British accent. Articulate and arrogant to the core, he was not only proud of this accomplishment but never hesitated to correct the grammatical mistakes of his German colleagues. According to a story told about him that had a ring of authenticity (if for no other reason than his flair for the dramatic and a tendency to show off), a discharged U.S. captain had paid his own way back to Germany to testify in Peiper's behalf at Nuremberg. The captain had been w(1938) Mercedes, the only model with a "Heckmotor" (in the rear like a Volkswagen).

INSERT

In 1957 Peiper was released from Landsberg on medical parole (he suffered from thrombosis in the leg,

Misprint page 24–Insert missing text to the 4th line from the bottom of the page:

in Peiper's behalf at Nuremberg. The captain had been wounded and was lying beside a road, virtually helpless to defend himself. When Peiper's jeep approached, Peiper ordered his driver to stop and announced in elegant Oxford English: "Well, captain, it's a long way to Tipperary!" Then he ordered German medics to attend to the American officer and left him to be picked up eventually by his own forces.

Peiper's interests were—especially for a professional soldier—extraordinarily catholic in nature. He was interested in everything from science to literature, especially the American movie industry (which fascinated him, although he devoutly disapproved of Hollywood's influence on contemporary society). After we had engaged in numerous discussions on a wide variety of topics, he invited me to come to his cell one evening and address an elite "discussion group" he had organized among inmates whose intellect he deemed in the acceptable range. I considered this the ultimate compliment, as only one other GI, my friend, Private Jim King, was invited to participate in this elite soiree. Peiper directed the evening's discussion with a firm hand and asked most of the questions. The others merely acted as though they were privileged to be included—and as a matter of fact they *were*.

Peiper was in charge of the prison motor pool, an assignment that provided distinct advantages for the Americans there, including me. For a year mechanics under his supervision kept operational, gratis, my ancient (1938) Mercedes, the only model with a "Heckmotor" (in the rear like a Volkswagen).

among other ailments) and became a salesman for Porsche in Stuttgart. An Air Force friend of mine who stayed on in Salzburg eventually bought a Porsche from Herr Peiper. I have no doubt that Peiper became an expert salesman who thoroughly understood every aspect of his product!

Some years later, this friend sent me a clipping from the Paris *Herald Tribune* with the following article reporting that Peiper had been assassinated in his home in Traves, about 150 miles southeast of Paris.

Herald Tribune, Paris (undated)
Nazi Commander
Believed Slain

Nazi Commander Believed Slain

DIJON, France, July 14 (UPI)—Joachim Peiper, the former commander of Adolf Hitler's elite bodyguard unit, apparently was killed today in a gunbattle at his house, police said.

Authorities said they found the charred remains of a human body in the ruins of Peiper's house in Traves, about 150 miles southeast of Paris.

Investigators theorized it was the corpse of the 62-year-old Peiper, who was condemned to death for ordering the execution of 71 American prisoners during the Battle of the Bulge in 1945.

The death sentence was commuted to life imprisonment, but he was released in 1957.

Peiper, who has been a publicist for an automobile company, recently was spotted by a former resistance fighter and the French Communist Party organized demonstrations calling for his expulsion.

Police found a revolver and Peiper's shotgun near the body. The house was littered with cartridges and remnants of fire bombs.

To this day, I remain mystified as to why Joachim Peiper ended up in France, a country whose people he despised. He must also have known it was the last place on earth he would be welcome. I have a feeling that there is more to this finale than meets the eye. We will probably never know the full truth.

Peiper's deputy and closest confidant was a Major Josef Diefenthal. Of all the Malmedy prisoners, I came to know Diefenthal the best as we worked for the better part of a year in the same office, where he was a trusty. His duties were in supply. He knew practically every supply manual in the U.S. Army by heart and was absolutely indispensable.

Diefenthal looked the quintessential hero of Nazi mythology. He must have been what Wagner had in mind when he created Lohengrin. Tall, very blond even in his early forties, blue-eyed, and muscular (there was a certain "grace" about all of his movements, even though he dragged a wooden leg around), he was the very symbol of the "Aryan." His black prison uniform did nothing to diminish his striking appearance. I never saw another human being who came close to resembling Diefenthal during my four years in Germany—except perhaps in glorified posters and advertisements.

He had lost a leg in battle and been awarded the Iron Cross, Germany's highest honor for bravery. His character, moreover, was in keeping with his image—and I came to recognize it, almost grudgingly, over an extended period of time. Despite his largely warped political views and distorted conception of the world at large (and the United States in particular), he was a man of absolute honor and integrity, who was incapable of even the mildest form of deception. Indeed, his outspoken opinions often got him in trouble—especially with his parole officer, whom he heartily disliked. Since he hated any form of Marxism in the extreme, I was surprised to find that he basically admired the Russian soldier, whom he considered the most blindly courageous and obedient member of any fighting force anywhere in the world, "even including the Turks."

He and Peiper told me stories of Russian soldiers being thrown out of low-flying aircraft into the snow—*without* parachutes—and then accomplishing their mission, at least those who survived!

For a time, at least, Diefenthal had served near Stalingrad, although he was later pulled back and reassigned to the western front during the Battle of the Bulge. In contrast to his generous feelings toward his Soviet enemy, he had nothing but contempt for the French, who represented—in his mind—everything the Germans had struggled *against* during two global conflicts in this century. He once told me that he would never go to war again against any country in the world—with the notable exception of France.

Diefenthal's bitterness and disillusionment were directed most scathingly at his own people, who, he felt, had accorded him and his colleagues total adulation and support until the war was lost—at which point they deserted him. Again, it was the perceived hypocrisy of the postwar German psyche that so deeply offended him. While he was on death row, he told me, he received a great deal of fan mail from German women who wanted him to father their children—out of wedlock. "These were the same 'whores,'" he believed, "who were telling their American boyfriends they never had any Nazi sympathies."

During an era when so many in the prison (and on the outside) claimed to have served the Nazi machine involuntarily and as a result of threats and pressure, Diefenthal's open acknowledgment that he was a volunteer in the National Socialist movement from the outset was an attitude I found enormously refreshing if regrettable. Also, there was another appealing side to the man. I could talk to him on almost any subject and get a sensitive and sympathetic response—even if not agreement.

Like most of the professional military officers I have known, however, Diefenthal refused to associate the German Army with Nazi atrocities—even though the army had become one of Hitler's main enforcement mechanisms. Doing their duty on the front lines of battle, people like Diefenthal believed, had absolved them of any Nazi excesses to which they were not a party.

Malmedy and the Wartime Role of the SS

Malmedy was the name of a village in Belgium, often described as the crossroads where bodies of a large number of American prisoners shot during the heat of the Battle of the Bulge had been found. It had many of the outward manifestations of the so-called My Lai massacre of the Vietnam era—except that Malmedy involved POWs while My Lai involved civilians as victims.

Malmedy has always been described as a massacre, which indeed it was, and the shooting of prisoners was certainly not in accord with the Geneva Convention. The question remained, however, as to whether it was an impulsive action, taken at the company or platoon level by soldiers who panicked in retreat during some of the heaviest fighting of the war—or whether it was the result of a conscious decision reached at the highest level and transmitted down the chain of command. In the latter case, everyone involved in transmission of such an order, as well as the man or men who carried it out, were subject to prosecution for war crimes.

What follows is the version of events recounted to me in the prison by German officers involved in Malmedy. According to them, much was explained by a fundamental difference between the two branches of the SS (the "Schutz-Staffel," roughly translated as protection echelon or detachment). This distinction has generally been lost on American and Allied veterans of World War II, to whom both categories represented a close identification with Hitler, the archenemy. Among German survivors of the war, however, the subtle differences were clearly understood—which may account for Chancellor Kohl's insistence that President Reagan fulfill his original pledge to visit a cemetery at Bitburg containing the graves of

Waffen SS personnel, despite protests from contemporary Jewish organizations.

SS troops were often referred to, rather imprecisely, as "Hitler's bodyguards." While the SS was closely associated with the Führer and the Nazi movement—to a far greater degree than the Wehrmacht or the regular army—only a handful of people in this category actually performed bodyguard-type duties.

The Allgemeine (or General) SS, under the direction of Heinrich Himmler, was a kind of paramilitary force (often with military titles) that performed most of the Nazi dirty work—the persecution of the Jews and internal opponents, or presumed opponents, of Hitler, as well as oppression of populations in the conquered territories (like Poland and Czechoslovakia). These were the Adolf Eichmann types who ran concentration camps and committed other unspeakable atrocities. Many believe that the Allgemeine SS actually lost the war for the Germans on the eastern front. Among Poles and Ukrainians, for instance, there was much disaffection with Soviet rule, and at first many even welcomed the German invasion. The ruthless and indiscriminate repression by the Allgemeine SS of all "inferior" Slavic "Volk," however, soon managed to drive these potential dissidents back into the arms of the Soviet Union.

The Waffen (Armed) SS, in contrast, was essentially a mixed bag. It consisted of some ethnic Germans from Eastern Europe, a number of whom reportedly held key positions in concentration and POW camps. However, Waffen SS elite troops were also combined with regular army forces. The difference was that these SS soldiers were carefully selected for such service and more closely associated with Adolf Hitler, the Führer. At first, all Waffen SS members were strictly volunteers (indeed, it was considered a high honor to be picked), but as the war dragged on, its ranks were also filled with draftees. In most cases the enlistees were chosen for their tall, strong Aryan-looking physical appearance.

All the SS officers I knew were from Western Germany and had served in the high-morale elite troops of the Waffen SS. All the Malmedy officers were in the volunteer category. From Sepp Dietrich on down to below the level of Diefenthal (that is, to the noncommissioned ranks), all had spent time on death row before their sentences were commuted to life imprisonment.

According to Diefenthal's version of events, the American lawyer or lawyers for the prosecution in the Malmedy case approached the defense with a proposed deal: if the defense would concede in open court that a certain order originating in Berlin (the code name of which I have forgotten) *existed* during the period in question, certain benefits (the details of which I have also forgotten) would be provided in return. The defense did not have to identify the order in any way—or define its origin—just concede that such an order *existed*. Since everyone had heard of this order—and it was generally regarded as common knowledge at the time—all of the Malmedy defendants agreed to the prosecution's offer.

The first witness called, however, was the corps commander, Sepp Dietrich. He had only one goal in mind, namely, to take full and sole responsibility for whatever happened—in the best German military tradition. He asked only that his subordinates be spared the hangman's noose. As the interrogation proceeded, however, it became increasingly clear that Dietrich knew next to nothing about detailed military operations and had been bypassed completely by Berlin during the entire Bulge exercise. The more he "lied" in claiming responsibility, the less credible he became as a witness, and he was finally (prematurely) dismissed by the prosecution.

Others apparently provided the desired information, however, and in any case all of the Malmedy defendants ended up for a time on death row, before General Lucius Clay commuted their sentences to life imprisonment. My recollection is that *all* were eventually released on some sort of parole if they lived long enough—albeit *after* my departure from Landsberg.

Other Aspects of Landsberg

While the inside of a prison complex is not an altogether favorable work environment—and the atmosphere can be depressing at times, especially during holidays—my detachment at the War Criminal Prison lived exceedingly well by any military standards. Our quarters were attached to, but remained outside, the prison walls, and with one or two exceptions we all had private or semi-private rooms, maintained meticulously by a former German army major and his colleagues. Not a bad deal for a corporal with a beat-up Mercedes who eventually had responsibility for issuing passes to the enlisted men!

Our cuisine was particularly outstanding—as could be attested to by several sergeants whose "mass" approached the 300-pound level at one time or another. About halfway through my Bavarian assignment, a new lean American general was installed as head of the entire Southern Area Command. He was firmly opposed to overweight soldiers and sent out patrols to pick up such offenders and take them to military hospitals for extended treatment. Fortunately for my colleagues, such patrols never made it to Landsberg.

Our detachment had one of the most innovative mess sergeants of all time, named Joe Barker, brother of Lex Barker of Tarzan fame. (Before I arrived in Landsberg, Lex and his then-bride, Susan Hayward, had dropped by for a visit—still the subject of discussion some two years later). Joe was tall, dark, and handsome (some say he was handsomer than his brother) and had a smooth, quiet, and persuasive way of talking. Although he was "R. A. [Regular Army] all the way" and had a limited education, he had learned a good deal about practical economics—especially the law of supply and demand.

Reminiscent of a real-life version of Corporal Klinger in MASH, Joe's modus operandi was to find out which consumable items were in relatively short supply throughout the Southern Command and then acquire the available stock. Finally, when supply personnel were desperate enough, Joe would trade the needed item for something desirable, like filet mignon. He used to drive around nearby barracks and enlisted clubs in a truck with one or two members of his "staff." While Joe talked quietly and persuasively to the man in charge, his helpers would often clean out the storerooms of the visited establishment—or so the stories went.

One day I remember we were visited by a colonel from USAREUR headquarters in Heidelberg, who announced that he had been assigned to inspect the "administrative operation" of the prison. Why, he wanted to know, were we all eating roast beef when the standard chart called for C-rations? As usual, Joe had a ready explanation, which somehow related to the special sensitivity of our "mission." All right, said the inspector, but why had he discovered in a locked storage area 159 cases of Lux soap? For fifteen men? Somehow, Joe talked himself out of that one too, as the inspector never returned. Possibly Joe bought him off with some item in short supply.

My original assignment to the prison was as a so-called censor-interpreter. While many of the inmates were fluent in English, only three enlisted men within the detachment spoke German at my approximate level of fluency. At first my duties consisted of reading the inmates' incoming and outgoing correspondence and screening out any language that might have "adverse policy or security implications." The distinction between adverse policy and national security was never made clear, and the censors like myself were merely told to exercise their best judgment. While my fluency in German improved quite dramatically during this period, I was immediately made aware of my obvious unfamiliarity with local dialects and the subtleties and nuances of vernacular expression. (In other words, any real security threat probably would have escaped me.) In any case, most of what I read struck me as being personal and none of my business. My future, I soon discovered, was not as a censor.

I once served as an interpreter in military-administered court-martial of an inmate who stabbed a colleague in the potato kitchen. A prisoner who served as a de facto staff aide to the prison director warned me that I would have great difficulty understanding the defendant, as he spoke in a totally obscure mountain dialect. Fortunately, I was able to get enough advance background on the incident from a cross-section of inmates in the kitchen to get some of the gist of what he was saying during the interrogation. His punishment, as it turned out, was not too severe, since he had already made amends to his victim. Mine, however, was a genuine recognition of my linguistic limitations.

Another more important duty of a censor was to examine carefully all incoming packages to screen out lethal weapons, liquor or drugs, and real or potential explosives. In this connection, the greatest challenge usually arose during the Christmas holidays, when many inmates received large quantities of chocolate "eggs"—hollowed out and filled with liquid cognac or schnapps. Since a number of prisoners tended to indulge themselves to extremes when given the opportunity (in the past, several had required medical resuscitation), the eggs were declared prohibited items and had to be returned to the senders (not consumed by the censors, I hasten to add).

The volume of incoming parcels over the holidays was staggering and kept the censors more than busy and out of trouble. This was also the season when a prisoner was discovered "missing" during head count, leading to the sounding of alarms and sirens. It goes without saying that I was highly embarrassed by a phone call I then received from the local Landsberg post office, where I had inadvertently left one of the inmates. He was a trusty who helped load the mail on the truck and would have returned on his own, but he was afraid his uniform might disturb the local populace and police. I told him to hold on and raced down to pick him up in my own car.

The censoring of packages led to one semicomic episode. I or one of my fellow-censors discovered a minute
"vial" among the coffee grounds, and the matter was
reported to higher authority. The prison security officer,
a highly nervous fellow to begin with, rushed to the
scene. "For God's sake, don't touch it," he exclaimed.
"It could be nitroglycerin and blow this place apart."
Then he sealed off the area and called everyone from
nearby bomb disposal units to the Air Force OSI (Office of Special Investigations) for assistance. A platoon
of "experts" soon descended upon the prison to investigate. After much discussion and consultation, one of
the experts had a bright idea: why not question the ad-
dressee or intended recipient of the item in question?
The latter was called and immediately confessed that
the vial contained "something precious" from his wife's
vagina. What this "substance" was used for I will leave
to the reader's imagination, but it was the last thing suspected and managed to tie up most of the resources of
the Southern Area Command for over a week. Naturally, everyone involved had to submit a report in tripli-
cate, which must have become required reading for
generations of subsequent agents.

Let me now turn for a moment from the bizarre to the
macabre. One "special detail" of interpreter service readily
comes to mind. In a small cemetery, very well tended (by
a prisoner-trusty) in a nearby churchyard outside the prison
walls, all persons who were hanged between 1948 and 1951
were buried unless or until the bodies were claimed by
the next of kin. Any family who wished to move a deceased from this prison cemetery to another resting place
was free to do so at any time; a security officer and one
interpreter were assigned merely to oversee the operation,
not to participate or interfere in any manner.

Digging up a grave after five years of burial can be an
excruciatingly painful ordeal, especially (as in one case I
"supervised") for the deceased's son. Although the
graves had been well tended and preserved, no mortu-
ary services had been performed on the bodies after

hanging. They had just been dropped into simple pine boxes, with part of the rope still around their necks, and placed underground. Hence in time both the bodies and the boxes would have disintegrated.

In this case, the gravediggers (all wearing gas masks) pulled open the box top with little difficulty, as the wood was quite rotten. Within the box, however, a vacuum had preserved a kind of mold around the body, which then disintegrated before one's eyes as soon as it was exposed to oxygen, leaving a skeleton instead. It was a weird and frightening experience to witness this sudden transformation, which seemed at best like a bad dream. I remember thinking at the time that Shakespeare had the right idea when he ordered the following instructions inscribed on his tombstone:

> Good friend, for Jesu's sake forebear
> To dig the dust enclosed here.
> Blest be the man that spares these stones
> Cursed be he that moves my bones.

Promotion to Sergeant

A few months after my arrival at the prison, I was transferred from the censorship operation into detachment headquarters, where I worked directly for the first sergeant. The original incumbent of that position was clearly unqualified for the job and needed all the help he could muster. The detachment commander turned out to be even less qualified, and the two quarreled most of the time. It is a rule in the army that neither the commanding officer nor the first sergeant needs to be a genius, but if both are incompetent, you have problems.

This situation soon changed with the transfer of the first sergeant and the arrival of Master Sergeant Joseph J. Passa and his family from Trieste. Joe was a natural leader and an inspired first sergeant, and morale improved considerably. Unlike his predecessor, he did not play favorites and knew how to delegate responsibility without losing authority. Soon I was drafting and then typing all of the correspondence for the "old man's" signature.

With Joe in charge, the captain was really superfluous. Fortunately, the latter soon recognized this fact and would normally come in only at the end of the day to sign all of the papers Joe placed before him.

This modus operandi suited everyone, and before long we were operating quite efficiently as a unit. Joe and I became good friends, and he often invited me over to his apartment. The secret of his success was that he treated everyone in the detachment with equal fairness and was open and aboveboard with all of his subordinates, whether he liked them or not. Joe had his cronies, and for a time I was one of them; no one, however, could accuse him of cronyism.

My ultimate reward came at the end of my tour, when I discovered that I could only get my new Mercedes 180 (which cost less than $2,000 in 1954) transported home if I were a "first three-grader." That meant a sergeant or above, and I seemed destined to remain a corporal for the remainder of my active service. The War Criminal Prison Detachment was top-heavy with sergeants already, and further promotions within our unit were considered out of the question. Finally Joe persuaded someone at the next higher headquarters in Kaufbeuren that he would not be adding a permanent sergeant to our rolls, since I was about to depart, and he was authorized at least to submit a recommendation for promotion. "You write it," Joe suggested, "and I'll get the old man to sign it."

It is not often that a corporal has the opportunity to recommend himself for promotion, so I overdid it a little— I even quoted Shakespeare in my behalf. The recommendation bounced and had to be reworded. It was not "standard promotion language," we were told. Besides, someone in Kaufbeuren knew our captain personally and doubted that the language was authentic. "The captain don't talk no Shakespeare," Joe was told. "That's for damn sure!" Consequently a revised form was prepared, signed, and resubmitted; and much to everyone's surprise, my promotion was eventually approved.

No one was more surprised than the captain when I appeared in his office one afternoon with "three stripes and a rocker." "When the hell did you make sergeant?" he asked incredulously. I responded by thanking him profusely for his outstanding write-up. Still looking a bit confused, the captain nevertheless had the grace to say: "Well, Chester—I want you to know that I only promote my best men!" Even though no one else had ever been promoted to sergeant while assigned to the prison, I still regarded that statement as a compliment. (And the Army transported my Mercedes home, while I returned by troopship, in 1955.)

Many years later Joe telephoned me from Las Vegas. He was desperately in need of funds for a complexity of reasons, the details of which I have forgotten, so I wired him the money. He never paid me back, a sin for which my wife never forgave him. I did, though, because I knew that if the situation had been reversed, he would have given me the shirt off his back. I should have given rather than lent him the money in the first place.

As of this writing, Joe has been dead for over a decade (1977—at the age of fifty-four). I still correspond with his widow at Christmas time. She lives alone on a farm in upstate New York and is understandably despondent. It is not easy to live only on memories.

Some time between 1957 and 1959, when I was a vice consul in Munich, I issued a visa to the German wife of the last American soldier at the War Crimes Prison at Landsberg. That soldier had officially terminated the American presence there and turned the facility over to the Bavarian authorities. My life, it seemed, had come full circle; now my service in the occupation was finally and officially over!

PART II
THE FOREIGN SERVICE

CHAPTER 2

Commencing a Curious Career

"Just one last question, Mr. Chester: Do you honestly aspire to a diplomatic career, or are you using the Foreign Service to escape a family obligation?"

It was a fair question, or at least a relevant one, asked by the assigned "hatchet man" on my oral board, otherwise known as the Board of Examiners for the Foreign Service (BEX). (Welcome to the world of letter-symbols and acronyms!)

Traditionally, a typical panel of BEX examiners consisted of three or four senior Foreign Service Officers, each with at least a decade and a half of service experience. Most questioned the examinee in a courteous—even encouraging—manner in an attempt to elicit strengths in one's background and education; then the "designated hitter" would pepper one with curve-ball, even hostile, questions in an attempt to probe for weakness. To the examinee, the latter tactic seemed to dominate the proceedings, so that I was actually surprised to learn I had passed muster.

I was also surprised at the amount of personal information about me that the panel had had at its disposal prior to my interview. Normally, the FBI does not initiate a so-called full-field background investigation on a Foreign Service applicant until after he or she has passed both written and oral examinations—mainly because of the cost involved. In my case, however, the FBI had conducted some preliminary checks on my previous employment—consisting of a few temporary summer jobs with the T. A. Chapman Company of Milwaukee, a family department store founded by my great-grandfather in 1857. I later discovered that one of my former "supervisors" interviewed in this connection was my Uncle Norman, the store's executive vice president, who not only gave me an extravagant endorsement, but even indicated I was "too good" for the government. In his view, I should "settle down" and focus my talents on the family retail business. Even though this evaluation was provided by a relative, its evident sincerity made a strong—and favorable—impression on the BEX panel, conveyed by the investigating agent.

From my family's standpoint, at least, the final outcome was positive. I have never doubted for a moment that whatever talents I possessed were *not* those demanded in the retailing industry. Perhaps the most significant and positive action I have ever taken in behalf of my family was to distance myself from the T. A. Chapman Company. Although it was an important and venerable landmark institution in its day, the store fell upon hard times following the Korean War. In other words, it had *enough* problems without me.

In retrospect, I tend to regard all ostensible career motivation as suspect. No callow individual in his or her mid-twenties can really make an informed judgment of what lies ahead, and sometimes I think too much eagerness may not be the quality desired in a diplomat. A degree of independence and detachment may be more useful. George F. Kennan once observed in a speech to the American Foreign Service Association that one of his early mentors, a very senior and distinguished career ambassador, originally joined the service because he wanted diplomatic passports for himself and his family—to facilitate border-crossings in Europe. Whether or not this was the right motive for undertaking a Foreign Service career, Kennan noted that the gentleman in question turned out to be one the most able and effective diplomats of his generation.

The Foreign Service was in fact a curious career. To outsiders unfamiliar with the workings of diplomacy, including many people who work on Capitol Hill (as I later discovered), both the State Department and the Foreign Service are what might be called, in Churchill's oft-quoted words, a "mystery wrapped in an enigma." In my own career, in what was to become a repetitive pattern of choosing "my way," I was able to select a number of offbeat assignments, partially because I was interested in and curious about them.

The BEX examiner was not all that far off: I *was*, in fact, resisting family pressures to a certain extent, and I was *not* ready to settle down in my hometown of Milwaukee. Besides, I had just returned from several fulfilling years in Europe, and serving abroad had a definite appeal. In the mid-fifties, the State Department, USIA, or the Marshall Plan's successor organization, known at various times as MSA, FOA, ICA, ECA, and AID, offered the only regular service overseas (aside from the military) with a career advancement program. The multinational businesses and banks were not yet in full swing. The government thus had a virtual monopoly on overseas employment. Above all, the Foreign Service offered me not so much an escape as a legitimate means to continue an international lifestyle to which I had become warmly attached. That wanderlust, to some extent unrequited even to this day, had included travel with my family, three months living in Vienna with an Austrian family, four months in Paris waiting to be sworn in to the army, and my army service in Germany.

Of course I didn't tell that to the BEX panel. Instead, I pointed out that I had spent a year of graduate study at Georgetown's School of Foreign Service in an attempt to prepare myself for "my life's work." In all honesty, however, I did not then anticipate that my State Department service would last the fourteen years it did.

While on the subject of preparation and motivation, I might just add a few retrospective comments. Back in the fifties or early sixties, a bill was introduced in Congress for the establishment of some type of "Foreign Service Academy"—to train career diplomats in a manner somewhat similar to that of the military service academies. Fortunately, senior career diplomats for once took a strong and unified stand in opposition to this ill-advised legislative proposal. As a result, the idea died a-borning. If there was one dispensable requirement for U.S. career diplomats, it was more uniformity or conformity. In terms of educational background and training in particular, what government needed then and needs today is *more* diversity, not less.

People have often asked me what sort of special preparation should be undertaken by an aspiring diplomat. My answer has always been to take as many courses in as many different fields as possible, then pursue more specialized studies in an area of particular interest. When you are finished, you may not want to be a diplomat at all, but your skills will undoubtedly be needed by the diplomatic profession.

My own family provides a good example of the futility of much advance academic planning. My older brother, George, went through Princeton's famed Woodrow Wilson School of Public and International Affairs with the Foreign Service ultimately in mind. He wrote his undergraduate honors thesis on Poland between the wars, entitled "Poland at the Crossroads." Following World War II, however, he went to Harvard Law School and ended up in Wisconsin's oldest and largest law firm for the remainder of his professional career.

By contrast, I majored in English and German literature at Princeton, and never gave a thought to the Foreign Service until after my discharge from the U.S. Army. And I effectively ended up in the "foreign affairs establishment" for over thirty years thereafter. So much for the value of "focused" preparation for a career in diplomacy and international affairs.

ORIENTATION — BASIC TRAINING

My introduction to Foggy Bottom took place on February 28, 1957, when I took the oath of office as a third secretary of embassy and vice consul. My commission was signed by Dwight D. Eisenhower and John Foster Dulles. My starting salary was just under $5,000 per year, which was in the above-average range for that decade. I make this statement with some assurance, as my Princeton classmate, Richard Kazmeier, who was the 1951 Heisman Trophy winner and most celebrated football player in the United States that year—having appeared on the cover of *Time* Magazine—was offered the exorbitant salary of $7,000 by George Halas, owner of the Chicago Bears. By contrast, a Heisman Trophy winner in today's world would receive a $10 million contract at minimum and probably an additional $500,000 "signing" bonus. Dick had the good sense to turn the offer down and went to Harvard Business School instead. Those were the years when Princeton was a football powerhouse—in my senior year, even rated by several experts as the No. 2 team in the country—and Harvard was in the cellar, even by Ivy League standards. I am told that more undergraduates of the "Crimson" persuasion went to see Dick Kazmeier play touch football for the Harvard Business School on Saturdays than went to the stadium. (Just another important digression for purposes of "context.")

The first assignment for all career FSOs was to the so-called A-100 course, administered by the Foreign Service Institute (FSI). It was the civilian equivalent of (army) basic training, lasting approximately three months. With the exception of a few lectures, it was a crashing bore, too, and confirmed one significant principle of Foreign Service life at that time: One did not have to be a polished speaker to get ahead. This is much less true today, as I will explain in due course.

Among my A-100 classmates were a few who later made headlines: One, Ronald Palmer, was an early, if not *the* first, black American career officer to be named ambassador;

another, Diego Asencio, became ambassador to Colombia, where he was kidnapped for several months before negotiating his way out of captivity, and later became assistant secretary of state for consular affairs and ambassador to Brazil; one, Marsh Thompson, subsequently became former Vice President Agnew's press secretary and ended up "holding the bag," so to speak, after Agnew had resigned; and the "notorious" John Hemenway spent much of his adult life fighting the entire State Department and Foreign Service "system"—as I will describe later on. Unlike Hemenway, who was both a mover and particularly a "shaker," most of my other classmates tended to be quiet academic types who disappeared into oblivion after the A-100 course terminated. All, I have no doubt, were intelligent, well-educated, and competent. Those qualities, I was to learn, did not *per se* ensure success in the Foreign Service. As I began these memoirs, only one of my classmates, Bill Clark, was still on active duty— first as ambassador to India and then as assistant secretary for East Asia.

I was never to see or hear of the class's three women again. In those days, the only way a woman was accepted as a career FSO was to convince the Board of Examiners that she had no interest in—or prospects for—matrimony. My three female classmates were certainly convincing in that respect. In case that sounds like a sexist remark, I should emphasize that I am merely telling it the way it *was*—without attempting to *justify* how it was.

The only part of the A-100 course that was of real practical value—especially to someone who, like myself, was later assigned to consular duties—was the final week of visa training under the personal leadership and direction of Dr. Frank Auerbach—the department's then-reigning and unchallenged expert on the Immigration and Nationality Act of 1952, as amended. This aspect of the course, in my view, should have been extended by at least two additional weeks, even if one would never be assigned to a visa section.

Dr. Auerbach had an even stronger German accent than Henry Kissinger, but he "knew the book" cold, plus all of the precedents and interpretations. One questioned his judgment at one's peril. I only wish I had absorbed more of his wisdom during my final week at FSI and had been able to consult him personally during my subsequent tours as vice consul and consul. He was— and remains—historically unique. Although the late Dr. Auerbach probably has no contemporary equivalent, the "Consulate General Arlington" course now provides intensified hands-on consular training of the kind that did not exist when I entered the service.

"Intensive" German Language Training

Perhaps my initial "break" resulted from a departmental blunder: The BEX office *lost* my German written examination, after informing me of the passing score. Because there were so few applicants for Foreign Service appointments who could speak a foreign language in the mid-fifties (and the situation is worse today), the *language* portion of the Foreign Service written examination did not "count" in terms of qualifying for appointment. The language test was entirely separate, but had to be passed (or a trainee had to be rated in the acceptable range by FSI) before a new appointee could be promoted. Thus, FSOs who had *not* passed a language-qualifying test were designated as "probationers" and were sent to FSI for three to four months of "intensive" language training—followed by a post in a country where that language was spoken.

Thanks to the BEX "snafu" (which was finally admitted to me orally but never in writing), I was technically qualified as a "probationer." After two years in Bavaria with the army my German was still in pretty good shape, and it soon became apparent that I did not belong in a basic German language class. Instead, I was placed in a "class" all by myself with one instructor assigned to me exclusively for several months. (If you are ever interested in private instruction from Berlitz for six or seven hours a day, you will discover that having a private tutor gratis *and* a salary at the same time is a very good deal, indeed.)

Eventually I was joined in my personal classroom for a few weeks of "refresher" training by a distinguished, very senior (to me) officer, W. Tapley Bennett, Jr., who had been assigned as political counselor to Vienna. By the spring of 1957, "Tap" Bennett had been identified as a potential "star" ("Ein hohes Tier," literally "a high animal" in the German vernacular). He also had a valuable sponsor in the person of the senior Career Ambassador of the Foreign Service at that time, Robert Murphy, for whom he had worked as a special assistant. Ambassador Murphy even visited our two-man class on one occasion to see how his protégé was progressing. This established Tap's credentials, which he had modestly hidden up to that time.

For better or worse, intensive language training tends to form more intensive relationships than might otherwise be the case, and ours was no exception. From then on, Tap Bennett was especially cordial to me and my wife, both on visits to Vienna and Athens (where he became deputy chief of mission), despite the great disparity in our respective ranks. He went on to a distinguished career as ambassador to two posts and assistant secretary of state.

CHAPTER 3

Vice Consul in Germany

In the late summer of 1957 my wife Clara and I, our one-year-old basset hound Heathcliff, and one steamer trunk plus fifteen pieces of luggage set sail for Bremerhaven en route to Bonn on the SS *America*. It was a pleasant enough crossing—not up to the standards of the *Nieuw Amsterdam* or *Queen Elizabeth*—but far superior to the American Export Line we mistakenly selected on our return. Our fellow passengers included an army general and a ranking member of the U.S. House of Representatives Armed Services Committee (both coincidentally named Gavin) and a large retinue of Defense Department aides. I learned then and there that members of Congress often have a much better time on trips than do generals.

The general did not seem to relish his new assignment (in charge of the U.S. Army's Southern Area Army Command in Bavaria), but the congressman took pains to enjoy thoroughly every aspect of the voyage, on the assumption, he once told me, that his good fortune and the good life could not last forever. He was a large, hearty, and imposing sort of fellow, who was actually quite good company, as he treated all of his fellow passengers like constituents—even to the extent of expressing interest in my foreign policy views. He also danced with all of the young wives on board, who basically appreciated the attention. His flamboyant personality was the exact opposite of that of his Senate colleague, the distinguished John Sherman Cooper, also on board, who was so quiet and reserved that one hardly recognized his presence.

The only problem with the SS *America* was that the kennel on the top deck was open most of the day to all dog owners who wanted to walk their pets in a prescribed area and generally keep them company. As a result, Clara and I took turns visiting Heathcliff, as it was virtually impossible to lie out on a deck chair or enjoy a game of shuffleboard while knowing that our hound was locked in his cage. (Nothing is more inhibiting in life than a guilty conscience.) On this crossing I also discovered that all the dogs in the *America*'s kennel (including even bulldogs and poodles) resembled their owners or vice versa. I began to examine myself in the mirror each morning to see if I looked as hung over as Heathcliff.

BONN—A THREE-DAY THIRD SECRETARY

Bonn was originally designed as a quaint university town, not as the capital of the Bundesrepublik. The nearby suburb of Bad Godesberg was probably not designed as anything, but in any case not as an oversized, sprawling mass of look-alike buildings such as comprised the U.S. embassy housing project. The large bureaucratic embassy complex and nearby housing development made a less-than-pleasing impression on me. It was comparable, I thought, to living in Rosslyn, Virginia, and working in one of the remote annexes of the Department of State. Fortunately, the embassy personnel section had already reached the conclusion that additional third secretary trainees (I was one of four) were superfluous for Bonn's requirements, and all four of us were farmed out to consulates general in various regions of the country. To my great pleasure and relief, I found myself headed back to Bavaria, just thirty miles from my old prison on the hill. Thus ended my three-day stint as a third secretary.

MUNICH — A VICE CONSUL'S MECCA

Only one thing was wrong with Munich as a Foreign Service post in the late fifties. The living there was so outstanding that every succeeding assignment would be regarded as a letdown, especially by one's spouse. By early fall 1957, most of the World War II damage caused by incendiary bombs had been repaired, with only a few ruins left in a park across from the Residenz-Palast (the former in-town palace of the Bavarian kings), for "symbolic" reasons, I was told. The limited traffic within the city limits and on the autobahns running both north and south made it easy to get around by car. Munich's location was ideal for weekend-or-longer excursions to Austria and Switzerland, and even to Italy. It was often said that when postwar Germany was divided into occupation zones, the Russians took over the industrial areas of eastern Germany, the British controlled the north German ports, and the French the coal mines of the Saar. The Americans, however, got the scenery.

The U.S. military establishment, recognizing the value of the Bavarian scenery soon after World War II, had taken over both Garmisch-Partenkirchen and Berchtesgaden as largely American military-run resorts, offering bargain rates for the military and for civilian government employees. In addition to such natural scenic beauty as the Zugspitze overlooking Garmisch or Hitler's former headquarters in the "Eagle's Nest" above Berchtesgaden, Bavaria also boasted a plethora of scenic and historic castles, thanks in part to the obsessions of King Ludwig II. Ludwig was supposed to have been stark raving mad, but he did a lot during his lifetime for the castle-construction industry. He also supported the arts, Richard Wagner, and everything French, even refusing to send Bavarian troops against

France during the Franco-Prussian War. Certainly he was a maverick, but a maverick in solid Bavarian tradition.

The following bit of history typifies the Bavarian outlook toward the rest of Germany. After German unification in the nineteenth century, with Berlin as the capital, each of the *Länder*, or states, sent a so-called minister to represent it in the capital. On New Year's Eve, the Kaiser and Bismarck would receive the chiefs of mission of the diplomatic corps, greeting each envoy in turn, followed by the ministers from the Länder. However, the Bavarian minister, Count Lerchenfeld, stood with the foreign diplomats, not with the Germans. Bismarck, so the story goes, decided on a pragmatic solution: He greeted the count like a foreign diplomat and spoke to him in French, the official language of diplomacy. In short, it is easier to ignore Bavarian eccentricity than to fight it.

While Bavarian peasant tradition was somewhat tribal in origin and even xenophobic when carried to extremes (especially the Bavarian outlook toward northern Germans), Munich by the late 1950s was a highly cosmopolitan center in every sense of that term. Its residents included many different types of refugees, not only from the Soviet-controlled eastern zone of Germany but from all of the countries of eastern Europe, including the Soviet Union. Refugees from eastern Germany were given stipends and discounts when they arrived in the west—advantages that often rankled traditional Bayern. The Bavarian Party was the parochial expression of this malaise—operating under the slogan "Bayern für die Bayern (Bavaria for the Bavarians)."

In addition to a number of world-class restaurants, Munich also had restaurants representing many nationalities—Hungarian, Yugoslavian, Turkish, Italian, Russian, and even Chinese. I never enjoyed such a good pizza in all of Italy or in the United States as was featured in an Italian restaurant just around the corner from the Feldherrnhalle. This town square, modeled after the Piazza della Signoria in Florence, was also a historic landmark: In 1923, the Nazis were arrested in the square just opposite its open-air-stage-like monument during the abortive "beer-hall putsch" that sent Hitler to Landsberg prison.

Munich also had its own Bohemian Rive Gauche–like area called Schwabing, a museum that housed the world's largest Rubens collection, another that contained reconstructed underground coal mines, a fine symphony orchestra, and an opera, not to mention the Wittelsbach castle and the china factory at Nymphenburg.

A bar in the center of town featured lady wrestlers who would change into low-cut evening gowns after each bout and sip beer with the clients (if they were too cheap to buy champagne). At each table was a numbered telephone, enabling a customer to phone over to a "contestant-table" and request the companion of one's choice.

THE CONSULAR WORKPLACE

Despite the hedonistic context described above, I reported for duty in early September 1957 as the eighth vice consul in the immigrant visa section of the American Consulate General. Munich was then considered the largest consulate general in the world. A large Voice of America programming staff was on the premises, and headquarters of Radio Free Europe (RFE) and Radio Liberty (RL) were nearby. When all of these government employees or government-sponsored employees were added to the U.S. military establishment, plus dependents, more Americans were residing in the Munich consular district than within the jurisdiction of most embassies. (RFE and RL staff were not considered government employees but employees of a private corporation. Until the early seventies, however, the radios' expenses were covered by the CIA. Later they operated with funding authorized and appropriated by Congress.)

The Munich consulate general was lodged in a large, venerable structure that once housed the Bavarian Ministry of Agriculture. It had high ceilings and endless corridors surrounding an inner courtyard. The visa section took up one entire floor and was quite a bureaucratized operation. An elderly German employee named Herr Sutor pushed a large file cart down the hallways between the central file room and the offices involved in varying stages of visa processing.

The amount of paperwork was staggering. In those days just about everybody, it seemed, wanted to emigrate to the United States, including GI brides (a distinct and separate category) and refugees from all of eastern Europe and the Soviet Union. The large backlog never seemed to change, no matter how many hours we devoted to their resolution. A plethora of public and congressional inquiries had to be answered either by phone or in writing. One vice consul even presided over a "correspondence unit" devoted exclusively to responding to congressional inquiries. I thought of this operation sympathetically in later years when I drafted letters for members of Congress requesting "status reports." The main challenge was not answering the letter or inquiry but finding the file. Herr Sutor always seemed to be sent on a wild goose chase because the file had just been checked out of one office or another. The consulate general never really solved this organizational problem until we moved into a new building on the Königinstrasse across from the English Garden, and John Hemenway's "far-out" recommendations were put into effect. That, however, will come later.

When I arrived in Munich, the chief of the visa section was G. Michael Bache of the Bache & Co. family. He was as conscientious and indefatigable as he was bereft of fatuous humor or guile. He took everything, including his job, seriously, and the government never had to pay him overtime. Mike was a Yale grad and Harvard lawyer and essentially a "case study" kind of leader. He saved the most difficult and complex visa controversies for himself, and he gave them his best efforts and judgment. (In all my thirty-three years in government I never knew anyone who was less self-serving!) Because of the organizational "backup" problems, however, an inspired administrator was needed, not an interpreter of immigration law. Being a less than inspired organizer or delegator myself, I can recognize the need, especially in hindsight.

Initially, at least, I made a highly favorable impression on my new boss, as I arrived exactly one hour ahead of schedule. At that hour, only Mike could be found at his desk, and he was pleased to observe that I was a kindred spirit. I must confess, that I arrived one hour early because my clock, for some unknown reason, had been set one hour fast. I guess I did not get around to conveying this fact to Mike until some years later.

I am not a "morning person" and have always had difficulty getting to work on time. During my fifteen years on Capitol Hill, my most productive periods were between 5:00 P.M. and 8:00 P.M., sometimes even till midnight when the House was not in session. This schedule was not possible, however, at Foreign Service posts abroad, as one often had a social function to attend early in the evening. My mother used to say that she was only "mentally fresh" at about 7:00 A.M. Unfortunately, she did not pass on that quality to her youngest son.

Although junior officer trainees like me were supposed to be rotated around various offices in the consulate, one was very lucky to spend a few months in nonimmigrant visa work prior to one's transfer elsewhere. Nonimmigrant visas were then the easy cases, involving German businessmen or legitimate tourists who required very little advance screening or complicated requests for advisory opinions from the State Department. The work volume was in immigrant visas, where most of the junior officer trainees were needed. Neither the Displaced Persons Act of 1949 nor the Refugee Relief Act of 1953 had been sufficient to solve the refugee problem. Additional Refugee Relief Act numbers had to be authorized. I spent considerable time at refugee camps around Nuremberg, working out security and processing problems.

In retrospect, I am entirely convinced that at large visa-issuing posts, consular work in general represents an institutionally guaranteed lost opportunity. Visa officers in particular constantly interact with the public; they also provide a needed service and have an opportunity to pick up quite a bit of useful intelligence in return. Nevertheless, most ambitious FSOs who enter the career service via the examination process disparage consular work and try to escape it as soon as possible. (At one time I was no exception.) In addition, at many posts if a junior consular officer tries to exploit his visa-related contacts by way of a political report, his effort is often resisted by the political or economic section as jurisdictional encroachment. Only at small posts does the cross-fertilization process seem to take root.

Conversely, in my view, those FSOs who have opted for a career in consular work often do not have the political or economic sensitivity to provide much useful input. They have more or less thrown in the towel on matters outside their "jurisdiction." It is a pity, but it is also a reality.

Admission of aliens to the United States works through a rather duplicative two-tier system. Consuls abroad—responsible to the Department of State—issue visas, while the Immigration and Naturalization Service (INS)—under the Department of Justice—admits. In the 1950s the INS tried hard to take over the visa function, with the strong backing of the House Judiciary Committee. The Eisenhower administration killed the proposal, thanks to the unified backing of all ambassadors and chiefs of mission, both career and political. Chiefs of mission do not want the visa function at their posts controlled by an INS inspector subject to the directives of another agency. The current system is inherently inefficient and redundant, but probably helps prevent undesirable aliens from entering the United States, and adds an element of political judgment— through the Foreign Service input—to visa decisions.

In postwar Germany, visa work provided exposure to the full gamut of human experience—from pathos to humor. Not only were refugees from Eastern Europe and the Soviet Union desperate to resettle in America, but many West Europeans who had lost money and property during the war were equally anxious to join a real or prospective relative or obtain employment in the dominant U.S. economy of that era. While the West German *Wirtschaftswunder* (economic miracle) was beginning to emerge from the ashes of allied destruction, it had affected relatively few German industrialists and businessmen by the late 1950s. Affluence was still an exceptional condition.

As a green vice consul, I was soon introduced to the vagaries of human nature—and to the Immigration and Nationality Act of 1952. An elderly lady appeared in my office one morning to explain her unusual situation: she had a "pen pal" who owned a farm in northern Vermont and had proposed matrimony. Apparently he was not the most ardent of suitors, but as an octogenarian in somewhat fragile health, he basically needed someone to cook for him and help him feed the animals. If the lady could join him in Vermont, he promised to marry her and provide her with room and board.

The problem was that my applicant was chargeable to the Austrian quota, which was then heavily oversubscribed (more so than the German quota). She had already been turned down for an immigrant visa in her native Linz and was now living with a relative just outside of Munich. If she did not travel soon, she cried softly into a handkerchief, her potential sponsor might expire.

I suggested that the farmer travel to Germany and marry her there. Then, as the spouse of a U.S. citizen, she would be exempt from the quota and her case could be processed immediately. "He has already turned down that suggestion," the lady wailed. "He said he would rather spend that kind of money on a new barn for his pigs."

As an overeager vice consul, I suddenly had a moment of inspiration: a marriage by proxy would solve the problem and remove the lady from her national quota. When I suggested this option, she cheered up immediately and rushed off to contact her fiancé. It was only after her departure that a veteran colleague showed me the paragraph in the law that specifically prohibited proxy marriages for purposes of quota "chargeability." Congress had evidently plugged this loophole, having considered it a potential device for fraud. Although Congress could not declare a proxy marriage illegal (since it was perfectly legal under many state laws), it could and did prescribe that "for purposes of quota chargeability," a marriage will only be "valid" if the contracting parties are married in the presence of one another or if (subsequent to a proxy marriage) the union is "consummated." In each case, it would require the U.S. citizen to travel to his or her intended's country before the prospective spouse could receive an immigrant visa.

Having misled this poor old lady on about my third day as a practicing vice consul, I instantly became conscience-stricken. With the help of a local (German) employee, I drafted a letter to the applicant, carefully explaining my mistake and quoting the exact provision of the law, both in German and in English. I asked her to come back to the consulate at her earliest convenience so that I could explain the problem in detail.

I never heard from her again, but I did eventually receive a letter from the Vermont farmer. It was barely legible and read more or less as follows:

> Dere General Consulate:
> My fianz done writ me that our (proxy) marriage performed by our local preacher ain't legal unless "consummated" by the Vice Consul.
> Please consummate and send. I need help.
> > Sincerely,
> > (name forgotten)

In subsequent speeches before public audiences, I have often cited this story as an example of the practical limitations of consular service even when an FSO might wish to be as helpful as possible.

In those days, and for years before and after my tenure in Munich, the front reception desk of the consulate general was presided over by the dominating personality of Miss Clementine (Clemmie) Le Cler. Clemmie was French to the very core of her being, although she had spent the entire war years in Bavaria and had somehow miraculously survived that experience. As a middle-aged spinster with no pro-German sentiments, she was a critical observer of German shortcomings—but always with a poignant sense of humor.

Clemmie had a wealth of consular stories, all based on personal experience. One in particular impressed me, since I was involved in the aftermath. The story concerns the special category of immigrant known as the GI bride. Throughout the fifties, unattached American servicemen (and even some who were "attached" to American spouses) seemed to fall for the German Fräulein in remarkable numbers. What may have begun as a need for sex and companionship often ended in an intense relationship. In the late forties and early fifties, many of the women who had lived through difficult war and postwar years viewed the American GI as a ticket to "freedom from want" and a better life. Despite cultural, language, and occasional age differences, plus a foot-dragging military establishment that tried to slow the process down with paperwork, by the end of the fifties any GI who was determined to marry a German national could eventually do so. Getting a visa for the spouse was a different matter, especially if she turned out to be a former prostitute, but even this hurdle could be waived in time, under a special provision of the law.

Clemmie was used to seeing just about every combination of American GI and German spouse brought about by World War II or its aftermath. One family, however, intrigued her especially: it consisted of a young

GI from the hills of rural Kentucky, who was a regular "Li'l Abner" type, and his German spouse, who was quite evidently approximately two decades his senior. She could have been his mother, most of the local employees agreed, and she had in her care her young, lovely, seventeen-year-old daughter from a previous marriage, who was classified as a dependent. The group appeared to be a bizarre misfit, but the papers were in order and they all received their visas in timely fashion.

Approximately one year later (when I appeared on the scene), the consular section received a long report from the Immigration and Naturalization Service, which had been investigating the possibility of fraud. The young GI had been reassigned to Fort Leavenworth, Kansas, and after months of domestic turmoil had asked to consult the post legal officer. During the interview, he confessed that his "family" was actually the result of a conspiracy. He had wanted to marry the daughter, but she was still a minor and needed her mother's permission to emigrate. The mother would only give permission if she could accompany them, so the young GI had to improvise. They worked out a plan for him to marry the mother and take the daughter along as his legal dependent. Then, after a decent interval in the United States, he would divorce the mother and (eventually) marry the daughter. Under this scenario, all objectives would be achieved and everyone would live happily ever after. There were only two "snags" in the scheme, as "Li'l Abner" explained to the legal officer: (1) the mother did not want a divorce; and (2) both mother and daughter were pregnant. Clemmie's comment: ". . . and you think YOU have problems?"

Lest the reader gain the impression that consular work in Munich was mostly fun and games, such was definitely not the case. We worked long hours—often on Saturdays—in an attempt to cope with our stubborn backlog. Finally the opportunity arose for a dramatic break with past procedures and the adoption of an entirely new "system." The timing was right when the

consulate general was moved from the old Agriculture
Ministry into brand new quarters on the Königinstrasse—
just across from the English Garden and perhaps a block
from the Haus der Kunst (art gallery). The new building was modern in design—resembling, some traditional
Bavarians observed, a "glass box on stilts." It was considerably smaller than the ministry quarters and required
a more efficient and organized use of the space available for all consulate offices. (Alas, how the situation
has changed: on a trip through Munich in the summer of
1991, I found the consulate general surrounded entirely
by a high steel fence—with several security checkpoints
between the main gate and the building.)

When we moved to the new building, John Hemenway (who had entered the Foreign Service about a year
ahead of me) had replaced Mike Bache as chief of the
visa section. Less interested than Mike in case law and
immigration precedent, John was determined to institute an entirely new organizational program. A graduate
of the Naval Academy and a Rhodes scholar, John at this
stage of his career was both a natural leader and a team
player. He also had an inspirational vision as to how the
immigrant visa section might be reorganized for maximum efficiency. Instead of moving files from one stage
of processing to another, and thus from room to room, he
suggested setting up three or four teams, each headed
by a vice consul who would supervise the local employees in the various stages of visa processing around a
large table and follow each case from inception up to
the final interview, which would be conducted in a separate room. The idea was to focus on processing, rather
than on finding files and reporting on their current status.

Those who subsequently tangled with him during his
long grievance fight with the Department of State would
call him loner, maverick, a man both vindictive and
obsessed, but he was none of these things in Munich.
He had strong opinions on most subjects, but he was
also disciplined in his outlook toward his work, in
characteristic Annapolis tradition. In other words, he

61

believed it was not only his right but also his duty to air his views as persuasively as possible during staff meetings or in the planning phase of policy formulation. Once a decision was reached by his superiors, however, he felt honor-bound to implement it. His character and personality had not the slightest element of deviousness, rebelliousness, or guile. He was up front with everyone and expected such treatment in return.[1]

John's idea about reorganization of the Munich visa section was a good one, but I didn't think it would work, and I told John as much, although I promised to give the proposal a fair trial. I seriously questioned whether the local employees, in particular, would ever cooperate in such a radical departure from the traditional practice, which also involved loss of room and space for them. John also had to sell the idea to the consul general, Edward Page, Jr., and especially to his deputy, Ray Ylitalo, who was directly involved in consular performance and who many years later became director of the Visa Office. Both were equally skeptical, but decided it was worth a try.

As it turned out, the new procedure was a spectacular success: within two months we had completely cleared up our backlog and were operating with maximum efficiency. In fact, the Munich visa section received an honor award from the Department of State, and one of the top officials in the Visa Office came out to Munich to examine our pilot program. Eventually our system was considered a model for other large immigrant visa sections around the world. We of little faith all benefited from the vision of a major Foreign Service iconoclast: we all got promoted. John Hemenway, perhaps to his subsequent regret, was selected for a year of Russian language training at the Intelligence school in Oberammergau, followed by a tour of duty in Moscow.

The Social Life of the Consulate General
Social life, often intertwined with official duties, was both pleasant and demanding. For a very junior vice

consul not yet thirty, it could be heady stuff. Some of the connections I made helped establish lifetime associations for me.

Catholic holidays, plus extended traditional celebrations, such as the *Oktoberfest*, the Christmas–New Year festivities, the *Fasching* (Carnival) season in February–March, and the Bock beer festival in the spring made Munich Germany's most "fun" place for visitors from abroad. A column by Art Buchwald in the Paris *Herald Tribune*, describing his experiences at a Munich *Fasching* (Carnival) party, tended to accelerate this trend.

Consul general Page, a senior old school diplomat, and his wife Teri took their representational (entertaining) responsibilities very seriously indeed. They had served in Riga, Latvia, and in Moscow before World War II and knew such old Eastern European hands as Chip Bohlen, Llewellyn Thompson, and Jacob Beam. A Harvard-educated, always impeccably dressed, handsome gray-haired diplomat, Page epitomized the "man of distinction," and seemed to have infinite reservoirs of charm to draw upon, attested to by all the women in the vicinity. He strove to make an invitation to the American consul general's residence (first, in the suburb of Grünewald, later moved to the in-town residential area of Bogenhausen) a highly desirable opportunity. He was eminently successful: whenever the Pages entertained, which was often, just about everyone showed up—from the local nobility to the Socialist *oberbürgermeister* (mayor) and a plethora of Bavarian state and municipal officials.

An integral part of the job for members of the consulate general staff was to arrive approximately ten or fifteen minutes ahead of time for parties at the consul general's residence to receive any special instructions from Mrs. Page, and then to mingle with and actively entertain the German guests. In those days wives were rated for their representational abilities on their husband's efficiency reports. A spouse's reputation as a hostess with charm and flair certainly helped her husband's career. Conversely, although a mediocre spouse rating might not be the key factor in an officer's promotion, it could limit his future assignments—which in turn could limit his career prospects.

Despite my lowly rank, Clara and I soon became very active in the Munich social whirl—primarily because Teri Page thought the world of my wife and involved her in as many wives' activities as possible. I was especially in demand during those extended periods when Teri's mother would come to visit. The latter was stone-deaf and largely uninterested in making conversation. I was one of the few Americans who could draw her out, and consequently was usually seated at dinner next to her deafer ear. The challenge was constant and considerable, but the rewards were plentiful. No junior officer at such a large U.S. mission could have been more actively engaged in society.

Aside from the Pages, the real impetus for party-giving came from the local nobility. The Baroness Gustava Rheinbaben-Hanna, in particular, was very active in Munich social life and soon took me and my wife under her wing. There were probably only a handful of functions at which Gustava was not in attendance, or had not organized, during our entire Munich tour. Gustava was indeed an unforgettable character. She must have been in her mid-seventies when we first met her and over ninety when she died. Although endowed with a bird-like beak and not beautiful in the classic sense, she was one of the two sexiest septuagenarians I have ever met. (The other was Clare Boothe Luce.) Her family, the Rheinbabens, were of distinguished background and, like many in that category, had seen their fortune depleted during World War II. (One of her ancestors had been finance minister under Kaiser Wilhelm.) The last of Gustava's three husbands was an American ambassador named Matthew Hanna, who died en route to Cuba, his last post. When we knew her, Gustava lived on a modest pension provided for her by Mr. Hanna and controlled by his former bank. Held in her medium-sized, attractive apartment on the Maximiliansplatz in the center of town, Gustava's cocktail parties included many consular corps members and representatives of local society.

We also developed a close and interesting connection with the Ungelter family. Baroness Johanna von Ungelter, known as Hannele, had worked in the Consulate General ever since the end of the war and the beginning of the occupation, primarily as a translator and interpreter. Endowed with a gracious, generous, and accommodating personality, she trained numerous succeeding generations of vice consuls in her subtle way until her recent retirement. Through her auspices I also came to know her brother, Baron Alexander (Gigi) von Ungelter and his lovely wife Lili—all of whom have remained among my closest friends. Gigi went into business after 1945, worked his way up through at least two commercial hierarchies that I know of, and was retired and living on Lake Starnberg just outside of Munich until his death a few years ago. That was his reward—together with several visits by the author (perhaps a mixed blessing). Both Gigi and Hannele spoke impeccable English—at least in part owing to their upbringing. Their mother was a Scottish noblewoman and their father was German consul general in three American cities (New York, New Orleans, and Seattle) prior to World War II. Consequently, the children were exposed to American culture early.

Gigi used to take me to a regular meeting of the Tafel Runde (roundtable) discussion group which met regularly in the Hotel Continental. It consisted of a selected erudite group of noble participants, including Wehrner von Braun's father and some famous wartime generals. I was the only commoner at the meetings, but was welcomed cordially as an honored guest. Old Fürst (reigning prince) Henckel-Donnersmarck was always in attendance in his wheelchair with an earhorn into which one shouted responses to his many questions. As a most interested participant, he usually waylaid the guest speaker with inquiries at the end of the evening.

To its credit, this group often invited controversial speakers to lead the discussion—including even one socialist professor. One evening this professor had been invited to talk about the Kaiser and World War I. His interpretation of history produced essentially negative reactions, but the audience maintained a high level of courtesy and allowed the professor to have his say. When he was finished, Fürst Henckel provided a full critique of his remarks as the others hurriedly left. This form of give-and-take, or open debate among disputants who were miles apart politically, was a new experience for many of the participants. Up to that time, most Germans had very little exposure to either parliamentary or democratic procedures, except during the totally discredited Weimar era.

Oktoberfest

In addition to its many permanent attractions in art, architecture and music, Munich is best known to the outsider for its Oktoberfests, actually celebrated mostly in September. The festival consists of large quantities of beer, *Wurst*, barbecued chickens, *Lederhosen* and *Dirndl*, and loud brass bands. Large circuslike tents, each sponsored by a different brewery, spread out along the Theresienwiese (Maria Theresa's meadow) near the Hauptbahnhof, or central railroad station. Inside each tent, however, the scene is very much the same: large numbers of chauvinistic Bavarians in traditional dress standing on tables with arms interlocked, and singing such original numbers as:

> *In München steht ein Hofbräuhaus*
> *EINS—ZWEI—Soufa . . .*
> (In Munich stands a Hofbräuhaus
> ONE—TWO—Drink)

I am a veteran of five such "fests," which is more than anyone's digestive system should be called upon to accommodate. Once is more than sufficient. You tend to get the hang of the routine in short order, and everything else is repetitious. One Oktoberfest evening was, however, to become the occasion of my greatest triumph as a junior vice consul. It all started when David Bruce, American ambassador to the Federal Republic of Germany, paid an official visit to Bavaria, purposely scheduled to coincide with the 1958 Oktoberfest.

Ambassador Bruce was one of our most distinguished and widely admired envoys of his day. Although a political appointee throughout his ambassadorial career, he was regarded by the Foreign Service establishment as a professional. Eventually he was to become the only diplomat in history to serve as ambassador to France, Germany, and Great Britain (and finally China). Eddie Page was determined to ensure that the ambassador's sojourn in Munich was a success. Consequently, he summoned me to his office to ask a special favor.

On the evening of his arrival, the ambassador and his entourage from Bonn were scheduled to have cocktails at the consul general's residence and then (about 8:00 P.M.) head for the Theresienwiese. Mr. Page asked me to go ahead of time to the second floor area of one of the major tents—reserved for VIPs—and hold a table for a party of approximately ten people. It sounded simple enough, and I dutifully complied. I arrived early enough to confiscate a long wooden table with benches in an ideal location—right next to the picture window overlooking the festivities already under way below. The head waitress was duly impressed when I explained that the *Amerikanischer Botschafter* (ambassador) *und Generalkonsul* would be in attendance. She promised to provide first-class service.

Much less impressed, however, were some tipsy members of the Bavarian *Landtag* (state legislature) who suddenly staggered upon the scene. They not only considered themselves qualified VIPs, but also eligible for the best table in the house, namely mine. They literally fell upon the benches and soon became impossible to move. The persuasive arguments advanced by the maitre d', the chief waitress, and myself fell upon deaf ears. Soon all such talk was drowned out by loud singing. By this time the other tables had begun to fill up and my options were disappearing rapidly. Only if you have ever attempted to reason with a plastered Bavarian will you sympathize with my thoroughly untenable situation.

Finally, after a suspenseful half hour, nature's call saved the day. The distinguished legislators suddenly stood up en masse and staggered in the direction of the men's room. By pure coincidence, the consul general's party arrived just at this moment. I practically pushed Ambassador Bruce down into his honored seat by the window. I then "ordered" all of the guests to be seated (there was no time for pleasantries) and had the waitress clear off all of the abandoned beer steins. That accomplished, we were in business. When the *Landtag* representatives emerged from the john, they had lost their table as well as their memory of where it was located in the first place. Eventually they drifted off downstairs. For the first round of beer, Consul General Page offered a toast to me for having made this occasion possible. "I knew I could count on you, Chips," he said with obvious sincerity, and I realized at that moment that I had successfully met the biggest challenge of my first year in office.

At the same time I learned that pure luck could be an important factor in one's career advancement.

Hotels and Restaurants

Of Munich's many fine restaurants during the decade of the fifties, representing many different national cuisines, three had official, hometown, or family associations for me.

Schwarzwälders was the only restaurant in town that did not serve beer—only wine—and it specialized in local game, such as pheasant and venison. The so-called Rehrücken, or backbone of the deer, is the only real venison delicacy, and only Schwarzwälders knew how to prepare it (in my experience). Although I dined there on various (not numerous) occasions, one evening stands out because my brother George (the attorney) was in town and invited Clara and me and his friend, Irwin Meier from Milwaukee, to a restaurant of my choice. I selected Schwarzwälders because of its authentic German-game atmosphere.

Mr. Meier, a man of strong convictions on most subjects, was at that time publisher of the *Milwaukee Journal*. He stated as an indisputable fact that John F. Kennedy could never be elected president, as the country was not prepared to accept a Catholic. (As a Catholic himself, he evidently thought himself an authority on the subject.) I thought of this statement some years later when I saw a photo in the *New York Times* showing President Kennedy in the Oval Office surrounded by leaders of the media, including Mr. Irwin Meier.

Boettner's, an exclusive restaurant on the Theatinerstrasse in the middle of the shopping district, was almost a state secret. The restaurant itself was located behind a well-known delicatessen and was largely unknown to the general public—including many clients of the deli. The restaurant had only a few tables, and one dined there by reservation only, usually after being introduced by a favored client. Clara and I were first taken there by John Ulhlein, a Milwaukee expatriate (virtually), who lived most of the year in his antique "palace" in Baden-Baden. The smoked salmon from the North Sea was the best I ever tasted, and the entrees were equally delicious. Subsequently, I asked Hannele von Ungelter to call and make a reservation for me there for a business lunch. She introduced me telephonically to the head waiter as "Mr. Chester of the American Consulate General" and apparently left the impression that I was *the* consul general. The food and service were so outstanding that I did not have the heart to disabuse the Herr Ober about my actual title—and from that moment on I was Herr Generalkonsul.

Finally my lack of total candor caught up with me. One night a local businessman took the *real* consul general and me to a restaurant that he promised we had never been to. I began to feel uncomfortable as our limousine turned into the Theatinerstrasse. Of course, it turned out to be Boettner's and the maitre d' welcomed me with open arms. "*Ach, Herr Generalkonsul, wie schön,*" he beamed, while virtually ignoring our host and my boss. Fortunately, Edward Page, Jr., was a man endowed with both sensitivity and humor, and he immediately grasped the situation. "Don't worry, Herr Generalkonsul," he laughed. "Just remember, you are responsible for both the food *and* the service!" Again, fortunately, he was not disappointed.

Throughout the fifties and well into the next decade, the Hotel Vier Jahreszeiten (Four Seasons) was the finest hotel in Munich—and some would say in all of Germany. It had been run for several generations by the Walterspiel family, and the *Café Walterspiel*, its restaurant, was once written up in *Life* magazine as among the top eight restaurants in all of Europe. The lobby was always filled with dignitaries of one kind or another—from politicians to movie stars to oil millionaires from the Middle East.

In 1958 my parents, accompanied by my maternal grandmother, Laura Chapman Miller, arrived at the Vier Jahreszeiten for a visit. My grandmother was then ninety-two, and had not been to the hotel since she had accompanied her mother on a trip to Munich sometime during the 1870s. When she announced this fact to the concierge, she not surprisingly created a stir—especially when she inquired whether King Ludwig had ever completed Neuschwanstein castle, which had still been in the process of construction during her former visit. (Ludwig built his castles mostly in the eighteenth-century style; thus many tourists and even local Bavarian visitors to these monuments did not always grasp that he was, in actuality, a late nineteenth-century monarch. Most visitors to Bavaria in any case regarded Ludwig's architectural creation as "ancient history.")

The then-manager, young Mr. Walterspiel, was hastily summoned. He pronounced my grandmother not only the oldest living but longest-served client of his establishment. Until grandmother's arrival, that honor had been held, he explained, by a tall, spare gentleman then seated in the main coffee salon, who happened to be Konrad Adenauer, the West German chancellor. Often referred to by the media as *der Alte* (the old one), Adenauer was perhaps a decade younger than my grandmother. He was exceedingly gracious when introduced to my grandmother and accepted his new second-class status in the hotel with all due humility and charm. Later, as I was accompanying Grandmother up to her room, she turned to me and asked rather plaintively: "I keep forgetting, my dear; who was that very nice young man we just met?" *Der Alte*, it seems, could be a strictly relative term!

My family's visit did a great deal to enhance my status and reputation. Mr. Walterspiel took me aside at one point and told me that certain privileges accrued from my grandmother's seniority: certain VIP rooms were saved for special emergencies, and if the need ever arose, I could call upon the hotel for help. I relayed this message to the consul general and on at least two occasions (when all hotels were solidly booked during one national holiday or another), I was able to obtain quarters for a member of Congress and his staff who arrived unexpectedly. If only I had had this privilege at *all* of my Foreign Service posts!

Alas, I am told that the hotel has degenerated enormously over the past thirty years and is now a third-class commercial establishment. The Café Walterspiel has been closed for decades. I have purposely refrained from revisiting the premises on recent trips to Munich to avoid disappointment. Better to recall this landmark's past glory than to witness its decline. Like *Der Alte* and Laura C. Miller, the Hotel Vier Jahreszeiten now belongs to the ages.

A DOG'S LIFE

No account of Munich in the fifties would be complete without a description of our basset hound Heathcliff and the prominent role he played in the life of the community.

North and south Germans are distinct species and often have little in common with one another. The vast majority of German *volk*, however, are dog lovers. Many prefer dogs to people, something I learned one evening when I showed up at a police precinct station to report the loss of Heathcliff, who had run off in the midst of a snowstorm. The desk sergeant was in the process of speaking quite sternly to a lady who had just lost—and subsequently recovered—her child. When I breathlessly explained my desperate situation, however, the officer immediately lost interest in the missing child and addressed my problem with sympathetic concern. He even sent me out with a patrol car to search for my errant canine. After an hour's futile drive around the center of town, I returned home disheartened—only to find Heathcliff wrapped in a towel and seated on the couch next to my wife.

To my surprise, I soon learned that the basset hound—well known in France (where the breed originated) and Great Britain—was hardly recognized at all in West Germany. Most people thought Heathcliff was either related to the *brake* (a slightly similar but larger German hunting dog that is no relation), or some sort of exotic *mischung* (mongrel). If anything, the basset is overbred and has a nose for following scent that is second only to the bloodhound (to which the basset *is* related), a fact that had escaped them altogether.

Walking Heathcliff in the vast English Garden was a daily ritual shared with a large majority of the downtown population. (The garden begins in the center of town right across the street from our former apartment house on the Königinstrasse and extends some twelve miles to the north). Each dog who spotted Heathcliff would rush up to greet him, and because our hound was so sociable and indiscriminately friendly, Clara and I ended up explaining Heathcliff's origins to almost every dog owner in the park. My wife was just beginning to learn German and ended up with a mostly pure Bavarian dialect she had picked up in the kitchen. I taught her a standard speech in German summarizing the history of the basset hound: In translation, it went like this:

> Originally from France, the word "basset" stems from the French word "bas" or low to the ground. These hounds, which have the second-best noses for scent in the world, are bred to walk close to the hunter. They chase primarily pheasants and hares and are popular in England and America—to which countries they have emigrated over time.

After committing this little talk to memory, Clara decided to try it out in the Garden. Along came a well-dressed young man who stopped her and said *"Entschuldigen Sie, gnädige Frau"* (Excuse me, Ma'm), at which point Clara launched into her five-minute description of Heathcliff's ancestry. When she was completely finished with her narration, she asked the very polite young gentleman if he had any questions. *"Ja, gnädige Frau,"* he responded. *"Ich möchte nur wissen wie spät es ist!"* ("I just want to know the time!")

On another occasion—following the birth of our older son, John—we were walking *en famille* along the Köninginstrasse, just about to turn off into the park. John was in his baby carriage. Suddenly a Volkswagen screeched to a halt and the young driver rushed over in our direction. *"Wie alt ist er?* (How old?)," he demanded breathlessly. Clara fondly stroked our firstborn and pulled his bonnet back from his face. *"Nur zwei Monate* (only two months)," she responded demurely. *"Nein, nein,"* shouted the youth impatiently—*"Nicht das* Kind, *der* Hund!" (Not the *kid*, the *dog*!). Fortunately, John never objected to taking second place to a *Hund*—he and Heathcliff were inseparable friends. The line was drawn eventually, however, when Clara found them drinking out of the same bowl.

Although I launched my Foreign Service career with considerable success in Munich, where I received two grade promotions, no member of our family enjoyed such universal acclaim as our *Hund*.

MUNICH POSTSCRIPT

One's past can indeed be prologue. In early May 1991, as I was about to leave my apartment building on Connecticut Avenue in downtown Washington, I received a call from the front desk informing me that two gentlemen from the Department of Justice wanted a "word" with me. At least it was not the IRS, I rationalized.

The gentlemen in question were both trial attorneys assigned to the Office of Special Investigations, which had been set up during the Carter administration to investigate those postwar immigrants (and later naturalized citizens) who were suspected of involvement in Nazi war crimes.

"Were you a vice consul in Munich in 1958?" one of the attorneys asked. When I answered in the affirmative, he showed me an original immigrant visa that clearly bore my signature. Needless to say, the applicant's photo did not ring a bell with me, since the immigrant visa mill in Munich used to issue some eighty visas per day in the late 1950s. The attorneys were extremely courteous and did not really expect me to recall this individual, who apparently had been a guard at Auschwitz for at least six months during the war. They asked me whether I might stop in at their office at my convenience and explain some of the security and screening procedures in effect at the time (to the extent that my recollection might be in any way useful).

That evening I compiled a list of all documents requested of an immigrant visa applicant, plus the various background checks we relied upon (again, to the best of my recollection). As I subsequently explained, a consular office is *not* an investigative operation. Consuls are, in fact, dependent upon the investigative services of other agencies. In our case we relied on two basic documents: a CIC (Counter Intelligence Corps) investigation report, and a police record, which had to be produced for all periods of residence over six months after a certain minimum age (perhaps eighteen or twenty).

One of the attorneys finally showed me a copy of the CIC report I must have reviewed in this instance. I took a deep breath, wondering if I had missed something of substantial relevance. But my "guard" had been given a clean bill of health, which was the ostensible problem: apparently a number of postwar intelligence agencies had developed a network of informants among ex-Nazis, among others—having promised, in the process, to help them eventually to emigrate (to both North and South America). In recent years, some of the more notorious "escapees" of this stripe had surfaced, such as Klaus Barbie, the "Butcher of Lyon."

As of this writing, I have no idea how many "cases" like this one were "whitewashed" by the CIC or how many such individuals were actually engaged in atrocities. The Immigration and Nationality Act of 1952, which applied during my tenure in Munich, only prohibited the immigration of persons *convicted* of war crimes. If they lied to the consular office under oath (on a *material* matter), they could be found guilty of fraud and their citizenship could be declared null and void. However, an interviewing officer would only have questioned an applicant about war crimes if the applicant's file suggested such a possibility. In this case the subject apparently never came up.

How to prosecute cases of this nature represents a considerable challenge for the Office of Special Investigations. Were I to be called at some time as a "general witness" in such a case, like all of my colleagues from that era I would be notably weak on specifics, a weakness any competent defense attorney would undoubtedly

exploit. Most of the people being investigated are undoubtedly ancient by this time (in their eighties), if not
senile. Of one thing I was certain, both in the fifties and
in the nineties: on any and all borderline cases, I would
certainly have requested an "advisory opinion" from
the Department of State. Ironically, the Auschwitz guard
eventually chose voluntary departure from the United
States in lieu of deportation. I was told that my scheduled appearance at his trial convinced him that he had
no other choice, although *my* testimony would probably
have been less than credible or persuasive.

I well remember the controversial cases. One was a
Ukrainian terrorist whose case was handled by a colleague of mine. The visa applicant had the code name
"Bandera" (and a different name on his visa application). He had fought everyone, the Allies, the Germans,
and the Russians. He was considered by all the experts
to be a hopeless fanatic and loser. One of my colleagues
interviewed him on several occasions and recommended
that the State Department refuse him a visa. He was
subsequently assassinated in Munich under mysterious
circumstances. He was thrown down some stairs and
either died from the fall or was murdered in the process. He most likely had many more enemies among
the emigre community in Munich than he ever would
have encountered in the United States. (A recent TV
program entitled "Spy-Tek" on the Discovery Channel
discussed the Bandera case. According to the commentator, the man was killed by an injection of a secret
potion, similar to the one used in London against a Bulgarian anticommunist broadcaster. The killing substance
was popular with Soviet and East European assassins,
as it allegedly left no trace in the body.)

The most controversial case I handled—and one
which I remember well after some three to four decades—was the immigrant visa application of His Excellency Ferdinand Durcansky. He had been foreign
minister of the Slovak "independent" (puppet) state set
up by the Nazis after they had taken over the Czech

part of Bohemia, following the infamous Munich agreement between Hitler and Neville Chamberlain. The Slovaks during that period did not have much of a deal: they could play ball with the Nazis and be permitted some degree of autonomy *if* they followed the German foreign policy line. The alternative was to rely on the Soviets or the Allies, who were not *there*.

I interviewed Mr. Durcansky on four separate occasions and was eventually convinced that he deserved a visa—or at least that there was no specific reason to deny him one. From the beginning, he admitted that he had collaborated with Hitler under pressure, but he noted that the Allies declined to indict him at Nuremberg. There was no evidence that he had been personally involved in the deportation of some 68,000 Slovak Jews to concentration camps, and he produced documents alleging that he had not cooperated fully with Nazi officials.

However, it was his direct question to me that seemed most persuasive: "What would you have done in the same situation—given the fact that the Germans controlled both your country and your people?" In captivity, perhaps, there is a time for valor, but also for discretion. I could not in all honesty blame the Slovaks for doing what was necessary for their survival—a conclusion I conveyed to the Department of State in a subsequent request for an advisory opinion. The Department agreed and I issued the visa under "instructions."

The next day I was surprised to find the following front-page story in the Paris *Herald-Tribune:*

Herald Tribune, Paris
(undated)

Ex-Nazi Puppet Talks to Slovaks At Waldorf-Astoria

NEW YORK, March 16 (A.P.).—Ferdinand Durcansky, once Foreign Minister of the Nazi puppet government of Slovakia, made his first public appearance in New York yesterday.

He spoke at a celebration of the 20th anniversary of Slovak independence, held under auspices of the Slovak League of America at the Waldorf-Astoria Hotel.

Earlier in the day, Rep. Emanuel Celler, D., N.Y., told an American Jewish Congress meeting that he was trying to learn "how a former leader of the Nazi puppet régime in World War II" had entered the country.

Mr. Celler said Mr. Durcansky collaborated with the iHteler régime and said allegations were made at the Nuremberg war-crimes trials that Durcansky had worked closely with the Nazis to deport 68,000 Slovak Jews to concentration camps.

Mr. Durcansky, in an interview later, said he was chairman of the Council of the Anti-Bolshevik Bloc of Nations, with headquarters at Munich, Germany. He said he arrived in the United States on a visa.

In the interview, he admitted he had collaborated with the Hitler regime and that he had been condemned to death by the Czechs in absentia. But he asserted that he did this under pressure and that other nations had refused a Czech request to indict him at Nuremberg.

He said the Slovaks had a choice of collaborating with either the Russians or the Germans—"we were between the millstones"—and they chose the Germans.

He also listed passages quoting German Foreign Office officials as saying he was not sufficiently Nazi and was no co-operating in implementation of German foreign policy.

Fortunately, no one ever told Congressman Celler, chairman of the House Judiciary Committee, *who* issued Mr. Durcansky's visa.

78

CHAPTER 4

A *Stint at Headquarters*

Washington assignment—especially following an initial tour abroad—can be a humbling experience. If one has been a fair-haired boy at one's first post, the return to one's capital city and headquarters can be more than humbling—it can be more like a jolt from a cattle prod.

The consul general had strongly requested my extension in Munich for another two years, as an officer in the political section, making me sound like a potential superstar in the process. The Department of State's Office of Personnel, however, had other ideas. At the time I thought Personnel had a purposeful plan to bring a young trainee–vice consul back to earth and deflate any ego trips I might have had, but their purpose was probably no more complicated than filling an open slot (I learned more about Personnel operations in a later departmental assignment).

Back at the department, unless you inhabited the seventh floor (offices directly associated with the secretary of state) or possibly the preferred areas of the sixth , you were nothing: no title, no perks, no diplomatic passport, no credentials assuring preferred access to anything, not even to a prison. Chiefs of mission or principal officers accustomed to having an assigned car and driver now stood in line for shuttle buses to State Department annexes or to the Foreign Service Institute across the river in Rosslyn, Virginia. Receptionists, who were mostly Civil Service rather than Foreign Service employees, were not invariably rude but often did not bother to look up when one entered an office. Being an FSO-6 in this environment was like being a second lieutenant in the Pentagon, where brigadier generals are a dime a dozen.

In the late fall of 1959, the Department of State was an organization in flux from prewar elitism and exclusivity to postwar growth and increasing specialization, reflecting America's growing influence as a world power. By the end of the fifties it was hard to believe that until 1947 the entire Department of State had been housed in that ancient if venerable structure just west of the White House now known as the Executive Office Building ("Old EOB"), currently holding White House staff exclusively.

The State Department underwent both expansion and consolidation during the fifties and sixties. The new headquarters, with main entrance on 21st Street Northwest just off Virginia Avenue (previously Selective Service headquarters), had proven inadequate to sustain operations. A new addition expanded the building west to 23rd Street, more than doubling its space. The diplomatic entrance was also moved from 21st Street to the intersection of C Street and 22nd Street. (The addition was initially referred to as "New New State" to distinguish it from "Old New State" headquartered on 21st Street.)

Consolidation, however, was harder than expansion. By the time of my return numerous State Department annexes were located all over town. (The CIA was similarly dispersed throughout downtown Washington, so that if one's assignment was not in the main building, one might be assumed to be engaged in a top secret project. This at least added an aura of mystery or intrigue to what might be compared figuratively to Siberian exile.) My first Washington assignment was in one of those annexes.

THE BUREAU OF INTELLIGENCE AND RESEARCH

I had three different assignments in the Bureau of Intelligence and Research (INR) in the next year and a half. INR was then an amalgam of various professional groups and interests, including area specialists from academia and both public and private sectors; intelligence experts representing the intelligence community (not just CIA), often in a liaison capacity; highly specialized intelligence operations requiring a higher-than-top-secret clearance (I was eventually assigned to one of them); and "Schedule C" political appointees, who may or may not have been competent but had good administration connections. Career FSOs were interspersed among the permanent positions at all levels (Schedule C excepted). Most of them would have preferred to be operational desk officers or country directors, dealing with foreign embassies at the government-to-government level.

Office of Biographic Information

Among the many INR subdivisions was the Office of Biographic Information (BI), located on the top floor of a broken-down World War II "temporary" annex just behind the National Gallery of Art on 7th Street, N.W. The World War II "temps" were considerably more temporary and fragile than those of World War I. Ours listed heavily to starboard, especially the second floor, where our offices were. (The ground floor was occupied by an unrelated government agency.) Most pedestrian traffic, therefore, ended up on the right side of the building, which led to an atmosphere of professional informality as one ran into one's colleagues (literally) and then apologized for knocking them down. Humbling, surely, for someone who had considered himself a fair-haired boy.

The upstairs quarters *did* have one distinct advantage over the downstairs, however: they provided many more hours of "heat leave" during the summer months. Our office's air-conditioning window box was often nonfunctional, and the work force was excused for the day when the temperature rose to above 85 degrees Fahrenheit. No one in our annex was too proud to comply with this regulation. (By contrast, in the winter months over at State Department headquarters, orders would be passed down from the seventh floor allowing "nonessential" employees to leave early during snowstorms. Such directives were often ignored, however, because no one wanted to be considered nonessential.)

BI differed from *most* of the rest of INR in that its product was widely read, widely requested, and useful. The rest of INR jealously guarded its independence and tended to establish its own priorities. A decade or so later, when I served as desk officer for Canada, I observed that desk officers often had no time, or sometimes inclination, to read INR's special studies and reports. BI had a different institutional approach: it produced *no* studies or memos or reports until requested to do so. Because people tend to make the world go round—in diplomacy and foreign affairs as in all other pursuits—the department and even other federal agencies always were interested in our product.

The BI files, broken down by area and then by country, consisted of relevant clips from newspaper articles, memoranda, broadcast summaries, reports (called despatches and later airgrams—then the major form of diplomatic prose communication between the posts abroad and the department), and intelligence and/or FBI reports that might shed light on the character, personality, or real or potential role of a foreign official. The major task of the BI assignee was to consolidate all of this disparate information and commentary into a (preferably) one-page summary for the benefit of those senior U.S. government officials—from the president on down—who needed such background prior to a meeting or discussion with or about the subject in question.

One-page summaries were preferred because the then-incumbent of the White House, Dwight D. Eisenhower, was supposed to have said that he would not read more than a one-page summary of official documents.

At the time I thought this rule too draconian, but now I feel differently: anyone who seriously attempts to force the bureaucracy in general, and the diplomatic establishment in particular, to condense what is of real importance, and then restrict rhetoric accordingly, shows a propensity for leadership. Alas, no chief executive, including Nixon, who launched a serious program to cut unnecessary paperwork, has been able to enforce such a rule over the long term. The rule eventually fell by the wayside and was abandoned. (Memoir writers are clearly exempt from such restrictions.) Nevertheless, in BI at least, we took the one-page dictum seriously. In retrospect, I believe it was not a wasted disciplinary exercise.

My new immediate boss in the German and Austrian branch of BI was a talented and memorable character, named *Miss* Brynhild Rowberg. Brynnie, as she was known to her colleagues, associates, and friends, has never (to this day) resorted to the designation *Ms.*—primarily, I think, because she did not welcome any ambiguity about her marital status. Brynnie was not someone who welcomed ambiguity of any kind: she always let you know exactly where she stood on any given issue. In the so-called "fudge factory," as the Department of State has been called, this was her most refreshing and endearing quality.

Brynnie was an excellent writer, but above all a superb editor. She required concise and explicit use of the English language—and she did not put up with officialese or "gobbledygook." Would that I had had her at my side during those later years when I was a congressional speech writer, on my *own*—without any feedback.

Above all, however, Brynnie was a distinguished and qualified FSO who had made it up through the ranks on her own in a man's world (as it then was) without any affirmative action program, women's movement, or grievance hearings to back her up. Of Scandinavian descent, Brynnie was essentially a Hubert Humphrey Democrat from Minnesota. At this time (January 1960), I suppose I was about as liberal as at any time in my life, which means that I was classifiable as an Eisenhower Republican, or moderate.

Another analyst of roughly my age, rank, and importance was considerably to the right of both of us. Our boss, however, treated us both with sympathy, generosity, and understanding, if not always agreement. Rarely in my executive branch or later congressional career would I find someone like Miss Rowberg, who could separate strongly held personal views so completely from professional judgment about ability and performance.

Although from my vantage point BI compared favorably with the rest of INR, I am hard put to list any positive accomplishments during my year there. I did have one very humbling experience, which began with a peremptory telephone call from the office of Secretary of State John Foster Dulles. The woman calling me was the secretary's personal secretary, and the tone of her voice indicated that she was accustomed to issuing direct orders without waiting for questions or reactions. "Secretary Dulles would like to see you here in his office as soon as possible...and please bring your papers." CLICK.

"The Secretary wants to see *YOU?*" Brynnie asked incredulously. "Well you better take a taxi and not wait for the next shuttle." Since I was not at all clear about what papers to bring, Brynnie handed me a few reports that had allegedly been prepared for the president and presumably might also be of interest to his senior cabinet adviser. As I was leaving the building, I ran into Brynnie's boss, Herbert Gordon, who at that time barely knew my name, although he probably suspected that I was one of the new trainees assigned to his division. "I'm on my way to see the secretary," I remarked as casually and nonchalantly as possible, leaving Mr. Gordon in a state of severe doubletake.

As I drove across town from State Annex Seven to the Halls of Valhalla, I also wondered what the second most important American official in Washington at that time might want from an FSO-6 on his first departmental assignment. Perhaps it was some family or Princeton connection which had finally permeated the seventh floor.

My *work* in BI, I concluded rationally, could not have been brought to the great man's awareness.

There were no security screening devices or procedures in the early 1960s, so one just took the nearest elevator to the seventh floor and reported to Mr. Dulles's secretary.

"Who are you?" a formidable senior citizen receptionist demanded. "I am John Chapman Chester from the Office of Biographic Information. The secretary evidently wants to see me."

"Mr. Chapman has already been in to see the secretary," the lady noted archly, "and YOU are *not* on his '*list*'" ... END OF MEETING. It turned out that the secretary had wished to consult the then Laos desk officer (during the first Laos crisis), Christian CHAPMAN. His name happened to be listed in the new State directory just above mine, and Mr. Dulles's secretary had apparently dialed the wrong number. Back to the boondocks, Chester. (Chris Chapman was not only a veteran of many decades and posts in the Foreign Service, but also a loyal Princetonian from the class of 1941. Chris achieved fame at his final overseas post, as chargé d'affaires in Paris, where an assassin shot at but failed to kill him.)

Another BI experience reveals that the collection and interpretation of meaningful "hard" intelligence remains a fragile undertaking at best. I will grant that the West in general and the United States in particular have enjoyed many intelligence coups and successes during the post World War II decades (the best probably remain undisclosed). Still, I recall reading a highly classified intelligence report based on the debriefing of a defector who had been the longtime personal physician of Wilhelm Pieck, the late figurehead president of East Germany. The report was evaluated "B-2," which is a high rating for reliability, and indicated that Mr. Pieck had almost every problem known to medicine: heart trouble, several strokes, circulation difficulties, and cirrhosis of the liver. The list of maladies filled two typewritten pages. The good doctor's professional opinion was that President Pieck could not survive for more than six months at best. Some ten years later, I read of the sudden death of Mr. Wilhelm Pieck, and I have been somewhat skeptical of our intelligence capabilities ever since.

Moments in the Mideast

My next assignment in INR was for exactly one month in the Division of Research for the Middle East. As a newly designated analyst, I had one great advantage over my office colleagues: since I knew next to nothing of any consequence about the Middle East, I did not represent a threat to anyone and was warmly received by my peers.

What I remember most vividly about that brief sojourn in an alien environment relates to the status of the branch chief, Dr. Harold Glidden, and the workings of the civil service system. Unlike me or most of my office colleagues, Dr. Glidden was a highly qualified academic expert with considerable experience in Middle Eastern affairs. He was also highly controversial, as one of those very few Arabists who generally disparaged Arabs. He was hired initially for his substantive expertise. In order to promote him, however, he would have to be moved up the ladder from *branch chief* to *office director*. In each case, his substantive knowledge, his basic credential, was of minimal value. What mattered most was the description of his *position* and how many people he *supervised*.

As I see it, this was the basic problem with the civil service. The position was all-important and motivated officials to build large empires. Once you landed the job, you were in it for life or until the job was abolished. You were not rated so much for performance, as you were in the Foreign Service, but for fulfilling the requirements of the *position*. Unless you were successfully prosecuted for malfeasance in office or some heinous crime (or the position was abolished), your tenure was assured. You could only be fired for cause, not ineptitude.

Apparently, the only way to promote an expert like Dr. Glidden was to make him a superexecutive, which he clearly was *not*. By his own admission, in fact, he was the *worst* administrator who ever inhabited a government office. I ended up cleaning out most of his files and reorganizing the catalogue system, while he ended up doing *my* assigned tasks as an "analyst." Many months after my departure, Dr. Glidden called me on the telephone to discuss my efficiency report. He was quite apparently confronted with this assignment at a time when he had absolutely no recollection of who I *was*! To his credit, he admitted as much and asked the right questions. (He was also delighted to learn that I had reorganized his files!)

Most amazing to me in retrospect is the existence of so many competent, qualified, and often dedicated civil servants in the Department of State who perform in a superior manner without any visible or understandable incentive to do so. The key must be interest or job satisfaction.

WELCOME TO THE INR WATCH

My departure from the Division of Research for the Middle East (RME) was an unnoticed departmental event based on a unique set of circumstances.

The INR bureau director (of assistant secretary rank) was former ambassador (to Indonesia) Hugh Cumming, Jr., a very traditional old guard (some might say stuffy) member of the Foreign Service establishment. He was probably one of the last of his kind and background to hold this position.

By today's standards, Ambassador Cumming would be considered an "elitist." He had attended all the right schools and colleges, belonged to all the right clubs, and owned a home in Georgetown and a farm in Virginia. He also knew all the right people of his generation and background. Like most of his old school colleagues, moreover, he was also "true blue," with a strong sense of noblesse oblige. I do not say this critically, since I was also raised in that tradition. In short, Hugh Cumming firmly believed that *duty* came *first*—ahead of all other considerations. He worked long, hard hours and expected the same from his subordinates.

On one particular weekend, however, the ambassador stayed at his Virginia farm, deciding—contrary to custom—to enjoy the rural scene until the very last moment and then return directly to the Department of State on Monday morning. He had, he felt, an entire week to catch up on his INR demands and responsibilities. Unhappily, he went directly to the secretary's staff meeting for assistant secretaries rather than to his office to brief himself in advance of that ordeal. It was perhaps the *only* time he had ever taken such a liberty. When he walked into the secretary's office, his ultimate boss recognized his presence and then submitted the fatal question: "Hugh, we are all waiting with bated breath to hear your analysis of last night's Iraqi coup. What exactly happened?" Hugh had not heard of the coup, which took place after midnight that day and ended the Iraqi monarchy. The King of Jordan's cousin was assassinated and a military ruler took over, changing the Iraqi political landscape for all time.

The Honorable Hugh Cumming was not only embarrassed; he was humiliated, especially as the top intelligence officer in the room. He determined from that moment on that such a scene would never be repeated. When he returned to his office, he ordered his executive director (his chief administrative officer) to identify approximately five young FSOs in his Bureau who would serve thereafter as his *personal* watch officers. The department had its own watch officers located in the Operations Center, but Mr. Cumming wanted hand-picked officers, responsible to him, to keep the INR director informed of all foreign developments that occurred during the night. I was one of the selected few, chosen for my "outstanding" Foreign Service record up to that point and also (I assume) because my continued service to RME could *not* be fully justified.

Ambassador Cumming, to his credit, was true to his word: he never upbraided a watch officer for waking him in the middle of the night. That task was left to Mrs. Cumming, who always ended up being the one who answered the phone. Because of the Iraqi experience, we were all instructed to err—if anything—on the overeager side: when in doubt, phone (and we did). The late Hugh Cumming invariably backed us up, even if Mrs. Cumming did not.

A watch officer's duties began either at 7:00 P.M. (until 1:00 A.M.) or at 1:00 A.M until 9:00 A.M It was a good way to get to know the nocturnal char force and security patrol, but little else. During the first three weeks or so, it was an exciting and even enlightening experience to read all of the incoming intelligence traffic in an office that required a very high security clearance, but eventually one tired of the assignment.

I was on INR watch duty on the night before the Kennedy inauguration, when all of the District of Columbia was paralyzed by a massive snowstorm. As I could see from my window on the top floor, people just abandoned their vehicles in the middle of the streets. My relief (who lived in Virginia) never showed up that evening so I spent a long eighteen–twenty hours in my INR "cell."

I also happened to live down the street in Georgetown from Senator and Mrs. John F. Kennedy. My late wife, Clara, had known Jackie Bouvier during their debutante years and had welcomed her and her daughter, Caroline, into her very informal "play group" for Georgetown friends and acquaintances and their children. On several occasions after the 1960 presidential campaign and before Kennedy's inauguration, when I returned from the department after 9:00 A.M, I was greeted at my door by individuals in fedora hats and double-breasted suits who asked me what I had in mind. "I live here," I remember stating affirmatively. "Who the hell are YOU??"

Eventually the logistics and security requirements of a presidential "play group" became too much for Georgetown. Instead, the entire operation was moved to the White House, to everyone's relief. A top White House floor, which had not been used for children since the days of Dolley Madison, was renovated as a kindergarten. All the three-year-olds in that "school" had a marvelous experience, in part because none of the children realized *where* they were and were entirely unselfconscious about their environment. That the President of the United States often came out to supervise their activities made very little impression on them. It was just "their school"!!

After six months of watch duty I was ready to move on. In retrospect, rotation in three INR assignments over a year and a half had not only humbled me; it had raised half-formed, yet serious, questions in my mind. Though I am sure that the work done in INR was important, I found the headquarters bureaucracy stifling. In its way it reminded me of the restraints I had chafed under since childhood. How could I, a mere cog in such a hierarchical structure, accomplish anything, compared with the useful and enjoyable work I had done in Munich, for example, or even as a clerk-typist in an army prison, where I had helped guard war criminals?

When the Department of State offered to lend me to the newly established Peace Corps in January 1961, I jumped at the opportunity. To be perfectly frank, by that time I would have accepted any assignment that released me from INR watch duty. At the same time, I recognized that the Peace Corps was a new and vibrant agency of the future. Participating in its inception from the inside eventually turned out to be a stimulating career challenge.

CHAPTER 5

The Peace Corps—
"Present at the Creation"

President John F. Kennedy had a dramatic impact at home and abroad in his slightly less than three years of incumbency. The Kennedy family glamour (the Camelot mystique) and the final tragedy of the JFK assassination contributed to this impact. But a certain restlessness Kennedy sensed among the electorate—a desire, if you will, for more direct engagement, or "action"—also played a part.

Kennedy's theme became "get America moving again," after eight years of unprecedented peace and prosperity under the paternal guidance of a war hero and father figure, General of the Army Dwight D. Eisenhower. JFK suggested that we had been lulled by too much peace, prosperity, and complacency. He cited the "missile gap"(which eventually turned out to be bogus) as merely one example of what he had in mind.

Indeed, the call to action—a constant refrain of the Kennedy campaign—and the concept of volunteerism ("Ask not what your country can do for you") managed to reach a substantial segment of the electorate. And the Peace Corps, more than any other Kennedy initiative, embodied the American response to that call. In his first year in office, in fact, the young president succeeded in getting only *one* new substantive program through Congress, the Peace Corps authorization and appropriation. He did manage to get congressional authorization to enter the "Kennedy Round" of the General Agreement on Tariffs and Trade (GATT) negotiations, but that was basically an ongoing undertaking.

The Peace Corps idea did not originate with the Kennedys but with Congressman Henry Reuss of Wisconsin and Senator Hubert Humphrey of Minnesota. Exactly who thought of it first has never been entirely clear, as the congressional staffs of both individuals have claimed credit for their respective bosses. My impression is that Reuss originated the concept. In a handwritten note after reading a draft of this chapter, he stated: "When I see you I'll demonstrate that my Peace Corps credentials considerably antedate Hubert's—but why dice over the vestments?" I never followed up on that offer, but his version is probably the authentic one.

After the election, JFK's brother-in-law, R. Sargent Shriver, not only initiated and organized the Peace Corps but founded and put into operation an entirely new government agency. The Peace Corps not only had no program but also no authorized or appropriated funds during the first four months after its creation. Therefore it had to take on initially unpaid consultants or borrow government employees from other federal agencies. I was one of two "borrowees" from the Department of State. The other was primarily involved in "administrative liaison" and largely disappeared from sight.

Being "present at the creation" of a brand new federal agency was an experience most of my contemporaries have missed—for the simple reason that all other agencies of the Peace Corps' scope had been around for decades. In recent decades a number of new departments have been created, such as the Departments of Energy, Transportation, Housing and Urban Development, Education, and Veterans Affairs (not necessarily in that order), but each was primarily a reorganization. Starting from scratch in the 1960s was an unusual Washington occurrence.

In early February 1961, when I reported for duty at the Maiatico Building (at Connecticut Avenue and H Streets, NW), the Peace Corps consisted of a number of half-empty rooms on one floor. Just a few desks were available for Mr. Shriver and his senior staff. These included such luminaries as:

- The late Gordon Boyce, President of the Experiment in International Living, on leave from his headquarters in Putney, Vermont;
- Warren Wiggins, a former senior ICA (International Cooperation Administration) official, most recently at the Transcentury Corporation;
- Harris Wofford, who became president of Bryn Mawr College and senator from Pennsylvania after his Peace Corps service;
- Ed Bailey, a reporter for the *Milwaukee Journal;*
- Tom Quimby, a Kennedy campaign organizer from the state of Michigan;
- Nancy Gore, daughter of the senator from Tennessee and sister of current Vice President Albert Gore (She died young of lung cancer, and was mentioned movingly by the vice president at the 1996 Democratic National Convention);
- Sally Bowles, daughter of the Under Secretary of State, Chester Bowles;
- William Haddad, a New York politico of Lebanese background who had had a prominent role in the JFK election campaign in New York and who subsequently ran for various elected positions in New York City;
- William Josephson, special counsel to the director, who was quite influential and is currently a law partner of Sargent Shriver;
- Morris Abram, general counsel (succeeded by Bill Delano); and
- Bradley H. Patterson, Jr., my boss-to-be.

The Reverend William Sloane Coffin, the chaplain at Yale, meeting with Haddad, played the role of devil's advocate, questioning how the Peace Corps could prevent a large group of young Americans from getting into cultural and related difficulties in the developing world. Finally, Haddad had "had it" (no pun intended) with this needling and blurted: "All I hear from are doubters—and now you are also giving me a pain in the ass." This incident stays with me because the Reverend Coffin became a leading campus radical of the sixties—constantly involved in civil rights demonstrations and anti-Vietnam War activism. He was the man of the hour who all conservative Yale alumni loved to hate, but in the Peace Corps case he was actually preaching caution.

Brad Patterson, like me, was essentially an anomaly: a career civil servant who had made his way to the top as a professional, having reached the pinnacle of achievement as the Eisenhower administration's cabinet assistant secretary for eight years. Despite his professional status, Patterson did not expect Sargent Shriver to hand-pick him for executive secretary of the Peace Corps. He thought that his long Eisenhower Republican connection would be a negative, but Shriver thought otherwise. Patterson had the job after one interview. A mixed blessing at first, his main assignment was to bring some kind of order out of total chaos, at best an impossibility. Nevertheless, he helped the new agency somehow hover on the edge of survival.

Normalization, however, did not come easily. Aside from the assigned staff, any number of "volunteers," who allegedly had been told by someone in authority (although there was no real authority except Shriver) that they "might" at some point be considered for a job, hung around the office. Sorting out the bona fide staffers from just plain hangers-on was a challenge at best, as was telling people with excellent credentials (or at least contacts) that they really would not fit into the headquarters organization. Eventually, the General Counsel's office partially resolved this situation by ruling that a federal agency like the Peace Corps could not take on unpaid volunteers as federal employees. Various senior staffers questioned this ruling, since it seemed to be contrary to the Peace Corps mission, but eventually it stuck.

The Executive Secretariat was supposed to be the channel for all communications between the director and his senior staff. This was closer to a utopian objective of Brad Patterson than a reality (as the executive secretary himself realized), since everyone who was anyone had his or her own method of reaching Sarge's ear, and everyone, it seemed, had a different idea about how the Peace Corps ought to operate.

Early staff meetings made this diversity of opinion especially clear. Numerous policy disputes arose over, for example:

- The ideal size of the Corps
- The generalist versus the skilled specialist
- Security clearances and background checks (how extensive and how thorough before applicants would drop out?)
- The wisdom of sending Jewish volunteers to Arab countries
- The organizational status of the Peace Corps

The last item turned out to be the most controversial and became the first large bureaucratic fight in the agency's early history. In March 1961, Kennedy proposed to reorganize the U.S. foreign assistance program—combining ICA, the Development Loan Fund, and Food for Peace into a new umbrella organization called the Agency for International Development, or U.S. AID. Henry Labouisse, the ICA director, advocated placing the Peace Corps under AID's control. Key members of the White House staff, especially Ralph Dungan and David Bell, director of the Bureau of the Budget, supported him in this view. The top echelon of the Peace Corps staff, however, totally resisted having the agency subservient to the aid programs' bureaucracy. The Peace Corps was founded precisely to create a *different* image from the AID bureaucrats and technicians. On this issue the staff was prepared to man the barricades. Although Henry Labouisse was a highly regarded Kennedy appointee and could be expected to give the Peace Corps both support and a necessary degree of leeway within his organization, the Peace Corps leadership worried about his successors.

After a long struggle, the Peace Corps emerged victorious as a semiautonomous agency, subject to policy direction from the Department of State. This was the ideal solution from the Peace Corps' standpoint, especially as Under Secretary of State Chester Bowles was a Peace Corps supporter. We at the working level always assumed that Director Shriver had won the battle by appealing directly and successfully to his brother-in-law. Now I stand corrected: according to Gerard T. Rice, in his authoritative book *The Bold Experiment*, Sarge Shriver had indeed appealed to JFK on numerous occasions but had finally struck out.[1] During the key period, Kennedy was preoccupied with the Cuban Bay of Pigs fiasco and left foreign aid organizational matters in the hands of pro-AID White House staff members, namely Messrs. Dungan, Bell, and Theodore Sorenson, his speechwriter, and Peace Corps autonomy seemed a lost cause. The Peace Corps obtained its ultimate victory through the intercession of Vice President Lyndon Johnson through his staffer, Bill Moyers. Johnson met with Kennedy privately on the subject and emerged as the prevailing influence. The first big battle had been won. It was clear, both to the bureaucrats and to the appointed members of the administration, that the Peace Corps had clout.

This brings me to a necessary if brief personal appraisal of the Peace Corps' first director, the Honorable Robert Sargent Shriver. "Sarge," as he was called, clearly got his job because he was the brother-in-law of the president, who had unlimited trust in him. It has also been hinted that JFK chose his brother-in-law for this assignment because he could be easily sacrificed if the entire program backfired. Whatever the reason or combination of reasons, no better candidate could have been found for the job at hand.

Sarge not only had the best contact an agency head could have, namely, the president; he could also afford to innovate and take chances in areas where "angels" (both political appointees and bureaucrats) feared to tread. To his credit, he nonetheless spent much of his time trying to win friends rather than exploiting his power.

Sargent Shriver was not a mere agent of the Kennedy family but a distinctive leader in his own right. He was an unabashed and dedicated "do-gooder" in the best sense of that term (and very much, in that respect, like my late mother, who led the Girl Scouts and founded the Junior League of Wisconsin). He believed absolutely in all of his causes, as well as those of his wife, Eunice Kennedy. This strong belief gave him a certain confidence and security that other program heads seemed to lack by comparison. He was also pragmatic about achieving his goals and welcomed the support of anyone, not limited to members of Kennedy's New Frontier.

Above all, Sarge was a super promoter, just what was needed to establish a new agency. He was also an optimist who was never discouraged, not even by the dire predictions of his closest advisers. If you were a mere borrowed FSO and underling of Brad Patterson, he still made you feel welcome and an integral part of his operation. In later years, the agency needed an inspired administrator and program instigator. To get the agency *going*, however, it needed Sargent Shriver.

When Sarge first came to prominence, all sorts of stories appeared in the press about how the Shrivers of Maryland were of considerably finer lineage than the Kennedys, who after all were descended from Irish politicians and bartenders. Sarge's mother was reputed to feel that Sarge had married "beneath him." This was all nonsense as far as Shriver was concerned, as he greatly admired John Kennedy *and* his family. Anyone who knew him well never could have doubted that claim.

In terms of his character, I particularly recall a letter I read among the mounds of incoming correspondence the Executive Secretariat had to deal with, from an enlisted

World War II buddy of Shriver's. After congratulating Sarge for his recent achievements, he reminisced about their past association, writing "I remember, Sarge, when you told one of the officers on our ship: 'I didn't need to become a gentleman by act of Congress.'" The writer was obviously impressed by that line of thought—and so was I.

The Executive Secretariat was set up primarily to deal with correspondence, and we did have a lot. When Kennedy first suggested the Peace Corps idea during the campaign, campaign headquarters kept the responses and sent them to the White House after the election. After the Peace Corps came into being, the White House sent us every bit of correspondence on the subject known to man, including everything that came in after the election. It was a deluge.

I devised form letters for most of this correspondence that were probably not totally responsive. I had to make some bland comment about "programs," because I didn't know (nor did anyone else) what we would end up with. Almost every day we received a letter from Mrs. Eleanor Roosevelt recommending someone she knew "intimately" for a Peace Corps position.

Eventually I devised a (satirical) form response, which was only partially appreciated by senior members of the New Frontier:

Suggested Form Letter
(Just fill in blanks)
My dear Mrs. Roosevelt:

    I want to thank you very much for your recommendation of your dear friend _____ from _____ (Hyde Park, New York, Washington, D. C., etc.) for service in the Peace Corps.

    Mr./Mrs./Miss _____ has excellent credentials, the confidence you have expressed in (her/him) being of maximum importance.

While the Peace Corps currently has no programs or policies which have been approved by a majority of the senior staff, I can assure you that _____will be given every possible consideration in due course.

In the meantime, I would appreciate your contacting all 435 members of the House of Representatives in behalf of this outstanding program.

With high esteem and renewed appreciation, I remain

Sincerely,

s/R. Sargent Shriver

Director

PUBLIC AFFAIRS

Not surprisingly, Peace Corps headquarters was inundated from the very beginning by requests for speakers. The demand for such services far exceeded the supply, particularly at the senior levels. Although many staff members found themselves confronted with unavoidable speaking engagements, most tried to put off such duties— especially before specific programs and policies had been approved. Nancy Gore, an attractive and congenial colleague with a good sense of humor, and her small public affairs office were simply swamped with requests which over time became demands. I understood the problem, as it was not dissimilar to the executive secretariat's correspondence workload.

In a new agency such as the Peace Corps, many questions arose, literally on a daily basis, for which there were as yet no "cleared" responses. When I was drafted into the speaking circuit as early as April 1961, I found that even as a junior officer in the executive secretariat, with little prior background in this area, I could contribute to policymaking in the form of speeches.

I had some misgivings. Still a diplomat and full-time employee of the Department of State and not an authoritative member of the Peace Corps staff, I did not have a direct influence or even voice in programs and operations and only an indirect channel to the director. I neverthe-less welcomed the opportunity. I could talk in very gen-eral terms about the goals of the Peace Corps and the way its policymakers and programmers *perceived* the basic Peace Corps mission. I could spell out some of the ca-veats and generally agreed-upon "don'ts." Fortunately, I obtained a copy of an early speech by Henry Reuss on this subject that contained a number of useful points (points, I realized, no one in the Peace Corps would want to dispute).

Particular speeches I made were at the Washington Hebrew Congregation to some 150 high school students and a major address to a Conference on Education for Public Service in Overbrook, Pennsylvania, on the Main Line from downtown Philadelphia. Among the speakers at the latter was Richardson Dilworth, then mayor of Philadelphia.

After the mayor's keynote address, the students were to be divided into three groups, each with a principal speaker addressing a different topic. All the students were interested in what I had to say on the Peace Corps, I soon discovered, and no one volunteered for the other two semi-nars. (The conference organizers had to distribute students arbitrarily among the three seminars.) This clearly indi-cated which program had caught the national imagination. I also learned that students were mainly interested in se-lection criteria and whether Peace Corps volunteers would be subject to the draft.

In my speeches on the Peace Corps, I emphasized cer-tain points:

- The program would try to fill manpower gaps in ex-isting private and public programs, rather than un-dertake new programs.
- Only projects for which there was an urgent need would be approved, mainly in health, education, ag-riculture, administration, and construction.
- Official diplomatic representatives could not carry out the programs in the direct and personal way

desired. The Peace Corps would consist of highly intelligent, qualified, and articulate volunteers, mostly in their twenties, working on projects requested by the host country, to help meet that country's urgent needs for skilled manpower.[2]

- Draft-age male volunteers would receive deferred status, not exemption.
- Training would cover such things as the host nation's language, history, and economy, as well as refresher courses in American government and history.
- Those running the Peace Corps were taking a practical approach to imaginative solutions for problems, without illusions or wishful thinking.

ARRIVAL OF BILL MOYERS—ON A "WHITE HORSE"

Perhaps no single event was as vital to the Peace Corps' early visibility (if not survival) as the sudden appearance of Bill Moyers—a gift from the vice president (if not from heaven).

Until this point in late March or early April 1961, I had had the uneasy feeling that the new agency was essentially floundering in amateurism. The few professionals with any governmental experience, such as Warren Wiggins, seemed to be regularly overruled, and only the steadfast determination of the director gave reason for optimism. (Brad Patterson, who was also experienced, was hired as an administrator, not a substantive planner or programmer.) Staff meetings reminded me of the proverbial Madison Avenue ad agency. Someone needed to take hold of ideas "run up the flagpole to see who might salute them," and bring these exalted ideas *down* the flagpole to earth and to work out a short-term strategy. The Peace Corps always had more than enough long-term thinkers!

What was needed at that moment in history was what we got: Bill Moyers. Slowly, almost imperceptibly, things began to change—and for the better. By this time spring had arrived, and just about everyone knew that the next major hurdle was to get an authorization and then an appropriation through Congress. Without the achievement of those goals, no Peace Corps program was possible.

Despite his boyish appearance and modest demeanor (you had to be modest to work for Lyndon Johnson), Moyers knew what he was about, and he particularly knew what had to be done on Capitol Hill. He recognized, above all else, that the Peace Corps had to be converted, to the extent possible, from a New Frontier program into a national program with bipartisan support.

His first action was to invite Dr. Walter Judd, a senior Republican congressman from Minnesota, to address the Peace Corps staff and impart to us some of his wisdom and inspirational oratory. Dr. Judd was a former missionary doctor in China and spoke fluent Chinese. In the late fifties he had proposed the establishment of a "Youth Corps," which many felt was the forerunner of the Peace Corps concept. Although he was eventually to become a keynote speaker at the Republican National Convention and was not bereft of good old-fashioned partisan rhetoric, he engendered a special brand of bipartisan appeal. (When I eventually joined the House Foreign Affairs Committee staff, I soon discovered that *no* Republican in the committee's memory had ever commanded such a high level of respect from a series of Democratic chairmen and senior staff—not to mention those members on the GOP side of the aisle who still remembered him.)

Whether Moyers was instrumental in recruiting a favorite young Republican protégé of Barry Goldwater's in Arizona, I cannot say with certainty; but it was certainly in keeping with his style. Toward the end of my assignment to Peace Corps headquarters, I attended a Princeton Club luncheon at which Goldwater was the guest speaker. He was asked about the Peace Corps and gave a surprisingly positive endorsement (having been an earlier skeptic). I remember reporting this incident to my Peace Corps colleagues with great fanfare, only to learn much later that this had essentially resulted from the appointment of a

Goldwater protégé. He may even have been well qualified for the job.

Under Moyers's guidance, the Public Affairs Office gained both authority and prestige, and put certain commonsense procedures into effect. My Foreign Service training led me (throughout my public career) to write a "memorandum of conversation" or a "memo of record" whenever appropriate on any public statements or speeches I had made. Moyers immediately used me as an example. He did not demand prior clearance by Peace Corps staff members (which was probably impossible to monitor anyway), but merely a record of what was said as soon as possible after the fact. Eventually, it began to sink in that it was very much in the staffer's own interest to comply with this reasonable requirement.

Although Moyers did his best to promote bipartisanship, he did not believe in wasting his time on the nonconvertible. He had an uncanny understanding about which members of Congress were pro–Peace Corps, leaning that way, or could be pressured politically in that direction. He also identified those who were intransigent and basically left them alone.

Soon a steady and protracted series of "intimate" breakfasts took place between Director Shriver and key members of Congress from both parties. Bill Moyers was always in attendance, always saying the right things. As a result, the essential groundwork had been laid when Director Shriver went up to the Hill to defend his program. The Peace Corps authorization and appropriation sailed through unscathed, despite some serious opposition on the part of senior members of the House Foreign Affairs Committee staff. (It is staff opposition, incidentally, which is really *serious*—but I will get to that in later chapters).[3]

In July 1961 I was selected for my second tour of language training at the State Department's Foreign Service Institute in Washington: this time for ten months of training in Serbo-Croatian (a so-called "hard" language), prior to assignment in Yugoslavia.

My six-month service at the headquarters of an exciting new agency, the Peace Corps, was intense and the hours long. But I think I departed at just the right time: my correspondence backlog was finally under control, although about to explode again as new programs were developed. Now the Peace Corps had an appropriation and could hire its own people. I was not one of them, but I wished them well.

I did not then realize that I would subsequently be confronted with a Peace Corps crisis in an African country—or that in the 1970s I would end up authoring the first two (and only) staff investigative reports for the House Committee on Foreign Affairs ever devoted to the Peace Corps exclusively. My findings in those reports on how well the agency (which in a minor way I had helped create) had been successful in achieving its original goals are discussed in chapter 15.

6

Consul in Croatia

rior to my next assignment, as head of the consular
section at the American Consulate General,
Zagreb, Yugoslavia, I underwent an academic
year's training in Serbo-Croatian at the Foreign Service
Institute. Training in a so-called "hard language" was
supposed to be an honor of sorts, as it represented a
long-term investment in one's career by the Department
of State. Those of us who opted for a Slavic language
probably did so primarily for reasons of inertia, prestige, or both: the big names in the Foreign Service like
Charles Bohlen, Llewellyn Thompson, and George
Kennan had made it with Russian, primarily in the aftermath of World War II and the emergence of the Soviet
Union as a superpower. Even though the Foreign Service by 1962 was filled with Russian speakers who could
only be assigned to one Russian-speaking post (Moscow), the aura of a Slavic language related to Russian
had appeal to the uninitiated.

Serbo-Croatian had certain advantages over Russian:
the language had been "reformed" by a Serbian monk
named Vuk Karadžić in the eleventh century and the
grammar had been standardized and simplified. There
were no silent letters to contend with and it was possible to pronounce any word in the language, even if

one had never seen it before and had no idea what it meant. Serbo-Croatian was thus considered a good Slavic language to start with, since it was closely related to Bulgarian and to a lesser extent to Czech, Polish, and Russian. The Croats used the Latin alphabet, as did Czechs, Poles, and Slovenes (who spoke a separate language all their own, even though they understood Serbo-Croatian). The Serbs used the Cyrillic alphabet, as did Bulgarians, Montenegrins, Macedonians, and Russians. Since our Foreign Service Institute instructors were both Serbs, we had to learn Cyrillic, even though I was eventually assigned to Zagreb, Croatia, where it was never used.

If I had to do it all over again, however, I would probably have opted for a world language like French or Spanish—both of which are infinitely more useful for a generalist like myself. By the time I discovered that my future did not really lie in Eastern Europe, it was too late to change.

In retrospect, I also feel the course was too long and the routine suffocating. Being locked up in a window-less room in the basement of Arlington Towers, an apartment building in Rosslyn, Virginia, across the Potomac from the Department of State, from 9:00 A.M. to 4:00 P.M.—with one hour off for lunch—is a much more arduous ordeal than working on Capitol Hill until midnight—as I later sometimes did. The official FSI explanation is that if one is starting a Slavic or other hard language from scratch, even the best of linguists cannot attain even a "useful" knowledge of the language (level 3) or a fluent level 4 (bilingual is 5) without the full ten months of concentrated training in the classroom. This is undoubtedly true. After five or six months one would probably be only at the 2 or 2+ level. However, if those months in FSI were followed immediately by service in a post where the language was spoken, I believe the overall result would have been preferable to a ten-month classroom period. In learning a foreign language, I discovered, there is nothing comparable to the necessity of using it on a daily basis.

That is the Chester theory of learning. The FSI method, definitely different, was similar but not identical to Berlitz. It emphasized oral usage of the language: the instructor was a native speaker with whom one conversed for six hours a day with the aid of an FSI-prepared textbook. The students learned grammar on the side—with the aid of a professional linguist, if necessary. Native speakers can tell you *how* to pronounce words and put sentences together correctly, but they are not qualified to tell you *why*. That is the general philosophy.

Our class was divided into two sections, each led by a Serb. The two instructors were brothers-in-law who had spent most of their lives together, first in their native village of Šabac (near Belgrade, capital of Yugoslavia) as students, attorneys, and cavalry officers in the Serbian-dominated Yugoslav army in World War II, as POWs in Germany for the remainder of the war after being captured, and finally as refugees and then U.S. citizens residing in the greater Washington area. The two gentlemen had married sisters, and the two families lived together in the same house.

Although they shared a similar cultural upbringing, the two men were quite distinct, despite their obvious devotion to one another. Janko Janković, the lead tutor, was the more soft-spoken and sophisticated of the two, while Dragutin Popović, my tutor, was somewhat gruff of manner and more overtly rigid in his thinking. However, both shared a set of largely unshakable core political and personal values. Serbs and Serbian culture, we were to learn, were not subject to change of any kind. It is their strength: it kept the culture alive and well during centuries of Turkish occupation. It is also their weakness: they cannot accommodate other cultures, customs, and peoples without trying to dominate them.

My fellow students included Lawrence Eagleburger, an FSO-6 like me who years later became ambassador to Yugoslavia and eventually secretary of state; David Anderson, another future ambassador to Yugoslavia; James Lowenstein, a future ambassador to Luxembourg; Charles S. (Stu) Kennedy, future consul general to a number of posts; Harry Dunlop, a very bright but somewhat abrasive and flamboyant young man whom Lowenstein would later encounter in Vietnam; and Jim Fletcher, a CIA "spook," who would eventually join me in Zagreb. For a few months we also had Richard Johnson and his wife Pat. Dick had served previously in Poland and was a naturally gifted Slavic-speaking linguist. He was able to pick up Serbo-Croatian a bit faster than the rest of us and then joined the political section in Embassy Belgrade. (After he retired from the Foreign Service, he served as president of the U.S. Business Council for Southeast Europe, formerly the US-Yugoslav Trade and Economic Council.)

In any event, the ten-month course was a success for me. At its end I tested at 3+ (very useful) in speaking, and 4 (fluent) in reading, Serbo-Croatian. Only a 3-3 was required. (After my return from Zagreb, I tested at 4-4.) With the exception of Jim Fletcher and myself, all the other students were assigned to the Embassy in Belgrade. Our later outlooks on Yugoslavia were very much influenced by our respective locales.

One final retrospective: the late Messrs. Janković and Popović were by no means candidates for sainthood, but they did represent the very best of Serbian culture and tradition. Honor, dignity, and integrity were their most salient characteristics. I try to keep this incontrovertible fact in mind as I read about Serbian atrocities in the international press. Unfortunately, ethnic groups tend to be represented in the media by their worst elements, who are always the newsmakers.

ZAGREB, CROATIA

Yugoslavia, the land of the South Slavs, no longer exists.[1] It was then ruled by a centralized Communist Party regime, with carefully balanced ethnic representation at the leadership level. The maximum and undisputed leader was Marshal Tito (né Josip Broz), an authentic war hero who, unlike all of the other communist leaders of Eastern Europe, had fought the invading German army. He had been surrounded six times, escaped six times, and survived. He was the product of a Croatian father and a Slovenian mother, but essentially adopted the Serbian cause of national unity, although not with the degree of Serbian dominance the Serbs might have preferred.

Ironically in view of its world image in the 1990s, Yugoslavia in the 1960s enjoyed a relatively positive reputation. Contrary to popular belief, Tito became one of the few "true believers" in the communist system during extended stays in the Soviet Union, where he was nurtured in conspiracy. As a pragmatist about power, however, he recognized that he could not long survive as an agent of Stalin.

Tito broke with Stalin and the Comintern in 1948 when Stalin forced a break by imposing such unacceptable conditions on Yugoslavia that Tito saw no other choice. As a defensive move Tito established relatively good relations with Western countries. Substantial Western aid and the import of Western products followed. Tourism became a major industry and hard currency earner, primarily by attracting hordes of West Germans, Austrians, and Italians to Croatia's magnificent Dalmatian coast. To some, Titoism was "socialism with a human face."

Despite outward appearances, however, the Yugoslav Communist Party was harsh and repressive in maintaining internal controls. The UDBA, or secret police (the Yugoslav equivalent of the KGB), was both sophisticated and brutal. It ruthlessly suppressed any hint of opposition but for the most part concealed these manifestations from foreign tourists and casual visitors.

As I drove my new Mercedes from the Daimler-Benz factory in Stuttgart to my prospective new home in the

Croatian capital, I was astonished to find a total absence of traffic south of the Austrian-Yugoslav border. On the *autoput* (similar to the German *autobahn*) that linked Ljubljana, capital of Slovenia, with Zagreb, I encountered no more than four vehicles. In terms of "development," as the term was understood in the West, Yugoslavia was strictly in the Third World category. (And Yugoslavia was then considered more economically "progressive" than its eastern neighbors.) When I parked my car in front of the Palace Hotel in the center of town, just across the street from the American Consulate General, a great admiring crowd surrounded the vehicle— as if it were a spaceship from Mars. The alarm device I had installed at the factory rang perpetually, it seemed, as everyone felt the need to touch the car in some fashion and set it off.

Taking a Mercedes, even if only a 180, to Yugoslavia was my first big mistake: the low-octane gasoline available in Zagreb caused the motor to knock, and local mechanics generally replaced new with secondhand parts. A Volkswagen Beetle, such as several of my colleagues owned, would have been a far better choice, as I learned to my endless regret. There was one compensation: upon departure I was able to sell my 180 to the local government for a good price, almost as much as I paid for it *new*. The party members who purchased it (with public funds) were especially impressed with the radio aerial, which rose automatically when the radio was turned on. Aside from this clever feature, what the comrades purchased in the summer of 1964 was a piece of junk!

Unlike Belgrade, which must rank as the ugliest metropolis in Eastern Europe, Zagreb was by and large a handsome city, constructed mostly in the Hapsburg style with a mountain backdrop. The new modern-looking structures, which were mostly falling apart before construction was even completed, were concentrated in one low-lying area across the Sava River. The Stari Grad, or old town, was especially picturesque, located high on a hill overlooking the rest of the downtown. The local communist regime carefully preserved it, not only as a Republic of Croatia government and party headquarters, but also as a "national treasure," used on several occasions during my tour as a movie set for wartime spy films produced by Western companies. (Curiously, communists tend to preserve old buildings more steadfastly, as in Moscow and East Berlin, than do we in the West, where such buildings are torn down and replaced with modern glass monstrosities.)

In keeping with the local architecture, the American Consulate General was an old-fashioned, decrepit-looking building located in the heart of the city. It was definitely not designed to withstand an assault of any kind, despite a number of thick old doors with special locks. In short order I was to learn just how defenseless this structure actually was.

I was greeted at the front door by a spare, almost deformed, old gentleman who resembled a street person. When he took off his cap and held it in front of his chest with both hands, I assumed that he was panhandling, and I reactively placed a few dinars therein. He turned out to be the live-in house master, named Dragutin. He accepted my largesse without complaint, as he was never known to turn down a gift of any denomination. Instead of Marine guards, we had Dragutin to protect and preserve the American interest.

During the first few weeks after my arrival, I stayed in the somewhat run-down Palace Hotel across the street. Soon my wife and our two young children (John, our firstborn, and Isabelle, just born) joined me. The Palace, which hardly lived up to its name, was one of two hotels in town designed primarily for foreigners, especially Americans. That meant that the UDBA had carefully bugged each room, an activity considerably more efficient than the room service. The best way to get a bellboy to come to the room was to unplug the telephone, which caused havoc at the front desk.

Another usual feature of the Palace was the tendency of all sorts of hotel employees, when they *did* show up, to enter one's room without knocking. On one occasion, when I was lounging in bed and my family was out, a fellow in overalls appeared with a ladder, climbed up to inspect the chandelier and changed the tape! One learned quickly enough not to share one's innermost secrets with the authorities.

On the second night after my arrival in Zagreb, I literally "ran into" Tito. The incident remains vivid in my memory bank. It was late evening and pitch dark in front of the Palace Hotel. (The street lights in downtown Zagreb were exceedingly dim if they worked at all.) In the absence of traffic, I was strolling in the middle of the road when I encountered a large mob walking—almost in march step—in my direction. I turned to face this apparent juggernaut, out of curiosity and because I felt I had plenty of time to make a hasty retreat to the sidewalk. As the marchers approached, I realized that in the front row were Marshal Tito and the visiting Leonid Brezhnev.

I remained transfixed until the very last moment. As I moved to the side, I saw Tito smile at me like a politician running for public office; he even extended his hand, which I was about to shake when two burly security officers grabbed me from behind and threw me unceremoniously to the pavement. I landed on my attaché case, which I was holding at the time and may have made me appear a potential subversive. Tito was displeased and sent two of his henchmen back to apologize for this rough treatment. Even at the time I was not offended, however, as I imagined that the U.S. Secret Service might have administered similar treatment to anyone suspicious getting that close to the president. It was a rather exhilarating adventure. (My experience the following year, when I followed Tito and his robust spouse, Jovanka, around the American pavilion at the Zagreb Fair, was rather mundane by comparison.)

AMERICAN PERSONNEL AT THE CONSULATE GENERAL

The American Consulate General, Zagreb, was definitely in the category of a small post. (Sarajevo, the only other American consular post in Yugoslavia, was smaller, and that two-man office was closed down soon afterwards.) The building we inhabited was, as noted, of prewar traditional construction, so we tended to blend into the local scene.

The consul general (the principal officer at the post) was a most unusual career FSO named Joseph Godson. He had recently been transferred from the embassy in Belgrade, where he had served as labor attaché. Joe was born in Poland in 1913 and reputedly spoke little English when he arrived in New York at age thirteen. The following paragraphs from his 1986 obituary are, I believe, quite accurate and highly revealing:

> The same transition from Europe to America, which took him through City College in New York, and then law school at New York University in the 1930s, also helped to shape his ideas about politics.
>
> A Marxist in his early years, he soon decided that Stalin held no attraction for him; but he also rejected the romanticism of the Trotskyists and was thereby saved from the exaggerated swing to the right which many Trotskyists subsequently went through by way of overcompensation.
>
> He belonged to that brave group of Americans who continued to search for a workable, democratic form of Marxism until the Nazi-Soviet Pact of 1939 made them dissolve their organization in despair.

By the early fall of 1962, Joe Godson was anything but a leftist. Having spent many years in the U.S. labor movement, he had reportedly fallen under the influence of—and was in fact much like—the late Jay Lovestone, the so-called Minister of Foreign Affairs of the AFL-CIO. Lovestone's background made even Joe's seem pallid by comparison. Although I never met Lovestone, I consider him an important figure in the U.S. labor movement who warrants a few descriptive comments.

In the mid-sixties the *Washington Post* featured a four-installment front-page series on Jay Lovestone's life and works, which should have been made into a best-seller. In the 1930s he was the leader of the Communist Party of the United States, but he eventually broke bitterly with Stalin. He was even quoted as having told the Soviet dictator to his face (in Moscow) that he, Stalin, "was unfit to lead the international Communist movement." Stalin allegedly replied, "Mr. Lovestone, there are graveyards all over this country for people like you!" This was rather foolhardy behavior by Lovestone, as he could easily have been disposed of in Moscow, and it is doubtful that the U.S. diplomatic mission at the time would have considered the disappearance of an American Communist a top priority concern.

Lovestone managed to escape, however, and eventually became an exceedingly forceful hard-line anti-communist—at the highest echelon of the AFL-CIO hierarchy. Like J. Edgar Hoover, he remained a bachelor throughout his life and had virtually no outside interests (not even the racetracks Hoover frequented). He not only spent long hours at AFL-CIO headquarters, but often slept there on a cot. His main mission in life was to keep the U.S. labor movement divorced from any East European or Soviet labor organization—whether or not sanctioned by the United Nations or other international bodies. Even the somewhat more "liberal" Yugoslav trade union organizations were off limits from his standpoint. He wanted no one to "mess" with them.

Many U.S. labor officials disapproved of this strategy, not because they were leftists, but because they believed in the usefulness of international contacts. "We lost the opportunity to influence these people in the right direction" was a complaint often heard. Nevertheless, Lovestone reigned supreme at the pinnacle of power, with the strong support of AFL-CIO President George Meany. No one served as labor attaché in a U.S. diplomatic post abroad without the express clearance of the Department of Labor.

And no Labor Department clearance was ever issued without the personal approval of Jay Lovestone.

I was subsequently amused to read one account about Lovestone in the *Post* series, shortly after my return from Europe in 1964. Apparently some AFL-CIO officials took a vacation in Europe and eventually decided to hold informal, unofficial discussions with their (allegedly) Croatian counterparts. When Mr. Lovestone was informed of these unauthorized contacts, the officials were recalled to Washington and severely castigated by their leader. It was not hard to figure out just how Jay Lovestone came upon this incidental information. (In other words, you also did not tread with impunity upon Joe Godson's turf without authorization!)

Godson had an intense, somewhat nervous personality that often turned people off, especially Americans. He was anything but the legendary smooth and polished diplomat whose effectiveness was largely founded on charm. On the contrary, he found it absolutely impossible to engage in small talk and preferred to obtain his objectives with pressure and the hard-sell approach. He did not appreciate my wife's representational skills the way Consul General Page in Munich had. As a consequence Clara never assumed an active role in the social world of the Zagreb consular corps, such as it was. Joe Godson liked to run a tight ship, and he generally reserved the important political, economic, and social contacts for himself.

Joe also had an acute sense of political reality and a reporter's nose for a story. He found out about internal local political developments because he was never afraid to ask. Once, when a naturalized U.S. citizen of Croatian extraction came to my office in the consulate to have his passport extended, he casually remarked that he had heard a rumor in his native village that the employees of a local *poduzeće* (or factory enterprise) had conducted a three-day strike. (No strikes were either authorized or recognized in Titoland, and any such reports were carefully suppressed.) When I took this gentleman in to see the consul general, the latter convinced this U.S. citizen that it was his patriotic duty to change his travel plans and go back to the village for further investigation. The man did so, and Joe reported the scoop.

When high-ranking Croatian officials who were recipients of USIA leader or specialist grants (designed to expose foreign leaders and experts to U.S. institutions, politics, economics, and culture) would come to the consulate general for their visas, Joe and I worked out what we called a "one-two" punch. As chief of the consular section, I was the official glad-hander—I would greet the dignitary with cordiality, offer him a glass of Šljivovica (Slivovitz), an absolute requirement for such occasions, and provide him with a glowing description of his forthcoming itinerary.[2] Then I would take the VIP in to see Joe. I am not at all certain what transpired behind those closed doors with Joe Godson, but I do know that when the grantee emerged he (or, rarely, she) was usually perspiring profusely—and Joe usually had something of interest to report to Washington.

This was the era of "bridge-building" toward Eastern Europe, designed as a strategy to wean East European satellite regimes away from Soviet domination. Since it was clear by the early sixties that none of the Western allies was prepared to "liberate" the Eastern bloc by force, this seemed a prudent course. Joe actually had no criticism of the policy per se, but he believed in *both* the carrot *and* the stick. With his East European background, he obviously felt more at ease than did many American diplomats in applying pressure where it was needed. And he was usually right, in my judgment. Yugoslav officials generally understood his approach, whereas they never truly fathomed the highly intellectual style of Ambassador George Kennan, who presided over the American establishment in Belgrade.

There could not have been two more contrasting personalities than Joe Godson and George Kennan, although they treated each other with a degree of mutual respect, if not high regard. When the ambassador came to inspect the Zagreb consular district on occasion, Joe would get extremely nervous and fidgety.

Kennan was notorious for forgetting names—even of people on his senior staff—and his wife, who was a most efficient and gracious hostess, tried to coach him in this regard. En route to their first trip to Zagreb, she must have reminded him that I happened to be the son of a good friend and business associate of his cousin, Charles James of Milwaukee, and that he should mention this connection. As we were all lined up at the front door of the consul general's residence, the ambassador was introduced to my wife. "How nice to see someone from Milwaukee," the ambassador observed. "Thank you," said Clara, "but I am from Washington." I still recall the look of shock and disillusionment he then cast at his spouse. Later that evening I managed to startle the guests by informing Ambassador Kennan that my grandfather, a neighbor and pastor of Milwaukee's Immanuel Presbyterian Church, had been called to his mother's bedside as she was suffering the pain of childbirth from which she subsequently died. The child was George Kennan, and, I hastened to add, my grandfather was in no way responsible.

Joe Godson's deputy and economic officer in Zagreb was another career FSO named George W. Jaeger, at that time not many grades or years above my own. Jaeger and Godson shared a few things in common: both were of Jewish or partly Jewish background and had fled from their native lands at a tender age. George had been born in Vienna and escaped first to England and finally to the United States prior to the outbreak of World War II. Both valued their American citizenship highly, believed in aggressively promoting and defending the U.S. national interest, and were extremely conscientious in carrying out their responsibilities.

The similarities ended there. In contrast to our consul general, George was smooth, polished, and sophisticated, and exuded continental charm. His soft, low, mellifluous voice was especially appealing to women, but he wisely eschewed romantic attachments in Yugoslavia. Although by no means a confirmed bachelor, he realized the risk of becoming compromised in one way or another by the UDBA. George lived in solitary splendor in his villa on Tuškanac (the posh hill overlooking the town where most diplomats and high government officials resided), supported by a devoted middle-aged servant named Ivanka. Each day Ivanka left her husband to take care of all of Consul Jaeger's most pressing housekeeping needs.

George was a hard-driving perfectionist who worked long hours and expected the same from his colleagues. Although I was nominally in charge of the consular section, including such functions as visas, passports and citizenship, protection, and welfare, George tended to second-guess my every move and check every detail until he became reassured that I had the situation fully under control. While I chafed at times under this system, I recognized even then that my overall performance always improved when subjected to the right kind of pressure! (George, I should add, has remained a lifelong friend. I often visit him and his wife Pat in Middlebury, Vermont, where they live in retirement.)

Finally, my FSI classmate, Jim Fletcher, ostensibly on the State Department rolls, was actually involved in intelligence, using his consular title primarily as a cover. He took his consular duties seriously and became highly proficient in all aspects of this work. Jim was so conscientious in carrying out his cover responsibilities that the UDBA had trouble figuring out which one of us was the "spook," despite numerous (and usually obvious) provocations.[3] We had both arrived at the post at approximately the same time, were of the same approximate age and grade, and had similar-sounding names. To the Yugoslav authorities, it must have looked like a plot to confuse, although that is giving the U.S. government too much credit.

Eventually the consulate was assigned a young "trainee," Robert Barry, who drew Zagreb as his very first overseas post. I thought I would have him on a permanent basis to help clear up my consular backlog, but he proved to be too valuable to both George and Joe, and even to the administrative section. (We must have trained him right, as he later served as ambassador to Bulgaria, Romania, and Indonesia, and was named the Organization for Security and Cooperation in Europe's chief representative in Bosnia in the mid-1990s.)

The USIS (United States Information Service) contingent was headed by Neely Turner, a career United States Information Agency (USIA) officer, who spent much of his time fighting with Joe Godson over turf. While the principal officer was nominally in control of the post, Neely was often at pains to point out that the USIA branch public affairs officer reported to the public affairs officer in Belgrade and to USIA in Washington.

A remarkable older woman on Neely's staff, Corinne Spencer, ran the USIS library located on the ground floor of our building. Corinne was a charming, soft-spoken product of the Deep South, with an attractive drawl, and was regularly surrounded by a devoted group of Croatian intellectuals. In terms of lasting impact, she probably exerted the most pervasive influence of any postwar American official in Croatia.

TUŠKANAC—WHERE THE LIVING AIN'T ALWAYS EASY

Tuškanac was essentially one of the several foothills leading from the base of Sljeme, the highest mountain above Zagreb, down into the central city. Located high above the smog and fog that was often trapped in the lowland, it was an area that housed Croatia's more prominent leaders plus members of the consular corps. The residents had included, in turn, the Austrian nobility and colonial administrators of Croatia, then the Germans and their local fascist *Ustaše* puppets during World War II, and finally the postwar Communist party leaders.

Despite its obvious advantages, Tuškanac also had drawbacks: all supplies for daily living had to be hauled up the mountainside. Preparing for the winter was especially onerous. Most of the houses had been constructed as summer residences, with large glass windows and no real foundations, and heating was very difficult, time-consuming, and frustrating. A state enterprise would eventually drop wood in the form of large logs in front of one's gate. The logs resembled large trees without limbs, and totally blocked the entrance and exit to one's property. Then one negotiated with the Albanian minority, which had a total monopoly on wood-cutting. If you were lucky, after two or three days a man would appear with a mobile saw powered by something resembling an outboard motor. He sawed the logs into small blocks that could fit in a furnace, and again stacked them in front of the entrance. Hired laborers would carry the wood from the gate through the living room and into the basement. We then would order and have delivered the peculiar-smelling brown coal (often called railroad coal) that polluted the atmosphere. Often the large chunks of coal had to be broken up to fit into one's furnace.

To get the wood fire started, we hired a stoker named Milan. He arrived at between 4:00 and 5:30 A.M. Each household had to keep the fire going through the day and into the evening by adding regular amounts of coal. Unfortunately, I have lost a photo once taken of my wife standing in our basement in a negligee, wearing reading glasses, and holding a shovel full of coal in front of the furnace. Below read the caption: "Smith College never prepared me for *THIS*." She learned by hard experience never to let the coal burn away or she would have to start a new wood fire all over again. All these procedures were priorities during our first winter in Tuškanac, which was the coldest on record for over fifty years. During one extended snowstorm, even the trains could not get into or out of town for three days!

Our section of Tuškanac was also situated above the municipal gas line. That meant we had to pick up and return (attach and detach) individual canisters of gas to run the stove. At least the gas was not affected when the lights went dim or off in the early evening because of a power overload, although a canister might go dry in the middle of a dinner party, and a heavy replacement canister had to be carried in from the garage by the head of family (me!).

What impressed me most about the above rigmarole was not only the effort but the *time* which had to be expended just to secure the basic necessities of life. Perhaps for those of us accustomed to turning on heat or air conditioning by setting a dial, this was a valuable experience.

Kindergarten

The *dječji vrtić* or kindergarten for Tuškanac residents was located about a mile down the road from our villa, in the direction of downtown. Since the office was closed for two hours at midday, in keeping with local custom, and everyone went home for luncheon, I would normally drive my four-year-old son, John, to school en route to the consulate and then pick him up at noon, mostly on my Lambretta motor scooter.

I was soon to become famous, or perhaps infamous, as the only diplomat in Zagreb to commute to town and back on a scooter, which I had purchased in Trieste. To the best of my knowledge, I was also the only owner in all of Yugoslavia of a diplomatic license plate custom-made for a scooter in Belgrade's Sremska Mitrovica prison. Unlike the Mercedes, the Lambretta was an eminently practical machine (except in deep snow): gasoline for it cost approximately $1.00 per month, and the motor never broke down. It could also pass all the heavy trucks traveling at snail's pace up and down Tuškanac hill, which a car could not. Above all, it freed up a car for my wife to use—and she needed it much more than I did. When we departed Zagreb, I sold the Mercedes and transferred the scooter to Washington. I continued using a Lambretta or Honda for the rest of my working life, a lifestyle that accurately reflects my personal value system.

John's adjustment from the comforting confines of the White House play school to a Balkan kindergarten was considerable. Fortunately kids readily adapt to changing circumstances. John and Jimmy Fletcher, son of my consulate colleague, were the only two American children in the school, but they were in different classrooms, so they were not able to support each other much. Neither spoke a word of Croatian when enrolled.

At first I worried about my son, as he seemed hesitant to leave me and even shed a few tears from time to time. I subsequently learned that five minutes after my departure he was happy and relaxed, and soon became a class leader. In time I found out why: the individual classroom instructors were really more like baby-sitters, of the very sympathetic, maternal variety. They were known as *"Teta,"* roughly translated as aunt. Their devotion to the children was warmly reciprocated: John became particularly attached to Teta Ljerka, "the nice *teta.*"

By contrast, the school's director was highly intimidating. She was known as Drugarica (pronounced Drugaritsa), the feminine form for "Comrade," and she was built something like a Washington Redskins linebacker, with her hair combed into a bun at the back of her head. Unlike the soft, motherly *tetas*, she was as tough as nails and had a partisan war record to prove it. She claimed to have fought alongside Tito during World War II and had a large picture and sculpture of the president in her office. She was also in charge of indoctrination and taught the children such concepts as "East is good" and "West is bad," and such songs as *Tito je dobar Vodža Naša* (in rough translation):

Tito is our good leader,
although he lives in Belgrade
he is with us in spirit . . .

Despite her ideological affinity for Marxism in general, and for the Yugoslav League of Communists (as the party was called) in particular, Drugarica eventually displayed one glaring weakness: she was soft on the son of the notorious capitalist consul! In other words, John became her pet and was often loaded up with candy provided by the front office, which he then shared with his schoolmates. And that, dear readers, is how you become a "leader" in a Croatian *dječji vrtić'!*

About six weeks after John started school, I stopped by to pick him up and was met by Drugarica in the hallway. She wanted to show me some of my son's rather primitive art work, which she had prominently displayed in her office. At that very moment, we heard shouting and laughter from the upstairs level—led by a familiar voice about an octave higher than the others. "Can that be my son?" I asked incredulously, as he was speaking not only in fluent Croatian, but with the local *kaj-kavski* dialect peculiar to the city of Zagreb. "Oh, yes," Drugarica replied, "John has no problem with communication!" Thus I learned the lesson that so many Americans stationed abroad learned: one's offspring—after six weeks in the country and with no prior training—was already speaking flawlessly in a language his father had just spent ten months trying to learn. Of course, John only needed a child's vocabulary, but the accent was virtually unattainable by an adult nonnative speaker.

Another example of youthful adaptability involved the annual trip by all schoolchildren in Zagreb to the Dalmatian coast. Every June an entire train transported the young kindergartners from Zagreb to the outskirts of Zadar, where various tent camps were located. Each car was reserved for a particular school and its respective faculty. My wife and I at first demurred, assuming that a full month's outing in a distant and alien environment was probably a bit much for a four-year-old. We acted without John's concurrence, however, and he seemed bitterly disappointed. Consequently, as parents often do, we reassessed our position.

On the evening of the train's departure, the Zagreb *Kolodvor* (railroad station) was packed with humanity—mostly children and grandparents (many of the latter were live-in baby sitters who cared for the kids while the parents worked). Slavic people, even heroic ones, have no inhibitions about public display of emotion, which means that just about everyone was in tears. As the train left the station, virtually every small child was leaning out of the window, waving and crying *"Do Vidjenja, Djed; Do Vidjenja, Baba"* (Goodbye, Grandpa; Goodbye, Grandma), while the old folks were behaving in similar fashion. The entire scene resembled something from a World War II film depicting the separation of families under desperate circumstances.

Amid this chaos and confusion, only two smiling faces were to be seen, both illuminated by the car's dim internal lights, namely, John and Drugarica, both happily engaged in some kind of checkerboard game. And thus, gentle reader, one small budding capitalist disarmed, at least temporarily, a communist "dragon."

SECURITY SHENANIGANS

All members of the Zagreb consular corps were subject to constant electronic and personal surveillance by the UDBA. Not only were our movements watched, our telephones tapped, and our rooms bugged, both at home and in the office, but our professional and social contacts were noted and often interrogated. To protect especially the latter, we generally made it a habit *not* to invite the same people for cocktails or dinner in close succession. Official contacts were less vulnerable in this respect, as their attendance at any consular function normally had been cleared in advance with the so-called chief of protocol, Mr. Petar Menac, who was nothing more nor less than a UDBA operative.

Every appointment, even of the most routine nature, had to receive Mr. Menac's advance approval, except high-ranking Croatian politicians who outranked him. This even applied to calls and conversations with midlevel government officials, which cramped the style of Joe Godson and George Jaeger in their efforts to find out what was going on in the political and economic life of the district. Since most of my clients came to the consulate to see me and obtain a service, I was somewhat less affected by these restrictions.

At one point Tito introduced a program of *rotacija* (rotation) for prominent government officials, mainly to combat "parochialism" (read nationalism) among Serbs and Croats by moving them to different locations. "Why is it," our consul general asked Mr. Menac with his usual bluntness, "that everyone in Hrvatska seems to be subject to *rotacija* except *you?*" Whatever the response, the real answer seemed to be that no one in Belgrade wanted Petar Menac either!

Our local security problems never received much sympathetic understanding from our American colleagues in Belgrade. The situation there simply did not bear out many of our expressed concerns. In the early sixties Belgrade played host to a broadly representative diplomatic corps: almost all of the Western Hemisphere countries, all of Western and Eastern Europe, most of the Third World, and even China. The Belgrade and Zagreb situations were really not comparable.

The Croatian UDBA's activities also included hostile clandestine operations designed to entrap, discredit, and/or blackmail foreign diplomats. The British had recently been targeted in this fashion. A sexually attractive (and active) spouse of one of the British officers had evidently been seduced by a Croatian official. On one occasion, when the couple were in bed in a remote inn, UDBA personnel broke into the room, took photographs, and attempted to enlist the woman's cooperation in espionage. Although very frightened, the lady did not cooperate and was immediately hustled out of the country by the British consul general. The incident received no publicity, but was recounted to new arrivals as a warning of the perils that lay ahead and were best avoided.

Most of the local (Yugoslav) employees of the consulate general had been enlisted, at one time or another, in the UDBA surveillance program. Those who did not cooperate were often threatened or, at least on one occasion that I knew of, beaten severely. Others, we assumed, submitted routine reports about the Americans' movements and contacts merely to retain their positions. It was best, I learned, to suspect everyone (for their sakes as well as our own) and to behave accordingly. Only Stojan Krnjajić, the major-domo of our establishment, who brought the coffee, delivered the mail, and placed large bundles of paperwork in our respective in-boxes, was above suspicion. If the consulate building had been totally destroyed, I have no doubt at all that Stojan would have gone with it—holding the American flag! Despite his many sterling qualities, however, Stojan was a compulsive gossip and probably provided more information unwittingly than could ever have been extracted from him with threats.

One of the UDBA spies turned out to be a valued assistant, Ana Ašperger, who was of Hungarian extraction and cordially disliked by many of the Croatian women. She was disliked especially by Neda Zepić. Neda was of equivalent value to Jim Fletcher and the entire post, as she had developed excellent contacts among government officials and proved invaluable in resolving protection and welfare problems. Ana was already an expert in passport and citizenship matters when I arrived. I later encouraged her to increase her level of expertise by enrolling in a State Department correspondence course in this field. She received one of the highest grades ever accorded to a local employee worldwide. At the end of my Zagreb assignment, in the summer of 1964, I spent many overtime hours with Ana, attempting to clear up a large backlog of pending cases relating to U.S. citizenship rights of Croatians who had become naturalized and had then returned to Yugoslavia.

During this period my wife received an anonymous letter claiming that Ana and I were having an affair. Fortunately no one believed this charge, beginning with my wife, as it was clearly preposterous, but it was evident that the animus was directed at Ana, not me. (Ana was in her mid-thirties and fairly attractive, though a bit corpulent.) I was just a convenient prop to get her into trouble. Eventually, several years after my departure, Ana confessed to a State Department security officer that she had been a regular UDBA informant and was discharged. No doubt her successor was similarly recruited, so that Ana's departure was in all probability a net loss to the American establishment. This comment may seem cynical, but, I fear, accurate.

Official surveillance was not limited to the office. Our next-door neighbor on Tuškanac hill was a "retired" police official, whose evident assignment was to keep track of our comings and goings, and especially our guests. The man was extremely unpleasant and reclusive, not a normal Croatian trait. He had a large wolfhound chained to an outside doghouse. Only twice did this neighbor make personal contact with me: first, when his dog, a killer, got loose and played happily with our basset hound, Heathcliff, on neutral ground until the wolfhound was recaptured and turned once again into a fierce, protecting, chained-up watchdog; and second, when the telephone technicians, in the process of installing a tap on our phone, managed to switch the wires so that we were receiving the neighbor's calls and he ours. The man appeared in a great state of agitation, practically ordering me not to answer my own phone. (Not that anything ever spoken on the telephone in Zagreb was in any way comprehensible; international calls were clear as a bell, but local calls were both weak and full of static—primarily, we assumed, because of constant tapping.)

All rooms in our residence were assumed to be bugged. At least, it was considered prudent to act on that assumption. My wife and I often communicated in writing if the matter under discussion was in any way personal or sensitive, then burned the paper. At times when we thought we were becoming overly paranoid, something would happen to confirm our worst suspicions.

At one point we hired Angelina, the best cook in town, who had been employed at one time or another by various ranking members of Zagreb's consular corps. In just a few weeks we understood why her tenure at each household had been strictly curtailed. Although an inspired gourmet chef, she had a frightful temper and quarreled with the rest of our domestic staff, even including Mara, our sweet-tempered nanny from Slavonia (the agricultural district of Croatia, not to be confused with Slovenia). When it was finally reported to me that she had banged my darling young daughter Isabelle's head against the kitchen wall in a fit of pique, I fired her instantly.

Returning from a brief vacation some weeks later, we spotted Angelina hurriedly departing our home in the midst of a snowstorm. Closely resembling someone who had just stolen the crown jewels, she looked furtively around, then disappeared into the night. According to Mara, she had returned ostensibly to pick up some forgotten belongings but made a detailed inspection of the premises instead, and then left empty-handed. Clearly Angelina was a UDBA spy, which, together with her bad disposition, accounted for her inability to hold lasting employment with so many of my colleagues. Everyone I consulted on the subject agreed on two points: while Angelina was on board, the family ate extremely well but the price was intolerable.

VACATIONS ABROAD

The vacation we were returning from when we witnessed Angelina's clandestine retreat from our residence was one of the more memorable out-of-country ventures of "Assignment-Zagreb." Together with our Belgrade friends, the Lowensteins, we had decided on a skiing vacation in Bad Gastein, a resort not too far from the Yugoslav-Austrian border.

If one's home base was anywhere in Yugoslavia—or indeed in Eastern Europe generally—planning vacations in Western Europe became a top priority concern. Vacations spent in-country were just not the same, and one needed to get out to retain one's sanity. Jim Lowenstein, both professionally and personally, was a meticulous planner and programmer. Unlike many people who thought about global foreign policy, he also checked on the details. Jim learned that instead of driving over one of the various passes leading into Austria, we could put the car on an auto-train and speed through the tunnel from Slovenia. Upon checking, I found out that it was indeed a viable option.

When we arrived in Jesenica (the key Slovenian town), we found ourselves in the midst of a blizzard. The snow was accumulating fast and vision became difficult. In desperation, we asked a passerby for directions to the train station; the latter stuck his head inside the front window and replied "Aaaaaaah..." He was, in fact, the village idiot, who could not speak in any language. He was, however, determined to be helpful and had me trudge after him in the deep snow all the way to the station, with Jim and the two wives following behind us by car in first gear.

At the station I was led to a back room where some uniformed officials were playing cards and drinking beer. "Here we are," I announced grandly, "the diplomats who made advance reservations, and we are ready to drive our vehicle onto the train." The officials looked completely stunned by this offer and, like the idiot, remained speechless for a time. Finally one official explained that yes, we could put our car on the train, but the freight train was not due to arrive for several hours and then we would have to take a different (passenger) train. The whole operation could take another twenty-four hours, I was advised, and we would be better off facing the challenge of the pass by road. And that is what we ended up doing.

In then-Yugoslavia, we learned by hard experience, it was not enough to get information from the top level of leadership. One must also consult the working level. During the entirety of my stay in Jesenica, moreover, I had the gut feeling that the village idiot knew all along that our goal was probably unattainable. In the last analysis, he knew more than we did.

JACK RUBY'S BLOND BOMBSHELL

Consular officers are often stuck with grubby detail, but they are also to be found where the action is. They may not always be confronted with world-shaking events, but individual human crises are their stock-in-trade. One such case happened in my function of protecting American citizens.

In fall 1963, shortly before the Kennedy assassination, Jim Fletcher and I had to rescue a very paunchy bald-headed middle-aged male in a drunken stupor in danger of losing his passport and money. Even after we sobered him up, his memory was gone, and he could not recall the location of the private home where he had left his luggage. I found him temporary lodging and left him in charge of a reluctant landlady.

The following morning he appeared in my office, quite sober, contrite, and in possession of all his faculties. He said he was an advance man for his wife, known as the "Blond Bombshell." She was scheduled to arrive in a few days to fulfill a month's contract as a stripper at a local club for party members only. Strip joints were off limits to the general populace, and as a matter of fact, this very private facility was the only one I had ever heard of in the entire Republic of Croatia.

The Bombshell and her husband were originally Swiss and part of a longtime circus act. The wife, who was in remarkably good shape for someone her age (late forties), had taken up stripping for a living after becoming a U.S. citizen and resident of Texas. The Yugoslav contract had appealed to the couple—primarily as a filler between European engagements elsewhere—because it also included a paid vacation on the Dalmatian coast. However, when they found out that the Bombshell's salary was to be paid in dinars (totally worthless outside Yugoslavia), the agent-husband was furious, though it was basically his fault for not reading the contract carefully. When the two left secretly for Austria after a few nights of work, the responsible Croatian officials were equally furious, but could not make a public row about the defection, as they were probably not authorized to hire the lady to begin with.

During her brief sojourn in Zagreb, the Bombshell had been very congenial and appreciative of the services we had rendered her spouse. He always went on a bender before her public appearances, she explained, as he did not really like her doing that kind of work, but they needed the money. For that purpose, at least, Vienna seemed a much more promising locale.

After their midnight disappearance, the case seemed closed. But as with Mark Twain's death, that judgment was premature. It just so happened that John F. Kennedy was assassinated on the day my wife and I departed for a brief vacation in Budapest and Vienna. Budapest had an almost total news blackout during the first forty-eight hours following the president's demise, so we were unaware of the dramatic events that followed, namely, Jack Ruby's shooting of Oswald. By the time we reached Vienna, however, the international media were covering little else. And there on the front page of the local Austrian newspapers (particularly the tabloids) was a full-page photo of the Bombshell, the feature entertainer at the Eve Bar and now an overnight celebrity. She had been one of Jack Ruby's girls and knew him well, she said, and thought highly of him. He paid his girls on time, she pointed out, and gave them many fringe benefits—also undisclosed. He stood out in her opinion as one of the few stripper-impresarios who was considerate and supportive of his employees. My wife and I went to see her at the Eve Bar, and she was most cordial, even posing between us (mostly unclad) for a photo. We thus became celebrities by association.

The Vienna publicity did not help in Zagreb, however, for in a few months I received a plaintive letter from the husband-agent, begging me to intercede with the Croatian government for arrears in promised payments. They were evidently short of cash again, but this was clearly a nonstarter, given the nature of their departure from Zagreb. Sic transit gloria!

SIMMERING SIGNS OF ETHNIC TENSION

Under Comrade Tito, the party line was *"Bratsvo i Jedinstvo"* (Brotherhood and Unity), and any manifestations of ethnic separatism or nationalism were ruthlessly suppressed. While the government in Belgrade, as well as the party, maintained a delicate balance among the various ethnic groups and provinces (called republics), the common goal was generally understood to be a united Yugoslavia. Only the "old generation" (those old enough to remember World War II or the era that preceded it) favored such concepts as Croatian or Slovenian nationalism. Such people were not only discredited, but their numbers diminished by attrition as they departed this earth. That party line was the recognized conventional wisdom. It was especially popular with Serbs, many of whose families had suffered grievously at the hands of their Croatian "brothers." They had everything to gain from the unity concept, since they were the dominant group in terms of numbers.

Although American diplomats tended to be skeptical of most government-sponsored propaganda, I think it is fair to say that most accepted the unity theme as valid and in accordance with Yugoslav national aspirations. That was less so in Zagreb—for good reason! While Serbs tended to play down the ethnic differences ("we are all Slavs, speak the same language with very minor variations, and have a similar Christian heritage," and so forth), the Croats would whisper into one's ear that they were "different"—the product of *Western* civilization—unlike the *Eastern* or Byzantine Serbs who, it was strongly implied, were clearly inferior in many respects. These sentiments were shared by Slovenes, except that they considered themselves superior to *both* Serbs and Croats (and indeed, although small in number, they were the most productive of all Southern Slavs). During the early sixties, these views were not proclaimed loudly or forcefully, but softly and subtly. Only those of us who served in Croatia were exposed to such heresy.

Realistically, the Yugoslav experiment never had a lot going for it: Created after World War I as the Kingdom of Serbs, Croats, and Slovenes under the Karadjordjević monarchy, the country underwent its first crisis in the twenties when the Croatian Peasant Party leader Stjepan Radić was shot to death in the national *Skupština* (parliament) by a Serb who evidently did not appreciate the man's remarks. Every year on All Saints' Day much of Zagreb marched up to Mirogoj Cemetery to place flowers on Stjepan's grave.

By the time World War II came along, resentments had reached such a peak that the independent state of Croatia was proclaimed, under Nazi sponsorship, led by the Croatian Fascist leader, Ante Pavelić, the Poglavnik (maximum leader). The Croatian leadership of that era (aided and abetted by a substantial element of the Catholic clergy, an endless embarrassment to the Vatican) then proceeded to commit hideous atrocities against Serbs living in Croatia, including chopping off heads with axes and burning people in churches.

Indeed, the wartime excesses of the Ustashi had the effect of persuading many noncommunists to support the partisans under Marshal Tito. The partisans at least were made up of all ethnic groups and were actually fighting valiantly against the German invaders. By contrast, the *Chetniks,* although honorable royalists attempting to defend their country against the Germans, spent more time trying to wipe out the Tito Communists, at times even with tacit German approval and assistance. The *Chetniks,* moreover, were a strictly Serbian force representing primarily Serbian interests.

Finally, when the carnage of World War II ended, there was an understandable desire to embrace the concepts of peace, brotherhood, and unity—a new "all-Yugoslav order," so to speak. It was a noble idea, but did not last very long.

Croatian Nationalism at the Opera

A hint that perhaps Croatian nationalism was not yet an anachronism—confined exclusively to the "old" generation of Austrian-influenced citizenry—emerged at the Zagreb opera house, after an evening of *Zrinsky,* a heroic opera with stirring musical and dramatic themes. In its last act a Croatian Count Zrinsky, after numerous patriotic arias and crescendos, walked out of his castle to face certain death at the hands of the Turkish invader, in a futile but martyred attempt to defend the Croatian homeland. As the music swelled into the final climactic scene, it brought forth from the audience chauvinistic emotion from the depths of the Croatian soul.

After one memorable performance, a chant arose from the cheap seats in the gallery, occupied almost exclusively by students. Some appeared not to have even reached university age, but clearly all were members of the postwar generation. "*Naša Zastava* (Our Flag)," they shouted, meaning the traditional Croatian flag in lieu of the hammer and sickle. After much commotion, a short squat official and member of the Zagreb People's Committee waddled onto the stage like a duck, and shook his forefinger at the young demonstrators, scolding them severely. This led to further shouting and booing plus a few undefined objects being thrown onto the stage. After what appeared to be a standoff, the authorities relented, hoisted the well-worn Croatian flag, and everyone departed after a highly emotional confrontation.

Americans who witnessed this scene felt unanimously that Croatian chauvinism was alive and well in the hearts of the young, even if mostly just below the surface. Our colleagues in Belgrade, however, did not fully appreciate our reporting of this incident to Washington. They feared that we were presenting a "parochially distorted" picture of youthful fervor, and suspected we were politicizing a purely antiestablishment student protest.

Within a year or two after my summer 1964 departure, a Zagreb university campus rebellion of sorts broke out, supported by a female Communist Party politician of Croatian origin. It was summarily suppressed by Tito, who sent in federal troops to quell the disturbances. No further trouble arose thereafter for some time, but discontent was clearly simmering.

Resurrection at Glina

Local ethnic tensions came to the fore on another occasion where I briefly became the center of attention. One of the Ustashi's worst wartime atrocities had taken place in the Serbian village of Glina. Although physically located within Croatia, Glina, like many of its neighboring townships, or *selos*, was populated almost exclusively by Serbs. Glina lies in the southern border area of Croatia known as Krajina.[4]

During World War II Ustashi forces rounded up all of Glina's Serbian residents—men, women, and children (most of the men were away, either fighting or captured by Germans), locked them in the local Orthodox church, and burned the entire structure to the ground. No one inside the church survived. This example of the Ustashi's grislier crimes managed to capture the special attention of the Serbian community worldwide. After the war, Serbian émigrés in Canada and the United States raised funds to build a new church on the original site. When construction was completed, numerous Serbian dignitaries assembled from home and abroad for a solemn dedication ceremony. Present were the ranking Orthodox bishop of Yugoslavia; several high-ranking government officials, also representing the *national* League of Communists of Yugoslavia; selected leaders of the Serbian émigré community from Canada and the United States, most of whom were strongly anti-Tito, but had been permitted to enter Yugoslavia for twenty-four hours just to attend this ceremony; and myself, representing collectively the American Consulate General in Zagreb and the U.S. government.

A large feast followed the dedication in the equivalent of the village hall, as was the custom on Serbian religious or secular occasions. Only the VIPs and village elders were allowed inside, while the villagers lined up around the building to catch as much as possible of the long-winded speechmaking. As the rhetoric proceeded, it occurred to me that each of the speakers in turn was acting in a highly restrained manner, especially for the normally emotional Serbian representatives. The bishop, realizing that the party was granting him "absolution" on this occasion, was careful in his remarks to stay away from the subject of religion. Likewise, the party officials did not press the Communist cause. The émigrés were especially careful not to press their luck, as they still needed government permission to exit the country. No one, I suddenly realized, had mentioned the word "God," even though we were all involved in consecrating a church.

Although I must confess that I am not very religious, I decided to make the most of this opportunity: when my turn came to make a few appropriate remarks, I ended up with the words "*Bog s vama* (God be with you)." That brought down the house—indeed, the entire Glina community. These were apparently the words everyone wanted to speak but felt constrained from doing so. I was under no such restraint. Even the party members present had to recognize my success: an official who had been notably solemn and unobtrusive during most of the speechmaking smiled at me for the first time, and in effect conceded: "You pulled a fast one on all of us here today . . . congratulations." As I shook hands with him while surrounded by well-wishers, I in effect told him: "Thank you, my friend, but you see, sometimes 'God' can help you more than the League of Communists of Yugoslavia."

Within the hall, everyone (except the party officials) cheered lustily, and outside I was mobbed by well-wishers all the way to my (consular) jeep. Never, in my memory, have I been the subject of so much adulation by so many. It was clearly a case of pent-up emotion which I had been able to release with three brief words (and banal ones at that).

Soccer SNAFU

Despite the Tito party line, ethnic differences were just as apparent within the party as in the real world outside. "Brotherhood and Unity" was without doubt an ennobling concept, but it had little relevance to "Yugoslav" reality. No better example comes to mind than a soccer case.

One day I received a call from a relatively high-ranking official in the Executive Council of Croatia, requesting an urgent meeting on a matter of "considerable sensitivity." The official wanted to bring along several of his colleagues, to which I readily agreed. When the group eventually arrived in my antechamber, they resembled a Grade B spy film scenario—with raincoats turned up in the back, hats pulled down over their faces, and dark glasses everywhere. I realized that something of monumental importance was about to happen.

The leader of the delegation asked me if he could speak "in confidence." I responded, "By all means, but it is my understanding that most of what is said here is recorded by your people. That surely would not be a problem for you!" Raucous but slightly nervous laughter followed. After a few more pleasantries and some Slivovitz, the spokesman came to the point:

"We have, Gospodin (Mr.) Konsul, information from our informants in Belgrade (read Croatian spies) that an international football (soccer) exhibition tournament is to take place in Philadelphia, Pennsylvania, next spring." I had not known about it, but said I hoped the Yugoslavs might be invited to participate. "We have been invited, Gospodin Konsul, but those 'bastards' (the actual word used) in Belgrade told the Americans that the best Yugoslav team was the Çrvena Zvezda (Red Star) team from Belgrade, and you know, Gospodin Konsul, that our Croatian *Dinamo* team just won the national championship!" I did know that important fact, as it was virtually impossible to live in Croatia and be unaware of the Republic's football prowess, especially when they were winning. I quickly reassured my Croatian friends that I would rectify this misunderstanding and keep them closely informed of the results. They all breathed a sigh of relief.

One phone call to Belgrade confirmed the fact that the USIS officer in charge of "exchanges" was a bookish sort of fellow who knew nothing about soccer. He promised to take my complaint up to the "highest level" if necessary and would definitely not send a second-rate team to Philadelphia. The Belgrade soccer officials— caught with their pants down, so to speak—assumed a dog-in-the-manger attitude: if the Red Star team could not go, no one would go. And that was the final outcome.

RARE RAPPROCHEMENT

For a brief period in my Zagreb tour, rapprochement between Khrushchev and Tito seemed possible. As I recall, it began with a Khrushchev initiative aimed at wooing the Yugoslav leader back into the "fold" (the Soviet–East European Bloc, as it was then called). At first Tito seemed to respond favorably, as he recognized that Yugoslavia had a considerable stake in keeping the relatively moderate Khrushchevs of the Soviet Union in power as long as possible. The U.S. government feared that the large Western investment in, and policy of, supporting Yugoslav independence might be in jeopardy.

The initiative, though short-lived, had unusual—even humorous—consequences. As the result of Tito's break with the Kremlin in 1948, Stalin had frozen all Yugoslav accounts in the Soviet Union and Eastern Europe. Thereafter Yugoslavia imported heavily from the West and developed a highly unfavorable balance of trade with Western countries, but it maintained a highly *favorable* balance with the East. In a gesture of amity, Khrushchev now unblocked those "Eastern" accounts, at least temporarily. Hence Tito ordered that imports from the West be curtailed and that the Eastern assets be used to import Soviet goods, at least while this windfall lasted.

What Tito ordered very soon became the party line, but many high-ranking party officials were far from pleased. No one, however indoctrinated with Marxism, wanted a primitive Russian car, for instance, but that is what he or she was about to receive—and in large quantities. Soon the building that the U.S. government leased each fall for the American pavilion at the Zagreb Fair was filled with imported Volga and Moskvitch cars. (A Volga, incidentally, was basically a 1945 Opel, as the factory had been transferred from East Germany to the Soviet Union.) Status within Yugoslav society, and in the party hierarchy especially, was derived from a Mercedes-Benz, or a least a modern Opel, not from a Soviet product. I remember being told by a Croatian party official of medium rank that he could not "afford" to be seen driving around town in a Russian vehicle, even if he wanted to be "patriotic" and fulfill Comrade Tito's expressed wishes: people would immediately assume that he had been demoted, and his authority would become seriously undermined.

Apparently this apparatchik's concern was widely shared among the upper echelons of the party, as the Soviet autos remained in storage for some time. Eventually they had to be presented as gifts to rural comrades who had no mechanized transportation at all and would presumably appreciate such largesse from headquarters. My own experience, however, led me to doubt that assumption. During trips through rural Slavonia, I often saw broken-down and rusting Russian vehicles, which, lacking spare parts or mechanics to put them in working order, had been abandoned by the side of the road. The horse and wagon remained the preferred mode of transportation in those areas.

The climactic moment of this brief rapprochement was a triumphal motorcade through the center of town, featuring Comrades Tito and Khrushchev standing in an open Mercedes (forget the Volgas, these were *leaders*) waving to the cheering populace. (Well, they were sort of cheering in a lukewarm manner—and mainly for *Tito*, not the "bloody Russian," as one Croatian onlooker remarked.) The contrast in the appearance of the two leaders was startling: Khrushchev looked decades older than Tito, although Tito was in fact a few years his senior. Clearly Tito had lavished a good deal of time and effort on his personal appearance, not to mention splendid uniforms.

Harking back to an eerily memorable occasion the previous year, the half-hearted cheering, mainly for Tito, still seemed vociferous compared to a similar motorcade when Brezhnev was accompanied by Alexander Ranković, a high-ranking Serbian official in charge of the security forces, at one time considered second or third to Tito himself. From my office balcony, which opened onto one of the main downtown streets, I saw a few children waving flags in the front row. But despite frantic hand-waving and smiles on the part of the parading officials, there was almost total silence on the part of the adult bystanders—like a TV parade with the volume turned off. I had never witnessed anything like it before, nor have I since! (Rankovic' eventually used bad judgment in ordering Tito's private quarters bugged, and his later downfall was precipitous.)

The rapprochement turned out to be a "blip" in postwar Soviet-Yugoslav relations and of little consequence.

AFRICANS ADRIFT

As a self-appointed leader of the nonaligned nations, Tito made every effort possible to attract students from the Third World, especially from Africa and the Middle East. Throughout the sixties, therefore, Zagreb became the home of a large contingent of foreign students, mostly but not exclusively from Africa. Following the activities of these Africans, in particular, became one of my subsidiary assignments—and, I reflect in retrospect, verged on the subversive.

Primarily through two medical students I knew at the University of Zagreb, one an American of Croatian background (Jerry Blasković), the other from Sri Lanka (Dr. Sarri Junaid), I initially made contact with a group of Nigerian students who had a lot on their minds. It didn't take me long to become their informal therapist. What they needed above all else was someone in authority (although mine was notably limited) who was willing to listen sympathetically to their various problems and frustrations. For me, it was an opportunity to gain some real insights into what it was like to be an African student in Eastern Europe.

The Nigerians' story was evidently typical—and traumatic. They had been happily enrolled in a college or university in Nigeria and had no plans to travel abroad. One day, however, the Yugoslav ambassador to Nigeria appeared, together with the top college administrator, and offered these lads a special "opportunity" to pursue their studies in Yugoslavia. The Nigerians frankly admitted that they had had no idea where Yugoslavia *was* and had the impression that English was the principal language there. The ambassador elaborated on his offer at some length, stressing all the alleged advantages. *All* expenses would be paid: tuition, books, housing, and even winter clothing would be provided. A generous monthly stipend was also part of the package—financed by both the Yugoslav and Nigerian governments.

The students, overwhelmed by this proposal, readily accepted. When they arrived in Belgrade in the midst of a snowstorm, however, they began to have second thoughts. No one was at the airport to greet them on arrival, and they couldn't speak the language. It was all downhill from then on.

Having arrived in Zagreb during the coldest winter in fifty years, they complained that the clothing they were given was unsuitable. They could have brought heavier clothes from Nigeria, if they "had only known!" The final straw was the language barrier: before they could pursue their university studies, they had to learn an entirely new and complex Slavic language—and they were only scheduled for tutoring twice a week! Ultimately the Nigerians solved their problems the "Bombshell" way: they slipped out in the dead of night and took a train to Munich, where they enrolled in the Goethe Institute, which gave crash courses in German to foreigners. (In the last letter I received from them, they reported a definite increase in their satisfaction level: German, they found, was not much easier than Serbo-Croatian, but they were being subjected to "total immersion" and felt they were making progress. Above all, "attention was being paid.")

Through the Nigerians and other African students, I learned firsthand about culture shock and de facto discrimination. While the government line guaranteed Africans the same rights as Yugoslav nationals, reality was different: the general populace treated these students with both jealousy (many Africans had better stipends than local students) and contempt. And, according to the Africans (who were unanimous on this point), the Croats charged them double for everything—rent, books, supplies, the works. The additional funding did not help much if you were always being fleeced.

Everything was relative, of course: treatment of African students in Bulgaria and the Soviet Union, we heard, was even worse. Typically, student protests about local conditions would bring down heavy-handed retaliation by the authorities. I reached the ultimate conclusion that Western influence on the African continent might have been immeasurably enhanced if we could only subsidize large-scale African study in Eastern Europe and the Soviet Union!

Before their clandestine departure, the Nigerians helped organize a famous "open house" at our Tuškanac residence. For months the students had been agitating for a cultural center of their own. The authorities had promised to take the matter under advisement, which meant that nothing was done. Finally one of the student leaders was advised to petition the appropriate government office in Belgrade, but when he took his appeal personally to the Yugoslav capital, he failed to find the office in question (the Croats had given him the wrong address). He then returned to Zagreb in a revolutionary frame of mind. At that point, I offered to stage an all-African evening.

The Nigerians suggested that we keep everything simple: just some beer, coke, plain fare, and records. A sit-down dinner was not the African way. We complied, and the event was a stupendous success. I had told all prospective guests to bring their girlfriends along, but at the last moment everyone chickened out (the girls were not all that respectable, it turned out, and the Africans were basically ashamed of them). Instead they all arrived simultaneously, having taken the bihourly bus from downtown, and stood hesitantly in the entrance way. At a moment of some awkwardness, my son John saved the day, or rather the evening. "Daddy," he exclaimed in a high-pitched voice, "they're all brown." He had never seen such a sight before, and his frankness was disarming. The students all laughed and loosened up. Soon all were dancing the limbo (which was in vogue at the time) and having the time of their lives. They didn't need any female partners anyway, although the two consulate wives in attendance ended up having a full evening (and had sore backs the next day from bending backwards under the limbo pole). It was the cheapest party I have ever given and the most appreciated. The African student community talked about it for weeks, and guess what? The government caved in and approved the construction of an African student center. For once, a modest American "demarche" had put leaders of the nonaligned world to shame.

THE LAST NIKOLIĆ

No Zagreb story would be complete without at least a passing reference to the Baroness Vera Nikolić, the only titled permanent resident of Tito's communist state. She was a very accomplished artist, and I happily state that I bought several of her works, one of which hangs near my front door. It is the only oil painting of flowers in a vase that I ever liked, but since I basically prefer animals to vegetation, I am no judge.

Though Vera's background is a mystery to me, the title obviously had to come from Austria, while the surname Nikolić was clearly Slavic. The family had obviously once had considerable wealth, power, and influence, as Vera was heiress to a large mansion and estate on the outskirts of town, a town house, and a villa on the Dalmatian coast. Most people with that kind of history no longer resided in Yugoslavia in the sixties, but Vera was indomitable as well as apolitical. She had a square build somewhat in the tradition of Gertrude Stein—only stronger, like Drugarica. As Somerset Maugham might say: "She had a man's mind—and also a man's mustache." She also had a deep gravelly voice and, believe it or not, an excess of charm.

Like much of the postwar nobility, she had a tenuous hold on property but no money. Being destitute never seemed to affect her lifestyle, however. Every Sunday she held court on her vast estate, in an old country mansion falling apart at the seams and needing total renovation. Inevitably, most of that property was confiscated by the regime, in order to build another Zagreb retreat for President Tito, who already had ten more palaces, islands, and country estates than the last Serbian king. Tito never even wanted Vera's place, but the local comrades thought it might be a way to gain his support and their advancement. They did not even want Vera's broken-down home, but cleared a large area high above it where construction was eventually begun.

Vera was the personification of mind over matter—or determination over power—or strength of character over the lack of it. As a representative of the degenerate "old order," she also represented the survival of old virtues, which decades of warfare could not totally extinguish. She had a strong will, but also a hearty sense of humor: she especially liked to compare the Tito one-party election slate to the Garden of Eden: "And God created Adam and then Eve...and he said to Adam: Choose thy woman!"

Thus when the communist authorities confiscated her property, Vera marched down to party headquarters and said, in effect, "Fine, take my land and everything on it—but in return, you should provide me with a place to work, since work is considered essential to your socialist system. I ask only for a studio where I can pursue my artistic profession!" This meeting must have made an impression on someone, as the authorities soon built Baroness Nikolić a fine if modest art studio on a hill across from the residence that Tito never used.

The Croatian Executive Council, if it had a choice, would probably have preferred to fight all of Belgrade than Vera. With Belgrade the conflict would at least have had some local support!

That she did not live long enough to witness what misery would descend on her native land was her ultimate reward.

DO VIDJENJA

The summer of 1964 witnessed two events of controlling significance: we had our beloved basset hound put to sleep, and we moved back to Washington.

Heathcliff was among the few residents of Croatia who fully embraced the concept of "Brotherhood and Unity," as he treated Serbs, Croats, and Slovenes with equally high regard. He was the only animal I have known in my life who never growled at anyone and never got into a fight. In his last months on earth, he became particularly attached to the Serbs who ran our neighborhood police station. (Under Tito's policy, Serbs manned the police force in Croatia, and Croats in Serbia. That way no one was inclined to be soft on law violators!) While roaming about the countryside, Heathcliff always made it a point to end up there, where he was fed and warmly received by the sergeant on duty. Whenever Heathcliff was missing, therefore, I knew where to look.

Alas, he developed cancerous lumps all over his body, which were easily removed by our able Dr. Vladimir Sertić. One on his windpipe, however, was inoperable and we had to put him down. Zagreb had a first-class veterinary clinic, staffed by doctors at the top of their profession. I never doubted that Heathcliff had received state-of-the-art care and treatment, but his departure was a milestone of mourning by all occupants of Tuškanac 55A.

Because this is mainly a personal memoir, I will not attempt to analyze the reasons for Yugoslavia's recent breakup and its lapse into civil barbarism. I would only conclude this section with two rather obvious comments: First, while those of us who served in Zagreb were more aware of ethnic tensions than were our colleagues in Belgrade, this was merely a matter of degree. And, *none* of us, it is fair to say, ever predicted the extent of the calamity that has befallen the people of Bosnia, southern Croatia, and Kosovo. Any Western observer who claims otherwise is less than credible. Although in the early sixties I had very little respect for the Tito regime, it was clearly preferable to what succeeded it, at least in Serbia and in Serbian Bosnia.

After my return from Zagreb, I spoke on Yugoslavia to the Milwaukee Rotary Club under State's Community Relations Progam. A reporter raised the "sister city" issue only after the talk had ended.

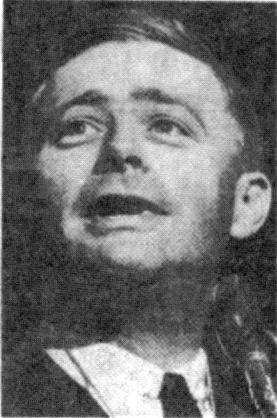

JOHN CHAPMAN CHESTER
—Sentinel Photo

Extend Sister City Idea, US Aide Suggests

Instead of abandoning Munich as a sister city to Milwaukee, "you should have sister cities in Warsaw and Tel Aviv also, a Milwaukee born foreign service o f f i c e r said here this week.

John Chapman Chester, who was in town to speak to the Rotary club, said in an interview that he considered the sister city concept an important form of international contact, one that should be broadened instead of restricted.

"Most people in eastern Europe as well as in the west like the concept very much," he said. "You should broaden the concept so that everyone is represented."

Munich Controversial

The city of Munich was recommended last February by a special committee composed of representatives of Milwaukee's ethnic groups. The recommendation was immediately denounced by some people because Munich had been the birthplace of the Nazi movement, and the recommendation was withdrawn. Other choices are now b e i n g considered.

Chester said he believed "we have everything to gain and nothing to lose by trade and cultural exchanges," especially with eastern Europe.

He said a sister city agreement with Warsaw might be only symbolic, but would be valuable because "the bonds are tremendously strong between eastern Europeans and their descendants here."

Notes Friendliness Abroad

Chester, who had been vice-consul in Bonn and M u n i c h, Germany, and consul in Zagreb, Yugoslavia, said that people he met in the hinterlands of Yugoslavia w e r e "pro-American. You can't get away from their hospitality. They tell you about their uncles in St. Louis."

U n d e r Tito's independent Communist leadership, he said, 75% of Yugoslavia's f o r e i g n trade is with western countries. In Yugoslavia and in other eastern E u r o p e a n Communist countries which are becoming increasingly autonomous from Russia, he said, "peace comes first and socialism second."

Chester is now in Washington as foreign s e r v i c e personnel placement officer for Germany Austria and eastern Europe.

147

CHAPTER 7

Headquarters Again

My second assignment to Washington lasted four and a half years, from late 1964 to the spring of 1969. It consisted of a year on Capitol Hill as a Congressional Fellow, sandwiched in between two years in the Department of State's Office of Personnel (what I call the "body-swap business") and about a year and a half on the Canadian desk. Since my sabbatical on the Hill became the prelude to the fifteen most satisfying years of my whole career in foreign affairs, I propose to talk about it separately, out of chronological order, after first recounting my two State Department assignments in this chapter.

PERSONNEL

I was less than thrilled with a "welcome" letter from my new boss, Bob Brown, informing me that I was to become a personnel staffing specialist in the European Branch of the Career Management and Assignments Division (CMAD). To the uninitiated like myself, an assignment to Personnel sounded like a rather pedestrian if not bureaucratic exercise.

I was to learn, however, that of all assignments one might receive in the Department of State, a tour in the

Office of Personnel (PER) was one of the most valuable—perhaps even self-serving. Personnel was, and I am certain still is, the key to and hub of the entire Foreign Service system. I eventually became amazed by how little some experienced and able senior officers actually knew about the system that governed their professional lives. Some details of the process may thus be enlightening.

Chester's "Body-Swap" Rules

A personnel staffing specialist—or placement officer— is essentially involved in assigning FSOs to posts at home and abroad. My area included the Soviet Union, Eastern Europe, Germany, Austria, and offices in the State Department that dealt with those countries. My responsibilities concerned all assignments other than for ambassadors and most senior officers.

I reviewed personnel files; worked out informal releases of the officers if they were in different geographic areas; and got the approval of career management officers (CMOs, or "Schmos"), who were supposed to look at each proposed assignment from the standpoint of the officer's professional development, rather than the needs of the personnel system. Then, based on my recommendations, my superior Bob Brown would attend weekly assignment panel meetings and bargain with his counterpart branch chiefs over bodies (hence the body-swap business, as I called it).

In case of deadlock, CMOs would cast the deciding vote, so it was always important to get them on your side if at all possible. In addition, for assignments to the Soviet Union and Eastern Europe, a special clearance from the Office of Security (SY) was needed. SY could veto the most carefully prepared and negotiated plans. In Bob's absence, I would engage in this continuing panel struggle myself.

While I no longer recall all the bureaucratic intricacies of the body-swap process, I firmly remember certain principles:

1. Keep in mind that any FSO in good standing highly recommended for transfer from another area of the world into your jurisdiction (recommended, that is, by the personnel assignments officers of that area) probably had a personality problem or some related difficulty which did not appear in his or her PER file.

2. Never give up "hot property" without getting someone valuable in return. In turn, however, if you wanted to transfer someone out of your area, you had to accept someone comparable (but, one hoped, not as disruptive) in return.

3. Despite points 1 and 2 above, remember that a few posts around the world would take almost anyone (usually because the officer assigned there had just resigned). In those days, Khorramshahr in Iran and Santiago de los Caballeros in the Dominican Republic were high on that list.

4. Never believe everything you read in a PER file without talking to people who knew the officer in question personally or who knew about him.

5. Keep in mind that political officers were a dime a dozen. The biggest fights on the panel were over consular and administrative officers, who were harder to find. Experienced economists of acceptable reputation were also few and far between in the mid-sixties, and in many instances were able to write their own tickets.

6. Never leave town for extended periods, or a virtual "turkey migration" into your area might well take place in your absence. My predecessor, John DeWitt, who evidently once experienced such a move, warned me of the dire consequences.

7. Be sure to read between the lines when reviewing a personnel file. What may appear at first glance to be a positive recommendation may actually be a "hatchet job."

Sacred Cows

When I arrived in PER in the late fall of 1964, Lyndon Johnson was at the pinnacle of his power and influence, having just been elected president in his own right for the first time.

The military buildup had begun in Vietnam, hand in hand with the pacification program, which was geared to political aid and required numerous civilian officers (from State, CIA, and AID) to be stationed outside of Saigon in the provinces. PER set up a Vietnam Task Force, with a relatively junior officer (then approximately my equivalent rank of FSO-5), Allen Wendt, in charge. At least, he was in charge at the working level where we were all negotiating for "bodies." The Task Force, however, did not need to negotiate. Under direct orders from the president, an FSO from anywhere in the world could be abruptly transferred to Vietnam if, in the Task Force's considered judgment, he or she were needed there in any capacity whatsoever. CMAD no longer had any input into this process and was ordered merely to rubber-stamp the decisions. It was not always possible under these circumstances to protect your bureau from arbitrary "raids." Fortunately, Allen Wendt was a sensible and reasonable young man who did not exploit his new-found power, which is probably one reason he ended up becoming an ambassador. If you had a reasonable argument in favor of retaining someone considered indispensable in EUR, he would sometimes refrain from exercising his *draft* powers.

In one case at least, that strategy didn't work. A political officer in Moscow, a West Point graduate, evidently became restless in the Soviet Union and wanted to "prove" himself in rural Vietnam. Without informing his ambassador, Foy Kohler, in advance, he wrote to PER requesting a transfer to Saigon on his next assignment. As to timing, he mentioned rather cavalierly that if he were needed immediately that would be no problem, as a number of his Moscow colleagues "could easily cover" for him temporarily. The ambassador was not at all pleased with this action and wrote the director of personnel a long and detailed rebuttal: the post was actually short-handed, with a trade fair in progress, and owing to other recent transfers, Bob X's presence in Moscow during the following six months was definitely in the national interest. "I have had a talk with Bob about this matter," the ambassador added, "and he fully supports my position." (The implication was clear: Bob had been severely reprimanded for his unilateral and "uncleared" action.)

All of this took place while I was acting branch chief, in Bob Brown's absence. Armed with the ambassadorial appeal, I pled the case of the Bureau of European Affairs with the assignments panel. Word even came down from the assistant secretary's office that Ambassador Kohler was counting on a successful outcome.

I lost. And I doubt that Bob X ever wrote such a letter again.

Latin America (ARA)

Another special LBJ preserve was Latin America. Normally, the Bureau of Inter-American Affairs (ARA), like all of the other bureaus, was headed by an assistant secretary, but LBJ wanted to upgrade the position to demonstrate his special concern about developments in the Western Hemisphere. He made a career officer, Thomas Mann (a favorite career FSO of his from Texas), a deputy under secretary, responsible both for State and AID programs in ARA. This organizational move led to a kind of separate closed-circuit personnel system for Latin America. William Lehfeldt, CMAD branch chief for ARA, could move officers around his area at will, without returning them to State after a prescribed number of years in the field or giving them up to other bureaus. However, he did not have the blanket *draft* authority the Vietnam crowd enjoyed. This meant that he could keep ARA-types in ARA, but had difficulty recruiting new and desirable "commodities" from other areas. Such officers, knowing that once they landed in

ARA they might never get out, often resisted with skill and determination.

Whether this system resulted in a desirable degree of area specialization, as was its purpose, or whether it encouraged Latino-oriented parochialism, as Henry Kissinger subsequently claimed, when he instituted his "GLOP" (Globalization Program), will forever remain a matter of controversy. My own subsequent exposure to the politics and culture of Mexico (as the congressional staff chief for the House Delegation to the Mexico-US Interparliamentary Group for eleven years) leads me to believe that at least a few out-of-area tours are definitely beneficial.

Sacred Spooks

A State-CIA agreement of long standing accorded diplomatic cover to intelligence officers assigned to our embassies and consulates throughout the world. The practice was universal, among friend and foe alike, except that the Soviets tended to go overboard to some extent. (The Soviet embassy in Washington, for example, was reputed to have been staffed by KGB officers on a ratio of about 4:1 over foreign ministry professionals. Rumors had it that an embassy chauffeur might outrank the ambassador in the KGB hierarchy!)

The Career Management and Assignments Division had nothing to do with assigning Central Intelligence Agency personnel, although State set up a special desk to handle routine processing of assignees prior to their departure overseas. Our position charts for the posts under our jurisdiction did not show who was "Agency." Only the names of incumbents and their Foreign Service grades (or equivalent grades) were shown on our records, which were amended as transfers were made.

While confidentiality in the assignment process was clearly necessary, too much secrecy, I learned to my regret, can cause a lot of heartburn. A career management officer counseling administrative personnel once asked me to try informally to introduce a kind of rotational approach in assigning officers. This CMO had spent several tours at hardship posts in Africa and Southeast Asia and resented the fact that numerous colleagues had spent most of their respective careers in "cushy" posts in Western Europe. In Vienna, for instance, the entire Budget and Fiscal Section, he complained, had been in place for some six years, and it was time to expose some of these people to the rigors of the underdeveloped world. Besides, he argued, most had come to Vienna from such posts as Paris, Bonn, or Berlin.

The idea sounded perfectly sensible to me. I would go along and release these high livers to the Africa and Near East regional bureaus, provided I received competent replacements from these same areas. My CMO friend promised to recommend only worthy assignees. After much preparation and consultation, we went to panel on this basis. With the chief administrative CMO in favor of the program, the transfers were quickly and easily approved.

At this point it "hit the fan." All the people being moved out of Vienna, it seemed, were "spooks," and soon there were recriminations at the highest level. The CIA leadership accused the under secretary of state for administration of "breaking faith" and capriciously abrogating a State-CIA agreement. When word finally trickled down to the working level, all the new assignments had to be brought back to panel and canceled, with a good deal of embarrassment. Talleyrand might have cautioned me: "Above all, not too much zeal."

The Gender Problem

Grover Cleveland's words "It is a condition which confronts us—not a theory" apply to the assignment process.

Economists, as noted, were at a premium, and at one point I thought I had found just the right person for Helsinki. My prospect was a highly qualified woman, and Tyler Thompson, a career ambassador, was known for his compassionate "nonsexist" outlook. As both economic analyst and commercial bilateral trade promoter, this woman could contribute substantially, I thought, to the embassy's overall mission, in a positive and friendly atmosphere that would be set by the chief of mission.

There was only one problem, the ambassador reluctantly pointed out. In Helsinki almost all the important business in town was conducted during the afternoon hours in the all-male sauna. Without entry to that hallowed institution, one was effectively cut off from the mainstream of economic life in the country. The institution of the coed sauna had not yet permeated Finland, and my candidate was not in a position to change a time-honored custom that had become such an unalterable part of the local culture.

The assignment was "broken."

A Memorable Personality: Elwood Williams

Of all the people I dealt with when I was a European "body trader" (as we were also called), the most remarkable was a senior fixture in the Office of German Affairs, the late Elwood Williams. No one was even a close second. He had been an FSO of considerable promise during the thirties and early forties until he was struck down with multiple sclerosis. This crippling disease would have sent most people into early medical retirement, but not Elwood Williams. His job was converted to a civil service position, and for several decades thereafter he provided both leadership and continuity to the German desk.

I first met him on my return from Munich in the fall of 1959, when he was already about 80 percent incapacitated, confined to a wheelchair. The department even hired a male secretary for him who could wheel him into the lavatory when necessary. His mental faculties, however, were in no way diminished. He even recalled a report I had written about a local Bavarian casino scandal, which had ended the careers of a number of strictly local politicians and the viability of the Bavarian Party. (Whether anyone *else* in that office had even *read* this outstanding airgram is questionable, but then, Elwood had exemplary taste.)

Elwood was also a bear for detail. He prided himself on knowing all about the character and abilities of FSOs serving in the approximately seven consulates in Germany, plus the two missions in Bonn and Berlin, and became the de facto personnel chief of German affairs. I never made an assignment to any post in the Federal Republic without clearing it first with Elwood. He had a status and virtually unmatched prestige within EUR. Office directors and their deputies, assistant secretaries and deputy assistant secretaries, would come and go, but Elwood was ALWAYS the one who knew "where the bodies were buried."

When I first came to see him in my Personnel capacity, I was shocked to discover that he could no longer hold a telephone. Instead he spoke into a phone box on his desk and the respondent's voice was amplified into the room at large. (I wondered how many confidential comments of my own had been blasted throughout the German office complex on the fifth floor of New State). He lifted cigarettes off his desk with his teeth and kept them smoldering in his mouth until he dropped them into the ashtray, as he could not hold them in his fingers. He had a way of turning the pages he was reading with his elbow and shoulder. He was the absolute embodiment of mind over matter.

Above all, however, Elwood was an accomplished raconteur, whose seemingly cynical, even sardonic, sense of humor temporarily concealed a genuinely compassionate concern for people. He always found something positive to say about those whose negative qualities he was also the first to discern, with one notable exception. In the 1920s, Elwood had been an American exchange student at the University of Munich. He liked to tell the story about his train trip south to Salzburg, where he ended up in the dining car with a group of German youths dressed in what looked like Boy Scout uniforms. Eventually they all became chummy, and the boys asked Elwood if he would like to see their "leader." "Sure, why not," the American innocent replied, so they all went down the corridor to a compartment occupied by a man with black hair combed to the side and riding boots, dictating to a secretary. The boys all waved at their *Führer*, and "*der schöne* Adolf" waved back. That, Elwood liked to say, was his first coincidental confrontation with consummate evil.

To those in the foreign affairs establishment who had any meaningful contact with him, it is no understatement to say that Elwood was more than a role model. He was plainly and simply an inspiration.

My Most Important Assignment: My Own!
One of the advantages of serving a tour in Personnel was the ability to influence one's onward assignment. This perk was sometimes resented by the average FSO without such connections, but after two years of hassle and pressure from every known source both at home and abroad, most of us felt we deserved this minimal reward. The main advantage was one of timing: as a PER staffer, you knew what positions were opening up, both *where* and *when*. My onward assignment turned out to be a sabbatical in Congress, the subject of the next chapter.

CANADIAN SUNSET

Poor Mexico—so far from God and so close to the United States
—attributed to former Mexican president Porfirio Diaz

In dealing with Canadians, one must accept the fact that the above sentiments are not merely Latin-based but are widely shared by our neighbors to the north. While Americans and English-speaking Canadians appear to have much in common, including language, culture, and the English parliamentary tradition, Canadians value their "separate identity." The worst American sin, in Canadian eyes, is to assume that "they are just like us."

In the late summer of 1967, when I embarked on what was to become my last assignment in the Department of State—as Canadian desk officer—Canada was in ferment. An academic-led movement toward economic nationalism was in full bloom, centered primarily in the province of Ontario but also supported by groups across the continent. This movement was based on the perception that U.S. investors owned too much of Canadian industry and that Canadian independence was being compromised as a result. These Canadians wanted to "buy back" their country and divorce the Canadian economy from the "profit-seekers" to the south, who were believed not to have pure Canadian interests at heart. Above all, and not entirely without cause, this group feared the insatiable American lust for Canadian resources—oil, timber, and especially water—and their exploitation for American instead of Canadian interests.

The "buy back Canada" idea eventually died a natural death, since it was altogether impractical, given the state and extent of Canadian financial resources. Resentment toward heavy-handed U.S. economic and cultural encroachment has lingered, however. The vast majority of the Canadian population lives along the U.S.-Canada border and is highly susceptible to U.S. "cultural imperialism" in the form of radio and, especially, television. To those few Americans who are even aware of such reactions, Canadians at times appear schizophrenic: they want all of the advantages of living next door to a superpower without assuming any neighborly responsibilities. To many Canadians, however, Pierre Trudeau's analogy about sleeping with an elephant ("The beast might be friendly enough, but he might also turn over accidentally and crush you"), struck a most responsive chord.

French separatism in the Province of Quebec also appeared to be in full bloom and growing. Following the highly charged 1963 visit of Charles de Gaulle and his "*Vive la Quebec Libre*" speech, France-Quebec relations seemed to be taking off. Every other week a French minister seemed to turn up in Quebec. The transatlantic *pull* was of ever greater concern to the government in Ottawa.

Most Americans never embraced Quebec separatism with enthusiasm. Nor, certainly, did any leading policymaker in the State Department or White House ever encourage the movement. Separatism never took on an anti-American flavor. Quite the contrary: Rene Levesque, the charismatic French Canadian separatist and leader of the drive for independence, believed a strong economic relationship between the United States and Quebec essential for Quebec sovereignty and viability. He promoted the separatist cause with U.S. bankers and Wall Street financiers and appeared on U.S. television programs like the Johnny Carson show to try to demonstrate that Frenchmen from the north were reasonable chaps without horns. I watched Levesque on numerous occasions and concluded that he was succeeding in creating the desired image. Ottawa, however, was concerned about this trend and always feared and suspected the worst on the part of U.S. officialdom, so "hand-holding" and reassuring was part and parcel of U.S. diplomacy of that era.

The far western provinces not only had no use for Quebec nationalism in general and bilingualism in particular but also viewed Ottawa with deep suspicion. The prime minister of British Columbia, W. A. C. (known as "Wacky") Bennett, based his entire political career on the concept of Ottawa-bashing. He considered "vertical" relations much more effective than "horizontal" ones. He never criticized the United States, and he maintained cordial ties with the state governments of Washington and Idaho, among others. He directed his blame only at Ottawa for failing to accommodate Western Canadian interests properly.

In sum, dealing with Canada was highly challenging and complex. For the Department of State and our embassy in Ottawa, just keeping track of all the vertical political and economic contacts between the United States and its largest trading partner was difficult enough; controlling events from the standpoint of foreign policy was clearly impossible. An example: J. Edgar

Hoover once addressed a police organization in Alberta, denouncing U.S. draft dodgers and the alleged lack of Canadian cooperation in apprehending same. His remarks were well received by his handpicked audience but caused a furor in the Canadian press. Justice had made no attempt to "clear" these remarks with State. The speech was already a fait accompli by the time the U.S. ambassador read about it in the *Toronto Globe and Mail*. This was par for the course: picking up broken crockery was a routine assignment for the Canadian desk.

Another problem was organizational. Ideally, Canada should have been an integral part of the Bureau of American Republics Affairs, not an appendage of the European Bureau. However, Canadians felt submerged among the Latin cultures and always lobbied for continued inclusion within EUR. Canada was not then a member of the Organization of American States (OAS) and fiercely resented being pushed in that direction by U.S. leaders. At least one president and one vice president who addressed the Canadian parliament on this issue were subjected to severe criticism.

American officials had no logical reason for being so uninformed about Canadian politics. During my tenure in EUR/CAN, the office director was Rufus Z. Smith, a highly knowledgeable and respected career officer. Rufus had spent at least two tours in Ottawa, as political officer and political counselor (chief of the political section), and was highly regarded by the then-assistant secretary, John Leddy. (Smith eventually became deputy chief of mission and minister, but not ambassador, a title he eminently deserved.) Smith's mentor and chief sponsor of his career was Walter Butterworth, the ranking U.S. career ambassador on active duty at the time as well as dean of the diplomatic corps in Ottawa. Despite this expertise, the upper echelon of the department was evidently shocked and even "stunned" when Prime Minister Pierre Trudeau announced that he was pulling a contingent of Canadian troops out of NATO. Rufus had been predicting this development at

EUR staff meetings for months, but apparently no one was listening.

My "Hands-On" Approach to $50 Million

Rufus Smith was not merely well informed; he was also a pragmatic man of action when the need arose. He proposed public hearings by the Canada-United States International Joint Commission (IJC) in local areas along both sides of the border, to motivate the two governments to resolve their mutual problems, primarily pollution of the air and of the Great Lakes. I followed the work of the IJC for a time, particularly when members of the commission came to town and held briefings for Canadian and U.S. diplomats, but generally found these presentations extremely boring.

One western border dispute, however, soon captured my fullest attention! Under the Columbia River Treaty of 1961, which came into force in 1964, three dams were to be constructed on the Canadian side of the border. In return for the flood control benefits provided by these dams to the contiguous U.S. states, the U.S. government was obligated to pay the Bank of Canada a specific dollar sum *as each of the dams came into full operation.* Apparently, a very experimental earthen fill method was adopted during construction of one of the dams, the Duncan Dam. If successful, it would bring the dam into operation several months ahead of schedule. Most of the engineers doubted that the system would work, but to just about everyone's surprise, it worked perfectly. On the day the dam began functioning, the Canadian government informed the U.S. embassy in Ottawa that the U.S. government owed Canada $50 million plus interest for every day the debt remained unpaid.

Of course, no official in the executive branch, from the president on down, could comply with this request until the funds in question were appropriated by Congress. Getting money out of Congress, moreover, is anything but an "instant" process. First there are hearings in the appropriate committees of each house, followed by committee mark-ups; then, hearings in the rules committees of both houses, floor debate, final passage, and negotiations between conference committees of both houses. While the executive branch could try to expedite this process to the extent possible (by emphasizing to key members of Congress that the necessary funds were part of a treaty commitment), it could not perform miracles. State Department lawyers argued that implicit in all treaty obligations is the element of good faith: the understanding that treaty-mandated funds would only be provided within a reasonable period of time required by our "normal legislative process." I sat in on several heated exchanges on this subject between the Canadian ambassador and an attorney on the staff of the Department's Legal Adviser.

My big moment came quite a while later, when a public works appropriations bill that included the Duncan payment completed its legislative hurdles and was sent to the president for signature. The Canadian embassy in Washington was determined to get the funds to Ottawa *tout de suite*—like the very next day. If there were any further delay, critics in western Canada would seize the opportunity to complain about Ottawa's inefficiency and negligence in promoting and defending their interests.

Canadian ambassador Edward Ritchie lost no time in contacting the White House and Secretary of State Dean Rusk personally on the subject, and all assured him that now that the bill was passed, the funds would be forthcoming immediately. The order "pay the bill now!" was passed down through various bureaucratic echelons till it reached Rufus Smith. Unlike the innocents above him, he suspected that delivering funds instantaneously would not be all that easy. He called me into his office, told me to drop anything and everything I was doing, and concentrate on getting $50 million out of the U.S. Treasury. Because of the high priority assigned to this mission, I was offered a State Department limousine and a driver to be at my disposal for an entire eight-hour period.

Fortunately, I was wise enough to decline this generous offer. A four-wheeled vehicle, I realized, would just slow me down, especially crossing bridges during rush hour. I relied instead on my trusty Lambretta (the motor scooter I had first acquired in Croatia), which could sail through bumper-to-bumper traffic.

What I was about to receive was a distinct object lesson in the essence of bureaucracy. Before *any* Treasury check of *any* denomination could be issued, certain iron-clad procedures had to be followed; and it did not matter what the President of the United States or the Secretary of State thought about the matter. Presidents and secretaries come and go, but tenured bureaucrats cannot be removed except for cause, and in this instance they had the law and regulations on their side.

At an office across the Potomac, in Rosslyn, Virginia, a document I had been handed required an impression seal, which could only be provided by one authorized official who had locked the device in his safe and gone on leave. Next Monday would be time enough, I was informed. No, I said, that would never do; I was under orders to settle this matter immediately. After a good deal of hassle and after being referred to several supervisors of supervisors, someone finally decided that the only way to get rid of me was to telephone the keeper of the seal and get the combination to the safe (and later change it for security reasons).

With the document now properly sealed, I headed downtown on my scooter, only to run into similar roadblocks at two other (essential) offices. Finally, all papers were in order, and I raced over to the Treasury for printing of the check. When I arrived, I was informed that the check-issuing unit was about to close, but if I came back next Monday, someone would be happy to accommodate me.

I am not the kind of person who creates a scene easily and hastily, but I did so at that moment. I had no other choice. After calling for three supervisors in turn and refusing to leave until I had the check, the office was opened under duress especially for me. I was regarded by everyone in that office, I am sure, as a form of hold-up artist, but the bottom line is that I left with the check in hand.

What might people think, I later fantasized, if they found me run over in traffic with a $50 million U.S. treasury check in my coat pocket?

As my Lambretta approached the driveway of the Canadian embassy (then on Massachusetts Avenue), I was greeted at curbside by a uniformed member of the Royal Canadian Mounted Police. The man clearly regarded me as some kind of bomb-thrower, but he asked politely if he could be of service. "Yes," I said, "I would like to see the ambassador." "So would a lot of people." the officer responded skeptically, "Do you have an appointment?"

"No," I replied, "but in this case, you will discover that *he* has an appointment with ME!" After he called the ambassador's office, he hurried out apologetically and said: "He is on his way down."

Mission accomplished, under harrowing conditions. Ambassador Ritchie—in words reminiscent of Edward Page, Jr., in Munich (in the VIP tent at the Oktoberfest)—put his arm around my shoulder and whispered: "I *knew* I could count on you, Chips!" I often wondered if he had any idea how close I came that day to being beaten by the system!

The Eisenhower Funeral

General of the Army and former president of the United States Dwight D. Eisenhower died on March 28, 1969. Soon kings and chiefs of state, from Haile Selassie to Charles de Gaulle, arrived from around the world for the funeral. At times it became, for those like myself involved in the arrangements, a security and logistical nightmare.

In Canada, the Quebec separatism problem had been laid to rest temporarily by the election and elevation to prime minister of a French Quebecer, Pierre Trudeau, a committed federalist. Trudeau, unlike any of his predecessors in anyone's memory, had both style and sex appeal. He evoked something called "Trudeaumania," especially among the female electorate, and people forgot about his specific policies, focusing instead on his personal qualities. At one time, he had a following not unlike Frank Sinatra in his prime and was often identified in the press as "another John Kennedy." Trudeau liked to wear "mod" clothing, especially silk scarves instead of ties, and although his policies were rather conventionally liberal, he was nevertheless widely regarded as a "swinger." The perception was undoubtedly more compelling than the reality.

The new prime minister represented Canada at the Eisenhower funeral. When the small, also stylish, Canadian Air Force jet landed at National Airport on the day of the funeral, Under Secretary of State Elliot Richardson, Ambassador Ritchie, and I were standing on the tarmac as the official welcoming party. "I wonder what he's going to have *on*," I whispered to the ambassador, who assured me, "When he is on the Queen's business, he always dresses properly." And then he added, in a whisper, "*I HOPE!*"

The door opened and out stepped the prime minister in morning coat and striped trousers, just as Ritchie had predicted.

Prime Minister Pierre Trudeau was accompanied to the funeral by Canada's ranking Canadian general, in full dress uniform, covered with ribbons and decorations, by Robert Stanfield, leader of the Tory opposition, and even, to my surprise, by former prime minister John Diefenbaker, who shook my hand repeatedly and managed to upstage everyone to the extent possible. Inviting Diefenbaker to accompany him was an act of great courtesy on the part of Trudeau, as Diefenbaker was no longer Tory leader but just an M.P. back-bencher. He had known Eisenhower personally, however, when he was prime minister, and was included in the Canadian delegation for that reason.

The moment I saw him descend from the plane, I knew we were in trouble. President Nixon was to host a reception at the White House following the ceremony for the official delegates *only*, and I knew that each country was limited to three such individuals. There would be no place for Big John unless someone made an exception. Needless to say, Ed Ritchie was thinking the same thoughts and asked me at the first opportunity to see what I could do to help.

When I arrived at the Office of the Chief of Protocol to make a special pitch on behalf of my client, I found the room filled with desk officers like myself, all pressing the chief, Emil Mosbacher, for extra tickets. Mosbacher was primarily an expert yachtsman who was never cut out for Protocol, either by temperament or experience. Becoming testy under pressure, he finally walked out in frustration. "No exceptions," and that was *IT!*

I felt I had as good a case as anyone in the room, as Mr. Diefenbaker was in the process of writing his memoirs, which were expected to complicate U.S.-Canada relations. Once during a presidental visit to Canada, the press reported, one of JFK's aides had left some papers in his room that contained a marginal note in longhand referring to Big John as an S.O.B. This incident was more than likely to appear in his forthcoming book and, as Ed Ritchie pointed out: "If he is left seething in my embassy residence, while the others go to the White House, there is no telling what that book of his might include!"

This time, however, I knew I had struck out, and told the ambassador as much. "You'd better take this up on a much higher level if you want results," I advised. Ambassadors don't normally like to use up political IOUs on compatriots who are *out* of office, but in this case Ritchie must have pulled out all the stops. John Diefenbaker went to the White House reception and apparently had a whale of a time.

Departures of the visiting delegations were less formal than arrivals, it turned out. No ambassador or under secretary, just Canadian desk officer Chester and his spouse stood next to the runway bidding the VIPs farewell. When Trudeau arrived, he was surrounded, as always, with "teenyboppers" from Canadian embassy families, all of whom gave him impassioned farewell kisses. My wife braced herself happily for the same treatment, as she was one of his current admirers. Instead, he pulled himself up stiffly and shook our hands with extreme dignity, leaving one relieved male and one unrequited female behind him on the tarmac. The party was over.

The Permanent Joint Board on Defense

As desk officer, I also inherited an additional function: U.S. secretary of the Permanent Joint Board on Defense—Canada-U.S. (known as the PJBD), one of those numerous intergovernmental boards that one only knew about if one actually served on it in some capacity, or knew someone who did. Its origins were rather impressive. Founded in 1940 by FDR and Canadian prime minister MacKenzie King, it was based on the Ogdensburg Agreement, named after the site of the meeting in northern New York state. Originally, the board was set up to coordinate the defense of the hemisphere at a time, Canadians liked to remind Americans, when Canada was a belligerent and the United States was still neutral.

Those not involved in Canadian or NATO affairs generally assumed that the PJBD had long outlived its usefulness. Possibly for that reason, the three meetings per year, alternately at naval bases in Canada and the United States, were actually funded out of the secretary of state's (emergency) discretionary funds. A seemingly permanent agenda never varied. It usually consisted of U.S. requests for base rights in Canada or joint projects along the DEW line, a defensive early warning system against hostile aircraft in northern Canada. On both sides the board consisted of one Army and one Air Force general, a Navy admiral, and one senior representative each from the U.S. State Department (Rufus Smith) and the Canadian Ministry of Foreign Affairs. The chairmen of the board were usually distinguished statesmen, retired. The two secretaries of the board made most of the preparations, took notes, and did most of the work.

The PJBD served one useful purpose: it was the only mechanism in existence that brought the military of both countries into direct contact with their foreign policy and political establishments. It was thus a useful informal debating society. What counted was not the formal discussion in the working sessions, which my Canadian counterpart, Jim Harris, and I faithfully recorded in the minutes, but the bull sessions in the dining halls and bars in the evenings. The important two-way learning process made a lasting impression on the participants. During my tenure as secretary, the two board chairmen were Arnold Heeney, former Canadian ambassador to Washington, and H. Freeman ("Doc") Matthews, one of the two or three most distinguished U.S. career ambassadors (retired) still alive during the late sixties.

Here's a bit of trivia mostly unknown to the world at large. *Question*: Who was the first U.S. chairman of the Permanent Joint Board on Defense? *Answer*: The late New York mayor Fiorello LaGuardia. What his qualifications were for such a position I cannot say, but I am certain that the Board was never as colorful an operation thereafter.

At one PJBD meeting in Halifax, Nova Scotia, the U.S. delegation, including myself, were guests of the Canadian Navy. We were put up in an elegant BOQ (bachelor officers quarters) across from the venerable official residence of the ranking operational admiral in the Canadian Navy, known as "Scruffy" O'Brien. The admiral's home was an ancient wooden structure, complete with a "captain's walk" on the roof, overlooking the harbor. Nothing could have looked more appropriate for an old salt. The admiral took great personal interest in the PJBD discussions, particularly those after hours at the BOQ bar lasting into the night. One night when we were talking about submarines, he impulsively gathered us all together and drove us down to the dock where a sub happened to be berthed. The ship's watch officer was somewhat bewildered to see the top boss with a motley crew of American and Canadian officers and civilians descending on him at 11:45 P.M., but he made the best of it.

The submarine's cramped quarters impressed me deeply. The captain's stateroom was about one-third the size of my room in the War Crimes Prison, when I was a corporal! One could hardly stand erect in those quarters, but they were clearly superior to the bunks for enlisted men, which were crammed one on top of another.

I have been known, in most organizations I have served, as the guy who provides the comic relief. Upon our departure from Halifax, however, I must admit that I overdid it a bit. We had just finished breakfast in the BOQ and were waiting for the fleet of Navy limousines to take us to the military airport. Everyone was reading a newspaper, and there seemed to be no movement whatsoever. I decided this was a good time for a "comfort stop," as there was no telling when we might have another such opportunity. When I emerged, the BOQ was deserted. I raced down to the front desk to confront a chief warrant officer in deep shock: "Oh, sir," he lamented, "They must have left without you!" The man was resourceful, however, and put a call through directly to the admiral's office. Within a few minutes the admiral's personal limousine arrived, and I departed in high style, with all flags flying and with the entire police force of Halifax holding back the normal traffic so that I could pass by at high speed. The populace waved at me, so of course I waved back. When we arrived at the airport, the military police guard at the gate saluted smartly and motioned us inside. The driver, as I recall, never even slowed down, as he was accustomed to take precedence over all other official vehicles in the province. As we careened around the corner to our aircraft, the two delegations were lined up facing each other and the band was playing "O Canada," having just completed the "Star Spangled Banner." All activity stopped, however, as I descended from my royal "carriage." While the expression on Rufus's face was one of pain and chagrin, the others gave me a royal welcome. It was the first time they realized I had been missing.

It was also a scene no one on the Board would ever let me forget!

Treasure Island

The second PJBD meeting, at the U.S. naval base on Treasure Island in San Francisco Bay, was somewhat less memorable, as the two secretaries had to work into the night on minutes and joint statements, while everyone else enjoyed the sights of San Francisco. After the meetings, however, we did fly out to the U.S. carrier *Oriskany*, then stationed in the Pacific within striking distance of the coast. Watching the jets take off and land with precision was more than impressive, especially on such a small runway and at such high speeds. The day before our arrival, a tragedy had occurred. A "cold cat" had occurred (malfunctioning of the catapult that launched the jets into the air), and one jet balanced for a time on the edge of the takeoff deck. The pilot decided to bail out and was propelled high into the air and killed when he landed on the deck. It was all in vain, unhappily, as the plane never fell into the sea and he could have been easily rescued. Operational decisions, however, have to be made in split seconds, and he made the wrong one. (If he had fallen into the sea, he might also have been saved.) The greatest fear of all jet pilots, we learned, was that of the cold cat.

The "Education" of Harold Linder

With only six months left in his final term in office, President Lyndon Johnson appointed Harold Linder, president of the Export-Import Bank, as ambassador to Canada. Linder was a highly regarded businessman with a generally positive reputation as a government banker, even if he was at heart a fairly partisan Democrat.

Getting Ambassador Linder confirmed by the Senate was relatively easy, but getting him to his post was a different matter. The dean of the diplomatic corps in Ottawa (as mentioned earlier), and the highest ranking career ambassador on active duty at the time, was the venerable Walter Butterworth (he called himself "Walt"), and he was not going to be dislodged in a hurry. Ambassador Butterworth had been Secretary Rusk's first boss in the State Department many years before, and they remained close friends thereafter. Rusk let it be known that he would *not* permit anyone to push Walt Butterworth out of Ottawa before he had made all of his farewell calls, had been honored at farewell dinners, and could depart with dignity.

My assignment was to keep Harold Linder busy in Washington until such time as Butterworth was fully prepared to depart. This was not always an easy task, as Linder was champing at the bit to get to Ottawa before the Johnson administration expired. (As it turned out, the Nixon administration, after taking office, kept him on for another six months.) Fortunately, I was able to establish a warm relationship with Mr. Linder and often ended the day having a drink with him and his devoted spouse at their elegant Kalorama residence. I arranged an endless series of briefings, which he attended at first with good grace if not total enthusiasm. "Good Lord, Chips," he would sometimes remonstrate, "how many briefings do I need from the Agriculture Department?"

Finally I was running out of make-work projects when someone in the White House (God bless him) came to the rescue: he suggested that Linder fly out to Colorado Springs to visit NORAD, the joint U.S.-Canada Air Defense Command, and while he was at it, make a formal call on the Air Force Academy. The Air Force secretary's official jet would be placed at his disposal. That was a fine proposal, and I accepted for the ambassador forthwith. Within twenty-four hours Harold Linder and I were headed off into the Wild Blue West on the most comfortable aircraft I have ever in my life inhabited. The seats had an excess of leg room, and the two AF stewards who accompanied us were more than sufficient, since we were the only two passengers on the plane. They cooked us steaks on a grill in the rear of the aircraft to our order—the only time in my life I have tasted meat on a plane that was sufficiently rare!

We had one intermediate stop in Omaha, where the commander of SAC (Strategic Air Command) came out personally to our aircraft to give us a full briefing on his mission, although we had not requested or expected one. When we arrived in Colorado Springs, we were taken to an almost empty Broadmoor Hotel and each assigned a suite of rooms, for an astonishing price of $25.00 per night.

On the day of our scheduled visit to the Air Force Academy, Harold Linder became ill and returned to the hotel after luncheon in the main mess hall, where he had been "hailed" by the Air Force cadets in thundering unison. I ended up being the VIP during the remainder of the tour, which was certainly impressive. Everything had been carefully worked out in advance, and I was personally subjected to the treatment: at one stop, a young lad on a ladder some fifteen to twenty meters above a deep pool shouted my name, saluted, and jumped off, all as part of training for being ejected from an aircraft over water. The academy's location, surrounded by mountains, could not have been more attractive, and even though I am not a fan of contemporary architecture, I was favorably impressed by the innovative style of the chapel.

In sum, unlike Ambassador Linder, I was not eager to return to Washington.

At last Ambassador Butterworth completed his farewell ritual, and elaborate plans were made for the transfer of authority: the Butterworth limousine crossed the border south, less than an hour before Linder's car crossed to the north. The new regime was on board, I was off the hook, and ready to go on to my next assignment in Malawi (see chapter 9).

172

CHAPTER 8

Capitol Sabbatical

I owed my ten-month sabbatical on Capitol Hill to a program administered by the American Political Science Association. The APSA program, known as the Fellowship in Congressional Operations, was the initiative of the Stern Foundation, a family foundation in Louisiana. It provided journalists and young professors of political science at the assistant professor level an opportunity to work on Capitol Hill in a congressional office or committee. Fellows would then presumably return to their respective professions with a better practical understanding of the workings of the mysterious legislative branch of government. The Ford Foundation approved of the program's objectives and expanded participation in it, taking it over after its successful launching.

Eventually the executive branch discovered that the program was useful in training its own midcareer officers, often isolated from the legislative process because of the all-too-effective separation of powers. One or, at most, two representatives of federal departments (State, Interior, Defense, CIA and others) were selected annually for participation. The federal fellows' parent department or agency, not the Ford Foundation, continued to pay their salaries during what became a ten-month program.

I was one of several State Department candidates. Fortunately, only a handful of FSOs knew enough about the program to apply. Jim Briggs, a veteran ARA hand, and I became the chosen "fellows" from State and entered the orientation program in October 1966. The move eventually led me to a very different midcareer life change.

Until fall 1966, my principal exposure to Congress had been as an assigned control officer for visiting congressional delegations to my two Foreign Service posts abroad. My interest in spending a year or so on the Hill was probably whetted by the transfer of a Foreign Service colleague from Yugoslavia days, Jim Lowenstein, from State to the Senate Foreign Relations Committee. Jim's move involved resignation from the Foreign Service, and I was not certain that I wanted to take so drastic a step just yet. Hence the congressional fellowship attracted me by offering a sabbatical taste of the Hill without commitment to a definitive break.

The Congressional Fellowship Program consisted of two months of orientation, followed by four months in the House and another four in the Senate, not necessarily in that order. During the orientation, one was free to negotiate one's own onward congressional assignments. Picking an office assignment was not all that difficult, we learned, as the program was well known and highly regarded on the Hill. Members of Congress realized that they would be getting fairly experienced executive branch assistance *at no charge*, a decisive consideration.

Since the last fifteen years of my public career were spent in the House of Representatives, more than enough attention will be focused in due course on my Hill experiences. Here I will briefly summarize some of the highlights of my ten-month interlude in Congress between Foreign Service assignments.

The orientation period, like most such exercises, was a mixed bag. We met with the House and Senate leadership (who predictably told us very little that was useful and recited the usual platitudes); with the national chairmen of both parties (mildly informative); and with lobbyists and key current or former congressional aides (very informative).

The best session of all was at the Cleveland Park home of Dr. Max Kampelman—a former aide to Hubert Humphrey—later to become a leading arms negotiator. That the details of his presentation still stand out in my mind is an early indicator of my fascination with the legislative process. In his early days in the Senate, Humphrey had faced the kind of hard choice often faced by conscientious legislators: deciding between the narrow interests of their constituents and the national interest. The dairy farmers of Minnesota, a main element of his political base, were up in arms over excessive amounts of dairy products they thought were being imported from Scandinavia, especially Denmark, and flooding the American market. They wanted, if not higher tariffs, at least *some* restrictions on quantity. Our ambassador to Denmark, Mrs. Eugenie Anderson, one of the first female envoys appointed anywhere (and a Humphrey protégé), argued persuasively against this. As she explained to the senator, the United States and its European allies were in the process of organizing NATO; if we wanted Denmark to join the alliance, the early days of the Cold War were not the time to establish quotas on Danish dairy products. During that era NATO's existence and the solidarity of its member states were considered crucial to the survival of Western civilization.

After much agonizing deliberation, Humphrey finally made the "national" as opposed to the "parochial" political decision and voted against the proposed restrictions on Danish dairy products. Ironically, according to Kampelman, it was the best thing that ever happened to the Minnesota dairy farmers, as Humphrey spent much of the remainder of his public career trying to make up to them for that adverse vote.

OFFICE OF REPRESENTATIVE
FRELINGHUYSEN OF NEW JERSEY

Eventually I signed up with Republican Representative Peter H. B. Frelinghuysen of New Jersey in the House and Democratic Senator Joseph Clark of Pennsylvania in the "other body," both members of the foreign affairs committees of their respective houses. Both were also maverick patricians, rather than veteran politicians, and very much alike in background and outlook, though their political orientation was quite divergent.

The 1966–1967 congressional year was a more than exciting time to be where the action was. Two monumental events characterized the period: the House expulsion of Congressman Adam Clayton Powell of Harlem, and the Senate censure of Senator Thomas Dodd of Connecticut.

Mr. Frelinghuysen's office was exceptionally good for the purposes of the APSA program, possibly because he was not a typical congressman and his office was not a typical office. Unlike the great majority of his House colleagues, at least those I had met, Congressman Frelinghuysen was not a "driven" personality motivated either by an intense desire for public recognition or political power. An aristocrat among politicians, he was a man of independent means and status, with as many interests outside of Congress as within. (He was a trustee of Princeton, for example.) In other words, Congress did not do for *him* as much as he did for *Congress*. A strong element of noblesse oblige marked his years of service on Capitol Hill. His service represented somewhat of a personal sacrifice for him, but he was continuing a family tradition—one Frelinghuysen ancestor had signed the Constitution and another had run for vice president on an unsuccessful Whig party ticket with Henry Clay.

For an "intern" or "fellow" like myself, the key to every congressional office was the role and status of the AA (administrative assistant), the person in charge at the congressman's office. If the AA was secure in his (in those days, the House was almost all male) dealings with his boss and was a decent office manager, everything ran smoothly and morale was high. If the AA was insecure and the legislative assistants went around him to deal directly with the congressman, the stage was set for mutually hostile factions and disaster. The politics of the member or his public reputation would be of little consequence. It was the AA that counted.

Fortunately, Bill Kendall, a New Jersey chemist who had left his profession decades before to run Frelinghuysen's campaign and then his Washington office, had his boss's total confidence and could speak for him as his alter ego at any time. He was so highly respected among his peers that he once headed up a bipartisan organization of staff members. He was *the* AA to whom other AAs turned for advice, most notably Democrats from across the hall. Bill was actually more of a partisan Republican than Peter, but he was always the thoroughgoing professional. Working for him was a cinch.

I used to write the weekly newsletter, explaining to the congressman's constituents why he voted the way he did, especially in foreign affairs. Bill insisted that I work out the language directly with Peter, although I tried to clear everything first with Bill, to get him on my side if necessary. My efforts were useless, as he was determined to delegate this task to me. (After Peter retired, Bill ended up running Senator Charles Mathias's reelection campaign in Maryland, and then went to the White House, where he was in charge of relations with the *Senate*, although he knew more about the workings of the *House* than just about anyone.)

Down the hall from us was the office of Adam Clayton Powell, perhaps the most controversial member of either house in that era. Peter, as ranking Republican on the Education and Labor Committee (before he resigned to concentrate on the Foreign Affairs Committee), had consistently fought with Powell, the committee chairman, and was pleased to relinquish this permanent frustration. Powell rarely seemed to care what anyone thought of him and acted accordingly. I used to pass him regularly in the hallway, and we would exchange winks. I never knew what they meant exactly, but he seemed to be saying: "*I* know that *you* know that we *both* know this is all a big game!"

On the day he was expelled from the House, a busload of his followers from Harlem appeared, shouting his favorite slogan: "Keep the faith, Baby." As he was holding a press conference in the Rayburn Building, I happened along with my motorcycle helmet in hand. He stopped in midsentence, pointed at me and said: "See, I told you a man needs maximum protection in this place!" He was evidently in his element, even though he had lost his power and seniority, as well as his seat. The expulsion was eventually ruled unconstitutional, but by then Adam was no longer alive.

OFFICE OF SENATOR CLARK OF PENNSYLVANIA

His critics called him a "limousine liberal," and the description was not that far off the mark. A Harvard-educated blueblood from Philadelphia's Main Line and related to Nelson Rockefeller's first wife, Joseph S. Clark hardly fit the mold of a common man's populist. But he was a genuine reformer. As the Democratic mayor of Philadelphia, he had broken one of the few *Republican* urban machines. Nonetheless, as one of his admirers among the Washington press corps noted at the end of his Senate tenure: "He soon found that it takes more than a white hat to reform the world's most deliberative body."

Joe Clark was at one time president of Americans for Democratic Action and a card-carrying liberal by conviction. He was also one of the original and most outspoken "doves" on Vietnam. He was a strong and consistent supporter of Lyndon Johnson's Great Society, but broke sharply with LBJ over his Vietnam buildup. In the initial stages, long before all the public demonstrations and hoopla that followed later in the 1960s, such antiwar criticism was very unpopular, and Joe Clark was immediately branded a Senate pariah.

Because of Clark's public stance on this issue, his staff was wary about taking on a congressional fellow who was still on the State Department rolls. Dean Rusk was still my ultimate boss, and the senator's AA worried that some of the more notorious Clark indiscretions at morning staff meetings might get reported back to his bureaucratic enemies at State and in the White House. Fortunately, my friend Jim Lowenstein, who at that time worked fairly closely with Senator Clark on Foreign Relations Committee business, was able to vouch for my reliability in this regard and to assure Harry Schwartz, Clark's AA, that I would not be a "security risk." (One of the cardinal rules of the Congressional Fellowship program was that the participants had to detach themselves from their home agencies or departments to get the maximum "educational" benefits from the experience of being an integral part of a representative's or senator's staff. To the State Department's credit, no one in authority ever requested me, even informally, to break this confidence.)

The senator's staff ranged from liberal to far left (except that all were "conservative" regarding Israel), and I was regarded as an establishment anomaly. The fact that I rode to work on a Lambretta motor scooter tended to confuse this image. Nevertheless, all staff members and especially the senator himself always treated me most cordially.

Senator Clark must have been one of the few senators, if not the only one, who held an office staff meeting every day he was in Washington, and I was invited to attend them all. The senator used this forum to vent his various frustrations, both about other senators and about ranking executive branch officials. While he could be bullheaded and stubborn and usually ended up doing what he wanted to in the first place, despite heavy pleading at times from his closest advisers, Clark always listened patiently to everyone in turn and welcomed adverse criticism and advice—and he got a lot of it. One exchange sticks in my mind:

> *Lou Phillips* (the press secretary): Senator, if you don't go down to the White House for the luncheon with General Westmoreland, people will say you are just a left-wing ideologue.
>
> *Clark*: You're right, Lou, I ought to go down, listen carefully, and then give them a piece of my mind. Actually, I can read the general's speech in the White House press release.

The senator ended up staying in the Senate, because of, he later claimed, a crucial vote.

On one occasion the discussion focused on the political ramifications of the senator's impending divorce and (third) marriage. The senator was contemplating these moves just prior to his reelection campaign, and his campaign staff were less than happy. I thought this subject was a bit personal for an outside observer to be involved with and offered to be excused. "No," the senator demurred firmly, "I want you to stay, Chips, because I definitely value your opinion." I wondered how many people in the Department of State could have made such a statement with a straight face. Strangely enough, the senator actually meant what he said (he usually did), and asked me several times how he ought to proceed and whose advice he was receiving that morning did I agree with?!

Perhaps the most abiding lesson I learned in the Clark office was the simple fact that political orientation has nothing *necessarily* to do with personal regard. To my great surprise, I discovered that the senator whom Joe Clark admired most was conservative Democrat John Stennis of Mississippi, although the two could not have agreed on a single subject, including the time of day. Stennis had the undesired assignment of chairing the ad hoc committee looking into the alleged misdeeds of a fellow member, Democratic senator Thomas Dodd of

Connecticut. He handled the job with great fairness and discretion, evidently one of his most redeeming qualities in Joe Clark's eyes. This was a job no senator would have welcomed, and all were sensitively aware of that fact. Later, when Clark chaired a subcommittee investigating poverty in Mississippi, he was scrupulous in consulting Senator Stennis in advance of every move, including selection of witnesses. Stennis, who was naturally opposed to the entire exercise, had no complaints about the subcommittee's modus operandi.

Thanks to my regular attendance at morning staff meetings, I received regular assignments from the senator personally, including drafting major speeches. One subject was gun control, of which he was an early advocate. Many believed his position cost him the western Pennsylvania vote and the next election.

I also worked on ABMs (antiballistic missile systems). The senator was the first in a public forum to oppose their construction. On the day he delivered his anti-ABM speech, only one other senator, Strom Thurmond, of South Carolina, was on the floor. Thurmond argued that Charleston was to be surrounded by ABMs only because it had so many vital military facilities that needed protection. The claim was valid, if only because Thurmond and Representative Mendel Rivers, House Armed Services Committee chairman, had been instrumental in getting so many bases located in South Carolina. Clark cited ex-President Eisenhower's warning about the military-industrial complex and denounced the ABM system as a waste of money. It wouldn't work, he protested, and he made that statement as a former Air Force colonel. "Well, you don't act like one," Thurmond responded. A member of the Thurmond staff subsequently expunged that remark from the *Congressional Record*.

The Six-Day War

By an accident of history, the June 1967 war between Israel and her neighbors took place during my spring tenure in the Clark office. As noted earlier, the staff was overwhelmingly pro-Israel and not merely because of the large Jewish representation in the office, from the AA on down to the logistical support team under the office manager, Mrs. Marie Littman. The senator himself was a strong backer of Israel, although he considered himself less demagogic and more statesmanlike than the other senator from Pennsylvania, Republican Hugh Scott. (Actually, Scott was a moderate Republican, and the two offices cooperated regularly on statewide projects.)

After the cessation of hostilities, Clark's enthusiasm for the Zionist cause in general, and the Philadelphia rabbis who swarmed into his office in particular, eroded rapidly. The rabbis tended to *order* Joe Clark to make statements which he probably would have made freely without the pressure. Those pro-Zionists overplayed their hand and caused resentment in the process. (AIPAC, the America-Israel Public Affairs Committee, had a similar image problem.) Although Clark continued his support for Israel after a cooling-off period, his commitment was never again as strong. I even heard him say once in anger: "Those rabbis can make an anti-Semite out of me, even though I know better." Strictly speaking, that was a politically incorrect remark, but most of his Jewish staff members nodded in embarrassed understanding, if not agreement.

In order to alleviate some of the tension surrounding this episode, I drafted a bogus press release that was widely circulated throughout the office. The senator liked it so much that he took it over to the hospital where his AA was recuperating from an operation and read it to him verbatim. Apparently Harry Schwartz laughed so hard there was real concern that his stitches might pop. The text follows:

For Immediate Release

CLARK PROPOSES FREEDOM RIDE

SENATOR JOSEPH S. CLARK CALLED TODAY FOR "ACTION, NOT WORDS" IN SUPPORT OF THE ISRAELI PEOPLE.

IN A PERSONAL GESTURE OF DEFIANCE, THE PENNSYLVANIA SENATOR OFFERED TO PROVIDE SEVERAL OUTSTANDING PRO-ZIONIST MEMBERS OF HIS WASHINGTON STAFF FOR DIRECT PARTICI-PATION IN A "FREEDOM RIDE" THROUGH THE STRAITS OF TIRAN.

LED BY PRESS AND APPOINTMENTS SECRTARY LOU PHILLIPS, THE DELEGATION WOULD IN-CLUDE MISS LESLIE GOTTLIEB, MRS. SARA EHRMAN, ONE UNIDENTIFIED CONGRESSIONAL FELLOW, AND THREE INTERNS. LOGISTICAL SUPPORT WOULD BE PROVIDED BY OFFICE MANAGER MARIE LITTMAN. "THIS ACTION CONSTITUTES A REAL PERSONAL SACRIFICE ON MY PART," SENATOR CLARK NOTED, "BUT CLEARLY THE TIMES DE-MAND SOMETHING MORE THAN BENEVOLENT NEUTRALITY."

THE SENATOR ALSO SUGGESTED THAT CER-TAIN DISTINGUISHED PENNSYLVANIANS LEAD THE BREAKTHROUGH FOR FREEDOM BY JOINING THE ADVANCE PARTY THROUGH THE STRAITS. WHEN PRESSED FOR SPECIFIC NOMINATIONS, THE SENIOR SENATOR MENTIONED JUSTICE MICHAEL MUSMANNO, 105 OUTSTANDING RABBIS FROM THE GREATER PHILADELPHIA AREA, AND MR FRANCIS SMITH AS EXCELLENT CANDIDATES FOR SUCH A VOYAGE.*

"MORALLY AND LEGALLY WE ARE AN ALLY OF ISRAEL," THE SENATOR OBSERVED, "AND IT IS HIGH TIME WE DID SOMETHING ABOUT IT."

STAFF MEMBERS IN THE SENATOR'S OFFICE WERE UNAVAILABLE FOR IMMEDIATE COMMENT. END

---

*Justice Musmanno was a primary opponent and founder of the ABC (Anyone but Clark!) movement. I no longer remember Francis Smith, evidently a Clark critic.

P.S.: The following year Senator Clark was defeated in the general election by Republican representative Richard Schweiker. When I last saw them, members of the Clark office staff generously assured me I was not responsible!

The press release was in the same vein as the fictitious acknowledgment I drafted to Mrs. Roosevelt, replying to her letters recommending Peace Corps applicants, during my brief tour with the Peace Corps. Never, however, in my wildest dreams would I have dared to do anything similar in the State Department itself. And that in itself says a great deal about my forthcoming career change.

The APSA program ended in the summer of 1967. The "honeymoon on the Hill" was over. In Part III, I give a fulsome account, including more anecdotes, of my later life on Capitol Hill that began in November 1970.

CHAPTER 9

Malawi Memorabilia

The drab atmosphere of the Department of State was a distinct letdown after my eventful year on Capitol Hill. In the late spring of 1969 I was ready for an onward assignment, which could well have been outside the Foreign Service.

Having traveled this distance in the Foreign Service, however, I decided that I ought to try one senior position at a small foreign post outside of Europe. I did not want to serve in the political section of another large U.S. mission like London or Bonn, as I had spent enough time in the bureaucracy already. I still had some contacts in Personnel who let me know what was available: not much for a junior FSO-3, at that time the lowest end of the senior grades.

The number two position in, to me, an obscure East African country called Malawi was about to become available. It was supposedly an attractive, mountainous ex-British colony, and the U.S. ambassador was a "prince of a guy." I accepted without further ado what was to become my last hurrah in the Foreign Service of the United States.

My assignment position to the small embassy in Malawi as deputy chief of mission (DCM), second in command to the ambassador, was such a completely new experience for me, and so unfamiliar to most readers, that a brief description of the country and its first postindependence president are in order.

Malawi, not to be confused with distant Mali (as it often is), takes its name from the Malawi, or Maravi, people. (The letters *l* and *r* are interchangeable in Chichewa and Chinjanja, the main languages of Malawi.) The Malawi once inhabited the lake region, having crossed Zambia from the southern Congo, and were practically wiped out by the dreaded disease bilharzia.[1] Their descendants, the Njanja, now reside in southern Malawi.

The famous explorer-missionary David Livingstone discovered Lake Malawi (or Nyasa) in 1859. After his death, the Church of Scotland established missions in the south at Blantyre, the name of his Scottish birthplace, and at Livingstonia along the lake, first at the southern tip of the lake and later removed to the north.

Malawi was originally called Nyasaland, and Lake Malawi, Lake Nyasa. In more modern times the Yao tribe populated its western shore. (*Nyasa* is the Yao term for lake, so that technically Lake Nyasa translates into "Lake Lake.") The Yao actively collected indigenous slaves and drove them north by foot to Tanganyika and eventually Zanzibar, where they were picked up by Arab traders. This is one reason Yaos and Arabs were traditionally unpopular in parts of Africa south of the Sahara.

In 1889 the United Kingdom established the Nyasaland Protectorate. From 1953 until December 31, 1963, the British combined the territory with Northern and Southern Rhodesia into the Federation of Rhodesia and Nyasaland (also referred to as the "Central African Federation," although geographically the area is east, not central). The federation soon dissolved. Northern Rhodesia became Zambia; Southern Rhodesia became Rhodesia by the Unilateral Declaration of Independence (UDI) of 1966 under Ian Smith, later to become Zimbabwe in 1980, under Robert Mugabe; and Nyasaland became Malawi. Kenneth Kaunda, Zambia's leader for several decades after independence, was actually from a Malawi tribe, as Malawians were often at pains to point out.

PRESIDENT BANDA OF MALAWI

After independence in 1964, Malawi was ruled by "the Life President, His Excellency *Ngwasi* (the peerless one) Dr. H. Kamuzu Banda," as he was invariably introduced or referred to during my tenure there. A few biographical comments about this remarkably durable autocrat may help provide the necessary backdrop for my final year in diplomacy.

Banda was born in 1905 (according to *Who's Who*), but that date has continually been under challenge. No one knows exactly *how* old the Ngwasi was, possibly not even the Ngwasi; the actual date of his birth used to be considered a "state secret." It certainly was a secret, since no representative of the state could produce any convincing proof one way or another. When I arrived in Blantyre in 1969, Dr. Banda was generally thought to be in his mid to late eighties. Some twenty-five years later he was reported to be in his nineties. Finally, a Malawian acquaintance told me, Banda began to "lose his grip" and show signs of senility. This is hardly surprising, as several years ago he underwent brain surgery in South Africa. He died in 1997.

The missionaries in Livingstonia christened him "Hastings," hardly an asset for a future nationalist. Fortunately someone had the foresight to give him the second name Kamuzu, by which he was subsequently known and revered as leader of Malawi independence. His childhood was marked by his small, slight build and his determined intellect, which various missionaries in turn recognized and subsidized. He ran away from Livingstonia, after being expelled from an exam because, unable to see the blackboard over the burly student in front of him, he had to stand. He made his way barefooted, first to Rhodesia, then to South Africa, where a group of American missionaries discovered his abilities and arranged for him to study at Xenia College in Ohio. He then went to Medical School at Meharry College in Tennessee. Before he could practice in Nyasaland, however, he required a British qualification, which he eventually received in Edinburgh. There he also joined, and later became an elder of, the Kirk of Scotland. After obtaining his British diploma in 1941, Banda seemed to have lost some of his nationalist zeal and contented himself with the life of a middle class— and relatively prosperous—physician in Edinburgh.

After World War II the siren song of African nationalism stirred Banda to thoughts of independence, nurtured by such leaders as Kwame Nkrumah of Ghana and Jomo Kenyatta of Kenya. (He spent some time in Ghana before being recalled to service as the "father-figurehead" of the Malawi nationalist cause.) Evidently the "Young Turks" of the Nyasa African Congress did not really know what they were getting when they persuaded him to return, in 1958, after some forty years in exile.

At first, he became a fiery nationalist orator, calling for the breakup of the Federation and independence for the Nyasaland appendage. The British obliged him by putting him in jail in Rhodesia, which merely enhanced his nationalist credentials. Once he acquired full power, first as prime minister and then as president-for-life, Banda began to change his tune. Unlike many of his peers, he did not immediately expel representatives of the colonial power from office, but rather urged them to stay on if and where they were needed. As a result, he received regular annual subsidies from Her Majesty's Government, plus aid from the United States and loans from international lending institutions. A strong anticommunist, he headed one of the last black African governments that maintained diplomatic relations with Taiwan in lieu of Beijing, a stance that enhanced his stature in some American eyes for much of the Cold War.

Banda consistently opposed what he labeled "decadent Western liberal ideas," many of which he felt a struggling young nation with minimal resources could not afford. Three of the four official "cornerstones" of Malawi life were work, loyalty, and dedication. (I have forgotten the fourth, but it is closely related.) Banda believed that Malawi could not afford the democratic process. He ruled the country and the single Malawi Congress Party, as well as Parliament, with an iron hand.

His policies were remarkably effective. Unlike leaders of many other newly independent African countries, he did not neglect the agricultural sector. Malawi's resources consisted of maize (corn), groundnuts (peanuts), tea, tobacco, and coffee, plus timber and bauxite too remote for exploitation. Eventually Malawi became self-sufficient in basic foodstuffs, especially maize, despite being one of the poorest countries in Africa. The World Bank often cited Malawi as an example of rare development success in a disadvantaged environment.

Although a dictator by inclination and disposition, Banda was not neglectful of grassroots aspirations. He had his own "intelligence service," which told him who was and was not popular or effective at the local level, and he acted accordingly. Although loyalty to the president was a sine qua non, local officials were otherwise promoted or demoted in accordance with their reputations among the populace at large. Disgraced politicians, like the minister of labor caught with his hands in the party till, could be rehabilitated after a period of penance and abject public apology.

Like many autocrats, Banda had one major blind spot: he could not delegate, and he resisted preparing and training a successor. He "sat hard" on the more talented or educated civil servants upon their return from study and training in England or the United States. He would often lecture them immediately upon their return to their homeland, emphasizing they had *yet* to prove themselves. Indeed, humility was enforced rather ruthlessly, and "divide and conquer" was a staple principle of his rule. The Ngwasi handpicked the politicians; few had much to recommend them aside from loyalty. Except for a few bright stars, whose character rarely matched their ability, most were primitive compared with the civil servants. A cabinet revolt a year after independence, led by Henry M. Chipembere, whom Banda had considered almost a son, established loyalty and reliability as the prerequisites for public service in Malawi. The dissidents all fled to Tanzania, where they formed a permanent anti-Banda cabal. Chipembere himself spent some time in U.S. academe, where he developed an American following of considerable stature.

Banda was a study in contrasts: a genuine and dedicated African nationalist, he nevertheless valued certain aspects of "white" culture, which he believed blacks needed for ultimate success. A staunch defender of African tradition, he also appreciated the benefits of a classical education for the Malawians. (Long after my departure, he founded a "classical education" academy for elite students.) He was the first black leader of a country south of the Sahara to establish diplomatic relations with South Africa, essentially for pragmatic reasons: the South Africans agreed to underwrite his new capital and airport in Lilongwe, after the British and Americans turned him down.

Banda was death on miniskirts, which were very much in fashion in the West during the late sixties, and he outlawed wearing them, even by foreigners, although short tennis skirts at private clubs were generally overlooked. On the other hand, bare-breasted females in public were perfectly accepted, as in keeping with tradition. (In African culture, breasts are considered primarily "functional," whereas the leg, or especially the thigh, can be considered dangerously erotic.)

An ascetic workaholic, Banda was a nonsmoker and teetotaler. No one was allowed to smoke or drink in his presence. Yet he was a strong backer of Malawi's tobacco industry and authorized the local construction of the first Carlsberg brewery outside of Denmark. He had an ambivalent attitude toward members of the Peace Corps: He appreciated the respect that many volunteers demonstrated for African traditions, in contrast to the attitudes of many British expatriates. He was extremely hostile, however, to the liberal, and to him subversive, "Western" ideals the program seemed to represent, especially in education.

Among African leaders, Kamuzu would always be considered a maverick-eccentric or worse. And he was clearly a dictator who ruthlessly suppressed opposition to—or criticism of—his rule. However, calling him an "Uncle Tom," as the Africa Bureau at State tended to do—if only tacitly—was simply inaccurate.

THE EMBASSY

When I arrived, Blantyre, and especially its sister suburb, Limbe, were the commercial centers of Malawi. Although Zomba, a small university town located about forty miles away, was considered the nominal capital, only a few ministry headquarters, plus the residence of the British high commissioner, were located there. Banda had taken over the former British governor's mansion there and used it for ceremonial functions, as well as for one of his several residences. Most of the embassies, however, remained in Blantyre. Lilongwe, now the capital, was then a primitive village with only a handful of buildings and no paved roads.

Our embassy was definitely *not* overstaffed. In addition to Ambassador Marshall P. Jones and myself, it included an administrative officer, several communicators, and two American secretaries. A junior FSO (on his second overseas assignment) performed all the consular and economic work plus a major share of the political reporting. This whiz, our working "stakhanovite," L. Paul ("Jerry") Bremer, handled all his assignments with aplomb and efficiency. I realized from the outset that he worked best under severe pressure. This propensity probably accounted largely for his later success in working for several secretaries of state, including Henry Kissinger, and his appointment as ambassador to the

Netherlands and director of counterterrorism in the Department of State.

Other embassy units included an AID director in the process of phasing out his operation, leaving me with most of his backlog; a military attaché, also accredited to Zambia and Rhodesia on a regional basis; a Peace Corps headquarters staff; a two-man United States Information Service operation; and a CIA political officer under State Department cover.

Ambassador Jones set the tone of the mission. The atmosphere was low-key, informal, and what I might describe as collegially congenial. A career FSO, Marshall's road to the top was unusual. A successful administrative officer for most of his career, his administrative prowess was based on a finely tuned sensitivity to *internal* State Department politics (real, even if unacknowledged by the average FSO), as well as to *external* diplomacy. Marshall negotiated good deals with bureaucrats, both foreign and domestic.

Blantyre's many administrative benefits, including embassy "rest houses" on the Zomba Plateau and along Lake Malawi, plus a 10 percent "hardship" differential, says a great deal about his administrative know-how. No one in management seemed inclined to deny him any request. He explained to me why we received a hardship allowance, in contrast to dreary, flat, and uninviting Lusaka, capital of neighboring Zambia, which was certainly worse than anything we had in Malawi. "Chips," he said, "their problem is that they don't know how to write a *request!*" (Our allowance request was based on malaria, still prevalent in Blantyre but eradicated in Lusaka proper—though not in Lusaka's hinterland.)

Marshall also used these talents to good effect in his diplomatic role. An American ambassador in Malawi had a sensitive role to play if he wanted to be effective. He must above all get along famously with British officials and expatriates, but he must also subtly associate himself with purely African aspirations. Jones was eminently successful at both. The British considered him a committed Anglophile, so much so that he was once invited to be the guest speaker at the annual tea planters' dinner, an honor accorded to no other American.

Africans who came to know Marshall Jones well tended to regard him as more sympathetic to their needs and desires than the average Britisher. His utter lack of pretense is what seemed to work so well. He called himself just a "simple guy" (he was anything *but*) from Indiana. He would don an outlandish baseball cap and walk around the city each morning talking with Indian shopkeepers and anyone else who came along. He picked up a remarkable amount of local intelligence that way, especially about economic trends, which often had political overtones. People would end up telling him secrets they would divulge to no one else.[2]

But Marshall was constitutionally unable to sit behind a desk for long, leaving his DCM to cope with most of the paperwork. That was perfectly acceptable to me, given the advantages we gained from Marshall's peregrinations around Blantyre. I wished there had been fewer early morning staff meetings, however. Though informative and entertaining, they lasted most of the morning and left me with a permanent backlog. That situation worsened after the AID program closed down and I took over the director's duties. Even though the program no longer existed, requests for things like feasibility studies and investigations kept coming in.

Marshall Jones had his priorities straight: "Nobody impresses me," he liked to emphasize, "by staying in the office after 4:30 P.M. It only indicates that you cannot get your work done on time!" The ambassador wanted his staff to be out in the community, not holed up in an office working on reports that probably didn't get read in the department anyway. This philosophy was intensely refreshing. (Competition among those wishing to be *seen* staying latest in their respective offices was a bane of many Foreign Service officers' existence. In my humble opinion, a tennis break after office hours, a Blantyre tradition, would have done the entire

Department of State a world of good in promoting clear-headed thinking, always in short supply, and increased efficiency and productivity.)

HOUSEHOLD STAFF

I arrived in Blantyre initially as a summer bachelor, because of an injury to my oldest son, John, which kept the family behind in Washington until September. Suddenly I was confronted with domestic responsibilities. Fortunately, my predecessor had been a gourmet diner and connoisseur of fine wines. I eagerly purchased his entire stock of food and drink. I also inherited his outstanding household staff, including:

- The best cook in town. When I left, he was expropriated from my successor by the new ambassador.
- Two house boys, one Christian and one Muslim, so that both Saturdays and Sundays were covered.
- A "dhobi," who did the laundry.
- Two gardeners, who at first did little work because our residence was on the edge of a jungle. They later built a tree house and a rope swing for my son John.
- A night watchman, who at least once fell asleep under a car in the middle of the night and almost was run over.
- My embassy driver, Duncan.

We later added a nanny, Katherine Phiri, trained in South Africa, primarily for my youngest son, Charlie, aged three. Katrine, as she was called, was devoted to him, and even walked him to his play school with a parasol over his blond head to shield it from the morning sun. (After our return to Washington, Charlie's standard of living deteriorated dramatically, and he suffered severe adjustment problems at first. He only partially succeeded in getting his brother to tie his shoes in the morning, but he is now our most independent free spirit!)

The monthly cost (including food) of maintaining this staff was about half of what I now pay my part-time cleaning lady in Washington per week. Even allowing for differences in time and place, all my employees were better paid and better housed than the overwhelming majority of relatively "skilled" workers in Blantyre. Within the local community, *all* were greatly envied their respective positions.

REPRESENTATION

About "representation," that is, official entertaining, I soon learned a few important guiding principles from the more experienced Ambassador Jones.

First, never invite Malawian civil servants and politicians to the same party. The two groups simply did not mix, primarily because civil servants were afraid of contacts with MPs or cabinet ministers. The latter were untrustworthy in the eyes of the intelligentsia and would only serve to get them in trouble with the president-for-life. Civil servants would not show up if they heard that politicians were to be present.

Second, sit-down dinners are in order for "Europeans" (read *whites*, including Americans), but never for Malawians. Always assume, Marshall cautioned quite correctly, that most Africans have already eaten when they arrive at your home, as they don't like and have difficulty digesting *your* food. Therefore, a stand-up buffet table with a wide selection of food, allowing guests to selectively choose what to eat, if anything, is the preferred option.

A particular incident, which I call the "shrimp test," made a lasting impression on me. At a buffet dinner the German ambassador gave for the diplomatic corps, the *pièce de résistance* was shrimp shipped to Malawi from Europe under special refrigeration. The Malawian chief of protocol, who had studied at the University of Wisconsin, had married a white American student, and eventually had been Malawian ambassador to Germany, tried three times to swallow the shrimp. Trying his utmost to be a good sport, and smiling helplessly at the guests, he finally placed it in his pocket when he thought no one was looking.

Lastly, do *not* attempt to force Western social customs upon an African guest list. Polygamy in Malawi was quite common. Malawian guests might bring their traditional wives from a village *and* their current educated wives or girlfriends to the same party. Traditional wives sat in one corner, supported by one another, and made no attempt to mix with the other guests. Such a scene could be anathema to a Western hostess, whose immediate instinct would be to break up this nest of wallflowers and move them about the room where they might meet other guests. This was invariably a mistake: the ladies felt uncomfortable on their own and desperately wanted to be left alone. Not even a Perle Mesta or a Pamela Harriman could alter centuries of tradition. Better to go with the flow.

Indeed, mixing categories and classes of people in Malawi was not a promising undertaking. British civil servants seconded to the Malawi government would generally welcome talking business with their African opposite numbers at cocktail parties, but they tended to socialize primarily among themselves. Africans, even intellectuals, seemed to prefer *not* to be overwhelmed by a European diplomatic or expatriate presence.

Notable exceptions to the last rule were Jerry Bremer and his wife Francie. They often held a kind of informal open house with a rather sparse "penny whistle band" (consisting of several blind musicians playing such instruments as bamboo pipes and a drum). These lively parties were always well attended by young educated Malawians with aspirations and prospects for future leadership. They regarded both Jerry and Francie as young, professionally astute, and glamorous, and somehow not intimidating. The guests were put immediately and permanently at ease. And they stayed until all hours of the night.

U.S. Independence Day

At most Foreign Service posts, July 4 is the day the principal officer normally hosts an elegant garden party for leading officials and prominent citizens of the host country. Not in Malawi. There the custom was to hold a picnic and baseball game for the numerous American missionaries in residence throughout the land.

Our missionaries' behavior abruptly shattered my image of people like Dr. Schweizer or those heroic humanitarians who serve their fellow man under incredible hardship conditions. The missionaries at the party were mostly of the uncommunicative variety who refused to mix with one another. As Marshall Jones took me around to introduce me to the various sect leaders, the apparent hostility of each of these individuals toward their colleagues from other denominations appalled me. Their unbridgeable differences, which seemed peculiarly irrelevant to the demands of the modern world, seemed to be related to obscure passages in the Bible.

Putting together two baseball teams under these circumstances was no small achievement: representatives of the Church of Christ were reluctant to be on the same side with those from the *United* Church of Christ, and so it went. The day turned out to be the most forgettable day I was to spend in all of my time in east Africa. I remain appalled at these so-called "Christians" who could not even play on the same team!

My July 4 disillusionment led me to begin to appreciate the wisdom of President Banda's somewhat ambivalent attitude toward missionaries. Although he was a leading Elder of the Church of Scotland, he required them to bring "something more than the Bible" with them. All were welcome in Malawi if they contributed to the country's welfare and development. They were not accepted, however, if they were only interested in spreading ideological propaganda.

The Jehovah's Witnesses were a prime example of religious fanatics who were definitely *un*welcome in Malawi. They tended to settle in the more isolated rural areas and made a sizable number of converts, whom the government considered subversive. The Witnesses' main pitch was that the local citizenry owed allegiance only to God and *not* to Dr. Banda, a nonstarter of a policy. The converts refused to carry Malawi Congress Party cards and were often persecuted as a result. Banda eventually ordered their operations closed down and their property confiscated. Under the Hickenlooper amendment to U.S. AID legislation, all American bilateral aid to Malawi therefore had to terminate. After much unhappiness on all sides, some face-saving formula was worked out and aid was resumed. Marshall Jones told me that explaining this amendment to President Banda was one of the two most difficult assignments in his four years in Malawi.

In all fairness, I should add that the only decent medical facility in Malawi was built and staffed by members of the Seventh Day Adventist Church. They certainly contributed handsomely to the general welfare and fit Dr. Banda's prescription. Several Catholic missions also performed important work at the local level in combatting blindness and maintained a nonsectarian reputation. These operations proved more the exception than the rule.

Malawi Independence Day

The Republic of Malawi gained its independence on July 6, 1964, and became a republic two years later, on July 6, 1966. Although the festivities for its third anniversary on July 6, 1969, probably resembled similar ceremonies throughout Africa, it was a first for me and made a considerable impression. I have drawn on a letter I wrote to my family to describe some of its more colorful aspects.

Independence celebrations sometimes lasted as long as a week, depending on the mood of the president. In 1969 the events took four days, after several weeks' preparation. Eventually every store and office building was covered by flags, colorful decorations, and life-size pictures of Kamuzu.

The festivities climaxed with a day in Kamuzu Stadium, from 9:30 A.M. until 7:00 P.M. Fortunately I was in the reserved section and did not have to start out at the crack of dawn to get a seat. Even my VIP section was jammed with last-minute arrivals, making breathing difficult at times. I sat in the front row, just below the speakers' platform and just above "Kamuzu's women," a group of ladies all dressed up in fancy new traditional African green robes for the occasion, most with children strapped to their backs. They preceded and/or followed the president wherever he went, and chanted and clapped when he arrived and departed. He stopped to say a few words to them before he got into his large Mercedes 300 limousine.

At 12:50 P.M. the presidential motorcade entered the main gate to the stadium, and the program was *on*. Ngwazi's ceremonial arrival was an impressive sight to behold. Security was tight. Although surrounded by motorcycle policemen and plainclothesmen, the president stood on the back seat of his convertible, a classic father figure waving triumphantly to "his people." Despite his age, he was an arresting personality with a distinctive, rather autocratic presence and a face that had character written all over it. It was hard to picture anyone else in the country, including all of his ministers, in that position, which was the way he liked it! Wearing, as always, a dark suit with vest and homburg (all from London's Savile Row), he usually waved a baton that resembled the kind of fly-whisk we used to use for horses in the country. It symbolized a chief's power.

After he and his retinue were seated, the traditional, or "tribal," dances began. Groups represented every section of the country. The dances were probably the most impressive feature of the afternoon's entertainment, as colorful as one might imagine, with many different costumes and headgear, and complete with snake charmers and witch doctors.

Then the Young Pioneers, the elite young cadre of the Malawi Congress Party, the country's only party, put on the "youth display." They were a healthy, good-looking group of men, all under twenty-five. Dressed in modern sports attire (white trousers with red, blue and green sports shirts), they performed gymnastics and lined up in parade formations.

The army show, which included several truckloads of soldiers, came next. The men, forming two teams of commandos, raced over a rather difficult-looking obstacle course and finally fired blanks at each other. On the return trip they had to carry one of their number on a stretcher over the hurdles, which seemed particularly hazardous, especially for the victim. (The commander of the army was a British brigadier, whom I met just prior to the scheduled events. Resplendent in full dress uniform, he sat next to our ambassador.)

Finally the president spoke. He could speak for several hours, depending upon the occasion, but this time he limited himself to approximately forty minutes. After stressing the benefits of Malawi independence, he elaborated on his favorite theme: everyone (black and white alike) was welcome in Malawi as long as they behaved themselves and contributed to the development of the country.

A late afternoon soccer game was meant to be the highlight of the day. Malawi was beating Swaziland, 3-0, when the lights went out and we were left in absolute darkness. The lights did not come on again, and the game was eventually called off. The Ngwazi's motorcade returned to pick him up, while the rest of us spent another hour trying to get out of the crowded stadium and find our respective cars without benefit of any light whatsoever.

That same day, the VIP section was the scene of what I call the *sardine fiasco*. Since I would be sitting in the stadium for at least seven hours, Marshall had warned me to bring some food and drink, as none were sold on the premises. The stores were all closed, however, I had no food at home, and the servants were on leave, so my options were strictly limited. I finally discovered a can of sardines left by my predecessor. I gratefully placed it in my pocket before leaving for the stadium.

Next to me in the VIP section were seated two princesses from Swaziland, honored guests representing King Sobhuza, the longest-reigning monarch in the world at that time. Swazi women have attractive and pleasing features. With fine complexions and cafe au lait coloring, they were among the most beautiful examples of femininity on the African continent, and my companions were no exception. Before long we were deep in conversation. Eventually, I offered to share with them some of my canned sardines, which they looked at with due skepticism. When I started to open the can, a gusher of olive oil like Yellowstone's "Old Faithful" rose from the can. I was totally unable to control it. How so much oil could have emanated from such a small tin is more than I can explain, but it just kept coming and spilled over onto the ladies' dresses. I only had a handkerchief, which was of little use. Finally a nearby spectator gave me his newspaper, and I began to mop up and clean off the ladies' long skirts, which were deeply dipped in oil by this time. Finally, a burly Swazi gentleman, who must have been a bodyguard, came over to inform me that it was improper to rub paper on the legs of a Swazi princess, so I desisted forthwith. The ladies didn't seem to mind, and actually took the whole catastrophe with good grace. It was, however, my worst African humiliation.

AMERICAN VISITORS

The only U.S. member of Congress to set foot in Malawi during my tour was Rep. Charles Diggs (Democrat of Michigan), then chairman of the Africa subcommittee of the House Foreign Affairs Committee and later to become chairman of the Congressional Black Caucus. Diggs, a rather moderate middle-of-the-roader by nature, had been pressured to adopt a more radical posture on African issues, especially regarding South Africa. In a private meeting, Banda lectured him in no uncertain terms, telling Diggs that he knew nothing about African blacks and in effect should keep his mouth shut. Ambassador Jones, who had been obliged to attend the meeting, felt constrained to intervene on his countryman's behalf, and the result was a high degree of tension. Diggs apparently sat quietly and made no attempt to defend himself, while helplessly looking to the ambassador for rescue and relief. He departed the country the next day and never returned. Malawi was probably the *only* country in black Africa that the peripatetic Diggs did not visit at least twice!

I have a plaque (see page 215) associating me with another visitor, Donald Brody, whose stay in Malawi was surely shorter than he had intended. His experience highlights the fragile and fleeting nature of Western prominence in an alien culture. On Independence Day, Brody was seated next to the president, high above the diplomatic rows. He was introduced at the outset as the "personal official guest" of the Ngwasi.

Brody's saga goes back to Lyndon Johnson's second term, when Dr. Banda paid a state visit to Washington. The State Department tried to keep the visit as low-key as possible. But when LBJ learned that the Malawian president was the *only* black African leader who publicly supported his Vietnam policy, the atmosphere changed dramatically. The red carpet was rolled out and a twenty-one-gun salute ordered, leaving Banda in a state of euphoria. "Tell me, Doctor," LBJ inquired during their first meeting, "what can I *do* for you?" "Well," Banda reportedly responded, "I have always wanted to develop the timber resources which lie in great abundance on the Vipya plateau" in central Malawi. LBJ called his friends at the Texas firm of Brown and Root and asked them to conduct an early feasibility study of such a project.

Nothing came of the Vipya timber project. The feasibility study concluded that development of the industry was not economically practical because of the distance and the transport infrastructure required, a finding in keeping with all such previous studies. However, Brody, a public relations expert, businessman, and honorary consul of Malawi in San Francisco, had accompanied the Brown and Root team to Malawi. Apparently he and Banda hit it off famously at their first meeting. Brody was evidently a persuasive talker. Banda, deeply impressed by the depth of Brody's PR knowledge and experience, was interested in having him promote and expand Malawi tourist facilities. Brody's salary was "topped off" with U.S. AID funds.

Before long, Brody held the official title of director of tourism. This, as it turned out, was his fatal mistake, because, in assuming his new duties, he managed to offend a number of Malawian officials who aspired to that position. He had never before been a presidential adviser, a concept he found exhilarating. He also lacked humility in his dealings both with the U.S. embassy (although I never had a problem getting along with him) and with his subordinates in the tourism office. His attitude of superiority soon changed to frustration. "I can't seem to get these people to carry out my instructions," he complained, and told me of one long-term project he had devised before his arrival in Blantyre that was "guaranteed to make over a million dollars in less than six weeks." It had been sent to the then-acting tourism chief. Six months later, however, he found it crumpled in the drawer of an empty desk, ignored and abandoned. Officials expert in bureaucratic intrigue had effectively undermined his standing.

One way to sabotage someone in Malawi was to ensure that negative reports about that individual were relayed to the president. For example, if the tourism director were told that an important delegation of prominent businessmen from abroad was scheduled to arrive on a Wednesday, when in fact they arrived on Tuesday, no one would meet them at the airport. The president's closest advisers would then hear about this dereliction of duty from one of their confidants. I *know* that this modus operandi was used to cashier at least one prominent South African official.

What scheme was cooked up for Brody I cannot say, as it took place after my departure. I later learned however, that Brody not only fell out of favor, but was ruled a "P.I." (prohibited immigrant, the nondiplomatic equivalent of persona non grata). He and his family were ordered to leave the country within forty-eight hours. Because his wife was over seven months pregnant, she could not travel by plane. Don Brody and his family had to *drive* over bumpy dirt roads in the direction of Rhodesia via Mozambique to comply with the expulsion deadline.

CHARGÉ D'AFFAIRES

About six weeks into my tour, Marshall Jones left for Washington on consultation, leaving me in charge. "Everything is in order," he assured me. "You won't have any problems." *WRONG!* The next day John Msonthi, a senior cabinet minister, stormed into my office, highly agitated. "This is an outrage," he shouted, as he threw on my desk a recently published promotional brochure released worldwide by TWA. It contained a map showing the complete land area of Malawi as an integral part of Tanzania. "What," the minister wanted to know, "are you going to do about it?" I gazed at the map helplessly and wondered if it had already been subjected to worldwide distribution. It had been, and the president-for-life of Malawi was not pleased. This might have seemed an idle threat, but Msonthi indicated that TWA *might* be prohibited from landing in Blantyre if the map was not corrected.

I promised to report the outrage to Washington and to *recommend* that the company issue a revised map but warned the minister that the U.S. government could not impose an economic decision on a private firm. I thought to myself that recalling all of these brochures and issuing new ones was likely to be a costly undertaking; *some* TWA executives might conclude that such a large investment in obtaining the goodwill of the poorest small country south of the Sahara was not cost-effective. As it turned out, however, TWA was deeply embarrassed by its mistake and apparently recalled all the offending brochures, printing new ones showing Malawi as a separate and independent entity. The first crisis of my "reign" was over.

My second assignment as chargé d'affaires was more complicated, and more serious. It happened during the annual weeklong meeting of the Malawi Congress Party. The faithful had gathered in Blantyre to hear the leadership give inspirational lectures on how best to implement the president's policies. The format of these conferences never varied. First came the ceremonial opening session, with leading representatives of the diplomatic corps in the front row. Marshall Jones had attended that session and received high praise from the president, who commended him and his government for aid already provided the Malawian people. Marshall was even asked to stand, and received generous applause from those in attendance.

After two or three days of secret meetings, the session was scheduled to end with a similar closing ceremony, also attended by diplomats. After the opening kudos, it could only be assumed that US-Malawi relations were not only good, but flourishing. As he boarded his plane later that afternoon, Marshall turned to me and said in jest: "Now, Chips, don't feel that the minute I leave you have to send a high priority telegram to the department about some emergency, calling attention to yourself!" It was a good joke, but as it turned out, the joke was on *me*. Approximately seventy-two hours later I sent the first NIACT cable ("Night Action," to be acted upon immediately at any time of day or night), at least in anyone's memory, from Blantyre to Washington. This is what happened.

At the closing session, the diplomatic corps assembled dutifully once again to hear what we assumed would be the same long-winded speeches of a few days ago. Only this time I was seated in Marshall's chair, directly in front of the president. A minor party official began reading a series of "resolutions" the delegates had supposedly "debated" and then "adopted," unanimously as always. Nothing was new about any of these resolutions, and the eyes of the distinguished chiefs of mission or their surrogates were beginning to glaze over. Then the speaker came to resolution #8: "Because of the detrimental influence of the Peace Corps volunteers on our youth, the program will be phased out in a timely fashion," or words to that effect. I was stunned, but remained momentarily motionless as I stared directly at the Ngwasi, who stared right back in a totally enigmatic fashion. Finally the South African chargé seated at my right whispered: "Did I hear what you heard or do I need a hearing aid?" As I watched the Reuters correspondent furiously taking everything down in longhand, I decided that *I* would need all the aid I could get in the next few days, as the news would be in Washington within the hour. Resolution #8 had been a real bombshell which no one at the highest levels of government had anticipated.

The next day, I was visited by Brian Roberts, President Banda's senior British adviser. Roberts was a wheeler-dealer disliked, but mainly feared, by British officials in Malawi. He prided himself on his "intimate" knowledge of current policy decisions. Surprisingly, he had known nothing of this Peace Corps pronouncement and was clearly at a loss to understand it. Even the recently revised five-year plan for Malawi's development had included Peace Corps projects in every phase of the planning process. "It must have been a back-channel decision," he remarked, which meant that it was made by Banda personally, without consulting anyone in advance.

Over the next few days I learned the relevant history. In 1965, during the country's first cabinet crisis, a number of Peace Corps volunteers had committed the cardinal sin of involving themselves in local politics. Some even joined in demonstrations before the parliament building in Zomba and cheered opposition leaders as they emerged after hours of heated debate. Not only did they take political sides, which no volunteer was supposed to do, but they opted for the *wrong* side, the losing one. Although Banda had never taken any disciplinary action, he had apparently never forgotten.

Now, to his mind, the timing was perfect: his "friend" Marshall Jones was out of town and a neophyte chargé represented the United States. The last bilateral aid project had been approved, and his beloved lakeshore road was at last under construction, together with a new capital in Lilongwe that South Africa had agreed to finance. Now was the time to put the Peace Corps in its place. Besides, reports that volunteer teachers at the grassroots level were instilling ideas of intellectual "reform" and lack of discipline into the minds of their students seem to have disturbed him. Such charges were vastly distorted, but Banda had always been somewhat paranoid on the subject.

In the days that followed, Peace Corps officials in Washington, backed by all members of Blantyre headquarters, decided to close up shop and move out immediately. (The Peace Corps had already been humiliated in neighboring Tanzania when it begged President Julius Nyerere to be allowed to stay when government leaders called for the Corps' ouster.) A main tenet of Peace Corps philosophy, as I well knew from my earlier association, had always been that only programs specifically requested by the host government would go forward. Now, PC/Malawi argued, it was time to abide by that principle.

While this reaction was more than understandable, the embassy (in the form of Messrs. Bremer and myself) counseled a wait-and-see attitude. Banda had threatened similar action before on other matters and then reversed himself. Resolution #8 was still just a recommendation, not a definitive order, and it too might be reversed. For the moment, we felt, the best action was no action.

As it turned out, one new Peace Corps program was canceled, at Washington's initiative, but the other programs and projects were allowed to continue. Eventually the *Malawi News* reported that at a local celebration attended by President Banda, several Peace Corps volunteers dressed in native garb participated in a traditional dance. "These are the kind of Europeans we favor," Banda was quoted as saying, "people who value and respect our customs." That was the signal that the Peace Corps was back in business. When new U.S. ambassador William Burdett arrived the following spring, he was in a position to offer a "new direction" for the Corps: henceforth the emphasis would be on carpentry, plumbing, auto mechanics, and similar trades, and away from education. Resolution #8 was never implemented.

The Moon Landing

The Apollo landing of U.S. astronauts on the moon occurred in late July 1969, during my first stint as chargé. I had to bluff my way through a radio interview without knowing any of the major facts surrounding the mission.

The return splashdown of the Apollo crew took place while I was on an official visit to Nsanje, a benighted sea-level village located beneath the escarpment at the very southernmost tip of Malawi, across from Mt. Chipperone in Mozambique. (Mt. Chipperone gives its name to the chill rain and wind that sweeps over most of Malawi about once a month during the winter season.)

The following April, I presented moon rocks, together with the Malawi flag (which had allegedly been to the moon and back) to President Banda.[3] The following article from the *Malawi News* gives the flavor of this presentation:

MALAWI NEWS

BUILD THE NATION

Newspaper.   PRICE 3d   TUESDAY, APRIL 7, 1970.

President receives Malawi flag which went to Moon

THE President shakes hands with the United States Charge d'Affaires ad interim, Mr. John Chester after the presentation of the Malawi Flag and moon perticles at the State Lodge.

Blantyre, Monday.

THE Malawi National Flag which was carried to the moon on the spacecraft Apollo Eleven and particles from the moon's surface, embedded in Lucite, have been presented to the President, Ngwazi Dr. H. Kamuzu Banda, by the United States Chargè d'Affaires ad interim in Malawi, Mr. John Chapman Chester.

The presentation was made by Mr. Chester on behalf of the President of the United States, Mr. Richard Nixon, at a special ceremony held at the Blantyre State Lodge.

During the ceremony Mr. Chester said he had been instructed by the American President to present the Flag and particles as a gift to the Ngwazi and the people of Malawi.

Receiving the gift, the Malawi Leader thanked Mr. Chester and asked him to convey to the President of the United States his sincere gratitude and appreciation.

ON SPECIAL PLAQUE

Later the American representative told reporters that the moon particles and the Malawi National Flag were presented to His Excellency on a specially made wooden plaque on which was inscribed the message: "Presented to the people of Malawi by Richard Nixon, President of the United States of America."

He said similar gifts had been presented to Heads of State in all independent African countries as well as in other countries of the world.

The purpose of the gift, he explained, was to indicate the American people's intention to share with other nations the results of their recent scientific achievements in lunar exploration.

The people of America feel that these achievements should belong not only to America but, also, to all mankind.

The "Voodoo" Murders

A spate of "ritual murders" began while I was still chargé and continued from that summer of 1969 until the following spring, just before my departure on safari in June. From beginning to end these events upstaged everything else taking place in Malawi. The experience of living in such an environment exposed me to the sometimes mystical aspects of a truly alien culture.

These gruesome attacks had no logical explanation. They usually occurred under a full moon and targeted the poorest elements of Malawi society. The traditional grass huts in and around Blantyre were especially vulnerable, as the killer or killers would normally enter through a smoke hole in the roof, hack the inhabitants to death with an ax or machete, and in most cases mutilate the sexual organs. Both robbery and rape were ruled out as possible motives: in most cases there was nothing to steal and the medical examiners found no evidence of semen. The whole ghastly affair took on an element of "voodoo," or mysterious witchcraft. Scotland Yard detectives came to Malawi to investigate, but neither they nor intelligence service officials could produce any clues.

The murders terrified Malawi residents, particularly those in the lower-class squatter areas, and all kinds of improbable rumors began to circulate. One of the murders took place in a hut two houses away from that of Duncan, my driver, who was in a desperate frame of mind most of the fall and winter. If someone were determined to destabilize Banda's rule, this was certainly an effective grassroots method of instilling fear among the population at large. Many suspected, without proof, that Henry Chipembere and his opposition cohorts in exile in Tanzania were in some way behind the attacks.

To most diplomatic observers, Banda's frequent public speeches did not seem to alleviate the situation. He denied vigorously that the attacks were caused by either the Red Cross—allegedly to get blood for its blood banks—or the government—suspected of sending blood to South Africa for loan repayments. As bizarre as such charges sounded to Western ears, the president seemed convinced that people probably believed such rumors, which escalated with every new full-moon assault.

As I drafted my first report on this subject, I wondered just how it would be received in Washington. I feared that some people might suspect that I had spent too much time in Africa and was "going around the bend." The whole thing sounded more and more unreal. As time passed, the need to scotch rumors became a high priority objective.

I also wrote to the district commissioner in Fort Johnson, who had jurisdiction over the embassy's rest house on the lake. My letter, reproduced below, reflected the surreal concerns we dealt with almost daily.

EMBASSY OF THE
UNITED STATES OF AMERICA
Blantyre

April 2, 1970

M. J .L. Arnold
District Commissioner
Fort Johnston, Malawi

Dear Mr. Arnold:

I am writing you at the suggestion of Mr. N.N.P. Thindwa, Permanent Secretary in the Ministry of Local Government, to whom I reported the following incident:

Last week an employee of this Embassy, Mr. Richard J. Tilley, was supervising a group of workmen who were installing new toilet facilities in one of the buildings adjoining the cottage we maintain at Nkudzi Bay, Lake Malawi. During the preliminary excavation work, the men accidentally uncovered two human skeletons, apparently of unknown deceased who had been buried on that site many years earlier. The bones were extremely brittle and partially decomposed, leading Mr. Tilley to conclude that death must have occurred long before the cottage and other buildings were originally erected on the property. (The Embassy has leased this property for recreational use only since July 1, 1968, and consequently we have no first-hand knowledge of its previous history.)

According to Mr. Tilley, the African workers became rather agitated and fearful as a result of this discovery and requested that work be suspended until after a local witch doctor had been summoned. This request was immediately granted; the doctor who appeared on the scene applied certain medicines to the men's bodies and succeeded in assuaging their fears. The work has now been completed.

The purpose of this letter is to provide a full and detailed account of what acutally transpired in the event that any misleading reports are circulated about the episode and eventually brought to your attention. I also wish to offer this Embassy's fullest cooperation in undertaking whatever measures you feel might be appropriate under the circumstances.

If I may be of further assistance in this regard, please do not hesitate to call upon me.

Sincerely yours,

J. Chapman Chester
Charge d'Affaires a.i.

cc: Mr. N.N. P. Thindwa
    Ministry of Local Government

211

Finally, a break in the case came in late spring. A baker's hat was discovered near the scene of one of the murders and was traced to a baker's assistant, who confessed to being the serial killer. At first I suspected a forced confession, but evidently he was the culprit, as the murders ceased following his incarceration. The man's full confession implicated a number of prominent Malawians in the crimes, including the former minister of agriculture, a primitive type named Kumtumanji. After many hours of interrogation, however, all the British police experts were convinced that the killer had acted strictly alone and that the people he implicated were innocent. (The defendant knew he was going to "swing," according to the experts, so he decided to take a few of his bitterest enemies *with* him.) Kumtumanji, who had made numerous enemies during his official tenure in office, was most vulnerable to this kind of retribution, or so went the theory. In any case, he was placed under house arrest for the indefinite future and may even have died in custody.

Whatever motivated these bizarre killings, other than one disturbed mind, was never made clear to me prior to my final departure from Malawi on July 6. I only know that the murders, and the government's worst crisis since the cabinet revolt in 1965, were now history.

IN-COUNTRY TRAVEL

Most of my in-country travel took place between July and November, while Marshall Jones was still sporadically in residence. With the "aid" of a mostly broken-down embassy Jeep Wagoneer, I moved from Nsanje and Chiromo in the south, to Lilongwe in the central region, to Nkata Bay and the Vipya plateau half way up the lake, and finally to the Nyika plateau (8,000 feet) and Chitipa in the north. (Appendix A contains letters to my family describing two of these trips.)

Archaic regulations emanating from Washington required the embassy to use American-made vehicles only, even though they were totally impractical. The steering wheel was on the wrong side—in Malawi one drove British-style on the left. Local service and parts were designed for British models exclusively. The Peace Corps had special dispensation to use British Land Rovers to travel into the bush country in support of isolated volunteers. The rest of us were not so lucky.

Most of my nevertheless enjoyable overland journeys were to represent the embassy at opening ceremonies for so-called "self-help" projects, still being carried out all over the country despite the phaseout of bilateral aid. Under this cost-effective program, the local populace would undertake construction of a schoolroom, health center, or the like, with USAID providing modest financing of materials like cement. It was a way of involving the entire community in a building project, and the response was invariably enthusiastic. The ceremonies usually included traditional dances and endless speeches by local politicians, but the appreciation of local residents at each stop was clearly genuine. I had never before witnessed scenes where between $50 and $100 could purchase so much goodwill.

The Chester Family Safari

Approximately twenty-seven members of my family, representing three generations, were scheduled to visit Malawi in early June 1970, after which my wife and I and two of our children were to join them on a safari in Kenya and Tanzania. My family visitors turned out to be, collectively, the largest tour group that had ever stayed in Malawi, even during the colonial era, and it caused somewhat of a sensation. I had warned all the ladies in advance about miniskirts and was relieved to find all three generations properly attired. All were taken to the VIP lounge upon arrival, where the "leader," my brother George, stepped forward to be interviewed by two reporters from the *Malawi News*. "Who is sponsoring this trip?" one reporter asked routinely. "A little old lady [my late Aunt Isabelle] from Milwaukee, Wisconsin, who is currently vacationing in Austria" was the answer. The reporter looked stunned and his editor called me in the afternoon to get the facts straight.[4]

From that point on the Chester-Read tour group (Read was my sister's husband) made the news in the local press and radio three times a day for the remainder of its visit. The *Malawi News* of June 19 covered the trip:

Malawi News, Malawi
June 19, 1970
*"Largest Tourist Group to Malawi in its
Colonial–Independence History"*

THIS group of twenty-one American tourists arrived in Malawi last week from Wisconsin in the United States of America for a three day visit. The group comprised of two families of Chester and Read.

During their stay in Malawi they visited a number of attractive spots which included the Zomba plateau and the Namig'omba Tea Estae in Cholo. Among the group was the mother of the Counsellor at the American Embassy, Mrs. William Chester of Milwankee.

The tour which was arranged by Percival Tours Inc. in Wisconsin in aid of Malawi's Tourism drive will take them to several African Countries. Pix by the Depart. of Inform.

214

A plaque signed by Donald Brody was presented only partially in jest,

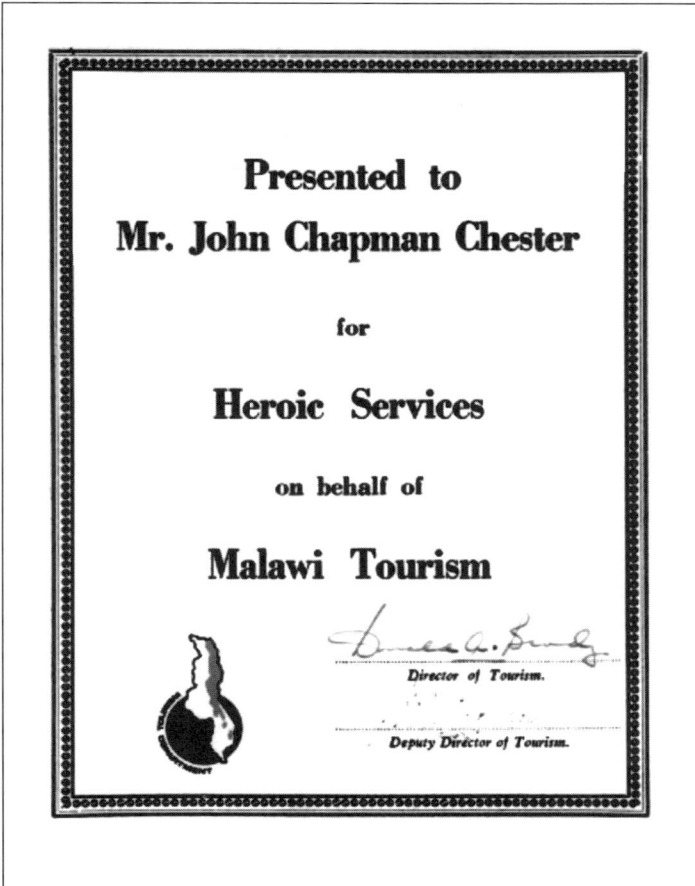

Presented to
Mr. John Chapman Chester

for

Heroic Services

on behalf of

Malawi Tourism

Director of Tourism.

Deputy Director of Tourism.

but the *Malawi Times* reported it in dead seriousness:

American gets hero award for tourism

Mr J. Chapman Chester Counselor at the American Embassy has received a certificate of heroism for his activities towards promoting Malawi's tourist industry.

The certificate was presented to Mr Chester by Malawi's Director of Tourism, Mr Donald A. Brody at a ceremony held at the American diplomat's home in Blantyre.

Mr Chester recently arranged for a party of more than 20 friends and relatives of his, to visit Malawi as part of a conducted tour of six African countries.

The party included Mrs William Chester, the Counsellor's mother.

The framed certificate bears the words, "presented to Mr John Chapman Chester for heroic services on behalf of Malawi Tourism."

It is signed by Mr Brody and Jack Muwamba, Deputy Director of Tourism and it is stamped with the Department's official seal.

Making the presentation, Mr Brody thanked the American diplomat for his courage in arranging for this visit.

He said that his Department hopes that more and more tourists from the United States of America will be coming to Malawi to visit the country's beautiful sights. — MANA.

I particularly liked the line about my courage. It takes guts to handle the Chester family! My wife lodged the only objection in connection with this award. She claimed that *she* was the one who made most of the arrangements and should have received the award. She had a point.

I learned later that I had completely upstaged Donald Brody with this visit: the following week he received a group of his friends and relatives from California, but it was only one third as large. It was all downhill for Don from that point on.

MY FINALE AS CHARGÉ

My final months in Malawi involved a series of interrelated events—Marshall Jones's retirement, his successor's presentation of credentials, the visit of the large Chester family group, and my own plans to resign from the Foreign Service. Though perhaps not critical diplomatic dealings, these events did require some fast footwork, much of it due to the nature of the Malawi regime and its leader.

Marshall's retirement meant that I served as transitional chargé from his departure in March until the new ambassador arrived in April 1970. As soon as I heard that William Burdett had been appointed as ambassador, I wrote him to try to find a DCM while he was in Washington. I had an ulterior motive: getting a timely replacement for me on board prior to the Chester family safari.

In February Marshall Jones went off to Zaire for a week to attend a regional chiefs of mission conference. After his return, he arranged for his final return to the United States on retirement orders. Just prior to his departure in March, we gave him and his wife, Virginia, a memorable farewell party at my residence, complete with costumes, prepared speeches, and skits. Everything that happened at the post thereafter seemed anticlimactic.

Presentation of Credentials

At the end of April Bill Burdett arrived to take charge of the mission. *CORRECTION*: he was in charge *internally*, but not *externally*. According to diplomatic protocol, to which Banda deferred rigidly, an ambassador is a *nonperson* until he presents his credentials. He cannot make any calls, even on his colleagues, or appear in public ceremonies until he is properly "credentialed," which means that for all practical purposes he does not exist. The chargé d'affaires remains the recognized chief representative of the U.S. government at all ceremonial occasions. No exceptions are made to this rule, and the transitional waiting period is not especially comfortable for the holdover chargé.

Ambassador Burdett was a much more conventional envoy than Marshall Jones. He had made his way up through the career system colorlessly and in low-key fashion. His last assignment had been as DCM in Turkey, and Malawi would probably be his final post. Although he was a bit of a fussbudget over details, I couldn't really blame him for the frustration that built up over the next three weeks. He arrived in Blantyre without having selected a DCM. The department had recommended that he try to talk me out of retirement, a nonstarter.

Problems with the Burdett credentials ceremony kept several American and Malawi officials, not least myself, on edge during the transition. The foreign ministry was presided over by a permanent secretary, John Ngwire, since President Banda acted as his own foreign minister. John was probably the least qualified individual in his organization for his position, and he was well aware of it. Once a week he would meet with the Ngwasi, who would lecture him about all of his shortcomings and then dismiss him peremptorily. John rarely got a word in edgewise.

Most of the foreign ministry's substantive work was performed by a Harvard-trained American lawyer named Jim Friedlander, who had served previously as a Peace

Corps volunteer, and a Malawi diplomat whose surname was Kotoki-Mwalalino. (His first name escapes me). Kotoki had previously been assigned to the United Nations, where his first wife jumped out of a skyscraper with all her children, an event covered extensively by the U.S. media.

When I first knew Jim Friedlander, he had left the Peace Corps and been hired as an employee of the Malawi government. As such, he did not feel it was proper to report "the inside story" of his ministry to his compatriots in the American embassy. He told us what he thought was appropriate, and we did not press him for more. His "diplomatic" position was clearly more sensitive than ours.

Every few days I would call John Ngwire and remind him that I had a new U.S. ambassador on board who was anxious to get going. John promised to bring the matter to His Excellency's attention, but he never seemed to get around to it. I should have gone over his head sooner than I did, but I felt sorry for him and wanted both the new ambassador and my eventual successor to start on the right footing. The person in John's position couldn't help you much if you were on good terms with him, but he could certainly mess things up if the terms were bad.

I finally realized that a crisis was approaching when we learned through our own sources that the South African prime minister, John Vorster, was about to make his first official visit to a black-ruled country, namely Malawi, for two days. Immediately afterwards, Dr. Banda was scheduled to depart for his annual three-week vacation at the Dorchester Hotel in London. What I knew, therefore, and John Ngwire did *not* know (and I couldn't tell him), was that *if* our ambassador were not credentialed by Banda's departure, he would remain a *nonperson* for almost another month. At this point I called Brian Roberts, the president's senior British adviser, who was flabbergasted with the news. "Why didn't you call me before?" he inquired incredulously. I explained that I didn't want to leave my successor with a sour, bypassed permanent secretary to deal with. "Well, never mind," he added casually: "John is already in so much trouble, you could not have caused him any more."

All the arrangements were made in no time flat, though not without a few glitches en route. Ambassador Burdett, having had nothing else to do for several weeks, spent much of the time revising his credentials draft, which had been prepared for him in the State Department. His final version was a considerable improvement over the original, but one problem remained: John Ngwire's suggested draft response for Banda dealt with the points raised in the *first* draft. If the response did not track with the ambassador's remarks, John would be in severe trouble once again. He begged me to get the ambassador to deliver his original speech, warts and all. Burdett at first resisted this request, but finally conceded that the rhetoric involved was not worth a diplomatic flap at the beginning of his assignment.

Another problem: The ambassador's cutaway was in a trunk somewhere between Turkey and Malawi, and he thus did not have the proper uniform. Banda was a stickler for protocol, so much so that I had to get our embassy in London to send me a *gray*—for daytime—top hat for my attire. Fortunately, Bernhard Heibach, the German ambassador and a friend of mine, was of similar stature to Ambassador Burdett. His striped pants outfit fit the ambassador perfectly.

Now we were ready for the ceremony. We drove to the president's palace in Zomba with a motorcycle escort. At the ceremony, the ambassador was flanked by Jim Thurber, the USIS director, by Lt. Col. Willie Haywood, the military attaché, resplendent in full-dress uniform, and the author.[5] The chief of protocol, E. H. Topham Thole, had carefully briefed us about procedure. First we would walk—all four abreast—into the president's chamber and stop after three steps. The president would then approach our position and the proceedings would begin.

Mr. Topham Thole was a giant of a man, with great superficial dignity. He may have had the right name for his job, and looked like a movie star, but he had the efficiency, alas, of John Ngwire. He had everything *wrong*. When we entered the room, Banda was at the far end, so far away, in fact, that we could barely see him. When we stopped after three steps, nothing happened. After a long and painful silence, we decided to move forward in unison and marched all the way to the other end of the room, where the president was waiting patiently. Words were exchanged and the stalemate was over. Great affairs of state had been resolved, and I was at last free to go on safari.

RESIGNING FROM THE FOREIGN SERVICE

My (professional) midlife crisis hit me exactly at age forty. I remember the date well, as I was vacationing in South Africa with my wife and two of my three children on my fortieth birthday, January 2, 1970. The reasons behind my decision to leave the Foreign Service are not really relevant to this continuing history, but suffice it to say that I suddenly woke up to the fact that *if* I wanted to change direction, *now* was the time to act, and act decisively.

I was determined to leave the service in an organized, even "tidy," fashion. I have always been a compulsive, clean-desk kind of operator who abhors leaving loose ends. At first I thought I would be doing everyone a favor by giving advance notice of my intentions. About late January I wrote the department, informing the current powers in Personnel that I would be resigning my commission in July of that year (1970), following completion of the second school semester.

I had fully enjoyed my diplomatic career up to this point and realized I had been extremely lucky most of the way. I had been promoted every other year since my swearing-in ceremony, but now I faced a few years at a plateau. From my years in Personnel, I realized that the next step toward promotion in the career service was to attach oneself to an influential sponsor—an assistant secretary or higher, perhaps as a staff aide—and then serve the incumbent with single-minded dedication and determination. That prospect had little appeal, and I realized that what I really wanted to do with my life was "freewheel" a bit on my own, outside of the organizational strait jacket. While I had enjoyed my seniority in Malawi and had done a good job there, I came to realize in retrospect that I had had more scope and fulfillment as a junior FSO than as a "leader," hemmed in with unavoidable responsibilities.

I could have let nature take its course, more or less, finishing my Malawi tour, transferring to the department, and then exploring other possibilities at leisure. But this course would have been fatal for me, and would merely have led me past the point of no return. *If* I was to act at all, I had to make a clean break. Otherwise, knowing myself all too well, inertia would take over. In retrospect, I feel I lucked into the right decision.

My successor, John Buche, principal officer in Hargeisa, Somalia, was available because the Department of State had decided to close the consulate there. Following my three-week safari, I returned to Blantyre, packed up, and prepared to depart on July 5. Our farewell turned out to be anticlimactic. Although we traveled to the airport in high style, with two Peace Corps friends serving as motorcycle outriders, the plane never arrived that day from Nairobi. We had a fine party in the VIP lounge and then went home again, to the surprise and consternation of the servants. The next morning only our faithful friends the Thurbers accompanied us to Chileka airport for a final farewell.

One professional career was finished, with another about to begin. Comparisons are odious, they say, so I will not make any. Whether my new career was to become better or worse is subject to interpretation. In any event, it was to become *different!*

PART III
AT HOME IN THE HOUSE

CHAPTER 10

Starting Out on the Hill

When Chips left the Department of State and joined the Committee, he raised the intellectual level of both places.
— Chairman Clement J. Zablocki,
House Committee on Foreign Affairs

The House of Representatives is an organization run by the members of Congress with the able assistance of the professional staff; the Senate, on the other hand, is an organization run by the staff with the unprofessional assistance of members of the Senate.
— Old House Proverb

The "totally unbiased" old House proverb contains a grain of truth, like all such apocryphal adages. In *both* houses, however, the staff actually perform most of the work. But staffers overstep their bounds and jeopardize their status when they attempt to create their own agendas or make political decisions that are the exclusive preserve of the elected representative or senator.

Is a staff member a necessary evil, someone whose job it is to take the blame when something goes wrong? Or is he or she a valued assistant who performs much of the work that a member of Congress cannot practically undertake? Perceptions about congressional staff aides run the gamut between these two extremes.

The journey across town from Foggy Bottom to Capitol Hill, however, was totally new and different. It removed any lingering doubt in the mind of any staffer about the constitutional "separation of powers," which has been implemented to an almost excessive degree. To the executive branch of government, the legislative branch was clearly a "riddle wrapped in a mystery inside an enigma" (Churchill's phrase about Russia), and the feeling was distinctly mutual.

The isolation of the Department of State and the Foreign Service from the day-to-day realities of domestic political life was virtually complete. During the early decades of the Cold War, State's focus was entirely abroad, trying mainly to sell departmental policies to senior executive officials, especially in the White House. Convincing Congress was secondary. The Vietnam War and the leading role Congress assumed in foreign policy changed this modus operandi dramatically. Congress even took on micromanaging foreign operations, a practice that happily subsided as the pendulum swung back toward the center. By now few inside the Washington Beltway question Congress's key influence on foreign policy. But the Department of State and congressional leaders still have a long way to go in terms of real mutual understanding.[1]

LEGISLATIVE ASSISTANT AND BEYOND

Except for an annual exchange of Christmas cards, I had not kept in touch with Representative Peter Frelinghuysen or with his administrative assistant (AA), Bill Kendall, since my 1966–1967 sabbatical in the congressman's office. After I resigned from the Foreign Service in 1970, however, I contacted Kendall. Peter had meanwhile left the Education and Labor Committee and was the second-ranking minority member of the

Foreign Affairs Committee to which he could devote all his committee attention. Since I had served as a congressional fellow in the office some three years previously, I was a logical choice to provide foreign policy background. When Kendall called to inquire, I gladly affirmed my availability. .

On November 1, 1970, I formally joined the office of Representative Peter H. B. Frelinghuysen of New Jersey as a legislative assistant and foreign policy adviser. Now I was introduced in earnest to the world of "Capitol confusion" (my term for the Hill, though it should be standard). My predecessor, Carl Golden, had been primarily a press secretary concerned with New Jersey state and district matters. He later served as press spokesman for the governor of New Jersey.

The Trade Act of 1970

I arrived in the Frelinghuysen office just in time to help prepare the congressman for the "great trade debate" of 1970. The venerable and powerful Wilbur Mills, chairman of the Ways and Means Committee, was about to bring H.R. 18970, the Trade Act of 1970, to the House floor.

Mills was not only the undisputed House leader in all matters involving trade and tax policy (he had singlehandedly written most of the Internal Revenue Code), but he never brought a bill to the floor that would not pass. Bills he crafted were delicately balanced, both politically and substantively. To allow a hodgepodge of amendments to be attached to these bills could have made their provisions both impracticable and self-destructive. Besides, every Ways and Means legislative proposal was considered under a "closed" rule, which meant that it could not be amended on the floor. The bill was voted either up or down, without the possibility of change. (Congressional reformers have often criticized the concept of a "closed rule" on principle, but it has its rationale in complex tax and financial legislation.)

Wilbur Mills was not a protectionist in any sense of that term, but H.R. 18970 had some protectionist features, especially in the form of retaliatory quotas for textiles and shoes. He had allegedly put this bill together for two reasons: (1) to demonstrate clearly and impressively that President Nixon could *not* provide favors to the textile industry without opening a Pandora's Box of cries for help from the steel, glass, and other industries hurt by foreign competition; and (2) to give members an opportunity to go on record with their local constituents' complaints and to express publicly their unhappiness with foreign trade practices perceived to be unjust. The bill eventually died in the Senate, with Chairman Mills's quiet and tacit blessing; the House debate was thus an essentially oratorical exercise of little lasting importance or impact.

Peter Frelinghuysen was by reputation and conviction a free trader and a determined opponent of the Mills bill. As such, he was the natural recipient of mounds of material provided by the Economic Bureau at State, as well as research from the Library of Congress. All of it contained many persuasive economic arguments, with valuable backup material, in opposition to the main features of the bill. Even as a neophyte, however, I immediately realized that *all* the material was totally unsuitable for House floor debate and had to be completely rewritten. I understood that political perception and "image," not necessarily intellectual profundity, were the keys to success in congressional debate. Opponents of a legislative proposal or provision would want to associate that provision in the public mind with some recognizably *negative* image or analogy. Meritorious arguments in a vacuum were next to useless.

No member of the House Foreign Affairs Committee was more adept at identifying the inherent weakness of a legislative provision, and then tearing it apart, than Peter Frelinghuysen. His precise legal mind had a way of zeroing in on the insupportable. He was also considered something of a fussbudget about language (nicknamed "picayune Pete"). His views and arguments were nonetheless highly respected. His most politically effective weapon, I believe in retrospect, was his ability to lend "prestige" to a proposal by *not* opposing it! He was less successful, however, in drumming up support *for* a legislative initiative by politicking and backslapping in the Republican cloakroom or the Speaker's lobby just off the House floor. As he once told me in a philosophical moment, "If I tried to be a classic working pol, I probably would not be credible, so I long ago gave up the attempt." He was undoubtedly correct in that judgment: the recognition of one's limitations as well as one's strengths may be the beginning of wisdom.

On the trade bill, Peter argued quite eloquently in general debate on the House floor that it "ran counter to U.S. national interest," stating:

> For almost four decades the United States has moved in the direction of trade liberalization, a policy which has resulted in our emergence as the world's leading trading nation. This legislation is exceedingly far-reaching, containing among other provisions mandatory import quotas for shoes and synthetic and wool textiles.
>
> The imposition of mandatory import quotas on certain items will lead to heavy pressure to provide the same sort of protection for other industries. . . . Moreover, a number of our trading partners have imposed controls of their own on our exports. Although some countervailing action is certainly justified, I believe that quotas constitute the wrong action at the wrong time. Quotas are more inflationary than other remedies available to us, such as tariffs, as they restrict supply and lessen competition. In effect, they represent a tax on the consumer.

As I watched the debate on this issue from the staff gallery, I noticed that whenever Peter seemed to be getting the upper hand in an argument with another member, the stentorian voice of Chairman Mills would come to the loser's aid: "Will the gentleman yield?" he would ask. "Yes," the hapless loser would respond, "I would be happy to yield to the distinguished Chairman" (a clearly accurate statement). Then Chairman Mills, with his photographic memory for details, would comment: "I think the Gentleman from New Jersey, if he would check Title II, Chapter IV, Paragraph 23–24, would see that we have taken care of the problem to which he is alluding." Of course, debate had long since proceeded in another direction by the time anyone looked up this particular provision. That was a day, I noted, when the chairman came to the aid of a number of "losers," although the outcome of the vote on final passage was never in doubt. Even if the vote had been close (which it wasn't), the chairman always had a few votes he held in reserve. This was a common practice with all chairmen and/or legislative floor managers: let a number of trusted loyalists "vote their constituencies," unless their votes were needed in an emergency, in which case they would support their leaders' positions.

Pride of Authorship:
My First Lesson on the Hill

I learned my first important legislative lesson in the aftermath of this debate: there is *no* (repeat *no*) pride of authorship on Capitol Hill. If you cannot accept this reality, you had better seek employment elsewhere.

Among my early duties was the drafting of a Washington newsletter from the congressman to his New Jersey constituents, explaining the background and rationale for his votes on specific subjects. As always, Peter was meticulous in editing such drafts, but soon I developed a facility for imitating his speaking and writing style. One newsletter in particular, entitled "A Return to Protectionism?" stands out in my mind as exceptional, as the text was left almost exactly as I had written it. Many of the arguments Peter had used during the floor debate on the Mills bill were summarized in three double-spaced pages. The peroration of this piece appeared in the penultimate paragraph, as follows:

> As the apostle of the free enterprise system, we cannot and should not abdicate our leadership in international commerce. We should not, in my judgment, erect a "Berlin Wall" around the United States because, while it may serve a short-term goal of keeping others *out*, it will have the ultimate effect of keeping us *in*.

My reference to the "Berlin Wall" was my most notable inspiration, as it conveyed a suitably negative image of that era. To my great surprise, however, I remember going through the mail hurriedly the following week and running across a newsletter from a Michigan Republican, also to his district constituents. The language sounded vaguely familiar, and very much like Peter's rhetoric. Finally I came upon the paragraph about the "Berlin Wall," and I realized that the Michigan congressman had lifted my language word for word. There had been no attempt to hide the fact, moreover, as the "author" had penned a personal handwritten note to Peter saying: "Many thanks, Peter, this was very helpful." The moral was clear: what counts in the House of Representatives is a member's *position* on legislation and his or her *vote*; language is cheap and is "yours" for the asking. Bill Kendall summed it all up perfectly: "Chips, this shows you have at last made your debut on Capitol Hill. If no one stole your stuff, it wouldn't be worth anything!"

In the Department of State, putting your name on someone else's airgram or report could get you fired if the charges could be proved, but on the Hill anything worthwhile spoken or written was presumed to be a ghostwriter's product. Members of Congress only tended to get into trouble when they pretended otherwise and were subsequently exposed, as in the case of the infamous speech by Senator Biden ultimately traced to the leader of the British Labour Party.

My second chairman of the Foreign Affairs Committee, the late Clement J. Zablocki, time and again would put the whole matter in perspective: "If you liked the speech," he would say, "it's mine. If you didn't like it, blame Chips Chester; he wrote it!" Unlike some members, Clem never hesitated to give credit to someone else for just about anything he did. That way, the *blame* was also assigned elsewhere. But then again, he was a lot smarter than most politicians!

WORKING FOR A CONGRESSMAN

Working in a member's office, as I did for only four months (twelve months if my prior service as a congressional fellow is included) is very different than working for a committee, as I did for some fifteen years. An office staff member is affected by almost anything taking place either on the House floor or in the congressman's state and district, whereas committee staff are only concerned with legislation falling within committee purview. In a member's office, when the (House) "bell tolls," I soon learned, "it tolls for *thee*." Even though I had been hired principally for my foreign policy experience and "expertise," I soon discovered that I needed to broaden my horizons considerably.

Opening and processing the congressman's mail is an excellent way to begin educating oneself. So I have subsequently advised hordes of young Princeton graduates regularly referred to me by the president of the Princeton Club of Washington and who aspired to "stimulating" Hill employment. Reading the mail may sound like a pedestrian activity, but it is an important key to understanding the major concerns of the member's constituency, the kinds of pressures that will regularly be brought to bear upon him, and which—inevitably if perhaps subtly—will shape his political response to most issues that come before Congress.

Even in a relatively affluent, sophisticated Eastern Seaboard district like the Fifth District of New Jersey, I soon discovered that foreign policy was *not* the highest priority item on the collective mind of the electorate. Those who responded to my foreign policy newsletters, in fact, tended to comprise a small but devoted segment of the League of Women Voters or similar organizations and of those business leaders directly affected by international trade decisions of the Congress. (The Princeton University community was an exception, but it was a minor influence on the Fifth District electorate. University people talk a lot and sometimes demonstrate, but they often vote elsewhere if they vote at all.) Actually, this relative absence of a strong emotional commitment to one or another side of a foreign policy issue, even during the escalation of the Vietnam war, gave Peter the freedom and flexibility, to an extent denied to many of his colleagues, to act in what he perceived to be the U.S. interest.

Such was not always the case with domestic matters, particularly the "great deer hunt" of New Jersey. Talk about emotions! When this controversy reached its peak, the congressman's office was flooded with mail, at four times or more the normal rate. Although New Jersey was, and I presume still is, the state with the highest number of residents per square mile, the deer population seemed to be taking over, even moving into highly urbanized areas. The state legislature had before it a proposal to trim the herd into manageable proportions via a one-time extended open season for deer hunters.

Everyone in the Fifth District, it seemed, had a strong opinion on the matter and there was virtually no middle ground. Moreover, the environmental movement was split between those opposed to all forms of hunting in principle and those who realized that the rampant overpopulation of deer in the state was destroying the delicate ecological balance of existing species. If there ever was a "no-win" issue for a politician, this was *it!* Fortunately for Peter, it was "not a matter before the U.S. Congress on which I will be called upon to cast a vote." This standard response to all correspondence on the subject included the suggestion to "make your views known to your state senator" (who surely had more than enough letters on the subject already). In terms of political urgency, however, I soon discovered that the "Berlin Wall" paled by comparison.

On another front, massive cutbacks were about to occur at New Jersey's Picatinny Arsenal, according to a January 27, 1971, front-page article featured in the *Daily Advance* ("A Great Family Newspaper Published for the North Jersey Lakeland Area"). The article was apparently based on a the rumor printed in the *Federal Times*, a Washington-based newspaper for government employees. Identified as "spokesman for U.S. Rep. Peter H. B. Frelinghuysen," I probably became involved in the crisis because Bill Kendall was out of the office at the time and I handled the incoming calls. "Chip (*sic*) Chester said yesterday he had tried to get some word out of the Department of Defense about the possible extent of the cutbacks here, but the Department is still maintaining official silence. *Federal Times* predicted Defense Secretary Melvin Laird would announce the cutbacks early in February." If you ever wanted to know how difficult it is for any defense secretary to close down obsolete U.S. bases, you ought to spend some time at the receiving end of a massive telephone campaign on the subject. On bread and butter issues like this one, a congressman has virtually no license to act in the so-called national interest, even though Peter was a lot less parochial than his peers.[2]

Bill Kendall also ran the Princeton summer intern program, which involved working out a schedule of activities, not just for the Princetonians assigned to the Frelinghuysen office, but for those assigned anywhere on the Hill during the summer vacation. For a chemist from Rutgers, he carried out his responsibilities with exceptionally good grace!

Each year, usually late in August, Peter would gather all of the Princeton interns to his office, provide a high-level speaker, and then take everyone to dinner at the

Capitol Hill Club. Because of Peter's seniority and prominence on the Foreign Affairs Committee, he was usually able to attract very distinguished speakers, from Henry Kissinger, to William Ruckelshaus (former deputy attorney general), to Nicholas Katzenbach (former attorney general and particularly influential among Princeton alumni). In 1971 our speaker was Colonel Alexander Haig, then deputy to Henry Kissinger as national security adviser to President Nixon. (Kissinger was out of the country at the time.) Haig was an obscure colonel, virtually unknown to the Princeton undergraduate body. He was a career military officer when students were mostly engaged in protest against the Vietnam involvement. I wondered just how this colonel would fare amid a good deal of obvious skepticism if not outright hostility.

To my surprise, he handled the situation with great aplomb and won over his audience by the manner of his presentation if not by its substance. In very direct and reasonable terms, he outlined the policy objectives of the administration and the rationale for achieving them. It was a superlative performance, and I was impressed. So were the interns. Haig was at his best that evening, clearly a strategic thinker who had a world view far above and beyond that of the average Pentagon colonel.

Yolanda Krol was an important reason the congressman's office ran so well. A permanent fixture in the office hierarchy, she was the case worker extraordinaire. Her role in providing services to the ordinary citizens of the district cannot be overstated. Her casework involved the gamut of problems, including lost Social Security checks, draft eligibility, veterans' benefits of one kind or another, and often just her willingness to *listen* to an individual's personal problems for hours at a time. The job required infinite patience and perseverance, as well as a genuinely sympathetic approach to human difficulties, and Yolanda had all of these qualities in abundance. This aspect of congressional activity is extremely important to a congressman's general reputation, and even to his political survival, especially when his positions on national issues are out of fashion. It is a gut reaction: people who have been helped, even in some small way, or whose friends or relatives have, generally tend to cast their ballots *for* the incumbent, even when they don't agree with him or her ideologically.

Yolanda was of Polish background and a leader of the local Washington Polish-American community, arranging dances and fund-raising "galas." She was a dedicated worker and never let her extracurricular interests interfere with her painstaking efforts in behalf of district residents. Yolanda once phoned Bill Kendall at home when a forty-eight hour blizzard, followed by a foot and a half of snow, covered Washington. Traffic came to a total standstill and the city was virtually closed down. Yolanda was at the office and wondered what had happened to the rest of the staff. (She had evidently had no problem driving all the way from McLean, Virginia, to the Capitol, as "the roads were empty"!) Yolanda was a jewel; no other description will fit.

Catherine Barrett, another caseworker, was a more complex personality. Very experienced and quite efficient in her own way, she had a tendency (unlike Yolanda) *not* to confront problems head on. She liked to squirrel away in her desk drawers letters that were difficult to answer and required extensive research. She meant to get to these eventually, but often neglected to do so. Bill Kendall used to raid her files from time to time to ascertain the cumulative backlog of unanswered correspondence and then administer a lecture. She always promised to do better, but like Dickens's Wilkins Micawber, procrastination was her major addiction. On the other hand, the work she *did* do, sooner or later, was of definite value, and she survived as a result.

In sum, a congressional office is very much like an extended family, and one I enjoyed being part of. The environment is warm and supportive when everyone is getting along and *hell* when there is domestic discord. Our AA, Bill Kendall, was the primary reason for this environment. Bill, Peter's alter ego, supreme office boss, and highest paid staff member, used to say in his own humorous and self-deprecating way that an AA's most valuable function was his ability to trade with other AA's for White House passes and tickets to the Army-Navy football game, and to obtain parking spaces in the Rayburn Building for visiting dignitaries. That his faithful executive assistant, Bobby Andrukitis, is still with him in his postretirement consulting business also says a lot about his qualities as a "boss."

In retrospect, I really think that Bill Kendall succeeded at his job because he identified problems early and took immediate corrective action.

11

The Influential House
Foreign Affairs Committee

On March 1, 1971, I joined the staff of the House Committee on Foreign Affairs (formal job designation: Staff Consultant) and remained with the committee until my retirement in 1986. After first working on legislative matters, starting in the mid-1970s, I traveled on overseas delegations with Representative Frelinghuysen, with other committee staff members, and as principal staff member for House delegations to interparliamentary conferences. Over the years I became more and more involved in speechwriting, primarily for committee chairmen. Circa 1980 I was promoted to Senior Consultant (my formal title, one I dreamed up myself, was Senior Staff Consultant for Special Projects). In my later years with the committee I also became the committee's de facto "poet laureate."

My first position with the Foreign Affairs Committee resulted from an informal agreement between the Democratic chairman of the committee, Thomas E. Morgan of Pennsylvania, and the two ranking Republicans, my boss, Peter Frelinghuysen, and William Mailliard of California.[1] The agreement was an indirect consequence of the Legislative Reorganization Act of 1970, which gave the minority party (the Republicans) hiring authority and/or control over 25 percent of all committee staff positions. However, when the new Congress assembled early in 1971, the Democrats (who had the votes) repealed that section of the law. The GOP called upon such organizations as Common Cause to give the opposition a fair shake.

Mailliard and Frelinghuysen suggested a deal: accept our two aides (Robert Boyer was Mailliard's choice) as members of the full committee staff, and we will cease our complaints about staffing percentages on the minority side. The deal provided for Boyer and me to be hired in a professional capacity and to work for the full committee, including the chairman and the chief of staff, not just the minority. The only proviso was that Republicans would have primary call upon our services when needed. The proposal was music to Chairman Morgan's ears in all respects. Dr. Morgan and his senior committee staff interviewed both Bob Boyer and myself, but our hiring was essentially a formality.

The new arrangement was a win-win solution from every standpoint. My presence on the committee enabled me to further Peter's positions on foreign affairs, which I could hardly have done from his congressional office. It gave the committee the benefit of my foreign policy experience, and me the opportunity for travel abroad. Most of all, the committee became the place where I would play a bipartisan role—congenial to my temperament—for the rest of my fifteen-year career on the Hill, all of it with the Democrats in control of the House. Even more, it was the job in which I formed close professional and personal friendships that have lasted until this day—where, in short, I was truly "at home."

Doc Morgan was later to save my job with the committee. When Peter retired, his ranking Republican successor, Bill Broomfield of Michigan, wanted to replace me with one of *his* aides. There was nothing personal about this preference, as Broomfield and I had never actually met. From that moment on, my destiny was essentially in the hands of the Democrats, although I retained my bipartisan image.

When I joined it, the House Committee on Foreign Affairs enjoyed considerable prestige and influence (and, I would like to believe, still retained that status when I left). It was steeped in history and tradition. The oldest standing committee of the House dealing with foreign affairs, it traced its origins back to 1775, when it was first known as the "Committee of Correspondence," later the "Secret Committee of Correspondence." Its original membership included such illustrious names as Benjamin Franklin (chairman), Benjamin Harrison, John Dickinson, and John Jay.

In the early 1970s the members' names were not so famous, but a prestigious political center remained, represented on both sides of the aisle by members who were "solid citizens" and influential leaders within the House establishment. Although the late senator (and later vice president) Alben Barkley is credited with the quip, "The House is still young enough to have 'affairs,' while the Senate has only 'relations,'" it nevertheless took a good many years of service in those days to attain meaningful seniority. (Bradford Morse, a relatively senior Republican, once told me that it took him eight years to get from the lower tier of seats to the top row.)

COMMITTEE CHAIRMEN

The tone of the Foreign Affairs Committee during my fifteen-year tenure was set by the three Democratic chairmen under whom I served: Dr. Thomas E. (Doc) Morgan of Pennsylvania, Clement Zablocki of Wisconsin, and Dante Fascell of Florida.

Doc Morgan

As the longest-serving Foreign Affairs Committee chairman (dating back to the first chairman, Benjamin Franklin), Doc Morgan was "venerable" in every sense of that term. Although a party loyalist and faithful bipartisan supporter of the president's foreign policy, he was clearly respected on both sides of the aisle, by political friend and foe alike. (Rumor had it that his long tenure as committee leader resulted from pressure by LBJ to stay on, rather than turn over the chairmanship to the next in line, Clem Zablocki, who was considered too independent-minded for Johnson's taste.)

Doc hailed from Fredericktown in western Pennsylvania. Washington, Pa., was the county seat. The city of Uniontown was also in his congressional district. His father was an early mine workers' organizer. Scabs of that era often harassed the family. Eventually the union rewarded his father by sponsoring a medical scholarship for Doc, who got his M.D. degree (and on retirement another honorary doctorate) from Wayne State University in Detroit.

Doc then returned home to become a highly popular general practitioner and surgeon. His patients, at $3.00 per visit, were initially mine workers and their families. Finally, when the incumbent congressman went off to military service, Doc was prevailed upon to run for the House seat. He won overwhelmingly. After all, who could vote against the family doctor? He maintained his practice on weekends in his home district throughout his congressional career. And he always retained an interest in health legislation.

My initial interview with him taught me an important lesson: *Never assume that party affiliation presupposes personal regard.* Since two Republicans had sponsored me, I thought it would be politic to indicate that I could also work compatibly with Democrats. I mentioned that as a former congressional fellow, I had been assigned to the office of Senator Joseph Clark of Doc's state of Pennsylvania and had profited from the experience. The chairman cast a glance up at the ceiling and then down at the floor before observing pointedly: "Well, as I said before, I have always had great admiration and respect for Peter Frelinghuysen!" I realized at that point that I had made exactly *the* inappropriate remark. Corollary lesson: *If you don't know for a fact what a member's relationship is with another member, keep still until you do!*

I later learned that Joe Clark and Doc Morgan had only one thing in common: both were members of the Democratic Party. While Doc was a party loyalist, Joe Clark was a maverick who espoused his own causes. Joe was an early and vociferous critic of our Vietnam involvement, while Doc supported the administration and the U.S. military. Joe was a Harvard-educated, Main Line blueblood, while Doc was the son of a mine workers' union organizer. The two were definitely not "made for each other."

Doc Morgan had a great deal of difficulty with names. He mispronounced the name of just about every witness who ever appeared before our committee: He referred to Fowler Hamilton, director of AID, as "Flower Hamilton." Leslie Gelb, a prominent *New York Times* correspondent who became director of political/military affairs at State (and only had a four-letter surname) was "Gleb" (which happens to be the Serbian word for "bread"). Doc never even got the name of his own chief of staff (Marian Czarnecki) right, referring to him as Marian "Char-nokki." At one point, Bill Mailliard, a close friend, even took the chairman aside and said rather pointedly: "Doc, you and I have known each other for a long time; I think by now you ought to know my name. 'Mallard' is a duck!" That little talk must have made an impression, as the chairman henceforth made a great effort to pronounce "My-Yard" phonetically.

Both in committee, where he generally spoke with a cigar in his teeth, and on the House floor, Doc tended to mumble, often incomprehensibly. I often thought he did this on purpose, to keep from being contradicted. Everyone trusted him, however, and members were not inclined to challenge him when he made such minor errors as saying "million" instead of "billion." It didn't really matter what Doc said—everyone knew what Doc meant!

Everyone also knew that Doc Morgan was eminently trustworthy, fair, and reliable, and would never throw a curve at an opponent of one of his bills. His reputation was indeed his major strength.

The Zablocki Era

Clement J. Zablocki of Milwaukee succeeded Doc Morgan as chairman in January 1977. Although he and I came from different worlds (and different sections of town, which in Milwaukee tended to restrict one's exposure), we hit it off instantly. Many began to suspect, quite inaccurately, that I was a veteran member of what was called the "Milwaukee mafia" (of longtime trusted Zablocki aides and assistants, many of whom ended up on the committee staff long before Clem's succession as chairman). Ironically, my Republican credentials might well have faded into oblivion were it not for Zablocki's attitude: he liked to treat me publicly as a "prominent" GOP functionary and then point out that I was the only Republican in the House that he could fully control! (The difference in our backgrounds may even have brought us together. I feared that at times he would put *too much* faith in my judgment, and that I might inadvertently let him down.)

Clem Zablocki's approach was not only good fun, but good politics: he was quite popular with members across the aisle, especially on foreign affairs, as he had been a traditional backer of the military, all veterans groups, and the U.S. effort in Vietnam over several administrations. He was particularly adept at getting Republicans to support (or at least not vigorously oppose) his mostly bipartisan foreign policy legislation.

The War Powers Act, which caused a lot of heartburn within both parties, was a case in point. It was clear to just about everyone in the House that only *he* could have led the successful fight, over a presidential veto, in behalf of that controversial bill. The committee staff, including Zablocki's former administrative assistant (for) and his then-current chief of staff (against), were split down the middle over the issue. Although he gained considerable prestige as the bill's floor manager and principal House sponsor, he evidently had strong initial reservations. He made a point of watering down the bill's most extreme provisions. However, when his objections had been met, he felt obligated to support the measure. The War Powers Act passed in the House despite the Republican minority's objections in principle. Zablocki's bipartisan strength, together with Richard Nixon's weakened political condition as a consequence of Watergate, carried the day.

Zablocki's bipartisanship in foreign affairs, and especially his position on Vietnam, had produced opposition to his chairmanship within the liberal wing of the Democratic caucus. Representative Benjamin Rosenthal of New York and like-minded liberals promoted Dante Fascell of Florida as an alternative candidate. (Fascell himself gave no encouragement to this movement.) Ironically, a staunch liberal, David Obey of Wisconsin, saved Zablocki's chairmanship. Obey addressed the caucus and vigorously supported his Wisconsin colleague. "This party," he pointed out, "has never imposed 'mind control' over its leaders" and had no business blocking a perfectly qualified—even if somewhat independent-minded—Democrat of long standing. In support of Zablocki's candidacy, some of his more liberally inclined but loyal staffers came up with some useful statistics: Zablocki actually had a better voting record in support of Democratic administration proposals than Ben Rosenthal. Of course, this included numerous votes on Vietnam favored by the Johnson administration and opposed by Rosenthal.

When Rosenthal and Company went down in flames, many politicians assumed that Clem would "get even." Instead the Zablocki approach was the exact reverse: he killed Ben with kindness and thoughtfulness, at times making him squirm in embarrassment. Even when the Democrats enjoyed a massive majority, the left wing rarely mustered a majority vote of the whole House. Clem gave the liberals every possible opportunity to present their positions to the committee, as well as to the House at large, before they were voted down. His tolerance for differences of opinion even included abortion: as a devout Catholic, he was antiabortion, but always treated colleagues with a different attitude respectfully. Clem's technique was masterful. Above all, it worked. At the end of Zablocki's first term as chairman, even Ben Rosenthal commended his leadership.

Of the three chairmen I served, Zablocki was unquestionably my closest mentor and strongest influence. Perhaps I am biased for that reason, but I also believe that the Committee on Foreign Affairs reached its zenith in prestige, effectiveness, and cohesiveness, in terms of both member and staff morale, during his reign.

I do not intend this as a criticism of either Doc Morgan or Dante Fascell. Both of these gentlemen handled with skill and aplomb the difficult challenges they faced during their respective incumbencies. Doc had to contend with the divisive Vietnam war, and Dante presided over a period of increasing partisanship and early "Balkanization," both in the committee and in the House as a whole, although the atmosphere was never as polarized then as it is today. Both men managed to hold the committee leadership of the two parties together under difficult circumstances and to pass significant legislation.

Clem Zablocki, however, enjoyed the best of all possible worlds: he had a strong following among Republicans and he had the left wing effectively neutralized. Committee members always entertained a large diversity of opinion on almost any subject, but usually along "issue"—not party—lines. And the staff, across the board, held him in the highest esteem. There was something very human and approachable about the man, as distinct from the leader, which appealed to people in all walks of life. The *Milwaukee Journal* summarized this distinctive quality in a feature article entitled "He Walks with Kings, but Keeps the Common Touch." As the reporter pointed out, Clem Zablocki could spend an entire afternoon at the White House negotiating with the president and his senior advisers, and then go home, don an apron, and cook Polish sausage for his friends and subordinates. (The leader of a visiting Polish parliamentary delegation whom Zablocki entertained at his home said to me: "We couldn't believe that your chairman would wait on us the way he did. Anyone doing that in Warsaw would be presumed to have lost his standing in the Party!")

The chairman also liked to drop by staff members' offices for a drink with the staff at the end of the day. There we would be exposed to much political wisdom, including a candid appraisal of his House colleagues, always mixed with perceptiveness and humor. He always knew ahead of time who was going to join or leave the Wisconsin House delegation via the next election, and he was always right. I particularly enjoyed listening to his analyses of Wisconsin politics, as I had been "out of the loop" for many years after my departure from home in 1947, the year Clem began his congressional career.

Jack Sullivan, his former chief of staff, told me that he once attended a political rally and shared the stage with Zablocki in his South Side district. When a woman asked, "What does that Irishman do that is so good that the job could not be filled by one of our fine Polish boys?" Zablocki defended his choice with vigor.

In my own case, Zablocki had no problem with the fact that my great grandfather founded Merrill Park, the current site of Marquette University, which Clem attended. Merrill Park was earlier inhabited by poor immigrant families (including the elder Zablockis) who had no electricity or running water. That I came from the Upper East Side instead of the South Side made no difference to him. (He was also an enthusiastic shopper and appreciated the quality of goods he found in the T. A. Chapman Company.)

In many respects, Zablocki reminds me of Harry Truman, especially since I read the monumental biography by David McCullough.[2] Truman, who surrounded himself with Ivy Leaguers like Dean Acheson and Averill Harriman, evidently had the same outlook. Only when cabinet officers like the late Henry Morgenthau thought they were indispensable did they suffer the consequences. (Morgenthau threatened to resign if he were not included at the 1945 Big Three meeting at Potsdam, and Truman accepted his resignation instantly. A number of years later, in private conversation, Truman summarized his attitude in succinct fashion: "Morgenthau didn't know shit from apple butter.")

That was the type of pithy and earthy observation the Hon. Clement J. Zablocki was fully capable of making. Like Truman, Zablocki judged people on their individual merits, not on their backgrounds. He had no hang-ups about privilege: if you worked for him loyally and conscientiously, you felt the warmth of his approval. Only those who acted "superior" (a sin not committed by any of the staff) ended up doing so at their peril.

Clem Zablocki died of a heart attack on December 3, 1983, just weeks after his seventy-first birthday, when the staff threw him a gala birthday party in the Committee hearing room, complete with male chorus line led by the author. He was stricken just down the hall from me in his congressional office as he and his Senate counterpart were preparing to meet with the prime minister of Israel. He went immediately into a coma from which he never recovered, which was just as well, as he would have suffered severe brain damage had he survived.

After a memorial service in Washington, Zablocki's coffin was transported by military plane to Milwaukee, where the main funeral took place. Although I had grown up in Milwaukee, this was my first visit to the South Side, where rows of schoolchildren lined the motorcade route, in an impressive demonstration of honor and affection on the part of the people he represented so long and so well. The priest who delivered the final eulogy managed to create something of a stir, saying that Clem had confided to the priest during his last visit to Milwaukee that he favored Senator John Glenn for president. The front pews were filled with Walter Mondale supporters (this was just before the 1984 presidential campaign, when Mondale, the Democratic nominee, was defeated by Ronald Reagan). They were anything but pleased with this dictum, but the Polish priest in a way reflected the independent frame of mind that characterized the deceased, from beginning to end.

Actually, those staff aides who knew Clem best doubted very much that he made such an endorsement (unless it was made in a confessional booth, which is even less likely). Zablocki may have expressed his admiration for the senator from Ohio in some manner, but it was not his style to make premature political endorsements, especially to indiscreet members of the clergy.

The Fascell Transition

Dante Fascell was a centrist within the Democratic Party. He was a traditional opponent of Fidel Castro, which was the only position a representative of Dade County, Florida, could espouse if he wanted to continue in office, but he also managed to maintain respectable links to liberals. Although he was a distinctly different personality from the man he replaced, I always thought of his tenure in terms of continuity: he retained Zablocki's chief of staff and just about everyone else from the Zablocki years. He added only his chief fund-raiser, Spencer Oliver, to the newly created position of counsel, and upgraded his longtime aide, Mike Findley, to deputy chief of staff. He emphasized "business as usual" (*not* a pejorative term in those days), especially during the period of mourning for Zablocki, but thereafter as well.

The first two years of Fascell's tenure were amazing. The chairman of the House Committee on Foreign Affairs respected and cooperated with his Senate counterpart, Republican senator Richard Lugar of Indiana (who himself had long espoused bipartisanship). The feeling was mutual. Together they passed a Foreign Aid authorization bill, in lieu of a continuing resolution under which the program had been extended from year to year over a considerable period. This atmosphere continued up to 1990, when the Democrats won back the Senate. Although no Democrat would admit it publicly, some considered Rhode Island Democratic senator Claiborne

Pell's assumption of the chairmanship of the Foreign Relations Committee somewhat of a letdown (even though he supported most Democratic foreign policies).

Fascell was a man of many parts. He was deeply interested in Latin America, and not only because the Cuban-American community in his district was breathing down his neck. Some years previously, he had had an important role in setting up the Inter-American Foundation, an innovative U.S. government entity aimed at promoting social development in Latin America. He was the original promoter of the National Endowment for Democracy, a bipartisan collection of business and labor leaders involved in showcasing or exporting the democratic process to countries that had been deprived of it, especially in the less developed world. He headed the original House delegation to the Commission for Security and Cooperation in Europe (CSCE), also known as the Helsinki Commission. He tried, in fact, to be all things to all people, and was more than partially successful at it. Perhaps his only weakness was that, like Doc Morgan, he had trouble saying no to members who wanted additional staff appointments that the committee could not afford. You cannot please everybody—in Congress or in life—but Dante certainly went the extra mile.

I had known Dante Fascell for many years, dating back to my service as a congressional fellow in Peter Frelinghuysen's office. In those days, Fascell, whose office was just down the hall, had had more time to socialize with the attractive young women in Peter's office. Fascell was not fussy about it: he liked the opposite sex, regardless of age, political orientation, or professional status. And he remained devoted to his wife of many decades, Jean Marie, who never doubted his basic loyalty. Bob O'Reagan, Fascell's longtime administrative assistant, reminded me that even in those years Dante was able to cope with demands on his time resulting from his chairmanship of subcommittees of both the Foreign Affairs and Government Operations committees.

That was a period, however, of less pressure on a subcommittee chairman.

Fascell's chairmanship of the full committee coincided with the beginning of the assault on the traditional House structure, led by the "Young Turks" of the Republican Party. People like Newt Gingrich, Vin Weber, and others equally frustrated by being almost forty years in the minority, started to give critical, highly partisan five-minute speeches in the period reserved for "special orders" at the end of the legislative day. They became such a pain in Speaker Tip O'Neill's large derrière that he retaliated by having the TV camera pan the chamber, showing row upon row of empty seats. The Republicans were outraged, and the atmosphere heated up perceptibly throughout the House side of the Capitol. Our committee did not have a role in any of these developments, but inevitably the strong bipartisan tone of the Zablocki era became increasingly fragmented. To his credit, Fascell did what he could to keep this movement under control.

Dante B. Fascell might be judged differently in today's climate, especially by feminists, but in those days no one really seemed to care. He was a much better chairman than most, and that was enough for his followers—and for *me*!

OTHER COMMITTEE MEMBERS

When I came to the committee, its other members included every shade of opinion, from H. R. Gross (Republican) of Iowa on the far right to Ron Dellums (Democrat) of California on the left. Nevertheless, control remained in the largely bipartisan hands of the senior Democratic and Republican members seated on either side of Chairman Morgan on the top tier of the committee hearing room.

Experienced moderates on the Democratic side included Zablocki; Wayne Hays of Ohio, a superpower in the House in the early 1970s; and L. H. Fountain of

North Carolina, who voted Republican most of the time and was never in contention for the committee chairmanship. Lee Hamilton of Indiana, a thoughtful and respected centrist not identifiable with any particular bloc, was the twelfth-ranking Democrat. He would eventually succeed Dante Fascell as chairman.

Other Democrats between Hamilton and those ranking four were Charles Diggs of Michigan and Cornelius Gallagher of New Jersey (both of whom were to spend some time in the slammer), followed by Robert N. C. Nix, a nattily dressed and elegant black from Philadelphia.

Below them sat the only "pocket" of true liberals who tended to hold together as a bloc: John Monagan of Connecticut, not totally identified as a liberal; Don Fraser of Minnesota, the human rights champion of later years; Ben Rosenthal of New York; John Culver of Iowa, a former Harvard roommate of, and administrative assistant to, Sen. Edward Kennedy; and Jonathan Bingham of New York, fifteenth on the Democratic side, but influential despite his low seniority. Dellums, in this group, ranked near the bottom in seniority (he later became chairman of the Armed Services Committee).

After Messrs. Mailliard and Frelinghuysen, the ranking minority members on the Republican side, came William Broomfield of Michigan; J. Irvin Whalley of Pennsylvania; H. R. Gross of Iowa, Edward J. Derwinski of Illinois; Bradford Morse of Massachusetts; former governor Vernon Thompson of Wisconsin; James Fulton of Pennsylvania; and Paul Findley of Illinois. Those below Findley were really too junior on the minority side to exert much influence, but John Buchanan of Alabama (a GOP "liberal" in many respects) and Pierre "Pete" Dupont of Delaware, the last man on the lower tier of Republican seats, were eventually to exhibit leadership qualities. In any case, there were no "bombthrowers" on this list, or, for that matter, on either side of the aisle.

Congressman Whalley was a buffoon of little significance. He was indicted for demanding kickbacks from his staff, a particularly egregious offense, as he was a multimillionaire. I remember him mostly in connection with two bizarre requests: Once while flying to Latin America, he asked the staff to let him know when the plane passed over the equator, so he could take a photo outside his window (of clouds and sky presumably!). He also tried to get a staff member to take him out onto Tokyo Bay to find the spot where the Missouri anchored for the ceremonial Japanese surrender in World War II. A hapless military escort officer ended up with this ridiculous assignment.

Jim Fulton, another Pennsylvania Republican, would have been the committee's ranking Republican if he had not been "disciplined" some years back for having deserted the GOP on a party-line vote. Even so, he had managed to work his way back from the bottom to the top tier on the Republican side. Fulton was not your average congressman: he filled his congressional office with works of art, especially Rubens paintings, in lieu of the usual photos showing the member shaking hands with the president or receiving an award from the local Rotary Club. He wore two-tone "suits" (the pants never matched the jacket), and presumably to disguise his advanced age, sported a flamboyant reddish-brown wig. Rumor had it that he was gay at a time when politicians of that persuasion were still in the closet. He was reportedly a multimillionaire and his behavior supported the rumor. Once when traveling in the Philippines, he came across a shop that sold crucifixes and religious souvenirs of various types. Fulton thought they were "quaint" and bought out the entire store, eventually sending the contents to his Catholic constituents as holiday gifts.

Fulton was a compulsive publicity hound. Another story about him placed him in a less-than-favorable light. When traveling in the Netherlands, he managed to meet Queen Mother Juliana, who was about to embark on a visit to the United States. Jim offered her and her entourage the peace and quiet of a "break" at his hunting lodge in the remote hilly region outside of Pittsburgh, between formal functions and commitments. She would have complete privacy, he assured her, and evidently the idea appealed. When the royal party arrived at the lodge, however, it was surrounded by reporters and a select group of Jim's political cronies, much to the queen mother's displeasure. In fact, the Palace was furious about the whole incident, but unfortunately, no one had checked out Jim Fulton with anyone on the HFAC!

Other committee members got a good deal of publicity and even notoriety during their terms in Congress. In at least some of those cases, the committee's overall accomplishments took place in spite of rather than because of them. Two of them, whom I label the Mover and the Shaker, merit further attention.

The Mover: Wayne Hays of Ohio

In the early 1970s no one in either house of Congress was more powerful, or more willing to exploit his power, than Wayne Hays of Ohio. A member of the Foreign Affairs Committee, and chairman of its International Operations Subcommittee, he became a major influence and/or headache for the Department of State and the U.S. Information Agency, for which he exercised oversight and authorized funding.

Hays's essential pragmatism contributed to his reputation as the "Hays juggernaut." He was definitely not an ideologue, and he could "get into bed" with just about any one politically if it served his purpose. Thus, his colleagues never knew just which way he might land on a specific legislative issue and bring at least some of his allies along with him. On foreign policy issues, for instance, he sided vociferously with liberals in opposing the Greek junta during the 1970s, but broke with them in supporting Radio Free Europe/Radio Liberty and in adopting a more hard-line position towards the Soviet Union and Eastern Europe.

Hays was a formidable debater, of the slash-and-burn variety. He could be a bully in debate and long had many of his colleagues intimidated. Every once in a while, however, he would overplay his hand. In one floor debate he blatantly tried to humiliate Peter Frelinghuysen by making various totally nongermane and uncalled-for references to Peter's "privileged" upbringing. But the technique backfired, and Peter received the bipartisan sympathy of the House membership. On our committee only Ed Derwinski of Illinois could handle Hays effectively in debate. Derwinski was particularly effective in using a partly humorous, partly sarcastic, style.

Despite his unattractive personal traits, Hays was also a formidable asset if he was on your side, and no one recognized this better than chairman Morgan. Even during the height of the Cold War, foreign aid (even security assistance) was not brilliantly popular, and getting Wayne Hays to support it was clearly a plus. Although Hays was inclined to exploit every possible political advantage, he was also rational. If you made a reasonable case for your cause, he could be won over. Despite the confrontation described above, Frelinghuysen and Hays supported each other's foreign policy positions more often than not. (I learned long afterwards that Hays was at least partly responsible for my continued service as a Republican appointee on the Democratic payroll after Frelinghuysen's retirement. Since he was in charge of the payroll, Hays announced to the committee's Democratic caucus that *he* would pay me if Doc wanted me.)

His debating strategy emerged, on one occasion I witnessed, in an uncharacteristically sympathetic mode. As chairman of the International Operations Subcommittee and floor manager for the State Department authorization bill, he was responsible for opposing floor amendments to the bill. A "knee-jerk" liberal, Don Bonker of the state of Washington, offered a floor amendment to the bill, calling for a fixed percentage of ambassadors to come from the ranks of

Foreign Service professionals. The percentage was not all that onerous, and may even have been met in most years. However, the provision was (1) probably unconstitutional, as it impinged on the president's appointment authority, and (2) from Hays's standpoint, more than probably undesirable.

Hays began his rebuttal with a degree of understanding rather than confrontation: "I recognize what the Gentleman from Washington is trying to accomplish," he said, "and I am not unsympathetic to his objective. We have too many unqualified political appointees to contend with as it is . . ." He then went on to praise the long and distinguished career of Ambassador Charles (Chip) Bohlen in his dealings with the Soviets. *BUT*, he said in his peroration, Chip Bohlen as a career professional was not in a position to take on the French during his assignment to Paris. Sargent Shriver, a public servant but also a political appointee, was more effective in standing up to DeGaulle and in supporting the U.S. position (on an issue I have long since forgotten).

Hays then discussed the Shriver stand, which had received much publicity at the time. "I would not want to deny the President the authority to appoint someone like *Sargent Shriver* to a position of this importance in the international field," he concluded. Hays's use of Shriver was most significant for purposes of debate, as Shriver was a liberal hero and someone that Hays knew Bonker especially admired. The amendment failed by a large margin. I think that even Bonker, the sponsor, voted "Nay" or abstained.

Hays's main power, however, came not from his membership on the Foreign Affairs Committee but from his chairmanship of the Committee on House Administration. Traditionally, an assignment to that committee was not considered much of a perk. It met irregularly and involved itself with routine and distinctly unglamorous housekeeping responsibilities. In the "old days," an assignment to Administration was almost considered a disgrace—an indication, perhaps, that the assignee was not really qualified for an important substantive committee.

Hays altered that perception dramatically. Unlike most of his peers, he had the foresight to develop the committee into a vital power base: every member, whether he or she understood it or not, at one time or another needed a friend on Administration. If you wanted acceptable office space, office equipment (which would become exceedingly important with the introduction of the computer), or a parking space in the Rayburn House Office Building or near the Capitol for your visiting governor or for vital constituents, you had to get approval from House Administration.

Originally the committee shared some administrative functions with the Office of the Clerk of the House, but Hays steadily undermined most of the clerk's prerogatives and reassigned them to Administration. I saw letters signed by Hays to all House members informing them that "henceforth" the House Administration Committee would be responsible for this-and-that administrative procedure, formerly under the purview of the Clerk's Office.

Since Hays also understood that opposing a winner is hard, he reportedly made a special point of bringing the poorly managed House restaurants into the black, mainly by placing guards at the kitchen doors to prevent the staff from stealing food, especially the chickens. After a year or two of minimal effort on his part, he highlighted his considerable managerial achievements on the House floor.

Above all, however, Hays had control over everyone's payroll, from mere representatives' offices to committee staffs. If a member got out of line, Hays would sometimes retaliate by removing that member's key staffer from one or another of his payrolls. More often, however, the mere threat of such action was just as effective. He ruled essentially through *fear*, and most members were reluctant (often because they did not have the time or patience) to take him on. By the same token, he was able to reward his allies and supporters quite generously.

Personal experience helped me to comprehend fully the political influence of Wayne Hays. I had two occasions to appreciate his assistance on personal matters.

Parking Space. Hays was chairman (and final arbiter) of the Parking Committee. For some fifteen years I commuted to Capitol Hill on either a Lambretta motor scooter or a Honda motorcycle. A special area had always been reserved for two-wheeled vehicles near the C Street entrance to the Rayburn garage, and all riders had long cherished this privilege.

One day, however, in a power grab by the Capitol Hill police, a note was left on all "bikes" informing us that henceforth we would be required to park in the lot across the street (without benefit of cover from the elements). Apparently the police wanted our space for a large van. With only one or two exceptions (staffers like me who wore a coat and tie), motorcycle riders worked as electricians or plumbers or in the basement "folding rooms," where House publications were produced, in a strictly technical capacity, and lacked political clout. An appeal to the garage superintendent was of no avail: he had no say in the matter.

Finally I turned to Paula Peak, a sensible, highly efficient and sympathetic member of the Foreign Affairs Committee staff, who just happened to be Wayne Hays's sister-in-law. I told her what had happened and especially the capricious manner in which the new policy had been implemented. "That doesn't sound right to me," Paula concurred. "I'm going to talk to Mr. Hays about this!" (I happened to know that among Mr. Hays's good traits was his sympathy for underdogs!)

Nothing happened for a few days and the easy riders had no choice but to comply with the new regulation. Then one afternoon a very polite uniformed officer approached me in the parking lot and told me, "I'm sorry,

Sir, but beginning tomorrow, you can't park here." Damnation, I thought, we will now be removed still further, perhaps to RFK Stadium. "O.K." I said resignedly, "Where will it be this time?" "Back in your old place in the Rayburn garage," he responded. "Our police vehicles are going to be parked out here!" And that, dear reader, is how one solved a parking problem during the Hays era. Even though Hays has long since departed— also from this earth—the motorcycles are still being parked in the old space in the Rayburn garage. The Capitol Police (who are paid by Congress) have never seen fit to challenge this perk again!

Railroad Pension. Paula Peak (and thus, indirectly, Wayne Hays) helped me once again, with a personal problem of our late devoted cleaning lady, Maud Carr. Maud's husband was about to retire and a receive a railroad pension. She wanted to continue working part-time for us indefinitely after he retired, which was fine with us, but she asked me if it was legal. My uninformed colleagues told me it was. I continued to pay her Social Security as in the past, but that was my big mistake. If I had just paid her in cash, I would never have been caught in an innocent error. Railroad retirement, it turned out, unlike Social Security, required that pensioners, *including the spouse*, cease employment with their *last* employer prior to retirement. Suddenly Maud had to pay $6,000, which she didn't have, before her husband's pension could be resumed. I paid the fine forthwith, as I certainly did not want Maud and her husband to be unfairly penalized.

This time Paula put me in touch with the "case worker" in Hays's office, who eventually was able to reduce my fine to $2,000, primarily on the basis of ignorance of the law, which is no excuse but can be considered a mitigating circumstance. In retrospect, I realized how important constituent service can be on the Hill, and how much a personal favor of this kind can mean in a strictly *personal* situation. It reminded me of Tip

O'Neill's observation that "all politics is local." If a politician, even an outrageous one, helps you out in a time of need, it is relatively easy to overlook his shortcomings.

"The Bigger They are, the Harder They Fall." Appropriately, a woman from House Administration ended the Wayne Hays saga. No member of Congress or of the executive branch had the political "balls" to take him on, but ironically his own mistress, Elizabeth Ray, finally brought him down. The media have fully documented the entire saga, which need not be recounted here. The moral of the story of his downfall seems to be: always remember to invite your mistress to your wedding. Hays's failure to do so allegedly led Ms. Ray to tell her story to a *Washington Post* reporter.

Mostly luck had kept Ms. Ray in House Administration and away from the House Foreign Affairs Committee, where we would *all* have been considered guilty by association. Marian Czarnecki, committee chief of staff at the time, had interviewed Ms. Ray. Fortunately for him, *she* decided she was not qualified for HFAC (after Marian made the position description sound especially challenging). Despite all the pressure from Hays, she effectively selected herself out of contention. It turned out to be the ultimate break for Foreign Affairs.

Having a mistress in Washington was not particularly newsworthy in the later decades of the twentieth century. Having her on the House Administration Committee payroll, however, was another thing, especially when she told the *Washington Post* that she could not "type, file or even answer the phone." In fact, it turned out that the "subcommittee" to which she was assigned had never actually met, and consequently her responsibilities tended to be limited to those personal services she provided, from time to time, to the chairman.

Within a few days after the nationwide publicity took over and dominated both the morning and evening news, Hays resigned from the House. In fact, he entered the committee office for his final press conference through my own hallway door (which Doc Morgan had often used in the past to avoid the press). By that time the arrogance was gone, and he resembled nothing more than a shaken, confused, slightly overweight old man. He was accompanied to this final ordeal by loyal friends from his political district in Ohio, as he had none left in the House of Representatives, with the possible exception of Doc Morgan.

He had lived and died by the sword, as the saying goes, and no tears were shed. The days of Hays were over.

The Shaker: H. R. Gross of Iowa

H. R. Gross was unique. He was the self-appointed watchdog of the House and the federal treasury, and he would very rarely let anything get passed by unanimous consent. As one of his colleagues observed: "We all need *one* H. R. Gross to keep us honest, but we couldn't live with *two* of him."

H. R. was in many ways an anachronism. He was essentially an isolationist and a protectionist in an era of U.S. world leadership. He didn't believe in a lot of things, like foreign aid, foreign travel for members of Congress, the United Nations, or the international financial institutions. Whether he even approved of diplomatic relations between the United States and foreign countries is debatable. To many "internationalists," putting him on the Foreign Affairs Committee seemed like a bad joke. And yet there was something about H. R. that evoked universal respect. The man was real, a work horse, not a show horse, and he was one hundred percent true to his beliefs. "What you see is what you get" describes the senior Gentleman from Iowa.

Before coming to Congress, H. R. had been a (naturally) conservative broadcasting pundit of some note in his native Iowa, so he understood how to "work" the media and maintained satisfactory relations with TV and the press. Whenever the House was in session, he would haunt the chamber, objecting to everything that sounded at all "spendthrift" and forcing committee chairmen and legislative floor leaders to spell out their proposals in minute detail. (In this respect, he undoubtedly performed a useful service.) It goes without saying that he was intimidated by *no* member, however high or mighty. Even Wayne Hays could not punish him administratively, as his personal needs were quite minimal. I've heard members say that the only way to get a unanimous consent request passed was to summon H. R. to the Republican cloakroom for a phone call, and then have a quick vote.

H. R. liked to harangue, in a loud voice, against what he called "international POO-BAHS." What exactly he meant by the term was never clear, but it seemed to include most of the sophisticated Third World delegates who inhabited the members' lounge at the UN. At one point in the State Department authorization debate, Doc Morgan provoked him on this subject, noting: "I am delighted to hear that the Gentleman from Iowa is so conversant with the . . . UN 'clubs,' because next year we plan to send him there as the House representative to the General Assembly. He will want to utilize all of these extensive facilities during his assignment." Gross responded in kind: "It will be a cold day in hell when I ever set foot in the POLYGLOT organization!"

Actually, Doc Morgan liked H. R. more than most members on either side of the aisle, and he had reason to. H. R. could have caused him a heap of trouble by shaving just a few million (which might possibly have passed) here and there off the foreign aid bill. Instead, his proposed cuts were so radical and steep that they were not taken seriously. Doc often tried to associate anyone who criticized the committee bill with the H. R. Gross position, and H. R. thus became a useful symbol.

Whatever his presumed shortcomings, H. R. Gross had one overriding virtue: he was invariably generous and sympathetic to staff. I was to learn this fact in a backhanded way soon after joining the committee.

After one mark-up session on some piece of foreign affairs legislation (H. R. always submitted "minority" views), I was given the assignment of asking the congressman for his draft comments as soon as possible, so we could proceed to the Rules Committee. Until we had his minority views in hand, we could not take our bill to Rules and thence to the floor. I was probably chosen for this particular assignment because I was a new "Republican" staffer and still essentially an "innocent." Following my instructions, I called the congressman on the phone and asked him when his comments might be ready and if I could help him in any way. As I recall, H. R. answered the telephone personally and blew his top. "Damn it all," he said, "tell those people to keep their G. D. pants on. We just passed the bill an hour ago. I will get them their views in my own sweet time." "Yes, sir," I responded, "whenever convenient." I realized then and there that the assignment I had been given was an unrealistic one for a greenhorn.

Approximately forty minutes later, H. R. personally appeared in my office and handed me a copy of his draft "views." "I'm sorry I talked to you the way I did," he apologized, "I know you were only doing your job!" I was speechless; no other member of Congress in my memory every spoke to a junior staff member in that vein. It made a lasting impression. From that moment on, H. R. was not a curmudgeon, but a legislator of infinite understanding and "vision."

Another story about H. R. is equally instructive. Once upon a time (it could be any time) H. R. was walking across Independence Avenue to answer an important roll call vote. Apparently, he ended up jaywalking, against a Capitol Police officer's signal. The officer was new and did not recognize H. R. as a member of Congress. (This is not surprising, as H. R. was among the most nondescript of legislators. In the winter, he often wore sweaters with a zipper down the middle underneath his suit jacket; some said he looked either like a janitor or the operator of a freight elevator.) "Go back," the cop shouted, and H. R. reluctantly complied. A few moments later the officer went over to the curb and explained, "I was just trying to save your life, sir, as you were walking against the traffic." At this juncture most members would have enlightened the young officer about their identity, and then told him it was his responsibility to stop the traffic while they went to cast a vote in the Congress of the United States. Instead, H. R. swallowed hard and agreed: "You were right; you were only doing your duty."

Unlike Wayne Hays, H. R. never had much influence, but he definitely did know how to shake up the place. Also unlike Wayne Hays, when H. R. finally retired, more than a few tears were shed, even by his most determined political opponents.

CHAPTER 12

An Eclectic Committee Staff

The Foreign Affairs Committee's effectiveness during my tenure there was largely attributable to its having the most able, qualified, and diversified staff of any committee in the House. I would place the high point of our staff ascendancy at a year to a year and a half after my arrival.

The key ingredient was diversity. My own case can serve as an example. With my Foreign Service background and especially my experience in Personnel, I knew my way around the Department of State. Above all, I knew where to go at the working level (the desk officer or country director) to get something accomplished. Going through a deputy assistant secretary or higher might be more satisfying to one's ego, but it was invariably a waste of time: you would merely be referred back to the people with substantive knowledge and ability to solve your problem, following a number of repetitive telephone calls and messages. (Many of my Hill colleagues never understood this distinction.) To a modest degree, therefore, I was of use to the committee in obtaining needed assistance from State Department officials. However, having two staffers with my particular background would have been redundant.

STAFF REORGANIZATION

The committee's time-honored organizational structure changed fundamentally shortly after I started working there. When I arrived, the full committee staff consisted of twelve full-time consultants like myself, all assigned to the full committee, thus giving considerable power to the full committee chairman vis-à-vis the subcommittee chairmen. The chairman of the full committee made subcommittee staff assignments as he deemed necessary and desirable. (He did not assign members to subcommittees, as that was done by a committee caucus. He was, of course, influential in that process.)

The "new look" granted each of the nine subcommittees authority to hire and maintain its own staff, usually a director, one or two "staff associates" (assistants to the director to work on legislation), and a secretary. The staff, both substantive and clerical, proliferated from the approximately twenty-five (including clerical employees) when I arrived, to over a hundred when I retired in 1986. Soon the minority joined in the fun, by appointing minority staff members, initially assigned concurrently to at least two subcommittees (and eventually, in some cases, just one, which meant more staffers).

Two distinct views emerged about the accretion of subcommittee staffs. The full committee considered the number excessive and likely to cause trouble. As in building more highways, you would just end up with more traffic and congestion. To justify their existence, many staffers tended to prepare amendments (many unnecessary and some mischievous) for their chairmen or members to offer, bogging down the legislative process. The full committee often—but not always—rejected these amendments.

On the other hand, the subcommittee view started from the fair premise that Congress did not always carry out its oversight responsibilities fully and efficiently. Given the vast resources available to the executive branch, the subcommittees needed additional help to even begin to level the playing field in carrying out much of the needed investigative work—detailed inspection and review of executive programs and operations. Thus, on my arrival in March 1971 the Foreign Affairs Committee did not even hold hearings on the State Department/USIA funding request; it merely provided an open-ended authorization, leaving the total review process to an appropriations subcommittee headed by powerful congressman John Rooney of New York. All that changed when Wayne Hays became chairman of the International Operations (IO) Subcommittee. Later, under Dante Fascell, IO spent a full year on Foreign Service reform legislation, with extensive hearings and long, detailed mark-up sessions. While the final product may not have enjoyed universal acclaim, it had clearly improved the proposal sent us by the Department of State.

Both views have considerable validity. My own feeling is that subcommittee staffs are clearly necessary, but that the number of both subcommittees and staffs can be drastically reduced, as happened in 1995. (I am told that in 1998 total staff was limited to sixty-five.)

CHIEFS OF STAFF

A series of outstanding chiefs of staff[1] were key to the Foreign Affairs Committee's effectiveness around the time of my tenure.

Boyd Crawford

My arrival at room 2170 of the Rayburn Building happened to coincide with the retirement of a memorable Foreign Affairs Committee institution: the late Boyd Crawford, staff administrator par excellence. In all my years in government, I doubt that I ever met anyone who rose—in the pure Horatio Alger tradition—from such humble beginnings to such behind-the-scenes heights of power and influence.

Boyd was a native Washingtonian who was not only "self-made" but essentially self-educated. His first job, either during or immediately after high school, was as an attendant in a Capitol cloakroom (a real cloakroom, where people check coats and hats, not the Republican or Democratic variety just off the House floor, where members assemble, receive telephone calls, and exchange views on current legislation). As a Hill employee able to check out books from the Library of Congress, he read voraciously. Later he enrolled in a business course and became an expert typist, winning numerous competitions for speed and accuracy. As a result, his typing requirements remained high: he once told me he never hired a secretary for the committee who could type less than eighty-five words a minute, a standard of proficiency never equaled during my employment with the committee.

On the basis of his clerical skills, Boyd eventually succeeded in getting a job as a "secretary" to a Republican representative from Michigan, from which humble position he was to launch a long and successful career as a committee staff "administrator" (he never used the title "director"). At one time he was the lone staff member, or "clerk," of the Foreign Affairs Committee, supported by a secretary, June Nigh, his cousin.[2]

By the time I arrived at committee headquarters in the Rayburn Building, Boyd's long and successful career had just ended. I learned about it thereafter via long luncheon discussions and in reading his draft memoirs (so far unpublished). He was a constant survivor of many changes in the committee chairmanship, not only from Democrat to Democrat, but from Democrat to Republican and back to Democrat. Every chairman in turn decided that keeping Boyd at the helm was a necessity. The secrets of his success seem to have been his absolute loyalty to whichever chairman he was serving at the time, his lack of a personal political agenda, and his unfailing determination to defend and uphold the best interests of his ultimate boss. On both sides of the aisle, committee members potentially in line to become chairman recognized that they would need someone like Boyd to sustain their leadership if they were ever in a position to wield the committee gavel.

Boyd's institutional memory encompassed the bonus marchers of the 1930s, the depression, World War II, and the Cold War. He would always accompany the committee chairmen to their White House meetings with the president (a practice no longer followed). Truman in particular paid him great heed, asking about him specifically on those few occasions when Boyd was out of the country or otherwise unavailable.

At one time in his career, Boyd shared the management role of the committee with a Harvard professor, Dr. William Elliott. The latter handled substantive issues and "policy"matters related to committee legislation, while Boyd continued to run the administrative side. Whenever a controversy arose between the two of them, as it inevitably did, Boyd always won in the end. Academic credentials do not always prepare one for "trench warfare" of the Crawford variety, and Dr. Elliott never really had a fighting chance!

Roy J. Bullock

Boyd's successor, Roy Bullock, was senior in age, though not in service, and highly educated, with degrees from Harvard Business School and Johns Hopkins University. Gray-haired, dignified, and distinguished-looking, Roy gave the immediate impression of being a bit stiff and formal, with a somewhat flinty personality. First impressions, however, can be deceiving: after you got to know him and he accepted you as an individual (as distinct from a colleague), he would open up and disgorge a remarkable combination of knowledge and experience and an especially sensitive understanding of human motivation and frailty, based on long observation. A superb raconteur, his stories about his early travels with the committee just after World War II never failed to hold one's attention. One might say that he deeply understood human nature without necessarily approving of it! His comment on a feature article in a Washington public affairs magazine, comparing the Senate Foreign Relations Committee to its House counterpart, revealed his dry wit and sense of humor. Referring to the committee's "aging staff," Roy was quoted as saying, "That doesn't apply to me, as I am already aged."

Roy held strong opinions on most subjects. I would describe him as a nonpartisan old-fashioned conservative with a notably independent frame of mind. He shared Boyd's outlook on the proper role of a staff member, carrying out his chairman's wishes rather than trying to make or influence policy. Providing his boss with a varied number of options, he believed, was part of his assignment, as was pointing out the possible or probable consequences of a policy decision. But the political decisions themselves were the prerogative of the member, not the staff, and Roy had little use for staffers who tried to manipulate their sponsors on behalf of their own political objectives or beliefs.

Marian Czarnecki

As Clement J. Zablocki's protégé and administrative assistant (AA), Marian Czarnecki had learned all about politics from a master in the business and knew instinctively how to deal with the many disparate personalities and prima donnas that collectively constitute the U.S. House of Representatives.[3] Getting legislation passed depended more on finding a way to get at the key members involved than on dealing with the issue as such. He was an expert at this, even if some members or staff tended to resent his "manipulative expertise"—a bad rap, since whatever actions he took were on behalf of his chairman, not himself.

Unlike Clem Zablocki or Edward J. Derwinski, a senior Republican from Illinois also of Polish origin, Marian was a Polish aristocrat. This was a factor of little significance, as the three Polish-Americans worked closely and effectively together. Derwinski liked to say in public that he and Zablocki were "Poles apart," but that was not the case at all. I doubt that the House ever produced any three individuals who were more generally intelligent and politically astute than those three Polish gentlemen. So much for Polish jokes!

Marian became chief of staff under Chairman Doc Morgan after Roy Bullock retired. When Zablocki assumed the chairmanship, Marian retired from Congress and moved to a position at the Inter-American Development Bank. Marian believed that he had managed to make a number of enemies among the House membership during his term as chief of staff under Doc Morgan and that Zablocki should start his chairmanship "fresh and unencumbered." Clem did not agree with this view, but he accepted it. Marian's instinct was probably correct—it usually was.

Colonel John J. Brady, Jr.

John Brady spent most of his formative professional years in the Pentagon, specializing in military intelligence. He rose to the rank of colonel and earned a Ph.D. from the London School of Economics while stationed in the United Kingdom. An "old" Democratic loyalist who would now be considered a more centrist New Democrat, Jack Brady possessed—outwardly at least—a somewhat curmudgeonly personality, regularly broken with an Irish horse laugh. Although his opinions on most subjects were well known (and not always appreciated by committee liberals), he was basically regarded as straightforward, approachable, fair, and above all a known quantity with whom everyone was accustomed to deal. While he had a low boiling point and was given to shouting rages from time to time, no one took those aberrations seriously, and he held no long-term grudges. These contrasting qualities probably account for his long survival as chief of staff for two chairmen. Brady, from Pennsylvania, was originally appointed by Doc Morgan, but served as chief of staff during all of Zablocki's and Fascell's chairmanships.

Because security assistance was a key section of the foreign aid bill under the committee's jurisdiction, Jack's military background was considered a plus. He was sympathetic to the military profession but never intimidated by the military-industrial complex. Before Jack became chief of staff, he and I were once assigned the task of researching a new senior position the State Department wanted to establish, under secretary for security affairs. Originally this position was to be held by a security assistance "czar," who would coordinate military aid programs with both the Pentagon and the National Security Council Staff in the White House. Jack was to investigate the position from the standpoint of the Pentagon, and I was to do the same via State. We jointly recommended that on balance creating such a position could be positive, if the right person were selected for the job. He or she had to be a professional of high standing not only in the State Department, but also in the Pentagon and the White House. Having professional respect, and above all political clout, was an absolute necessity. Otherwise such a position would be next to useless.

As it turned out, our worst fears were realized. The position became a dumping ground for high-level political appointees. Only Frank Wisner, Jr., a Foreign Service officer who was appointed to the position many years later, had the proper qualifications, but he was soon transferred to the Pentagon and then to India as ambassador. The position had no conceivable justification for existence and should have been abolished long ago. Or perhaps it never should have been established in the first place.

OTHER STAFF MEMBERS

Several other highly capable staff members worked for the committee during this same period.

Dr. Albert C. F. Westphal

Albert Westphal was selected for the staff in the "old days" by a bipartisan search committee (consisting of equal numbers of Republican and Democratic committee members), who chose staff strictly on the basis of professional qualifications, experience, background, and "merit," supposedly without regard to political considerations. Despite the lofty ideals of this mechanism, it was not totally immune from politics: nothing that took place on the Hill could ever be, and the panel was by no means infallible (as seen in the case of Franklin J. Schupp below).

Al Westphal was an entirely creditable candidate. A political science professor at the time of his appointment, his Ph.D. thesis was a study of the Foreign Affairs Committee's wartime and postwar role. Having referred to a couple of its members as inept, Al had to wait for those members to retire before his staff appointment could be finalized. Al had a dry sense of humor, very much in the Roy Bullock tradition, but less active than Roy. When I knew him, he was definitely "aging," albeit still competent, experienced, and knowledgeable. His relations with the upper echelons of the Department of State were usually more than satisfactory. Since Al generally accepted the executive's "party line" as gospel, "oversight" was thus not really his "bag."

Harry C. Cromer

An experienced accountant with the General Accounting Office (GAO), Harry Cromer had served tours of duty in Rome and Tokyo. He was discovered in the late fifties by Roy Bullock, who immediately recognized his skills. Harry could look at a page full of numbers provided by the Agency for International Development (AID) and immediately discern what was wrong with the projection or what did not add up. Eventually, Harry became such a central figure in the oversight of the AID program that the agency made him its auditor general at a time when it was considered in deep trouble (when has it not been?). He was sworn in by the Speaker of the House, Carl Albert, as a gesture of congressional confidence in his mission.

Harry was one of the great characters I knew in my thirty-one-year government career, and I cannot do him justice here with a summary appraisal. His character and personality were too filled with contradictions, from apparent abrasiveness and arrogance to actual sensitivity and understanding. A self-made man like Boyd Crawford, he began in an orphanage and reached a position of executive branch leadership. He was above all else the soul of reliability. Although definitely not a candidate for sainthood, Harry could always be counted upon to fulfill any promise or obligation. Dependability was his greatest strength and was the justification for his chairmanship of the Friday luncheon group (later described in full detail).

Dr. John H. Sullivan

Another Zablocki protégé and former AA, Jack Sullivan was born and raised in Toledo but educated primarily at Milwaukee's Marquette University. Once a journalist by profession, as a reporter for the *Milwaukee Journal,* Jack Sullivan continued to write eloquently and effectively for the HFAC before becoming assistant administrator of AID for the Asia/Pacific region during the Carter administration. He had strong ties with committee liberals. Despite some grumbling by elements of the center, such contacts were generally recognized as useful, both to Chairman Morgan and eventually to Clem Zablocki when the Democratic caucus first elected Clem committee chairman. Jack and I were to undertake two memorable staff study missions, in East Asia and Western Africa, respectively, recounted in chapter 15.

Lewis Gulick

Lewis Gulick was also a journalist by profession, for many years the AP correspondent covering the State Department. He joined the staff within the first year after my arrival. Renowned as one of the most thorough and responsible representatives of his profession, he brought these same qualities to all aspects of the committee's work, with considerable distinction.

Robert K. Boyer

As mentioned previously, Bob Boyer and I were hired under unusual guidelines, namely, as Republican staffers working not for the minority but for the full committee and its Democratic chairman. Although we were appointed with the proviso that the minority had first call upon our services, we became increasingly identified with the majority, as our respective Republican sponsors left the committee, and were eventually placed on the Democratic payroll.

Bob was bright, attractive, and articulate, and highly adaptable in taking on almost any assignment required of him. He was considerably younger than I was, and except for a few years in the Air Force had far less experience in government. He was a quick study, however, and soon became indispensable to his sponsor, Representative William Mailliard, and to the chairman and staff administrator. He continued working on legislation for the committee staff, whereas I eventually opted for speechwriting and "special projects."

Over the years Bob developed valuable contacts in other committees, like Appropriations, and clearly was the most qualified candidate to succeed Jack Brady when Jack retired in 1992 as chief of staff. Staff appointments in House committees, however, were not always guided exclusively by merit, and Bob did not get the job. His only drawback initially (alas, too much Hill service can dampen one's enthusiasm and breed a degree of cynicism) was a tendency toward impulsiveness. He sometimes spoke before he thought; I recount below how this once caused me a good deal of unintended heartburn.

Ray Sparks

Finally, Ray Sparks, the committee editor, was among the committee staff veterans at the time of my arrival. Ray was another self-made man in the Boyd Crawford/Harry Cromer/Horatio Alger tradition. He rose from a background of considerable deprivation, if not outright poverty, to become an expert in a variety of fields. At age sixteen he became a senior roller-skating dance champion and eventually attended Clemson College on an Air Force Reserve training program. After his discharge, he became an expert journeyman printer, or linotype operator, traveling from city to city in pursuit of his trade. In 1958, he was hired by the Government Printing Office (GPO), assigned first to the Pentagon and later (under Eisenhower) to the White House Conference on Children and Youth. Finally, the GPO detailed him to the House Foreign Affairs Committee to manage the publication of all HFAC documents under GPO supervision. In 1970 he became the committee's editor and a full member of the HFAC staff.

Ray spent much of his time in his Rayburn office across from the cafeteria, proofreading and editing the enormous volume of committee hearings and reports in line with GPO standards and sometimes arbitrary requirements. He was nevertheless a thoroughly integrated member of the old boy (staff) network and regularly attended what has become for me, in retirement, an important element in my life, Friday staff luncheons, first at the Watergate and then at the Tivoli restaurant in Rosslyn. Every so often we dined at the Cosmos Club as Roy Bullock's guests; on one occasion in particular, we learned of another accomplishment of Ray Sparks's allegedly misspent youth. As a top-rated pool player, he managed to humiliate Bob Boyer in the Cosmos poolroom after luncheon while the rest of us witnessed the one-sided contest.

Other talented and influential consultants were to join the full committee staff in the years ahead, including George Berdes (another former Zablocki AA who was particularly involved in the war powers debate), Marian Chambers, Gerry Pitchford, George Ingram, Margaret Goodman, and Peggy Galey, to name a few, but those described above were the core cadre when I marched into my new quarters on March 1, 1971.

My "Cubicle-Mates"

The committee staff did not consist only of paragons of virtue and accomplishment. There were also my two "cubicle-mates."[4]

Melvin O. (Benny) Benson was an authentic and highly decorated World War II hero. An accomplished OSS hand, he had distinguished himself first in Norway and then, after being dropped into the mountainous countryside of Yugoslavia by parachute, as the first American to make contact with Tito, who was then engaged in guerrilla warfare against the Germans.

Unhappily, the luster of his wartime accomplishments did not carry over into civilian life. For a time he had a CIA cover job with the Pepsi Cola Company in South Africa, but he was restless and unsatisfied as a phony "executive." Finally, with the backing of Mrs. Frances Bolton of Ohio, once the ranking minority member of the committee, he was more or less imposed on the staff.

Writing reports was definitely not his forte. As a result he soon became downgraded in the eyes of his peers. He tried his best to be of some value to the committee and eventually accompanied Rep. Charles Diggs on forays around the African continent. (I described one of those Diggs visits in chapter 9.) Benny made all the arrangements, paid the bills, kept the financial records, and wrote the thank-you notes. The study mission reports he produced usually had to be severely edited and rewritten. The point to be emphasized, however, is that he tried.

Franklin J. Schupp had seniority over just about everyone (except Roy Bullock and Al Westphal). A bipartisan panel of committee members selected him in the mid-fifties on merit grounds. He had excellent "paper" qualifications as an attorney and general counsel of the War Claims Board in Japan and liked to reminisce about those days in the past when "believe it or not, I was a key player on this team." That was evidently some time ago, as he never received an assignment of any kind while I was on board.

Frank had no substantive responsibilities but kept busy and preoccupied answering the phone with the smooth professional knowledge of an insider. He could predict exactly what legislation would be taken up by the committee, its chances of passage both in committee and on the floor, and the changes that would most likely be approved in conference. He was a past master at convincing everyone outside the committee that he was a "key player." (He was also a master at generating incoming calls and putting everyone, at least for a while, on hold!) Both Boyd Crawford and Roy Bullock had begged Chairman Morgan for permission to fire Frank, but to no avail. The good doctor just could not bring himself to take this step, perhaps out of loyalty to a departed colleague. Finally, when Marian Czarnecki took over as chief of staff, he convinced Frank to "retire," probably without the chairman's full approval.

Frank had managed to thoroughly discredit the back row of cubicles where I initially sat. All the other cubicle-rows had access to the Rayburn hallway via a side door, but Boyd Crawford had permanently locked our door before my arrival, and we were without keys. (Boyd had found the door next to Frank's desk unlocked one day, and this was our collective punishment.) I did not really suffer by propinquity, being considered something of an improvement over my two roommates!

"MY SOVIET CONTACT"

Once a year, the Soviet embassy invited all congressional staff members involved in foreign affairs to a reception hosted by its deputy chief of mission. The routine never varied. First, everyone was subjected to a blatantly puerile propaganda film, which caused much laughter from the American guests (and considerable embarrassment to the Soviet hosts). Then we all assembled in the great reception room for vodka and caviar. Boyd Crawford and Roy Bullock generally frowned on these sessions and declined to participate. If anyone was guilty of even a relatively harmless indiscretion, they felt, it would reflect adversely on the committee staff. Bob Boyer and I once decided to accept, however, primarily out of curiosity.

During the week prior to this function, Roy had asked me to put together a general briefing paper for the new chairman of the Middle East Subcommittee, Lee Hamilton, pending appointment of a subcommittee staff director. I requested and received the relevant material from the Near Eastern and South Asian Affairs Bureau (NEA) at State. Aside from editing it, I had no further Middle East connection.

At the Soviet Embassy, however, Bob and I were both approached in the reception area by a typical apparatchik of that era, a heavy-set, humorless bureaucrat in a double-breasted blue suit. We asked him what he did in the embassy, and he said he was involved almost exclusively in following Middle East developments from the Washington vantage point. "Oh," Bob responded, "then you ought to talk to Mr. Chester here, as he is our committee's current expert on the Middle East." The remark was made half in jest and in a totally offhand manner.

"You dunt say," the Russian countered in heavily accented English. "Haff some more caviar and ve haff very fine vodka here . . ." Thus began my cultivation by a Soviet operative. The man called me every day for two weeks, inviting me to luncheon. Finally, when he suggested the Watergate, where I was headed anyway, I decided to accept on a one-time basis, if only to explain in detail my total noninvolvement in Middle East affairs.

The Russian appeared in trench coat with his fedora hat pulled down over his eyes. Our meeting had all the appearances of a grade-B spy film as he pulled me over to a corner and looked furtively in all directions. At that point, I realized that we were surely being watched by the FBI. The luncheon conversation was guarded, to say the least. Sample dialogue:

> *Russian:* Vell, vot is Congress going to do about MFN? Vill the Jackson-Vanik amendment pass?
>
> *Author:* Good question. What is the Soviet Union going to do this year about Jewish emigration?
>
> *Russian:* Very good question . . .

At least the luncheon had two overall benefits: the Russian paid the bill, and he became thoroughly convinced that I had zero experience in Middle East or Arab-Israeli affairs. I never heard from him again.

Again my State Department background saved me from censure. I wrote a detailed memo about the "contact" and sent copies to the Soviet Desk at State, the FBI, Chairman Morgan, and Roy Bullock. The latter was not at all pleased with the entire episode, but he accepted my memo as accurate and conclusive.

I never went to "Congressional Staff evening" at the Soviet Embassy again.

To the best of my knowledge, neither did Bob.

CHAPTER 13

The Committee's Legislative Activities

My account of the Foreign Affairs Committee's operations is clearly inadequate, and purposely so. Learned books have been written on the subject, but I consider the character and personality of the "movers and shakers" on Capitol Hill far and away more significant than the substantive issues with which they dealt. In my judgment and experience, people tend to make history and not the other way around.

My initial years with the committee mainly involved me in regular legislative duties. I found that the committee's top echelon generally agreed on most major issues. They confined their haggling and give-and-take to details.

The major legislation was the annual Foreign Aid authorization bill. Unlike the Senate Foreign Relations Committee, which spent little if any time considering the House bill, our committee spent weeks on hearings and protracted mark-up sessions.

Normally, the first witness before the committee would be the secretary of state, who would speak in global terms about the need for development aid worldwide (although the lion's share always went to the Middle East in general, and to Israel in particular), and why an aid program was an important tool of U.S. diplomacy and very much in the U.S. national interest.

Questioning would then begin, not necessarily related to the bill under consideration—more often on timely political controversies. Again unlike the Senate, which permitted unlimited questioning and debate, House committees operated under a five-minute rule. After five minutes, "the time of the Gentleman has expired," the chairman would intone, and then cut him off with the gavel.

This was a rational procedure for a committee of forty-plus members, but the more junior members often became disgruntled: all the important questions had already been asked by the time their turns were reached. The so-called "Findley rule" (proposed by Representative Paul Findley of Illinois soon after I arrived at the committee) changed the procedure: junior committee members in their seats when the chairman called the meeting to order could ask questions in order of precedence, ahead of senior members who arrived late, as many did owing to competing commitments. This helped assuage the institutional frustration of junior members. (Only those who *lacked* seniority, however, objected to the seniority principle. As one member put it to me in private: "Chips, we have to do something about seniority *this* year, as next year I will have too much seniority to fight it!")

After the secretary's testimony, the AID director would testify, followed by assistant secretaries and AID administrators at the bureau level—Near East and South Asia, Africa, Latin America, and East Asia—wherever aid was dispensed. If arms sales or direct grant military assistance were involved, the secretary of defense or his surrogates from the Pentagon would testify. Finally, knowledgeable or concerned private citizens, representatives of private organizations, or the public at large could give testimony.

When the weeks of hearings were concluded, we would then go into mark-up, where any section of the executive branch proposal could be (and often was) amended by any member of the committee, provided he or she received a majority of members voting. When I first arrived, mark-ups were carried out in "executive sessions" without the public or media in attendance. In my judgment, those meetings were businesslike and productive, allowing members to negotiate in relative privacy. After mark-up sessions were opened to the public, we had an increase in five-minute speeches intended for home or national consumption. The great pressure, then and now, was for more "openness," however, so the move was inevitable. (As any diplomat will confirm, the negotiating *process*, especially on complex issues, is more effective if carried out in private, after which the results can and should be debated in public.) The "open" mark-up procedure merely meant that the real negotiating would take place off the committee floor. I was never directly involved in the process, but I sat in on several hearings and helped with drafting amendments when called upon.

In 1971, the draft foreign aid legislation provided for financing part of the development assistance program with borrowed funds. Although Treasury borrowing had been used over several decades as a method of financing a number of government agencies and corporations, the so-called "backdoor spending" issue had arisen in 1961, during the Kennedy administration, and was threatening to do so again. Critics of the procedure objected to the tactic of bypassing the Senate and House Appropriation Committees.

My major contribution was a 1971 staff memorandum entitled "Treasury Borrowing and Foreign Aid—A Recapitulation."[1] The memorandum reviewed the history of this controversy and suggested some of the problems which would evidently lie ahead. (Harry Cromer, who had previously been exposed to the issue, helped me with the legislative history.) In particular, I concluded that in 1971 the "backdoor spending" tactic would be even less likely to succeed than in 1961, when it had failed. Because of diminished enthusiasm for foreign aid, as well as in other fields, Congress might not be in a mood to assign even modest additional discretionary powers to the executive branch. Any attempt by the executive branch to bypass the regular authorization and appropriations processes, therefore, would appear to be doomed from the start. As a method of financing, "backdoor spending" would represent little more than "old wine in a new bottle."

As I reread the text, I am impressed with the detailed information I seem to have obtained. It was hardly an earthshaking document, but I was heartened to learn at the time that the chief librarian of Stanford University had called our committee document room to complain that this "very important report" had *not* been forwarded to him in a timely fashion as requested. (To the best of my knowledge, no similar complaints were registered by House members' offices. My late wife always used to say that I was particularly articulate in discussing subjects I knew nothing about, since I was not inhibited by minor facts and details—and perhaps she was right.)

My principal legislative assignments originally involved the Peace Corps, as well as the Board for International Broadcasting, which funded Radio Free Europe (RFE) and Radio Liberty (RL). I also did some work on the State Department/USIA authorization bill, but did my best to shy away from this area, as I feared becoming deluged with requests from former colleagues and then being regarded by staff members as a conflict-of-interest liability. The "Chester Amendment," which I discuss below, was an exception.

By the 1970s the Peace Corps was a going concern and enjoyed a comfortable degree of majority support within the committee. I recall only one horrendous error. The committee's highly competent legislative counsel, who rarely made such mistakes, somehow cut in half the committee's increase in the authorization for Peace Corps volunteers' readjustment allowance following their overseas service. The parliamentarian, a House staff official who provided guidance to members on parliamentary procedure, found that one provision in the bill somehow negated another. We had to get Wayne Hays to take the bill back to the floor and ask for a "minor technical correction" by unanimous consent. The problem could have been embarrassing in the extreme, giving the impression that the committee did not really know what it was about. Fortunately, Hays had so much political clout that no one was inclined to challenge him as he mumbled the massive correction through by voice vote.

BOARD FOR INTERNATIONAL BROADCASTING (BIB)

The Board for International Broadcasting was a different challenge. For years after World War II and during the Cold War, the two radios had been staffed by East European and Russian émigrés and funded clandestinely by the CIA. Radio Free Europe broadcast to Eastern Europe and Radio Liberty to the Soviet Union.

After their cover was blown in the early 1970s, a presidential commission was appointed to look into the possibility of open and public funding for the radios, which many still believed served a useful national purpose. Although critics tended to dismiss the radios as "propaganda" operations, they served as surrogate news services providing the target countries with information and commentary denied them by their own governments. The millions of dollars spent by the communist regimes to jam the radios gave some indication of their value.

The commission, chaired by Dr. Milton Eisenhower, Ike's brother, eventually recommended establishing a public body, the Board for International Broadcasting. The board would receive regularly authorized and appropriated funds from Congress, allocate them to the radios, and perform certain limited oversight functions. The first board chairman was the late John Gronouski, former postmaster general in the Kennedy administration and ambassador to Poland under LBJ.

The first hearings I attended on the BIB authorization request turned into a total disaster: critics of the radios, mostly liberals who favored détente and "bridge-building" with Eastern Europe, considered the RFE/RL émigré staff to be made up of reactionaries and hardliners (for the most part they *were*, but the programs were not as provocative as alleged). Critics of RFE pointed in particular to the 1956 Hungarian Revolution as illustrative of how the radios tended to "incite" the local populace to revolt when the West was not prepared to back them by force of arms. In short, RFE was accused of misleading the rebels into their subsequent destruction. Our hearings confirmed that 99 percent of the broadcasts merely provided news of what was taking place and repeated the rebels' own publicized demands, all legitimate news. One independent expert who studied all broadcast tapes during the period in question said he could identify only two that might possibly be considered to have "provocative" overtones.

The small opposition group on the committee, led by Representative Ben Rosenthal of New York, was out to discredit the radios in any way it could. They asked a lot of far-out questions, for which I was unprepared, to put it mildly. The late John Baker, a Russian and East European expert from the State Department, tried to help, but we could never put our hands on the exact information required.

Roy Bullock was not pleased with my performance and let me know it: "You made us both look bad," he admonished, "and you need to make amends." I did so immediately by putting together a "Fact Book" filled with data on the origins, objectives, composition, funding requirements, and just about everything you ever wanted to know about RFE and RL. At the next hearing, one of the pro-BIB members (who probably hadn't read more than the first page himself) stood up and commended the staff for providing "such a full and informative document which ought to dispel all of the reservations expressed previously by the Gentleman from New York (Mr. Rosenthal)." It didn't, of course, but it silenced the critics for the time being and my reputation was salvaged in the process. From this experience I learned another important lesson: *Always overwhelm the committee members with more paper than they can possibly absorb at one sitting, but never expect them to read more than one page.* It is the impression of knowledge that counts, not necessarily the reality.

Chairman Morgan's difficulty with names was another problem, mostly out of my control. I knew we were in trouble when the witness list was submitted on behalf of RFE: Dr. Zbigniew Brzezinski, then of Columbia University; Aloysius Mazewski, president of the Polish-American Congress; and Dr. Ilgvar Spilners, president of the Baltic-American Alliance. With help from the Eastern European Bureau at State, I carefully spelled out each of the names phonetically, in large capital letters, in the chairman's briefing paper, but to no avail. What he managed to do with the Russian names he encountered can only be surmised. It was essentially a hopeless case.

THE "CHESTER AMENDMENT": THE INSIDE STORY

My brief fifteen minutes of fame came on the annual State Department authorization bill. As noted earlier, I tried to steer clear of State Department requests because of my Foreign Service background. However, when asked for advice, I suggested a change in one minor State Department retirement provision. The story relates less to me than to the Carter administration, the president himself, and the capricious way in which bills become law.

The Foreign Service Act, when first enacted in 1946, assumed that everyone eligible for retirement with a pension would have by then attained the grade of FS0-3.

A bottleneck developed, however, in promotion from class 4 to class 3: as a result, FSOs who had not gone above class 4 faced retirement without a pension. The amendment I proposed would merely qualify FSO-4s who had reached the age of fifty, had served twenty years or more, *and* were not in the low 5 or 10 percent of their class, for a minimal pension, as was the case for FSO-3s and above. I happened to know some talented officers at the 4-level who were being "time-in-graded," as it was called. At least one of them had been recommended for promotion by the selection board, but had been cut from the list for strictly budgetary reasons. My amendment could give the worthier losers a midlife break while they sought other employment.

Democratic Representative Dante Fascell of Florida, then chairman of the International Operations Subcommittee of the Foreign Affairs Committee, accepted the idea without giving it much thought, and the full committee approved it routinely. No one really understood or cared about the details when I was called upon for an oral explanation of the provision. Finally, when the bill reached the House floor, a representative of the State Department took Jack Brady aside and informed him that the president of the United States opposed the amendment. (The executive branch usually invoked the president's name in support of its positions.) "Too late," Jack responded. "He should have thought of that earlier; we have enough problems with this bill without amending *our own version*."

So the bill passed, including the provision that was to become known as the "Chester Amendment," since only a staff aide named Chester seemed to know what it was about. The next step was to go to conference with the Senate, which had also passed an authorization bill *without* the Chester Amendment. As we were walking over to the Senate Foreign Relations Committee for negotiations between Senate and House conferees, Dante Fascell, the floor manager of the House bill, observed rather offhandedly: "Chips, I have to tell you that we have fourteen major substantive differences with the Senate which we have to work out in some way; I'm afraid we will have to sacrifice your amendment in return for something more important." I had already assumed as much and accepted this judgment as unavoidable. As usual, the senators were much less familiar with the bill's provisions than were our members. The Senate conferees on this issue were under the leadership of the late John Sparkman of Alabama, who, as the relevant subcommittee chairman, had responsibility for the "Chester Amendment." He had a hard time staying awake. Senator Fulbright, the full committee chairman, sat next to him and prodded him from time to time as he dozed off.

When we reached a discussion of the Chester Amendment, Sparkman read into the record a letter from President Carter strongly objecting to the proposal, primarily for "precedent" reasons. The Office of Management and Budget had evidently convinced him that all of his plans for reorganizing the executive branch of government would be nullified if this amendment passed. This was a perfectly asinine assumption, but the president apparently swallowed it whole. "Mr. Chairman," Democratic Senator Claiborne Pell of Rhode Island began, "I also oppose this amendment because it sets the wrong precedent for the military..."

At this point our side jumped on him. Our members may not have known much about the amendment, but they did know that *that* interpretation was dead wrong. On the contrary, the military provisions were far more liberal than anything in the State Department bill, as a member of the armed forces could retire with twenty years' service at *any* age or *any* grade. "In that case," Pell retreated, "I withdraw my reservation." Sparkman looked around the room for someone from the executive branch to speak up. A representative of "H" (the congressional liaison bureau at State) stepped forward and said that although the president was opposed to the measure, the department understood and appreciated the action taken by the House. (In other words, the department favored the move, but had to defend the president's position, at least in lukewarm fashion.)

Finally, Senator Clifford Case of New Jersey, a Republican, spoke up as follows: "Mr. Chairman, I have just read this amendment for the first time, and it makes sense to me. I don't see any precedent problem as we can easily add report language to specify that this is *not* intended to be a future precedent but is merely a retrospective attempt to clear up a past injustice. I suggest that we recede, Mr. Chairman, and accept the amendment." And so the amendment was adopted, although, ironically, *our* side had been counting on its *defeat* for bargaining purposes.

At the time, it seemed almost frightening that the President of the United States should have been defeated in a head-to-head confrontation with an obscure staff aide named "Chester." I learned subsequently that President Carter *had* been personally involved in this process, as he never should have been, in my judgment. (Surely a chief executive has matters of more consequence to take up his time.) My old boss, Vic Dikeos (from EUR personnel days), was then serving as senior deputy assistant secretary of state for administration. One day, when the assistant secretary was out of town, Dikeos took a call from the White House. To his consternation, he suddenly recognized a familiar voice with a Georgia accent: "What are you folks doing to kill this amendment?" the president asked. "I can't even sleep at night worrying about it. OMB tells me it will ruin all of my future plans. . . ." or words to that effect. Vic was almost speechless (and realized only later that *I* was the original author of the amendment), but he promised to do what he could. It wasn't enough.

I often reflected on what Lyndon Johnson might have done under similar circumstances. One telephone call and the amendment would have been killed. Carter just did not have the rapport with or understanding of the Congress. Reagan, in contrast, would never have lost any sleep over the matter, as he would never have *heard* of it in the first place.

As it turned out, only four FSOs qualified for the amendment's provisions, although only *one* received any benefits (for a few months before he died). So much for the "adverse precedent."

RULES COMMITTEE

Once the Foreign Affairs Committee reported out any major legislation, the House Rules Committee had to grant a "rule" specifying debate time allotted to proponents and opponents of the measure before the bill could be scheduled for general debate and final passage on the House floor. A "closed" or "open" rule would also specify whether amendments would be permitted. Attempts to bypass the Rules Committee have rarely worked. Going to "Rules" was in effect the *sine qua non* for passage of legislation.

The Rules Committee is not like any other committee of the House. For one thing, only members of Congress are called there to testify before other members of Congress. There are no outside witnesses. Also, those who testify, sometimes for at least an hour and often longer, are usually senior committee or subcommittee chairmen and ranking minority members. All are traditionally intimidated to some extent by this august body, which acts collectively like an arrogant, if fraternal, inquisition.

In olden times, I was told by Doc Morgan, Rules Committee members had a real "hazing" tradition to reduce senior House barons to pleading supplicants. Such treatment was no longer in evidence by the 1970s, but the aura of authority still permeated the crowded hearing room in the Capitol. One of the great powers had been old Judge Howard Smith (Democrat of Virginia), who presided over Rules with an iron hand for decades. (His power was broken somewhat by Speaker Sam Rayburn, who "packed" the committee during the early days of the Kennedy administration to allow New Frontier legislation to move forward to a vote. "Mr. Sam," a formidable power in his own right, only barely won that particular vote.) Members were still hesitant to go on record in opposition to "Judge" Smith. In his heyday Judge Smith would let it be known that he had "gone fishin'" and closed up shop if he disapproved of a particular piece of legislation. Then when he returned he would cite the "press of business" and time considerations as excuses for inaction.

Judge Smith was eventually replaced by another octogenarian, William Colmer of Mississippi, who was almost a replica of the haughty Virginian. Other senior chairmen included such personalities as Ray Madden of Indiana and Claude Pepper of Florida, both of whom became, successively, the oldest members of the House. At some point along the way, the gavel fell to Richard Bolling of Missouri (a mere child in his early sixties), and the question was asked whether he was old enough to vote.

I personally disliked going to the Rules Committee above all other congressional duties. There was always some curveball question thrown at my chairman that I was supposed to be able to answer. "Doc, what was the ratio of administrative to program costs in the Peace Corps' Nigerian project last year?" The chairman would then look helplessly at me while I leafed through reams of briefing material, trying to find the answer and sweating in the process. Finally, the chairman would give up and throw out a figure like "Oh, I guess about 25 percent." Inevitably, we would later discover that that figure was off by at least 10–15 percentage points, but so what? Doc knew one thing for sure: the questioner most probably didn't know the answer either, and if he found out subsequently, it would be too late to matter. Leaving the Rules Committee behind was one of the great benefits of my later transfer from legislation to speechwriting.

One final note: Since my retirement, dramatic changes have occurred. As of 1999, the chairman of the Rules Committee is my friend David Dreier, Republican of California. At one point during my House incumbency, Dreier was the youngest member of the entire House, and his party was in the minority. To say that I never expected in my lifetime to witness such a development as the most junior Republican, David Dreier, becoming chairman of Rules is a bold understatement.

CHAPTER 14

Around the World with
Congressman Frelinghuysen

Together with my sponsor, Peter Frelinghuysen, I traveled on two Foreign Affairs Committee study missions to eleven countries on three continents in 1971 and 1974. CODEL Frelinghuysen 1971 went halfway around the world and back; CODEL Frelinghuysen 1974 went around the world completely. (CODEL is the acronym used for "congressional delegation" in communicating with Foreign Service posts abroad.)

Frelinghuysen was about to become the ranking minority member of the Foreign Affairs Committee and the main Republican proponent of the Nixon-Kissinger foreign policy in the House. Both trips thus involved meeting and consulting with foreign officials at the highest level. Both were topical, relevant, fascinating, *and* exhausting, especially when the staff member had to sit up until all hours of the early morning transcribing notes into sentences while they were still fresh in mind.

If you were interested in "fun and games" abroad, I would *not* recommend Peter Frelinghuysen as a traveling companion. There was probably no other member of either house of Congress more committed to foreign affairs and the learning process. He went to every meeting, conference, luncheon, or dinner the State

Department arranged for him, and then asked for more. The only night life consisted of dinners hosted by a chief of mission.

Aside from note-taking, I was also responsible for assisting the CODEL (namely Peter) in a variety of administrative capacities. Since I was both absentminded and less than competent in money matters, this was obviously not my forte. Peter used to observe good-naturedly that *he* was taking care of *me* most of the time rather than vice versa. Finally I was able to point out in my defense that at about midpoint on one of our global ventures, Peter had cumulatively lost or left behind his pajamas, a shirt, a belt, and a hat, while I still had all of my possessions. That was, the congressman countered, because I was constantly being reminded and assisted by my mentor. Well, he had a point there. I'm sure we were perceived by the U.S. diplomatic establishment abroad as the "odd couple": Peter was the precise detail man, while I was the vague one (often thinking about what I would finally include in our committee report). In any case, our association was a highly amicable one.

CONGRESSIONAL TRAVEL

Let me here digress to expound my deeply felt views, developed from both my executive branch and Hill experience, on congressional travel, probably the most controversial aspect of congressional service. From the time of columnist Drew Pearson and his successor, Jack Anderson, any member of Congress (or to a slightly lesser extent, a congressional staff member) who ventures abroad on official business has been automatically accused of embarking on a "junket." In recent years both the print and electronic media have focused increasing attention on this subject. Political candidates (always *before* they are elected to office) have found it difficult to avoid the temptation of attacking an incumbent for "wasting the taxpayers' money" by roaming the globe while allegedly relegating district concerns

PART I
INTRODUCTION

*John Chapman Chester
Sr., age 3, at the family
summer home on
Oconomowoc Lake,
Wisconsin
c. 1933*

*Age 17, dressed for the Oconomowoc Hunt—
founded by Milwaukee brewer Fred Pabst Sr.,
1947*

PART II
THE FOREIGN SERVICE

State Department A-100 course for new Foreign Service officers, Foreign Service Institute, Spring 1957. Author is in second row, fourth from right.

Oktoberfest, Munich, 1958—with wife Clara, son John, and Basset Hound Heathcliff. (The author was a veteran of five Oktoberfests in the 1950s).

LIFE *magazine (March 17, 1961) photo of Sargent*
Shriver and his original Peace Corps headquarters staff—
including "borrowees" from State Department and A.I.D.
Author is in center in front of pillar.

American Consulate General, Zagreb, Yugoslavia (now Croatia), 1964.
Front row prinicpals: USIS Director Neeley Turner (left), Consul General
Joseph Godson (second from right), and two Foreign Service inspectors.
Author is at left, second row,

Contrasting roles: (above) As consul and chief of Consular Section, American Consulate General, Zagreb; and (below) as a visitor to the family of Mara Mustac (the Chesters' Zagreb domestic) in her very poor farming village in rural Slavonia (the agricultural region of Croatia—not to be confused with Slovenia, which is a separate country). Author and son, John, are on the right; Heathcliff is in the center, next to Mara (kneeling).

Zagreb Consulate General, circa mid-1960s (below), and staff entrance (right).

Windy arrival in Blantyre, Malawi, 1969; new DCM is welcomed by boss, Ambassador Marshall P. Jones.

PART III
At Home in the House .

Photo: Ashit Mukherjee

Representative Peter Frelinghuysen visits camp for Bengali refugees near Calcutta, India, 1971, with U.S. Consul George Griffin (right) and author (behind congressman). Refugees in this camp enjoyed higher living standards than street people in Calcutta.

Photo: I. D. Beri

Meeting with India Foreign Minister Tikki Kaul (at right behind desk), who assures us no invasion of East Pakistan is contemplated. (It took place three weeks later). U.S. Ambassador Kenneth Keating is at far left beside Representative Frelinghuysen and author.

*Staff Study Mission to East Asia,
1972. Author and Korean baby on
plane between Seoul and Tokyo.*

*Motorcycle diplomacy:
inspection of Peace Corps in
Thailand, 1972.*

*Representative Frelinghuysen (right) and author (behind) arrive at
Islamabad airport in Pakistan, 1974—on fifth stop on round-the-world study
mission—greeted by U.S. Ambassador Henry Byroade (third from left).*

Staff Study Mission to West Africa, 1975. Author inspecting Peace Corps project in Sierra Leone.

Author in Ghana on 1975 Study Mission to West Africa.

Nigeria, 1975; same Study Mission: HFA staff investigative team of John H. Sullivan (second from left) and author (far right) with USAID mission director Bill Ford (far left) and AID officer Don Parker (second from right).

"Poet Laureate" immortalizes Foreign Affairs Committee Chairman Thomas E. ("Doc") Morgan at retirement party, November 1976. (left to right) Morgan, author, and Secretary of State Kissinger.

Photo: Dev O'Neill, K. Jewell

Photo: Dev O'Neill, K. Jewell

At Morgan retirement party (another view) (left to right) House Speaker Carl Albert, Majority Leader Thomas P. ("Tip") O'Neill, Representative Clement J. Zablocki (behind Doc Morgan), and "Poet Laureate" (at microphone).

Photo: K.Jewel

Semiannual exchange between delegations of the European Parliament and the U.S. Congress (US-EP), Washington, early 1980s. Foreign Affairs Committee Chairman Clement J. Zablocki is in center, with author, as usual, behind him, flanked by European delegation Chairman Zagari (right) and ranking Republican Larry Winn (left) .

Extended consultation with Dante B. Fascell, chairman of House Foreign Affairs Committee, at US-EP reception, about 1984.

"Take Back Your Mink" sung by author after emerging in drag from papier-maché cake at 50th birthday party for Bill Kendall, Adminstrative Assistant to Representative Frelinghuysen, 1970s.

Reprise performance at 59th birthday party for Foreign Affairs Committee Chief of Staff, John J. Brady, Jr. (lower left).

With Representative Eligio (Kika) de la Garza, Chairman, House Delegation, annual Mexico-U.S. Inteparliamentary Group meeting, Colorado Springs Colorado, 1986.

"Beauty and the Beast"—author flanked by Committee Budget and Fiscal specialist Shelly Livingston (left) and Elizabeth Daoust, Protocol (right) at Colorado Springs conference, 1986.

Author flanked by two leading Republican delegates to the Colorado Springs conference: Representative David Dreier (left) and Representative Robert Lagomarsino, both from California. (Note: Dreier was once the youngest Member of the House, but is now Chairman of the prestigious Rules Committee).

to secondary importance. This issue is all too easy to demagogue.

That there have been abuses in the system is un-questioned. In my own diplomatic career, I learned early of the strains that a visiting congressional delegation (of *any* size) can place on the time and resources of a U.S. post or mission. To many diplomats in the field, CODELS represent an occupational hazard, to be avoided to the extent possible. The objective tends to be to tie up the members with extensive official meet-ings (and social functions, where required) to keep them out of trouble until they can be offloaded onto another post.

Abusers of power and privilege among the 435 mem-bers of the House of Representatives are fully capable of placing unreasonable demands upon the hard-pressed and often unjustly disparaged Foreign Service. The U.S. Congress is, in fact, fully and accurately representative of American society in general: some crooks and pimps at one end of the scale, and some self-sacrificing and high-minded leaders at the other end. And just about everything in between.

Despite any and all of the above considerations, I remain to this day a firm proponent of congressional travel. In this respect, my career eventually came full circle. While an FSO abroad, I spent a good deal of my time as as a so-called (congressional) "control officer," assigned to handling most of the low-level details of a congressional visit. In the second half of my public ca-reer, I was the recipient of such services, either directly or indirectly. Thus I feel qualified to express an opin-ion which will undoubtedly be subject to challenge.

The education of a member of Congress in the for-eign policy field can only be successfully achieved *out-side* the United States. Foreign policy briefings or congressional hearings held in Washington just do not fulfill the same purpose. Only when legislators are placed in an acutal foreign environment and can view conditions at first hand, meet with foreign officials and opinion-makers, especially in fields of their particular interest or competence, can they approach an understanding of what the problems actually are and how U.S. diplomacy might begin to deal with them. (Even H. R. Gross might have benefited from travel abroad, although I grant that is a dubious proposition.) Above all, a "junketing" member of Congress is usually confronted for the first time with the complexity of the issues involved in modern diplomacy. I have witnessed substantial changes in general outlook, as well as in specific policy positions, as a consequence of a member's personal experience in a foreign land. In no way is this metamorphosis possible in Washington, where there are just too many other distractions.

A senior Foreign Service colleague once told me that he had once served in Iran as a control officer for a junior congressman named John F. Kennedy. At the end of his stay, the congressman observed philosophically that most foreign policy choices were not between ascertainably good and bad options but only between degrees of "bad." The trick was to adopt the *least* detrimental course of action under mostly unacceptable circumstances. That always struck me as an unusually perceptive observation.

In my judgment, the Foreign Service often misses the boat with congressional travel. *Most* members of Congress (admittedly not all) are interested in what is happening in country X and susceptible to persuasion, giving a chief of mission and his staff a rare opportunity to preach to a captive audience and present the State Department's case. The department's representatives ought to (and occasionally do) make the most of such rare occasions when they have a congressman's undivided attention. For there is nothing a member would rather say in House floor debate than "I know— I was there." This is really the only path toward enlightenment.

The end of the Cold War has intensified an obvious tendency on the part of U.S. politicians to focus on domestic problems and ignore what is happening in the rest of the world (and an "interdependent" world at that). The Clinton administration has seemingly encouraged this dangerous tendency, not so much by its foreign actions as by its attitudes and emphasis.

If the "American people" truly want to be represented by parochial, uninformed, and inevitably special interest–oriented members of Congress, then that is what they are likely to get with a cutoff of foreign travel.

CODEL FRELINGHUYSEN 1971 TO PAKISTAN, INDIA, AND GREECE

Normally, the Foreign Affairs Committee's venerable chairman, Dr. Morgan, would insist that CODELS consist of at least three members (including two Democrats and at least one Republican). Peter Frelinghuysen, however, was an exception: the chairman not only thought highly of him but must have sensed that an investment in his form of globetrotting would be highly productive. In 1971 and again in 1974, therefore, CODEL Frelinghuysen consisted exclusively of Peter and myself.

Pakistan

A major crisis appeared to be brewing in Pakistan in the spring of 1971. The country's eastern and western territories, separated by India, were about to come apart. West Pakistan seemed determined to hold onto its eastern sector, while the Bengalis of the east were equally dedicated to independence, under the leadership of Bengali hero Sheik Mujibor Rachman.

Because of fears of airline sabotage, security was extremely tight on Pakistan International Airlines, departing from Amsterdam for our first stop, Islamabad, Pakistan's capital. As we walked down the runway to the plane, a huge Dutchman enveloped us both in an embrace and began an extensive body search on the spot, smiling benevolently the whole time. The procedure was somewhat startling, especially for Peter, who was not used to having a stranger push his hat down over his eyes and put his hands into every available pocket. I guess this was the substitute of the day for the current security pass-through machines now in use at all airports. In any case, we had no real objection to the procedure, which we found reassuring.

Islamabad was a rather makeshift capital near the more authentically Pakistani city of Rawalpindi. On the outskirts of the city, on the direct route from the airport to Islamabad, a prominent sign in English outside a medical doctor's office seemed to warn all visitors what to expect! It read, to the best of my recollection:

Dr. Khan [a common surname in Pakistan]
Specialist for:
>   Heart disease
>   Piles
>   Venereal diseases
>   Hysteria

General Yahya Khan, who had come to power via military coup like many before and after him, was president. Our meetings with him and others were unmemorable, except that every Pakistani official we met tried to impress us with the importance of keeping both Pakistan intact and the military aid pipeline in operation. All of the problems in the east were ascribed to the hostile "meddling" of the Indians.

At our next stop, Dacca, the capital and largest city of East Pakistan, accompanied by a planeload of West Pakistan soldiers dressed in mufti, our arrival was less than auspicious. We had traveled by Pakistani aircraft on an overnight trip from Karachi around the horn of India, the only route a civilian aircraft could travel at that time, as India would not permit any crossing of its airspace. Tensions were clearly mounting in Dacca. The looks we received from the local populace were at best quizzical. Wherever we went from that moment on was by car, preceded and followed by a truckful of West

Pakistan soldiers armed with Sten guns. (I remarked to Peter that we were perfect targets from the *side,* and would have had more real security if we had driven around in an old unmarked Volkswagen.)

The tension in Dacca was very high. At dinner one night, the military governor of East Pakistan tried to sound optimistic about the clearly deteriorating situation. His "mansion" was practically devoid of people, except for West Pakistan guards in the corridors. (He was one of the first people arrested after the Indian invasion. I saw his mournful photo, taken in an internment camp, in a Western newspaper just a few days after the change in government and the resulting creation of the nation of Bangladesh.) It was only a matter of time, we decided, before something drastic was bound to happen.

At the time East Pakistan was under water for about half the year. One day we flew down to the port city of Chittagong, most of the way over flooded fields. In addition to floods, periodic typhoons managed to clean out remaining areas along the coast. The climate, both in Dacca and Chittagong, is insufferable all the time: like the worst hazy, hot, and humid day of the Washington summer. The Bengalis and the tribes of West Pakistan seemed to have only one thing in common—they were all Muslims. The westerners had the reputation of making good soldiers, the Bengalis good poets.

India

Our first stop in India was Calcutta, where much of the population of East Pakistan had taken refuge. Refugee camps were extensive and full, and pressure on India to act was steadily increasing. That many of the refugees in the camps we visited were living in better conditions than many of the street people of Calcutta added to local tensions.

Calcutta, as many writers have noted, is indeed a city of great contrasts, from the traditional "black hole" to palaces of incredible opulence. Except for a large park in the center of the city known as the "lung" of Calcutta, everything literally stinks. People dry cow dung by plastering it against the wall, then burn it for cooking purposes, in about 90 degree heat and accompanying humidity. As a result, a visitor sweats profusely and breathes only with difficulty. The beauty of the place, nonetheless, was quite staggering. Peter and I stayed in the handsome residence of U.S. Consul General Herbert Gordon (my old boss in Biographic Information in the State Department). At a dinner hosted by the consul and Mrs. Gordon in Peter's honor, one of the guests, a Sikh, was one of India's highest-ranking generals, in command of all Indian troops in the eastern region. A classmate of his at the British military academy at Sandhurst had been Pakistan president Yahya Khan, whom he considered "a very good soldier, but a poor politician." Speaking gloomily of the situation in East Bengal, the general hinted ominously of a "breaking point" in the near future. When Peter pressed him repeatedly on this point, the general mentioned military action in three weeks, if no solution to the problem had been found by then.

The general turned out to be the most forthright Indian we met on the visit. The foreign minister in New Delhi later assured us—and Prime Minister Indira Gandhi also told President Nixon on a state visit to Washington—that there was no timetable or plan for an invasion. However, after I had returned to Washington and picked up the *Washington Post*, almost three weeks to the day, there on the front page was a photo of the general, unmistakable in his turban, seated on a tank that had just led the armored forces into the heart of downtown Dacca. The invasion was already complete and successful, and the general, it turned out, was right on target with the truth.

Calcutta was chronically plagued by some form of unrest. Revolutionary groups, mostly of the left, sprang up from time to time and were eventually suppressed. And life went on. During our stay there we met with the appointed governor of West Bengal in his opulent palace. Elected governors were sometimes replaced by central government appointees, usually when trouble was afoot, with some sort of military action contemplated. I vaguely recall that the governor appeared to be somewhat tense. The German consul general had been assassinated about a week prior to our arrival as his car was held up in a traffic jam. (He was shot from the side, despite security troops fore and aft, so my apprehensions in Dacca had not been unreasonable.) The subsequent invasion of East Pakistan, however, served to upstage these local events before very long.

Our last stop on the subcontinent was New Delhi, the Indian capital, where we were guests of Peter's former colleague and close friend, Ambassador Kenneth Keating (a former Republican congressman and senator from New York). Keating was not only a cordial host, but a delightful gentleman with an infectious sense of humor. That quality, I soon discovered, was an important prerequisite for dealing with Indian officialdom.

Just to give us a firsthand exposure to what he was up against, Keating took us to an official meeting with the Indian foreign minister, Tikki Kaul, a thoroughly disagreeable individual. He seemed to combine all of the traits Americans in particular find offensive. He was arrogant almost to the point of being blatantly rude and tended to "talk down" to Americans the way an autocratic schoolmaster might lecture to a callow first-year student. He reminded me of the late Krishna Menon, India's longtime ambassador to the United Nations, who had a unique genius for arousing hostility among Western audiences.[1]

The foreign minister was disdainfully critical of Pakistan's postindependence "aggression" toward India, especially the current government's inept treatment of its eastern province, which was causing India no end of undeserved problems. U.S. economic and military aid to Pakistan, he added, further complicated matters.

Peter, however, was able to separate policy considerations from personalities. Ultimately, to my surprise, he modified his position on the India-Pakistan controversy after long and detailed discussions on this subject with both Indian and U.S. officials. In his press statement at the time, he indicated that the amount of military supplies still going to Pakistan via the traditional "pipeline" was so marginal that it was not really that vital to Pakistan, while the supply operation "bedeviled" (his exact word) our relations with India disproportionately. I decided on reflection that this unexpected announcement was a characteristic attempt of his to bend over backward, putting personal impressions aside and promoting a course of action he believed in the overall interest of the United States. That we both found the Pakistani officials more congenial than the Indians was strictly secondary.

"The Athens Affair"

Until now everything had gone rather smoothly and the main purpose of our trip—to review and evaluate the situation in South Asia—had been successfully accomplished. The return stopover in Athens, however, was a different story. Just before we stepped onto the plane in New Delhi, the embassy control officer handed me a disturbing telegram from Athens that infuriated the congressman. Our long-held reservations at the Hotel Grande Bretagne had been canceled owing to "circumstances beyond the embassy's control." The embassy blamed the hotel, which had allegedly "overbooked"; it all had something to do with Vice President Spiro Agnew's impending official visit to Greece the following week. Instead we were to stay in "first class" facilities in the port city of Piraeus, somewhat distant from the capital's center. Peter was not at all pleased with this last-minute change and the more he mulled over it, the more it seemed like an affront.

This was the period when Greece was ruled by a group of second-rate colonels who had come to power in a highly unpopular military coup. Sentiment among Greek-American organizations, strongly reflected in

Congress, was distinctly hostile to the military government. There was pressure within the Foreign Affairs Committee to cut off relations with the colonels and subject the government to severe sanctions. Peter was definitely in the minority of those (on either side of the aisle) who supported the administration's policy, namely, to maintain relations with the military government and try to influence it in the right direction. Peter did not think much of the colonels either, but he believed, as always, in maintaining contact with the new leaders. (This outlook was consistent with Peter's view of the United Nations at a time when it was less than popular with the American public. We should pay our dues and fight our battles *within* the organization, he always advocated, not merely kibitz from the outside.)

The Department of State, especially in the form of the congressionally astute assistant secretary for Near Eastern affairs, Joseph Sisco, recognized and appreciated Peter's position on this issue and sent instructions to Athens to afford CODEL Frelinghuysen every courtesy, emphasizing the inherent wisdom of the congressman's approach. The message, for some unknown reason, did not quite get through. The U.S. ambassador and chief implementer of the administration's unpopular policy was the late Henry Tasca, a career minister in the Foreign Service at the time. The qualities that helped him reach that exalted rank were never quite discernible to the casual observer. In fact, his lack of just plain common sense was truly appalling. The physical arrangements for our visit were only part of the problem, but they managed to set the tone for subsequent disaster.

We arrived at the Athens airport at approximately 2:00 A.M. and were met by a Greek driver from the embassy. Peter started to upbraid him for all the embassy's sins until it became apparent that he spoke no English. He only had orders to take us to our "luxurious" first class quarters, which turned out to be a kind of motel complex with individual cabins located in the middle of nowhere.

"Don't get comfortable," Peter told me as we checked into our cabin. "We are definitely not staying *here!*"

The next morning our control officer arrived. He turned out to be an innocent young third secretary on his first assignment abroad. He had never before been assigned to a CODEL and was substituting for the administrative officer, who allegedly had a scheduling conflict. (The administrative officer, we learned in due course, had fouled up our reservations in the first place.) "I think your reservations at the Grande Bretagne were in place for some weeks," our young escort naively said, "until they gave your rooms to some Secret Service agents." At that point I knew we were in for trouble.

After one heated telephone call to the ambassador's office, we were transferred to the "presidential suite" on top of the Athens Hilton. This facility included several bedrooms, kitchen, large dining room and living room and clearly exceeded our needs. The vice president and his party were to stay in those quarters, it turned out, the following week. When I left to stay with my Foreign Service friends, Douglas and Debbie Hartley, Peter requested a more modest single room. He was instantly accommodated with a small cabana next to the noisy swimming pool.

That evening we called on the ambassador, who was to give us a political briefing over cocktails. The only other guest was a Greek-American tycoon named Tom Pappas (also an eminent Republican fund-raiser). Pappas was not only a friend and adviser of the ambassador. He was also known to have influence with the colonels. It was said that he owned most of the Esso (now Exxon) stations in Greece and used his political connections to promote his business. Though this last was undoubtedly accurate, he was probably not the sinister influence and behind-the-scenes decision-maker that some of the government's opponents alleged. He was clearly a multimillionaire who didn't hesitate to throw his weight around, both in Greece and the United States.

Unlike the ambassador, Pappas seemed to know all about Peter, claiming to have met him on numerous occasions. (Peter, on the other hand, had only a vague recollection of the name.) During the briefing, Pappas did most of the talking, providing the standard rationale for a continued relationship with, if not active support for, the military government. At least he could articulate a position, which was altogether lacking on the part of the president's personal envoy. Also unlike the ambassador, Pappas was immediately responsive to our material needs. "Why didn't you let *me* know you were coming?" he inquired with a reproachful glance at the ambassador. "I keep a VIP suite at the Grand Bretagne Hotel which is always at your disposal." Mr. Pappas apparently could have solved all of our logistical problems in the first place if only the embassy had had the presence of mind to give him a call. Now he insisted that Peter move to his suite in the Grand Bretagne.

Since Peter was getting little sleep in the cabana by the swimming pool, he readily accepted this invitation (for only the last night, as it turned out). When he went to pay his account at the Hilton, he was informed by the cashier that everything had been taken care of by Mr. Pappas. Peter strongly objected to this procedure and insisted on paying his own bill. The cashier responded that he could not accept any such payment, as Mr. Pappas would have him fired. By this time we were surrounded by embassy officers, including Doug Hartley and George Warren, among others, and were creating a notable scene in the main lobby.[2] Finally it was agreed that Peter would be informed of the total charges and reimburse Mr. Pappas by check after his return to the United States. Peter followed up with a check and accompanying letter of appreciation, which was kept meticulously on file. Pappas never cashed the check.

Eventually, some weeks after our return to Washington, Peter received a letter of apology from Ambassador Tasca, which I was told was requested by

Assistant Secretary Sisco. The best feature of our Greek sojourn was that it only lasted a couple of days and was finally over.

CODEL FRELINGHUYSEN 1974

My trip with Peter from February 7 to March 3, 1974, turned out to be the longest uninterrupted world tour in my fifteen years with the Foreign Affairs Committee. Our itinerary included Greece, Egypt, Israel, Iran, Pakistan, Afghanistan, India, and Vietnam. Again we were the sole participants. By this time, Peter Frelinghuysen was the ranking minority member of the committee and *the* leading Republican spokesman for the Nixon administration's foreign policy in the House of Representatives. The Department of State took his proposed itinerary quite seriously and sent specific instructions to the field to have the congressman meet with top officials all along the way.

At least three of our meetings were of historic proportions. We were the first congressional group to meet with President Anwar Sadat of Egypt following the Yom Kippur War. We also interviewed Mohammad Daoud, the prime minister and chief of state of Afghanistan, and President Nguyen Van Thieu of South Vietnam, both of whom left office (in different ways) approximately a year after our visits. We were certainly one of the last CODELS, if not *the* last, to have extensive talks with either of these gentlemen.

During our trip the world price of oil rose dramatically. For a brief period OPEC (the Organization of Petroleum Exporting Countries) was riding high, while gas lines formed, especially in the northeastern United States. Our fact-finding mission was perhaps most memorable and striking in that every foreign official we met expressed genuine respect and admiration (not necessarily approval) for the Nixon-Kissinger concept of Realpolitik. Our interlocutors seemed to think that Nixon and Kissinger had a world view and a "master plan," indicating that they knew what they were about. Ironically, this sense of confidence by foreign leaders (unequaled, I dare say, in administrations that preceded and followed Nixon) seemed to flourish at the very time the president's position was beginning to deteriorate domestically. We subsequently learned that even Mrs. Gandhi, who was known to dislike Nixon intensely, shared this perception. Whether the beleaguered administration actually had such a plan is debatable.

Soon after we boarded our plane for Athens, our first stop, Peter described in somewhat gloomy terms a recent White House meeting he had attended with the president and a number of key Republicans from both houses of Congress. Nixon, Peter thought, did not have a realistic grasp of his situation, and his distracted manner in responding to questions was cause for concern. Barry Goldwater summed up the sentiment of the meeting when he asked: "Mr. President, what we all want to know about Watergate is, when is the 150th shoe going to drop?" or words to that effect.

Greece

This time our very brief stopover was both uneventful and unmemorable. Peter had become increasingly disillusioned about even the basic competence of the military regime and tended to dismiss the colonels' pleadings as hopeless. His outlook was aptly summarized in a newsletter he sent to his constituents the following summer, after the junta had fallen owing to a notorious miscalculation over Cyprus:

> The course of events in Greece was not totally surprising to me. I had forewarned my colleagues, following a visit to Greece early this year, of the lackluster quality of the military junta and the increasing instability of the Greek government. At that time, there were ominous signs of uneasiness and political unrest. It was apparent to me that the mood of the military regime had deteriorated to one of uncertainty and drift.

... I also reported, in a statement to the House on April 3, that the alienation of Greek citizens from their government had been spreading, not only among students and intellectuals, as in the past, but also among the previously quiescent middle class, a group whose support is generally essential to the efficacy of any government.

Listening to the colonels at this stage in our travels seemed, and turned out to be, an exercise in futility. We went through the motions and then flew off to Cairo.

Egypt

Our sojourn here of several days proved to be the highlight of our entire study mission. It began inauspiciously when the desk clerk at the hotel could not find any record of Peter's reservation, despite the fact that our embassy control officer insisted the reservation had been made and confirmed "*weeks ago.*" It turned out that the reservation had been filed not under F for Frelinghuysen, but under C for Congressman. Ah, well. Minor mixup.

The embassy was technically the U.S. Interests Section of the Swiss Embassy and was headed by Hermann Eilts, a career FSO. (Eilts was soon to become our fully accredited ambassador following resumption of U.S.-Egyptian relations, which Nasser had broken after the 1967 war.) Our first two days were devoted to interviews with such ranking Egyptian officials as the foreign minister, the former foreign minister (then secretary general of the Arab League), and the deputy speaker of the People's Assembly. President Sadat, we were told, was totally preoccupied with the state visit of the president of Sudan and was unfortunately unavailable.

On the eve of our departure for Israel, where Kenneth Keating, now ambassador there, was planning an elaborate dinner in Peter's honor, Peter received a personal telephone call from President Sadat. After apologizing for having been incommunicado for several days, Sadat requested a meeting the following day at

Gianolis, a sort of "summer White House," formerly the estate of a Greek landowner and agricultural developer. Sadat was insistent and said it was a matter of some urgency. Despite all the inconvenience this would cause, Peter decided he had no alternative but to accept. Even Ken Keating, who saw his dinner party going up in flames, agreed that a one-day change in plans was a virtual necessity.

The next morning we started off in Eilts's limousine, headed by instruction for one of King Farouk's former palaces in Alexandria. There we sat looking over the lovely formal gardens and surrounding woods, wondering what would come next. We must have killed several hours there until finally four motorcycle "outriders" appeared. These official escorts were to guide us across the vast desert to the presidential palace, which was strictly an isolated oasis.

For a time, all went well until suddenly the motorcyclists disappeared over a sand dune and were lost from sight—forever, as it turned out. The driver seemed not to know the way and Hermann Eilts looked disturbed, to put it mildly. He had some kind of walkie-talkie in the car which he tried to no avail. I wondered at this point whether we were just lost or being set up for an act of sabotage. Fortunately, the driver's basic instincts saved the day and after driving "blind" for another hour on a desert road with no signs, we finally lucked into the estate. Whatever happened to our escorts was never explained, but we had reached our destination, even if by accident.

The meeting was a memorable one—four participants in a small room. I was the only note-taker. Peter began the interview by asking the president if his "aide" could take notes. "By all means," Sadat responded. "I hope he will take good ones." That the president brought no such aide of his own was quite surprising. Apparently, according to Eilts, he considered this a gesture of trust.

Sadat was impressive in this intimate setting. He spoke softly, but with a rich mellifluous—almost musical—

voice, which he would raise for emphasis and lower for dramatic effect. Unlike his public appearances on television, which I had watched on several occasions, here he had a gripping hold on his audience, who listened intently to his every word. Following is the gist of his remarks.

Unlike anything in the past twenty-six years (since the establishment of Israel in 1948), the United States and Egypt had begun a new relationship following the October 1973 war that could really help solve problems. The decent fight put up by the Egyptians in October 1973 made progress toward peace possible. Sadat trusted Kissinger in particular as a competent friend, and favored lifting the Arab boycott of Israel, even acting unilaterally if the other Arabs did not go along. The Soviets would likely attempt to obstruct lifting the boycott, since they saw Egyptian-American rapprochement as a threat to their interests in the Mideast. Nevertheless they had lost 80 percent of their influence there. He looked forward to full resumption of diplomatic relations with the United States, which would be a "severe blow" for the Soviets. He understood that if Israel moved too fast in improving relations with Egypt, that could cause domestic political problems in Israel. In answer to Frelinghuysen's query as to how Congress could help, Sadat pointed a finger at him and said with feeling: *Support Nixon.* (At this, Peter rose almost two feet in the air. It must have been a long time since he had heard such words in a domestic context. "Indeed, Mr. President," he responded. "I will do my best.")

This was an extraordinary interview, especially in the context of early February 1974, just about three months after the conclusion of Arab-Israeli hostilities. While Congress had generally been informed of some improvement in U.S.-Egyptian relations, none of us had any idea of the extent. Nixon and Kissinger had managed to keep this development almost as secret as the China venture. Peter was evidently chosen as the first congressional recipient of this information, probably for two reasons: (1) he was a senior and presumably influential member of the Republican party in the House; and (2) some years back, when Sadat was merely speaker of the Egyptian Parliament, he had visited Washington on a USIA-sponsored "leader grant." A State Department officer escorted him on a visit to Capitol Hill to meet a representative group of members from the Committee on Foreign Affairs. The timing turned out to be disastrous, as a major floor debate took precedence and no one showed up for the meeting, with one exception: the Honorable Peter Frelinghuysen. Even if Peter had only a vague recollection of the incident, the then-speaker and current president of Egypt had not forgotten.

At the end of the interview we were at pains to get to the Cairo airport as soon as possible, and the president granted us permission to use the fortified direct route (with a pill box every few yards) along the Suez Canal. We were the first Westerners to receive such permission following the October war.

Israel

We finally arrived in Tel Aviv on February 13, exactly one day late. Ambassador Keating did his best under the circumstances to reschedule his dinner party, but the prime minister could not attend, and a number of cabinet ministers had to regret. Shimon Peres was the ranking official guest. Peter and I stayed once again at the ambassador's residence, together with Senator Harry Byrd Jr.

The most vivid and impressive aspect of our Israeli sojourn was our one-day visit to the Golan Heights, just above the Sea of Galilee. A tour of this area was standard fare for visiting members of Congress, and for good reason. One really had to see the topography of the area, where before the October War Syrian guns had been pointed down at Israel, to understand its strategic importance for Israel. An embassy political officer and the embassy's army attaché, a ranking Israeli foreign ministry official (their former consul general in San Francisco), and an Israeli army lieutenant accompanied us. The latter may have been the lowest-ranking member of our entourage, but he was clearly the most articulate Israeli, in charge of our "education." Rank, we soon learned, meant very little in the Israeli context, especially among reservists. The lieutenant was evidently an important business leader in civilian life, merely fulfilling his temporary active duty obligation.

The "heights" consisted of a fortified mountain plateau, which clearly loomed large as a security control point for Israel. From the highest elevation, we looked down upon a field littered with destroyed Syrian tanks, apparently left in place for didactic purposes. One could not view this scene without recognizing its importance in the defense of Israel. The following, drawn from our CODEL report, illustrates our impression.

> As one flies over the far side of the Sea of Galilee and proceeds up the Golan foothills, which prior to the 1967 war were dominated by the Syrians, the vulnerability of the Israeli kibbutzim and agricultural settlements in the bottom-land area to hostile sniping and shelling becomes immediately apparent.
>
> This impression is intensified when one passes over the summit and inspects an Israeli fortification on the former Syrian side of the Heights, overlooking an expansive Hermonite Valley, which only three months earlier had been the scene of heavy fighting.[3]

What I had not realized up to this point was how close Israel had come to being overrun by Syrian tanks during the early days of the war. The U.S. army attaché, who had personally observed much of the ground action on the Syrian front, gave us a firsthand account. The Syrians had launched a well-planned and coordinated offensive and made an important breakthrough. If sustained, the Syrian attack could have led them, without serious opposition, deep into Israeli territory. (If led by a General George Patton, the Syrians might have made it all the way to Tel Aviv.) As it turned out, however, the Syrian infantry and logistical support troops lagged far behind, forcing a temporary halt in the tank offensive to allow these forces to catch up. This enabled the Israelis to deploy small numbers of tanks in a holding action, until Israeli reserves were assembled to contain and then counterattack to within twenty-five miles of Damascus.

The Syrians lost 250 tanks (others withdrew), while the Israelis lost 50 of their 70. Tank strength in the overall conflict between the two sides was similarly disproportionate: 5,100 Egyptian, Syrian, Iraqi, and Jordanian tanks arrayed against 2,100 Israeli tanks. (By comparison, the Germans deployed 3,200 tanks against the Russians at Stalingrad in June 1941.)

In addition, Arab antiaircraft missile effectiveness prevented close-in air support for Israeli ground forces during the entire war, except for the last two to three days on the Egyptian front in the Sinai *after* the Israelis overran and destroyed missile sites on the west bank of the Suez Canal.

These facts and figures, together with an on-site inspection of the Golan Heights and the Hermonite Valley, would understandably give pause to an Israeli, as it did to us. While there was little justification for the manner in which Prime Minister Menachem Begin later virtually annexed the Golan into Israeli territory, Israeli concerns over their security in that area were real and legitimate. That was the conclusion our visit was designed to draw—and in that respect it was successful.

What impressed me the most about Israel was the apparent kibbutz-like "team spirit" of the population and its willingness, even enthusiasm, to undertake relatively menial work for the good of the nation. (This general impression may be less valid in the late 1990s, as Israeli society has become polarized and divided between religious hard-liners and secular peace advocates.) One example of that spirit was the ambassador's valet, an Israeli graduate student working on his Ph.D who performed his valet duties willingly and with satisfaction. Additionally, Peter gave me a day off during our stay to allow me to visit Jerusalem and Bethlehem, while he met with the usual government officials on his own. I ended up taking a taxi from Tel Aviv to Jerusalem with a driver who evidently knew every biblical and historic monument along the way and was an expert guide. He later told me that he had been a full professor of history at the university in Bucharest, Romania. Despite his former high standing in the academic world, he left no doubt at all that he felt far more satisfied and rewarded driving a taxi in Israel. I found this type of outlook both pervasive and refreshing. Its loss would be a tragedy for the Israeli body politic.

Iran

Our stay in Tehran was somewhat disappointing because Shah Mohammed Reza Pahlavi was out of the country during our entire visit. Comments made by our ambassador, Richard Helms, nonetheless provided an interesting window into U.S.-Iranian relations.

Perhaps our most substantive meeting was with the Cornell-trained finance minister, Jamshid Amuzegar, who was later to become Iran's oil minister. As noted earlier, this was the period of dramatic oil price increases worldwide. Iran at this juncture was looking forward to a $16 billion dollar oil windfall. Of that amount, $12 billion was to be allocated to domestic development, with $4 billion for investment abroad and/or foreign aid. Amuzegar's primary challenge seemed to be how to spend these latter funds wisely and effectively.

A number of alternatives had already been ruled out, namely: (1) deposits in a bank or banks, because of the risk of dollar devaluation; (2) investment in industrial countries, because of possible nationalization; or (3) land purchases, for example, in Arizona, because these would force real estate prices up, making future investment more costly. Instead Iran proposed to increase contributions to the International Monetary Fund and the World Bank, to improve international liquidity and funding for lending purposes, and provide *bilateral* aid to such countries as Jordan, Tunisia, Morocco, Pakistan, and India. This bilateral aid would be in loans, not grants. The U.S. grant-in-aid principle was unwise over the long term, Amuzegar felt, as it generated feelings of jealousy and resentment in recipient nations: "Never give something for nothing."

Above all, Amuzegar defended recent Iranian oil price increases, which he said more accurately reflected international market conditions and would have the beneficial effect of moving the Western industrialized countries in the direction of self-sufficiency based on developing alternative sources of energy. Ambassador Helms, a former CIA director who had developed very strong ties with the leaders in the shah's government over the years, explained this theme in detail.

The shah, Helms pointed out during our background briefing at his handsome residence, originally adhered to a position that oil prices should remain relatively stable and *low*. The rationale was that Iran needed food imports and manufactured goods for industrial development and did not want prices of these imports to rise as a result of oil increases. In the past year, however, the prices of imports had risen dramatically, particularly wheat, soybeans, and vegetable oil. This was a tremendous shock for the Iranian economy and led them to rethink oil-pricing policy. Faced with a large increase in import prices, Iranians suddenly discovered that oil prices did *not* reflect then-current market conditions. A six-months experiment showed that the market price for crude oil could reach $17.35/barrel, compared with the previous price of $4.00/barrel. In just six months, Iran was to realize $1.5 billion on oil sales; under competitive market conditions the higher price still proved profitable for the buyer. This discovery changed the entire picture for oil-producing countries: *one* price increase agreement with *one* producer set the pattern for the others.

For the future, the shah (whose oil policy arguments, Helms emphasized, had invariably proved "right" in the past) saw the future of Iran not as a source of crude oil but as a producer of petroleum and petrochemical products. The shah was opposed to burning oil for heating, for instance. Oil, he felt, should be used for more productive and economical purposes. Petrochemical exports had a far greater potential than crude oil exports and were eight times more remunerative. The petrochemical industry in Europe and the United States, he understood, was prepared to make substantial investments in developing this capacity. According to this theory, therefore, the shah needed to raise crude oil prices to provide an economic incentive for alternative development (shale oil or coal liquefaction, for example). In effect, the Iranian government was interested in *discouraging* U.S. oil consumption so that the shah could concentrate on developing a domestic petrochemical industry while Iran's 65 billion barrels of oil reserves were still available for exploitation.

Despite Helms's superficially persuasive presentation of the shah's case, the shah's determination to bring Iran into the twentieth century via the country's most apparent economic asset, oil, was doomed to failure. His expansive plans, which included a massive land reform and distribution program affecting the mullahs, among other large landholders, and the "liberation" of women, were all more than Islamic fundamentalism could tolerate. As former protocol chief Marion Smoak once observed: "Perhaps if the Shah had lived twice as long and moved half as fast, he might have seen his expectations for Iranian development reach fruition." (Would that our differences with Iran over oil-pricing policies were the major problem today. The Western world would gladly pay the 1974 prices.)

Upon our departure at the Tehran airport, the prime minister presented Peter and me each with a large tin of Iranian caviar. As someone who could easily eat caviar like mashed potatoes, I remember this act of generosity with enormous longing and appreciation. Alas, we decided that we could never get these precious items through South Asia and the Far East before they spoiled, so we reluctantly presented them to our ambassador in Pakistan, our next stop. Needless to say, he was only too happy to accept. Now that the Caspian Sea has become polluted, according to current news accounts, I wonder how much of this treasure is left.

Pakistan

Our host in Pakistan was Ambassador Henry Byroade, an unusual general-turned-diplomat, who described with much gusto his colorful post–World War II career in China. At one point he had even ferried Chou en-Lai around in his plane. Eventually he was to become envoy to the Philippines, having already served in South Africa and Iran. Because of his military background, he got along famously with Pakistan army leaders, a distinct plus.

I did not attend Peter's meetings with Zulfikar Ali Bhutto, then prime minister. Bhutto had to contend with many old and new problems—establishing diplomatic relations with Bangladesh, delayed because of the fate of some 195 POWs from Pakistan held in Dacca; devastation caused by recent floods; oil price increases (which affected Pakistan less than India); and problems with neighboring Afghanistan, believed to have aggressive designs on Pakistan's Pushtu-inhabited territory. Above all, Bhutto wanted a resumption of military aid to mollify his army, even though he was personally more concerned with economic development. (His worries about his army were well-founded, as that institution eventually deposed and hanged him.)

We spent one night in Lahore, once considered the nation's likely capital city, in the principal officer's lavish residence, which had been prepared for an American ambassador. Our final stop was in Peshawar in the north, where authentic-looking tribesmen of various ethnic backgrounds mixed with heavily veiled women. The scene resembled something out of an old British film about colonial conquest. The central marketplace, in particular, had evidently seen little change in a hundred years.

Afghanistan

We then headed north by car over the Khyber Pass to Kabul, Afghanistan, a journey which proved to be both memorable and adventurous. This landmark of the former British Empire has many historic and some romantic connotations. Its raison d'être has not changed very much over the centuries. Because it marks the border between Pakistan and Afghanistan, the main industry is and always has been smuggling.

At first glance, one was impressed that border-crossers in either direction had little else in mind. In 1974 the principal traffic consisted of large old beaten-up American cars of 1950s vintage, back when fins were in style. The cars were filled with goods and people, mostly bandits considered highly dangerous. People traveling toward the border from either direction were warned not to stop along the roadside for any reason at all, as they would almost surely be held up at best and murdered at worst. The smuggling, not at all subtle, relied on a blatant modus operandi: the rattletrap vehicles, upon approaching the customs shed and checkpoint on the only road leading through the pass, would simply detour into a field behind the shed and then reappear on the road again on the other side of the border. We watched several cars perform this exercise with no interference from the authorities. About a week before our arrival there, a customs official who stopped a car had been shot dead for his pains. The entirely outmanned customs forces had evidently gotten the message *not* to interfere with the activities of the "mob."

Peter and I traveled in two separate cars, staffed with armed guards sent down from Kabul to fetch us in Peshawar. I was in the first car, apparently as a kind of advance party and buffer for the dignitary behind me.

We moved rapidly, even passing cars filled with desperadoes who cast hostile glances in our direction. We stopped only momentarily at the customs checkpoint, where we were waved through. There seemed to be a general recognition on all sides that dillydallying around could prove hazardous to one's health.

After we had driven about thirty minutes into Afghanistan, what looked like a full harem of women, all clad in colorful garments, some even carrying baskets on their heads, appeared along the side of the road. They were followed by a single man with a whip who appeared to be in charge of the ensemble. As we approached, I rolled down the window to catch this scene on camera. To my shocked surprise, our car caught something else: ROCKS. Each of the women reached under her long skirt, pulled out pieces of stone and hurled them at us with considerable force. Fortunately, only a few projectiles landed on the car. By the time Peter's car passed the group, a few more rocks reached their mark, even though no one in that vehicle had tried to take any photos. Apparently, the ladies did not wish to be immortalized on film, and I quickly got the message.

The women's reaction seemed to be quite spontaneous, as the man with the whip made no overt attempt to incite them (or to stop them). Either he had them well-trained or they acted entirely on their own. No one in the car seemed to know. One of our local security guards said it was not at all clear that my prominent camera was the problem: the ladies may have acted out of feelings of general hostility towards strangers. In any case, they were not mollified by my smile and friendly wave. As I have learned over a lifetime of dealing with difficult women, you can't win them all. Fortunately, our cars were not badly damaged, and we never slowed down until we reached the outskirts of Kabul.

While we only spent one day and two nights in that relatively primitive capital city, we managed to have extensive meetings with leading Afghan officials, all of whom stressed the need for Western economic aid for the development of what can only be described as a backward nation. Since the bloodless coup of July 1973, Afghanistan had been in a period of "transition," to put it mildly. At the time of our visit the man firmly in charge was Mohammad Daoud, prime minister and chief of state (also referred to as "president," although the term was not exactly accurate). He was a cousin of the king whom he had overthrown, largely over a royal draft constitution that concentrated too much power in the royal palace, according to Daoud. The prime minister was reputed to be a "man of the people" (despite his noble lineage) and a genuine Afghan nationalist, not to be confused with the so-called Young Turks, midlevel army officers who had been trained in the Soviet Union and were known to be pro-Soviet in orientation.

Daoud received us in his very modest-looking office, dressed in a sweater buttoned down the front. He seemed to be at pains to project the image of a commoner. The interview was long and painfully drawn out, even if highly informative, as his interpreter-secretary first wrote down and then translated each sentence in turn. (The contrast with the Sadat meeting could not have been more striking). The prime minister spoke very slowly and distinctly and seemed intent on making certain his underlying meaning was not lost in translation. After an initial discussion of the Pushtunistan boundary problem with Pakistan and the rationale for Afghanistan's neutralist foreign policy, the prime minister confronted Peter's key question: To what extent is the Soviet Union, in the form of the young radicals, influencing the Afghanistan government's policy?

Seeming to welcome this inquiry as indicative of the basic Western outlook toward Afghanistan, the prime minister began with a history lesson: "We have 1,700 kilometers of undefended border with Soviet Russia." Throughout long periods of history, Afghanistan was caught between two great imperialist powers, Tsarist Russia and the British Empire. Despite poverty and obvious weakness, many young Afghans gave their lives to preserve the country's independence and national identity. The British invaded the country three times in the past, but Afghans were willing to suffer and make the necessary sacrifices to maintain the country's independent position, *which is the Afghan position today*. Maintaining this independence came at the expense of "civilization" (roads, railroads, education, and such), which *could* have been provided by the "imperialist" powers. Afghans chose poverty and isolation over "civilized" despotism. Clearly, Afghans are a proud people, not willing to accept any foreign domination.

The prime minister admitted the danger of infiltration, however, which could result in the loss of independence. Afghanistan's two major problems were (1) severe social and class distinctions, and (2) poverty and economic differences between Afghans and their northern neighbors. (Residents in the north, in particular, watched Soviet television and were made aware of their relatively low standard of living.) Moreover, in addition to the bearded mullahs, other bearded teachers preached communism and spread Marxist propaganda. Raising the people's standard of living was necessary to block this trend. "There is no other way."

After this somewhat lengthy introduction, the prime minister then made the case for foreign aid. An investment in the economic well-being of poorer countries is in the U.S. interest, he stated repeatedly, and a more effective method of blocking the spread of communism than the approximately twenty-to-thirty-billion-dollar investment in Vietnam, which had been largely unsuccessful. The present Afghan government, the prime minister emphasized, was reformist and progressive, but *not* communist. Although future events were not entirely predictable, he was personally convinced that three factors—*tradition*, *nationalism*, and *religion*—were strong bars to the introduction of a communist system in Afghanistan.

Although the prime minister obviously downplayed the influence of the Young Turks in the military, who

321

eventually overthrew and assassinated him, his long-term predictions and projections were not far off the mark. The Soviet Union paid a high price for its initial success and long-term defeat. That the Daoud regime was the last to succeed in governing the entire country has been the real tragedy for Afghanistan.

Eventually, at a reception hosted by U.S. ambassador Theodore Eliot, we were able to meet a sampling of the young radicals, mostly army captains, majors, and colonels. All gave the impression of being intelligent and well educated. They seemed to exude confidence, mixed with an air of cockiness, which did not last long.

Our morning flight to New Delhi was delayed for some four hours, so we killed the time in Kabul's central city bazaar. This leads me to my favorite story about my *least* favorite pastime: *shopping*. With nothing else to do, however, as we roamed the streets lined with goods for sale, I ended up buying a number of furry items: fur hats, fur-lined coats, fur slippers, and the like. All of these purchases were sent, in bulk, to the congressman's office in the Rayburn House Office Building. About a month after our return, Peter called me to his office, where we attempted to sort out our respective purchases. Among my acquisitions was a sleeveless, fur-lined wrap which I remembered had been made out of a distinctive breed of "Afghan alpaca," or so the seller had claimed. I presented this outstanding item to my wife who had the temerity to turn it down. She took two Persian rugs and suggested I give the alpaca garment to her sister, who also gave it back. Finally, I threw it in my closet until I could find a more appreciative recipient

Shortly thereafter, Peter approached me at a committee hearing and asked quizzically: "Chips, do you remember that when we left Kabul for the tropics, I sent the liner to my raincoat home by diplomatic pouch? I never received it, apparently. The raincoat wasn't all that valuable, but it really isn't much good in the winter without the liner." "Was it long and sleeveless?" I inquired with some hesitation. Peter nodded and I said sheepishly: "I think I know where it is!" I have always been grateful for the good taste of the ladies, which saved me from ultimate disgrace. This is further proof, if any is needed, that I was not cut out for the retail business.

India

Ambassador Daniel Patrick Moynihan enjoyed a very different atmosphere among the upper strata of Indian officialdom than the one we encountered during our 1971 visit. The abrasive Tikki Kauls in the government were no longer in evidence. The change in outlook was the most striking aspect of this brief visit. The major problem of the moment was oil: not its availability, but its price. How could India pay for the petroleum supplies it needed, especially for the production of fertilizer? This was the dominant topic of conversation at a luncheon the ambassador hosted at his residence. Guests included Professor P. N. Dhar, personal secretary to the prime minister (who was out of town), Mr. P. K. Dave, secretary in the Ministry of Petroleum Chemicals; and Dr. Manmohan Singh, chief economic adviser in the Department of Economic Affairs.

Though the oil crisis turned out to be strictly temporary, it was certainly very real in the spring of 1974. An air of gloom and deep pessimism hung over the entire luncheon meeting. Not even a whiff of the customary Indian arrogance was discernible. Ambassador Moynihan did his level best to raise spirits and even urged Peter to assist him in this effort. Now was the time, he pointed out, for an Indian offensive vis-à-vis the oil-producing countries. Certainly the political IOUs India had acquired over the past twenty-five years should count for *something!* (He referred to such matters as the Arab-Asian voting bloc in the UN, and support for the Arab cause against Israel.) Now was the time to "cash in" a bit and exert some international pressure on the OPEC countries. He noted that of all countries in the world, India had the most at stake and was the most vulnerable.

According to my notes of that meeting, the ambassador's pep talk did not have much effect. The Indians evidently felt they had little leverage in the situation and that pressure would not be effective. Thus, if the developed countries meeting in Washington had not succeeded in reaching a consensus and bringing oil prices down, how could a poor country like India prevail? Peter's observation that OPEC countries tended to be more critical of pressure from the West than from the LDCs fell on deaf ears. Professor Dhar even expressed sympathy with the Arab states, whose "windfall" was acquired purely by accident. If India found itself in the same position, he said in all frankness, it might very well act the same way. Conversion from oil to coal as an energy source would help eventually, but the process would take two to seven years to implement. Moynihan tried another optimistic note: because of India's excellent reputation internationally for repayment of debts, the Bank of America had made available a $500 million line of credit for any projects India might wish to undertake. But commercial loans of this nature, Dr. Singh noted, involved 8 percent interest rates, which India could not afford.

Vietnam

Our final three days outside the United States were spent in South Vietnam. We entitled this section of our trip report, *Vietnam—A Changing Crucible.*[4] I invented the title, which turned out to be an inspiration, as most people did not understand what it meant and were too embarrassed to ask. To those few bold enough to inquire, the answer was simply "read the report and find out." Not many did.

Our visit took place at a crucial period in the long and bloody conflict that was to become the most unpopular such engagement in American history. Very few people, however, grasped that reality at the time. The apathy in the United States was of particular concern to Peter Frelinghuysen, who noted in the report's introduction:

> It is perhaps one of the supreme ironies of the mid-seventies that a country which has been the focus of international attention—and controversy—for over a decade is suddenly in danger of being forgotten by a Congress preoccupied with domestic problems, such as impeachment, the energy crisis, and the fall elections. That country is the Republic of Vietnam.

The Nixon "Vietnamization" program was now in place, and no U.S. troops were serving in combat any longer. The prospects of further military and economic aid to the country seemed to be in jeopardy, in a Congress that had grown tired and disenchanted with the whole business. The real test for the Vietnamese forces in the south was whether they would be able to hold up on their own, without the material and personnel support to which they had become accustomed. The best military intelligence at the time indicated that although the North Vietnamese had been rebuilding their forces in the south in recent weeks, they were not contemplating a major action in the immediate future, as they had in the spring of 1972. The Russians and Chinese had not been resupplying Hanoi to the extent believed necessary for a widespread engagement. Still, the acid test, or "crucible," would not be put off indefinitely. The South Vietnamese reaction to such a test would clearly demonstrate whether both the regime and Vietnamization could survive.

Peter Frelinghuysen had not always been an enthusiastic hawk on Vietnam. During the Cambodian incursion, he had publicly expressed dismay at the apparent escalation and extension of the fighting to a nominally neutral country. At this crucial transitional stage in the conflict, however—with a tenuous peace agreement in place and U.S. troops withdrawn—he felt strongly that the United States should follow through and provide the necessary level of aid. As he stated in our report's conclusion:

> Again, the question arises—especially in Congress—as to what is, in fact, reasonable and necessary. Past expenditures and past experience also play a significant role in the annual authorization-appropriation exercise. There is always, it seems, an endless need and an "eternal" U.S. contribution required. I understand such sentiments and the history which has led to their emergence. However...there is at last some "light at the end of the tunnel," if we do not "abruptly and unwisely turn off the switch." Given the immense sacrifices which have already been made—in U.S. lives and U.S. treasure, for better or for worse—it would be particularly harmful to the entire U.S. position, both in Southeast Asia and elsewhere in the world, to turn our backs now on a situation which shows some signs of improvement.

These arguments coincided almost exactly with the views of our last envoy in Saigon, the Honorable Graham Martin. To Ambassador Martin, Peter Frelinghuysen was a dream come true—a last hope and perhaps one of the few members of Congress he had met in recent years who had his head screwed on straight. The two men, both articulate and perhaps somewhat "elitist" in outlook (Peter was often called that, although exactly what the term meant was never clear), developed an instant rapport. In fact, their respective views seemed to reinforce one another to such an extent that I had the instinctive feeling from time to time that a degree of objectivity might be lost in the process. This is not to say that both were wide-eyed idealists—quite the contrary. But in their view, any policy initiative or strategy required an element of professional optimism to succeed, or it would get bogged down in cynical "defeatism." In that sense, they had a point.

Graham Martin, like Peter Frelinghuysen, was a man of many parts and also some complexities. Surprisingly enough, he had risen in the career Foreign Service via the administrative "cone," although his interest clearly centered on policy matters when I first met him. Earlier in his career, he had served as administrative counselor in Paris, which was one of the top management jobs in the Foreign Service. Like my last ambassador, Marshall Jones, Martin must have excelled in the administrative field. Unlike Marshall, however, who received his reward in a small out-of-the-way African post, Martin was selected for the top job in one of the most sensitive and challenging foreign missions anywhere. When first appointed envoy to South Vietnam, Martin said he had been quite skeptical of that country's future. After studying the situation closely, however, he had become convinced that a short-term infusion of U.S. aid could produce real results. Both Peter and the ambassador recognized what Congress viewed as the "bottomless pit" problem. After years of massive expenditure, no solution ever seemed to be in sight, and now that American "boys" were no longer serving there, an aid cutoff seemed a logical and inevitable move. Ambassador Martin's plans for Vietnam were designed with this problem in mind and provided for a finite end to the aid process. He proposed to set forth a clear two-year requirement for South Vietnam: $800 million for fiscal year 1975, and $600 million for fiscal year 1976. Then assistance should cease.

This infusion, Martin hoped, would in turn stimulate other potential donor nations such as the Paris-based Development Assistance Committee to follow the U.S. lead and make important follow-up contributions. The obvious problem was that Congress had already cut the current year's appropriation substantially, and a hard sell would be required to get the ambassador's plan implemented. Both he and Peter were determined, however, to give it an all-out college try, the ambassador especially so.

One evening (or actually early morning) stands out indelibly in my memory. In an attempt to cover more ground, Peter and I had decided to attend different social functions on our three nights in Saigon. I, needless to say, had cocktails or dinner with the slightly lower-level parliamentarians and other (forgettable) officials. One night, as I recall, my parliamentary hosts kept me up quite late, and I did not get to bed in the ambassador's guest house, where Peter and I were staying, until after midnight. I fell instantly, as always, into a deep slumber, only to be awakened an hour or two later by someone seated at the end of my bed. Although I almost never suffer from hangovers, no matter what I consume, I must have had one that morning. At least I had a difficult time focusing on the figure staring at me with cold blue eyes (which, unlike mine, were very much awake), who faintly resembled the ambassador. As a matter of fact, it *was* the ambassador! Apparently he thought this would be an ideal moment for a "strategy session." *What*, he wanted to know, did I think the chances were of getting his aid request through the House, and how should the proponents go about it?

My mind does not normally function well in the early morning hours, and by this time the dawn was definitely coming up like thunder and my head was buzzing from lack of sleep. I had the distinct feeling that what I was about to say would not be all that profound. I didn't want to tell the ambassador what I really thought, which was that his proposal had little chance of passing in the current political climate. Such a statement would seem to undermine Peter's position (even though at the bottom of his mind, if not his heart, Peter might have suspected as much) and be construed as an act of disloyalty. After all, I was there to *support* the committee's ranking Republican, not to obstruct his plans and proposals. However, I did not want to mislead anyone with unjustified optimism. And above all, I realized, I was not thinking all that clearly in the first place

I have the vague impression that I made two groggy points: (1) getting $800 million for FY 1975 was going to be a difficult challenge; and (2) if the ambassador considered it an essential appropriation, he should consider coming back to Washington and pressing his arguments personally with key congressional leaders. That turned out to be the course he later adopted, although I take no credit for it. I think he had that in mind all along and needed little encouragement.

This highly unusual nocturnal "conference" is cited merely as an example of the ambassador's fierce determination to explore every possible avenue of assistance in attaining his goals. I am certain that he viewed me, not as a person he admired or even liked in the same way he did Peter, but as a potential asset in his forthcoming struggle. That, indeed, was the way he viewed most of his own subordinates.

My skepticism, I should hasten to explain, related only to the prevailing congressional mood, not to conditions we found in Vietnam. Like Peter, I was both surprised and impressed by the high morale exhibited both by Vietnamese government officials and the military. The end of the "patron-client" relationship with the United States had evidently produced a national mood of self-confidence, a mood that unfortunately was not to last indefinitely. As our report proclaimed:

> Public confidence in the South Vietnamese Government (GVN) has been demonstrated in a series of public opinion polls conducted by the government under U.S. auspices. At the end of 1973, 82 percent of the respondents throughout the country expressed confidence in the South Vietnamese Government's ability to maintain its position during the coming year, as compared with only 48 percent in February. Another measure of the South Vietnamese Government's standing among the people is the large number of "ralliers" or defectors from the Communist side recorded in 1973. Our embassy in Saigon estimates that some 9,000 Communists came over to the government during the year, roughly the same number who rallied in 1972 at the height of the fighting.

The large but selective spectrum of officialdom we met might be expected to reflect optimism.

However, high morale cannot be faked on such a large scale, and the mood was clearly quite genuine. This impression was fortified by a one-day helicopter ride into the Mekong Delta in the south. We flew over countless green rice fields which certainly appeared to be flourishing despite the continuing hostilities in this region. Brief stops at the port of Rach Ghia on the Gulf of Thailand and the provincial capital of Can Tho tended to reinforce the self-confidence finding: the military commander of the Can Tho region, a general, exuded both pride in his forces and an evident conviction that victory was at hand, despite the guns which boomed from time to time in the distant background. I still have difficulty believing, even with the benefit of hindsight, that these observed conditions were totally superficial at the time. Yet the South Vietnamese forces collapsed in panic and the South Vietnamese Government fell approximately a year later.

The climax of our study mission was clearly our meeting with President Nguyen Van Thieu on the last day of our visit. Contrary to the constant sniping by much of the Western press (which characterized him as a corrupt right-wing extremist of sorts), the chief of state presented an image of matter-of-fact rationality and realism. He spoke quietly and persuasively in propounding the South Vietnamese case, or, some might say, the party line.

The president began by recognizing the current situation as a "delicate" one, owing to the forthcoming U.S. elections. Despite U.S. diplomatic efforts, however, there would be no real peace as long as the Hanoi regime continued to pursue its long-term objective of taking over South Vietnam by force. This was a tragedy, he said, not only for the south, but for the people of the north, who had suffered enormously during the past two decades. The economy of North Vietnam was in very bad shape, even worse than in the south, but the Communists only cared about attaining their objectives, not about the people.

The leaders of North Vietnam were not "politicians," President Thieu stated, but "old doctrinaires," almost all of whom were over sixty, and still cherished dreams of controlling all of Vietnam, Laos, and Cambodia. Although the goals remained unchanged, the means were currently lacking, as they had been unable to play off the Soviets against the Chinese in obtaining needed supplies and equipment. Both countries, he noted, had traditionally competed with one another for Hanoi's favor. North Vietnam, like South Vietnam, could only use the equipment it was "given." For that reason, it was important to maintain a "balance." If the United States cut off support, the balance could be tipped in favor of Hanoi. At this point the Chinese did not favor a strong and independent-minded North Vietnamese regime on their southern flank while they were busy with a hostile and menacing neighbor to the north. When the Chinese were "less busy," they could constitute a danger.

The president spoke of a two-Vietnam solution as the most realistic course. His current policy, moreover, was *not* to criticize friends (or former friends) who recognized Hanoi and extended it aid. The only South Vietnamese concern was that such aid reached the *people* and not contribute toward *undermining* the cease-fire. (In other words, only *military* assistance was ruled out). With regard to congressional attitudes, Peter suggested that an invitation be issued to Senator Fulbright, a dedicated aid opponent, to visit South Vietnam and air his policy differences with the South Vietnamese government. Even if the invitation were declined, as appeared virtually certain, the gesture might be beneficial and help neutralize hostile U.S. opinion.

The president concurred with this proposal and referred to recent meetings with prominent doves, Senators Edward Kennedy and George McGovern. Senator McGovern, he claimed, after hearing the president's case, had agreed with the president's analysis of the military situation. After boarding the U.S. plane, however, McGovern played the role of general by telling the press he supported the "enclave theory," essentially a defensive strategy of giving up widespread prosecution of the war and falling back into protected "sanctuaries" or "enclaves."

Nyugen Van Thieu concluded by expressing his conviction that with current resources and minimal assistance from the outside, the South Vietnamese economy could "take off," like those of Korea and Taiwan. South Vietnam had even better natural resources and potential than those two countries had had when they started "moving" economically. U.S. leadership was essential, however, to get the process started. As to the ambassador's short-term "infusion" plan, the president fully concurred with the proposed timetable. "It is better to give a large initial dosage of medicine to a sick man than an inadequate dosage over a period of time."

For reasons that are now history, military assistance was severely cut and the FY 1975–76 aid was not provided. The rug had clearly been pulled out from under the South Vietnamese regime. Their military eventually panicked and fled in the face of a new North Vietnamese assault. In April 1975 Saigon fell and what was left of the American mission—plus a handful of South Vietnamese supporters—were evacuated by helicopter. The long undeclared war was over. Whether the military would have made an adequate defense had it not felt abandoned by its principal patron, or whether the regime would have fallen anyway in due course, is and will forever remain an unanswerable hypothetical question. In any case, I ended up with most of the copies of *Vietnam—A Changing Crucible*, which were considered no longer useful once the summer aid debate was over. They are available to those still interested in this "before the fall" era, free of charge and with my compliments

Graham Martin was later severely criticized for his unwillingness to share intelligence with the American community in a timely manner and for his failure to make adequate preparations for the evacuation from Saigon until the very last moment. I understand that he feared any such action would send a signal to the Vietnamese government that it was about to be abandoned and thereby hasten its collapse. Thus, he refused to act until (many felt) it was almost too late to rescue many Vietnamese supporters of the U.S. mission. Though he was known to pursue a solo and perhaps devious modus operandi, I would never doubt his sincerity. He lost a son in the war and clearly was committed to the cause.

A Fascinating Last Stop: Honolulu

From Saigon we headed back to Washington, with a one-day stopover in Honolulu, the usual refueling stop for most airlines. It was also the usual place for a congressional briefing by the CINCPAC (Commander in Chief, Pacific). Unlike his predecessor, the colorful, curmudgeonly old salt Admiral John McCain (the senator's father), the admiral in charge turned out to be urbane, glib, articulate, and unmemorable. Briefing members of Congress from both houses had evidently become a routine chore for him, and he delivered the standard Pentagon line almost by rote.

By this time I had become thoroughly exhausted and spent the better part of one morning sound asleep on the beach. That same evening, Peter had a dinner date with former playwright, congresswoman, and ambassador Clare Boothe Luce. Mrs. Luce had been a close friend of the Frelinghuysen family, especially Peter's older brother, George, a collector of antiques and Mrs. Luce's traveling companion on a number of foreign tours. Peter treated this dinner engagement primarily as a family obligation, but then almost as an afterthought, he asked if Clare had any objection to his bringing his "aide" along. She answered graciously that I would be most welcome.

For some reason we arrived late at the appointed restaurant, which was quite elegant and located on the second floor of a large office building in the downtown heart of the city. This was unusual, as Peter was always quite punctual. Mrs. Luce was already on her second martini and in a mellow, reflective frame of mind. I remember being struck by the rather nostalgic mood she displayed, at such odds with her image and reputation as a feisty and dominant personality. Unquestionably she felt at ease with Peter and spent much of the evening quietly reminiscing about past political events, expressing particular regret about the current difficulties that had befallen the Nixon administration. Needless to say, I listened, fascinated, to her every word.

The simple fact is, and was, that Mrs. Luce was clearly and distinctly the most attractive and appealing septuagenarian I had ever met. Her native intelligence and strong (some might say biased) opinions did nothing to obscure a most compelling femininity reflected in her every word and gesture. Plainly the years had not destroyed an innate sex appeal which she most *naturally* (and I stress that adverb) exuded.

After much delicious food and drink, however, she needed a break. Grasping my hand beneath the tablecloth, she announced: "Let us take a walk, while Peter pays the bill." It was a direct order which Peter and I both obeyed without question! The "walk" took place on a narrow second-story walkway that encircled an open Spanish courtyard. Before long, the ambassador was leaning on me, first lightly and then almost completely, so that in effect I was carrying her light and lissome body altogether. As we rounded one corner in this mode, we must have made an unusual scene, and I remember thinking to myself: "If only my Friday luncheon cronies could see me now!!"

When Peter finally reappeared, we "escorted" the ambassador to her chauffeur-driven stretch limousine below, and I placed her tenderly within. When she bade us farewell and honored me with a perfunctory kiss, I had the distinct feeling that CODEL Frelinghuysen had just been brought to a satisfactory conclusion.

CODEL Frelinghuysen's end marked another milestone: on the day after our return to Washington, Peter held a press conference announcing his intention to retire after the completion of his current term in office. (He had meant to take this action the last time around, he told me in confidence, but the minority leader, Gerald Ford, had talked him out of it. "Nixon needs all the support he can get," the leader argued, before his landslide victory over McGovern. This time Peter was determined, and successful, in getting the jump on Mr. Ford.)

In his public statement, Peter noted that he had arrived in Washington with Eisenhower, and after twenty years it was time to step down in favor of some "new blood." It is just as well that he did not say "young" blood, as he was replaced by the notably older Millicent Fenwick. A neighboring congressman from New Jersey, the late William Widnall, did not appreciate these sentiments, as he was an aging incumbent running against a young and vigorous primary opponent. Peter's aside to me was typical of his sense of the absurd: "Bill Widnall, although a worthy Republican, was just exactly the kind of prospective retiree I had in mind."

CHAPTER 15

Staff Missions to Asia, Africa, and Latin America

During the 1970s I undertook three staff study missions. Two extensive and memorable ones were with my colleague Jack Sullivan to the Far East in 1972 and West Africa in 1975. The third was to Latin America, with George Ingram and Gerry Pitchford, in 1976.

The staff delegations (or STAFFDELS) that undertake these study missions differ from CODELS in one important respect: STAFFDELS are infinitely easier on staff members. Without the "care and feeding" of one or more members of Congress (no matter how congenial and cooperative), staffers have the luxury of working out their meetings and schedule of activities with maximum convenience and efficiency. This does not mean that staff trips are classifiable as vacation tours: quite the contrary.

In fact, U.S. embassy control officers usually do not hesitate to "front-load" visiting staff members' schedules with a full agenda of meetings, with side trips as appropriate. From the principal officers on down, they generally realize (if they know anything about Congress, and most of them increasingly do) that staff members often have a lot to do with what ultimately appears in legislation. Many FSOs may have given up the attempt to influence members of Congress (quite mistakenly, as I mentioned earlier), but they tend to consider *reasonable* staffers their last best hope. Professional staff members from committees also tend to be less ideologically committed than are members or their legislative aides, simply because they have to accommodate a diverse set of committee members from both parties.

EAST ASIA: THE PEACE CORPS IN THE 1970S

Our report on the Peace Corps in the 1970s was based on our trip to four countries, Korea, the Philippines, Malaysia, and Thailand, from November 10 to December 3, 1972. Its observations were limited to those countries, but, as the report concluded, might well point up problems confronting the Peace Corps worldwide.[1]

Jack Sullivan, with whom I traveled to the Far East, was an experienced journalist and congressional hand, having served as Clem Zablocki's administrative assistant before joining the full committee staff some years before my arrival. (Eventually he was to become assistant administrator of AID for East Asian affairs in the Carter administration.) As the senior member of our investigative team, Jack was a distinct asset: an experienced investigative reporter (originally for the *Milwaukee Journal*), he had traveled on previous study missions, especially in the Far East, and was an excellent writer, one of the very few on the committee at that time.

Our assignments were to inspect and evaluate AID and Peace Corps programs in selected countries and report our findings to the committee chairman, since the Committee on Foreign Affairs handled authorizing legislation for both agencies. Jack reviewed AID projects in the various countries we visited; I covered the Peace Corps, at least in part as a result of my earlier assignment to Peace Corps headquarters in its formative stage (see chapter 5). After each trip we submitted separate reports on the two programs, which we both signed, although

Jack wrote the ones on AID/Population Planning, while I wrote exclusively about the Peace Corps.

Following is a summary of the report's findings and conclusions:

1. Emphasis in Peace Corps programs had shifted from the traditional toward a "New Directions" concept in staffing and programming (older and more experienced volunteers and assignment of volunteer families).
2. Peace Corps programs were becoming more fully integrated with the host country's overall development effort.
3. Volunteers were assigned to positions within the regular bureaucratic structures of host governments.
4. The Peace Corps had not been able to fill the gap caused by AID's retrenchment in technical assistance.
5. Preliminary screening of volunteers, in many instances, had been grossly inadequate. More careful analysis of a candidate's qualifications and suitability for the Peace Corps was needed.
6. The day of the Peace Corps generalist was by no means over.
7. Peace Corps effectiveness should not be judged in quantitative terms.

We also made supplementary general comments on Peace Corps training, the image of volunteers abroad, the cultural exchange aspect of the Peace Corps, and drug usage by volunteers.

New Directions versus Tradition

In the early 1970s the Nixon administration, under Peace Corps director Joseph Blatchford, initiated a New Directions program, which placed greater emphasis on recruiting volunteers with a higher level of technical expertise and experience to "meet the higher priority needs targeted by the developing nations." In effect, it sought a balance between so-called generalists and specialists, whereas until 1969 liberal arts generalists accounted for some 75 to 85 percent of the Peace Corps' available manpower.

The Peace Corps came of age in the 1970s in more ways than one. It was originally conceived as a tangible response to President Kennedy's call for a renewed commitment by American youth to the concept of national and international service. Young college graduates with Bachelor of Arts degrees in—by and large—history, English, or the humanities were recruited in large numbers, more often than not to serve as English-language teachers in the host countries. English-language programs were popular with the Peace Corps staff in Washington, primarily because the so-called B.A. generalists were the most enthusiastic about the program and could fill the ranks rather quickly with a minimum of formal training.

The Peace Corps soon gained worldwide visibility and momentum, as thousands of potential volunteers offered their services to the cause of peace, international understanding, and economic progress. It seemed to have the most "pizzazz," as one commentator put it, of all the original New Frontier programs. Volunteerism in this early period became almost an end in itself. It was not the job or assignment that mattered so much as the willingness to serve and help out in any way possible. For lack of a better term, this concept might be called volunteerism per se. It was based largely, if not totally, on spirit and enthusiasm, qualities which appealed strongly to the American psyche.

By the 1970s, though idealism still permeated the organization and its participants to a considerable extent, the early thrill of volunteerism per se had become largely a thing of the past. This trend was inevitable, not only because the initial momentum of the program could not be sustained indefinitely, but because the developing countries wanted it that way. A decade or two after independence, those nations were demanding quality assistance and much greater control over all forms of foreign aid dispensed within their borders.

Quality did not necessarily mean specialization in all cases; in at least two countries we visited, certain generalist programs were the most successful. But it did mean that volunteers, to be acceptable to governments of the 1970s, had to be job-oriented and qualified to perform their assigned duties; the duties, in turn, had to be in accord with the host government's own views of its development priorities.

Quality versus Quantity. Peace Corps recruiters also favored larger programs because "numbers" would presumably impress Congress. Though probably true at first, the "numbers game" clearly could not be sustained indefinitely. It and larger English language programs in some countries (not all) had begun to outlive their usefulness.

In presenting their case to Congress, Peace Corps officials made much of the fact that the New Directions program had led to the reversal of a five-year downward trend in recruitment. Viewed from the standpoint of our four-country mission, that was not the case. The Peace Corps had been unable to meet the quantitative requests of foreign governments for volunteers in higher skill categories. When Washington tried to fill the gap with marginal candidates, on the apparent assumption that in-country training could make up for basic technical deficiencies, problems arose. What seemed to be happening might be described as the filling of New Directions requirements under "old directions" psychology, a basic premise of which was that if a volunteer had the *will* and enthusiasm, he would find a *way* to serve productively. Our observations led us to question the validity of this theory.

We concluded that quality was an absolute prerequisite to success and that if highly qualified personnel could not be supplied in the numbers desired, some retrenchment in the program would be unavoidable. We approved of the New Directions approach as having much intrinsic value not necessarily reflected in recruitment statistics. Where volunteers were able to perform adequately, their contribution was disproportionate to their numerical strength. However, where these circumstances did not apply, the program had backfired.

We did not propose a specific level of Peace Corps representation abroad, but advocated a more careful matching of volunteer qualifications with program requirements. The Peace Corps would not be any less effective if this were to result in a smaller organization than originally contemplated. On the contrary, a more streamlined corps of qualified individuals with a reputation for efficiency and professionalism would be more likely to receive both the recognition and the candidates it was seeking. A 1978 book by Kevin Lowther and C. Payne Lucas discussed the issue of quality versus quantity in more detail. It also quoted from our report.[2]

Training of Volunteers. In the countries we visited, we found that in-country volunteer training was cheaper, more relevant to future assignments, and more realistic than training in the United States. Training in their assigned cultural environment enabled volunteers to evaluate whether they were up to the challenge. But the large investment of time and money involved in travel to distant parts of the world increased pressure on both volunteers and in-country staff to *make* the assignment work, sometimes with unhappy results. This in turn placed greater responsibility on Peace Corps headquarters to improve inadequate initial screening procedures before accepting volunteers.

Volunteers' Image: Myth Versus Reality. The image of Peace Corps volunteers as long-haired youths, alienated from their own society—particularly as a consequence of the Vietnam War—and essentially "doing their own thing" abroad, produced an adverse reaction at home that was reflected in Congress. We found this characterization misleading. The volunteers were, by and large, practical, mature, and job-oriented, at pains to avoid involvement in local or international political controversy, and aware of the need to conform to local customs and traditions.

Cultural Exchange. From the start, the Peace Corps has emphasized its cultural exchange role, to present a dimension of American life other than that of U.S. military and AID officials, businessmen, or tourists. Volunteers were expected to promote in their host communities a realistic understanding of what Americans are "really like." We found numerous successful examples of volunteers who through their own initiative, patience, and perseverance made seemingly unglamorous and difficult tasks worthwhile. We also found that the cross-cultural benefits of a volunteer's assignment were most often realized when the volunteer's job situation was essentially positive. Conversely, a frustrated or unhappy volunteer could generate a cross-cultural boomerang, again pointing up the need for careful volunteer recruiting and placement.

Drug Usage. The Peace Corps policy on volunteer use of drugs was strict: immediate termination of employment. Since the drug problem permeated all aspects of American society, inevitably the Peace Corps had its share of incidents. Peace Corps directors in countries we visited, however, believed—and we concurred—that drug usage was not a major problem.

Korea

The Korean Peace Corps program was atypical because of the overwhelmingly military nature of the U.S. presence and the priority given to security considerations in the minds of most Koreans. Americans and Koreans alike regarded the relatively high visibility of the Peace Corps as an asset: by its participation in the educational, cultural, and community life of Korea, the Peace Corps tended to modify the military image of America.

The TESOL program (Teaching English to Speakers of Other Languages), the main focus of our visit, was a high priority of the host government. This made Korea an exception to our generalization about English teaching. Well over half the 286 Peace Corps volunteers there were engaged in TESOL activities. As described in our report: "For Koreans, English is not a luxury but an absolute sine qua non for the modernization of the country and for the advancement of the individual. Because Korean is an extraordinarily difficult language for foreigners to master, English—the international language for politics, trade, industry, science and scholarship—is essential for world communication and competition. For this reason, English has been made compulsory for all Korean students beginning at the middle school level, roughly equivalent to junior high school. Most importantly, advanced training abroad is only open to those who speak a foreign language, which for almost all Koreans means English."

Jack Sullivan and I spent a day and night on a field trip to the provincial town of Chun Chon, where we slept on the floor, Korean-style, wrapped in blankets, on a kind of pad that could not accurately be described as a mattress. We also ate on the floor in a (less-than-comfortable) seated position. I visited a few TESOL classes and saw highly disciplined Korean students. Desperate to learn, they realized that English was the key to their future. If they made the grade, all doors were open to them, but if they failed, their respective careers would have reached a ceiling. It was touching to watch them valiantly trying to master a language that would provide them with training abroad, the ultimate, universal goal of all trainees.

The most remarkable, and memorable, moment in our entire Korean sojourn, however, had nothing to do with the AID program or the Peace Corps. It occurred just prior to our departure, as I was about to climb the portable stairs to our aircraft. A uniformed airline official handed me a Korean baby, wrapped in swaddling clothes and zipped up in a cloth sack. He asked if I would carry it on board and give it to a stewardess. (I say "it" because the swaddling clothes and the sack would have made it highly inconvenient to distinguish the child's sex.) The stewardesses were all quite preoccupied with seating passengers, so I put on my seat belt and held the child in my lap.

After takeoff, various passengers stopped by to chuck the baby under the chin and make a fuss over it. Finally the stewardesses fell in line and followed suit. "I was supposed to turn this baby over to you," I commented to one of them. "Would you like to take him (or her) now?" "I don't know anything about that baby," she protested, "and in the absence of instructions, we aren't allowed to take possession."

At this point my colleague became agitated. "My God, Chips," Jack complained loudly, "you can't take that baby all over East Asia. We still have four more countries to cover!" I was thinking the same thoughts, but what to do? The baby never once cried and just smiled up at me sweetly, apparently completely confident that it was in safe hands. If possession is considered nine-tenths of the law, at least in Western jurisprudence, I now had the automatic responsibility. The American embassy in Tokyo, I fully realized, would never assume jurisdiction over such a case, although it might help me make phone calls. But whom should I call? The pilot, who was informed of my dilemma, got nowhere over his radio. Perhaps I could find an adoption agency somewhere in Tokyo, I pondered, but then I would miss my connection to Manila. (We had already missed one flight from Seoul by forgetting to reconfirm our reservations).

With considerable consternation, I bounced the baby in my lap with false bravado as we approached the landing strip in Tokyo. As I deplaned, with baby in arms, a lady in uniform suddenly appeared and took "it" from me enthusiastically. I was momentarily stunned. "Thank you so much, sir," the lady beamed at me. "The baby is on the way to the Netherlands for adoption. You were so kind to care for it." (I never did get the sex of the child or I have at least forgotten this minor detail.) I can only say that somewhere in Holland a Dutch family was rewarded with the best-behaved baby this side of Paradise. Never before or since have I seen (or heard) another one so good-natured and placid.

Philippines

In Manila, President Ferdinand Marcos had just dissolved parliament and invoked military rule on an emergency basis. No one we talked to seemed to mind. A little military repression seemed to come as something of a relief after a period of complete anarchy, with rampant crime and shootings in the streets. The Marcoses had not yet been thoroughly discredited.

Of the 265 Peace Corps volunteers, 125 were skilled agricultural workers in government programs for swine, fish, feed grains, vegetables, and cattle production. The rest worked in physical education and an area broadly labeled "social development," including community development, rural health, urban planning, and family planning.

The "New Directions" were firmly in place, with mixed results: on the one hand inadequate screening of volunteers and their assignment to jobs for which they were unqualified; on the other, underuse of highly qualified volunteers by a bureaucracy not organized or prepared to accommodate them at the local level. For example, the fisheries vocational education and training program, staffed by thirty-seven volunteers handpicked by the deputy Filipino fisheries commissioner, was evidently a great success. Another agricultural program, however, was only saved from certain extinction by the personal intervention of the Filipino secretary of agriculture.

On our visit to two of the Visaya islands, Cebu and Negros, I saw my first and only cockfight. It was a bloody spectacle, even more grisly than bullfighting, as the fighting cocks never gave up until the moment of their demise. The animal rights people on those islands were not very well organized.

Malaysia

I ended up flying to Kuala Lumpur solo, while Jack was inspecting population planning programs in Indonesia. Family planning in Malaysia, I learned, was a sensitive subject, as the mostly rural and traditional Malays who ran the government feared that the Chinese community, which ran most of the country's economy, would become the majority of the voting population. Serious communal riots had marred the past, and everyone in authority was determined to prevent the recurrence of such a disaster. (Actually, the Chinese, unlike the Malays, practiced birth control.)

A sudden and barely controllable attack of diarrhea spoiled my first full day of meetings with government officials. The embassy had gone to a good deal of trouble getting me appointments, so I felt I had to adhere to the official schedule, especially since I was alone and had no sidekick to make excuses for me. This was, to put it mildly, a day lost in anal preoccupation, which has a tendency to take precedence over all other concerns. Fortunately, I recovered quickly and was able to visit a number of Peace Corps sites outside the capital.

Malaysia was a showcase for New Directions. Since the Malaysian government had ruled generalists unacceptable, the 335 volunteers had a diversified set of skills, backgrounds, and forms of expertise. Officials at all levels of government were receptive to the Peace Corps, living conditions were generally favorable for the volunteers, and embassy–Peace Corps cooperation was at the highest level we found anywhere on the trip. A real star was serving in the College of Agriculture in Sedang: a volunteer with a doctorate in chemistry and ten years of prior teaching experience in the United States.

At dinner at Ambassador Jack Lydman's residence I met Anna Chennault, widow of famed U.S. Maj. Gen. Claire Chennault, who led the "Flying Tigers" over the "hump" from Burma to China during World War II. Anna was then the chief executive officer of the commercial Flying Tigers airline, which subsequently closed down.

Thailand

Jack and I joined forces again in Bangkok, where getting around by car was a major problem. The traffic was totally impossible. For a half-hour official meeting, one needed to set aside an hour for a few miles' ride.

As in Korea, the government in Bangkok placed great emphasis on learning English, which ranked as the most important second language in the school system. Because of a critical shortage of teachers, particularly in the rural areas, 180 out of 253 PCVs assigned to Thailand were engaged in Teaching of English as a Foreign Language (TEFL).[3] We met with a number of TEFL volunteers in Khon Kaen, a mountainous city in northeastern Thailand. All seemed to be satisfied with their assignments and working well with their host government counterparts. Within the past year, however, the Peace Corps program had suffered from an unusually high fallout rate among those who had successfully completed their in-country training. We heard reports that these dropouts had included a number of immature individuals who had clearly not been adequately screened before becoming volunteers.

Thailand was definitely a mixed bag in terms of programmatic success. A New Directions emphasis was needed in agriculture, but had been somewhat lacking. A critical shortage of qualified volunteers, particularly engineers, and a high dropout rate for civil engineers had contributed to the problem. The number of engineers went from twenty-three to six in the first year of the program.

Because of leadership problems, Peace Corps contacts rarely reached the top level of the Thai government. As a consequence, Thai commitment to the Peace Corps program was not strong enough. The Peace Corps director for Thailand was a former astronaut, Donn Eisele, who had participated in the Apollo Seven mission. He and his deputy had both arrived at the same time, without any prior experience in directing such a program or in dealing with foreign governments. Both had to feel their way by trial and error, without benefit of an overlap with a veteran peer.

"Scandal!" In Bangkok an incident essentially quite innocent and of minor import could easily have been blown out of all proportion by a scandal-minded press and humiliated and disgraced us. But we were in luck: the story never got back to Washington. On our last night there, after a good dinner and a stop in a night-club so dark that the waiter had to bring us the bill with a flashlight in his mouth, Jack and I were both tired and about to retire when I suggested we get a bath and massage, for which the Thais are famous, before facing the prospect of a twenty-plus hour flight back to Washington. The concierge gave us directions to a place nearby, but did *not* tell us that a military curfew was in effect after midnight and that we would essentially be breaking the law. (In Bangkok it was generally assumed that anything was possible for a foreign tourist if he was willing to pay for it.)

Thai massages can involve erotic procedures. However, the institution of the massage is also an advanced art form. Small masseuses can walk up and down one's back, snapping and cracking each muscle along the spine to provide comfort and relief of stress. (I wish all of my many friends with back problems could have been so blessed.) Before sitting in a plane for hours on end, a Thai massage is a chiropractic delight. The only problem in our case was that the military staged a postmidnight raid on the place before either of us could enjoy any of the establishment's benefits. Probably someone had forgotten to pay someone else in authority, and this was the penalty being assessed. Somehow my masseuse got me out of the building and into an alley, where I hid from marching troops. When I reached the car, I found Jack already in it, and we sped off to sanctuary in the Bangkok Intercontinental.

That night I had a dream: On the front page of the *Washington Post* was a minor headline: "HILL AIDES ARRESTED IN RAID ON BANGKOK MASSAGE PARLOR. COMMITTEE CHAIRMAN CONFIRMS VISIT NOT AUTHORIZED AND PROMISES DIS-CIPLINARY ACTION." I think Jack Sullivan had a similar lack of repose that night. At least we both slept pretty well for a change on the plane home

WEST AFRICA:
THE PEACE CORPS, 1975

Three years later (November 28 to December 18, 1975) Jack Sullivan and I undertook a similar study mission to six countries in West Africa: Sierra Leone, Côte d'Ivoire, Upper Volta (now renamed Burkina Faso), Ghana, Nigeria, and Senegal. Again our assignments were divided along the lines of our Far East trip, with Jack inspecting AID/family planning programs, and I focusing once again on the Peace Corps.

As on our 1972 East Asia mission, this study mission to West Africa evaluated the New Directions program, aimed at recruiting volunteers with technical expertise and experience. We concluded[4] that the New Directions concept was essentially inoperative in West Africa, which was not at the same stage of development as Asia or much of Latin America. Few volunteers with advanced academic degrees or specialized skills were being assigned. Instead the traditional B.A. generalists, liberal arts college graduates, usually in their twenties, were ostensibly best adapted to West Africa's needs. Their technical preparation was limited to several weeks of in-country training. No volunteers had families with them.

We also found that the Peace Corps of the mid-1970s reflected changing times. The glamour days of the early 1960s were over, as was the U.S. involvement in Indochina. The Peace Corps no longer represented an alternative to military service. Demonstrations by individual volunteers against U.S. government policies seemed to be a thing of the past. Volunteers now joined the Peace Corps for personal reasons and because of a desire to serve. Those we met appeared to be practical, realistic, and job-oriented. The Peace Corps problems cited below in no way detracted from the solid achievements by those many volunteers who persevered and succeeded, often under difficult circumstances.

The Peace Corps in West Africa had a more erratic record of accomplishment than was generally apparent in East Asia. Operations in West Africa had suffered and were still suffering from lack of clear direction and firm leadership at the top, as well as inadequate headquarters staff support, mainly for budgetary reasons. These shortcomings resulted mostly from either a shortage or a high turnover of staff.

Some of the staffing problems we had flagged three years earlier in East Asia had not been solved. Again implying that problems in West Africa, like those in East Asia, might well apply to the Peace Corps generally, we repeated our comments from that report: "If the Peace Corps is to survive in the 1970s it must face the fact that quality is an absolute prerequisite to success and that if highly qualified personnel cannot be supplied in the numbers desired . . . some retrenchment in the program will become unavoidable."

Recruiting methods had changed radically. Primarily because of costs, trainee applicants—rather than going through preliminary screening in the United States— were directed to report to U.S. staging areas and then sent directly to their countries of assignment. This left the task of eliminating unacceptable candidates to the overburdened in-country staff, which was rarely up to full strength. Staff complained about "tourists" who elected to return home after less than a week at the training site. One could assume that anyone who left so soon was not seriously committed to the program in the first place.

Nevertheless, in-country training had advantages that deserved further study. Although it ran a higher risk of trainee attrition, it was still cheaper overall than establishing PCV training centers in the United States. Training could also be made more relevant to future assignments. Trainees could visit job sites and meet host country nationals with whom they would work. Language instruction could be tailored to individual needs. The volunteers could be exposed directly to the local cultural environment and could evaluate more realistically whether they would be up to the challenge.

In the agricultural field, we noted, PCVs with farm backgrounds or basic agricultural training could be useful if selectivity were maintained. A relatively low level of technical input into the agricultural sector by the Peace Corps could produce positive results in much of West Africa. Soil conditions were generally favorable for growing a variety of vegetables and grains. With the benefit of some intensive training in rudimentary techniques of irrigation and cultivation, volunteers, even those with limited farm experience, could be usefully employed in rural areas.

Numbers of volunteers in the countries we visited were considerably less than in East Asian countries:

Sierra Leone	202
Côte d'Ivoire	77
Upper Volta	85
Ghana	131
Senegal	92

Sierra Leone

In Sierra Leone, our ambassador was Michael Samuels, an old friend who had previously served in the congressional liaison office (H) at State. That assignment had involved him very closely with the Foreign Affairs Committee. Mike and his attractive wife, Susan, were enthusiastic hosts. Mike took the opportunity to plug both his policies and his material needs.

Health needs were uppermost. A recent outbreak of Lassa fever, an exotic and potentially fatal tropical disease, pointed up a health danger to volunteers common to all the countries we visited. No U.S. doctor was stationed in the country. Instead, Peace Corps volunteers in Sierra Leone, like those in Upper Volta, Niger, and Mali, all high-risk areas, were serviced on an occasional, irregular basis by regional Peace Corps doctors stationed in Abidjan, Côte d'Ivoire, and Dakar, Senegal. (Bureaucratic restrictions prohibited State Department physicians from attending to the volunteers' medical needs, although they did so informally in emergencies.)

Apparently recruiting qualified physicians for the sole purpose of attending to the medical needs of volunteers was not easy. However, recruiting an American doctor from the Communicable Diseases Center (CDC) in Atlanta to perform Lassa fever research in Sierra Leone, while administering to volunteers on the side, eventually solved the problem. Our ability to get Doc Morgan, our venerable committee chairman (who, as a practicing physician, always had medical requirements close to his heart) to support this effort also helped get Mike the level of support he clearly (and understandably) needed.

Ghana

In Ghana, Jack and I were accorded a rather lengthy personal interview with Ambassador Shirley Temple Black, who had a strong interest in both of our respective missions. We had been warned ahead of time *not* to mention Hollywood or her previous film career. Now she was the chief of mission and all business.

Ambassador Black was well informed about and deeply interested in Peace Corps activities in Ghana. She had objected strongly to PC/Washington's practice of sending out trainees who had not completed the series of inoculations and injections required by Ghanaian law; the practice had been quickly discontinued. Since PC/Washington had never sent the post a list of recently arrived trainee-participants or other accompanying data, delivering an emergency message for one of them required a personal search of training sites. Ambassador Black observed that the Peace Corps, a volunteer and action-oriented organization, harbored an institutional resistance to management and administration, terms they seemed to associate with bureaucratic concerns rather than with people.

This outlook, fortunately, was beginning to change: in three of the countries we visited (Sierra Leone, Upper Volta, and Ghana) the incumbent Peace Corps directors had executive-management backgrounds. Clearly, good programs don't just happen; they have to be organized, coordinated with both host government officials and PC/Washington, planned, and monitored.

When we first arrived at the embassy, we were met at the front door by the ambassador's husband, Charles Black, who made it clear from the outset that he was merely a temporary visitor and would take no part in his wife's diplomatic duties. He was a successful businessman who served on several corporate boards and evidently had far-ranging business interests in the United States. At the time of our visit, he was planning to return home for an important meeting, although his spouse was trying to talk him out of it. In any case, he was clearly quite comfortable in his role as the spouse of the chief of mission and had no discernible competitive hang-ups. It seemed like an ideal relationship.

Nigeria

Nigeria was a special case. The Peace Corps was in the process of phasing out there at the time of our arrival, as a result—at least in part—of problems not dissimilar to those I discovered in Malawi a few years earlier (as noted in chapter 9). In Nigeria volunteers serving in the breakaway province of Biafra had expressed some sympathy with the Ibos of that region, and their comments had eventually made their way back to the central government, which took umbrage. Nevertheless, yet another new Nigerian regime was renewing talks for the possible resumption of Peace Corps projects.

Lagos, the capital, was also a "special case," not at all representative of conditions in the hinterland. The city is constructed on a series of islands connected by bridges inadequate for the automotive traffic of the day. As a consequence, if just one or two bridges were bottled up for some reason, traffic for the entire area would be brought to a standstill. Traffic jams were even worse than in Bangkok. On the morning of our departure, we had to cancel all our appointments and spend the entire time just driving to the airport—about 15 miles away.

Oil was beginning to flow freely, and every Western huckster had come to Nigeria to sell, not just products but whole economic "systems." What a labor-*intensive* society clearly does not need are labor-*saving* devices in the form of John Deere tractors and other accoutrements, which tend to need constant service and nonexistent spare parts. Moreover, someone in the preceding regime had ordered an endless supply of cement (probably for a healthy fee), and ships were lined up in the harbor as far as the eye could see. Many, we were told, lined up just to collect demurrage charges for each day the goods were not unloaded. Because of the moist climate, much of the cement had turned into concrete by the time it reached the shore. The government was evidently spending money like a drunken sailor, and the universal fear was that when the oil reserves were finally depleted, the country would be back to square one.

Côte d'Ivoire (Ivory Coast)

The capital of Côte d'Ivoire, Abidjan (called the Paris of francophone Africa), was a special case in a different way. The architecture, the culture, food, and drink were all decidedly French, with a French adviser, we learned, behind every public Ivorian official. Everything had to be imported from France, at a price which was definitely *not* a bargain. (Two beers at a fancy night club cost almost ten dollars, not counting any cover charge, which was quite a lot of change in those days). The elegant Hotel Ivoire had, to the best of my knowledge, the only operable indoor ice skating rink in all of Africa.

In Abidjan I was able to help my friend, Goodwyn Cooke, the deputy chief of mission (DCM) in Côte d'Ivoire, get rid of his ambassador, a non-Foreign Service appointee with an AID background. I tended to be particularly sympathetic toward DCMs, having been one myself at my last Foreign Service post. And "Goodie," as he was called, was the quintessential "good soldier" of the career service. That meant holding the post together under trying conditions and preserving morale in the face of an eccentric or otherwise impossible chief of mission. Above all, one never complained about one's fate to an outsider.

I was not exactly an outsider in the strictest sense of the term, and finally, late one evening, over a nightcap or two, the story came out. This time the problem was not the ambassador, who was both professionally qualified and endowed with an easygoing, straightforward personality. It was his much younger new wife, who exhibited highly neurotic tendencies that were making life unbearable for everyone at the post. For example, she had all the embassy wives prepare food for a luncheon by the pool for all the diplomatic spouses of chiefs of mission and then was so critical of the finished product that she threw everything into the pool and retired to her bedroom in a fit of pique. Basically, she was way out of control by anyone, including her husband. Apparently her reputation had made its way to Washington, which caused Goodie additional grief: no one wanted to serve in Abidjan and FSOs resisted assignments there, leaving numerous personnel vacancies, especially that of administrative officer. This meant that Goodie had to take up the slack. Goodie's wife and daughter were apparently beside themselves over the embassy "first lady's" behavior, and the mission clearly was about to explode.

When we returned to Washington, I took it upon myself to phone Lawrence Eagleburger and fill him in on the details. (Larry, my former Serbo-Croatian language colleague at FSI, was by this time the State Department's under secretary for management.) "That does it," he responded. "Yours is now the third report I have received about that post, and it looks as though I'm going to have to pull the guy. It's a pity, really, as everyone tells me the ambassador is very good on substance." (Indeed he was, as Goodie was the first to admit.)

This scenario played out, however, in a somewhat bizarre manner. After the ambassador was ordered home on extended "consultations," Secretary Kissinger was evidently approached by Ivorian President Felix Houphouet-Boigny at the UN (or perhaps it was Paris), who asked him point blank: "Am I to understand that you were miffed because I was not in Abidjan to greet you on your recent visit there?"

Kissinger was flabbergasted: "By no means; I knew you were going to be away before I arrived there on short notice. If anyone should be offended, it should be *you*!"

"If that is the case," the president continued, "please do me a favor and return the ambassador to Abidjan for a decent interval, so that I can kill all these rumors," or words to that effect. To assuage the Ivorian president's feelings, therefore, the ambassador returned to his post, while Goodie was sent on temporary duty to some other post in Africa until his chief was safely out of town. I had never heard of such a procedure before, but apparently it happened. The turmoil that enveloped that post, requiring the temporary banishment of the DCM, can only be imagined.

Eventually (and this is also a rare circumstance for a DCM in trouble), Goodie was "rewarded," if that is the word, with an ambassadorship, probably for having to put up with so much nonsense. The Central African Republic, where he was sent, was not the world's garden spot. It was ruled by a psychopath who called himself the "Emperor Bokassa"—eventually overthrown in a coup after he reportedly brutalized and killed a number of schoolchildren, but that is another story. At least, a humane gesture by the State Department (which is not known for its sentimentality) gave Goodie some necessary vindication prior to early retirement.

Senegal

Our study mission ended in Dakar, capital of Senegal, where Jack had some especially important AID projects to inspect. A Peace Corps staffing problem had also arisen. The post had received no information from the Senegalese authorities about where twenty-five new volunteers scheduled to arrive in March (after our visit) would be placed and under what conditions. Meanwhile Washington-based recruiters, who require considerable lead time, were selecting participants in the program without adequate information.

Nonetheless, Jack and I ended up with a free weekend for the first time on our trip. We decided to spend it on the beach at a resort about an hour's drive from Dakar. The resort was a most unusual one, run by a German promoter named Neckermann in the heart of French-speaking Africa. *"Neckermann machts möglich"* (roughly translated, "Neckermann makes it all possible") was his operating slogan, and he had worked out quite a remarkable program with the Senegalese authorities. Every Saturday a large plane loaded with German tourists would arrive in Senegal, drop off its human "cargo," and pick up the vacationers who had been there the preceding week. The program was designed to appeal especially to middle-class office workers who had had enough of the European winter and were dying at a one-week sun break. The resort itself was a fenced-in enclave on the Atlantic Ocean, with only German spoken within the compound. (I particularly enjoyed listening to the African waiters and bartenders speaking German with a decidedly French accent!) Except for a slightly grass-hut ambiance, there was no suggestion of African culture. One might just as well have been at a German resort on the North Sea in summertime.

On the beach, the standard bathing wear for women was topless, leading Jack to remark: "This is no place to be nearsighted without your glasses!" In fact, the only *nontopless* woman on the beach was an attractive young lady from somewhere in northern Germany, whom I took sailing one afternoon. We developed an instant rapport. The whole exercise was restful for exhausted bodies and good practice for one's rusty German. But it was hardly an African cultural experience.

Mr. Neckermann's ingenious project for the rotating masses had served its purpose. It provided a relaxing break for me, much as Hawaii had done for me in a very different way at the close of *CODEL* Frelinghuysen II (recounted in chapter 14).

INFORMATION AND CULTURAL PROGRAMS IN LATIN AMERICA, 1976

My only other staff study mission of any consequence was to South America, from October 17 to November 2, 1976. George Ingram and Gerry Pitchford of the full committee staff, who accompanied me, focused on the U.S. economic assistance program in Latin America. They cosigned my report, which reviewed U.S. information and cultural programs in Venezuela, Colombia, Peru, and Brazil.[5]

Our staff delegation reviewed operations of the U.S. Information Service (USIS), as the U.S. Information Agency (USIA) is called in the field, and the degree of coordination and cooperation between USIS and other elements of our embassies. An additional (and really the main) objective of our trip was to obtain the reactions of USIS and embassy officials to the recommendations in the so-called Stanton report (see below).

Embassy-USIS Relations

In terms of embassy-USIS relations, I found an unusually favorable climate of cooperation at all four posts, not always characteristic of those relations elsewhere in the world. USIS operations appeared to be an integral part of the country team's activities, enjoying both the confidence and direct support of the chief of mission. As I reported, "The atmosphere was one of interdependence rather than passive acceptance by the embassy of a Washington-imposed USIS presence." USIS officers were of high caliber, although the possibility of *fewer* officers accomplishing equivalent results warranted investigation

Conditions peculiar to the Latin American context affected the embassy-USIS relationship favorably. The U.S. presence tended in one way or another to be *the* central issue, and often the lightning rod for criticism, given the long history of alleged U.S. political dominance in hemispheric affairs. Problems included the real or perceived "exploitation" of Latin America by U.S. business interests, and the economic dependence of the region on fluctuating U.S. markets for Latin products. As a consequence, all mission personnel operated in an environment in which even minor shifts in U.S. policy emphasis could produce immediate public, media, and official reaction. That reality in turn increased awareness of the USIS function and its relevance to the mission as a whole.

The Stanton Report

USIA had survived as a separate and distinct agency of the U.S. government since its inception in 1953. Proposals to reintegrate its operations within the State Department, however, have remained alive (in fact, into the late 1990s).[6] Expert opinion is often divided on the subject.

The issue surfaced most dramatically in March 1975 with the release of a report by an independent Panel on

International Information, Education and Cultural Relations, chaired by Dr. Frank Stanton, former president of CBS. It called for a drastic reorganization of the United States Information Agency to bring about a closer relationship, both in Washington and the field, between U.S. policymakers and those responsible for articulating and interpreting U.S. policy to foreign audiences.

The Stanton report engendered extensive debate in the executive branch and Congress, including our committee, where opinion was divided. Our staff survey team undertook the limited assignment of discussing the Stanton proposals with State and USIS officers in the field, with specific focus on recommendations for restructuring USIS operations *overseas.*

USIS attitudes toward the Stanton proposals in general, and the panel's overseas recommendations in particular, were accurately summarized in a document entitled "USIA and the Future of Public Diplomacy," endorsed by 148 USIA officers. It rejected the recommendations. (More than half of our staff study mission's report consisted of two appendices, the Stanton recommendations and that document.)

USIS personnel in the four Latin American countries I visited confirmed, almost unanimously, the arguments in the rejection statement, namely that:

1. The distinction in Washington between information programs (under USIA) and cultural programs (under the State Department's Bureau of Educational and Cultural Affairs) was arbitrary and awkward. Both programs related to policy and to the society we represent.

2. The Stanton proposals for reorganization would compound that fragmentation, *and would create fragmentation overseas where none existed.*

Leading State Department officials in the field had more divergent views, ranging from strong skepticism to clear approval. The recommendations would have less direct effect on State Department officers, who could perhaps afford a more relaxed and noncommittal stance; in any case, most thought that the changes, if implemented, would not dramatically alter existing USIS operations. In practical terms, much would still depend on the relationship between a chief of mission and USIS personnel. "We could probably live with the situation either way" was the consensus of the Foreign Service people who expressed an opinion.

In any case, the report concluded, these different opinions merited a full and impartial hearing by the Committee on International Relations in the months ahead. (Final note: The Stanton proposals were never adopted.)

CHAPTER 16

The Interparlimentary Circuit

In 1978 I became coordinator for House participation in interparliamentary groups. In February of that year, at the request of Democratic Representative Lee Hamilton, I had produced a study (Appendix B) on the four such groups created by specific House statute, plus nine informal groups that existed or had existed at one time or another.

My original brief as coordinator of all of these groups turned out to be a designation in name only. My actual efforts became focused upon two specific groups: the annual Mexico–United States Interparliamentary Group, and the semiannual exchange between the House of Representatives and the European Parliament. For both groups I served as the principal House staffer until my retirement in 1986. I wrote several speeches for Foreign Affairs Committee chairmen Zablocki and Fascell and for the chairmen of U.S. delegations to these groups, and drafted reports on the meetings after their conclusion. I was in charge of administrative and logistical support for both groups, particularly when the meetings were held abroad.

Interparliamentary activities of members of Congress originated in the last century: U.S. representatives attended the first meeting of the Interparliamentary Union

(IPU) in 1889 and have participated almost continuously since, except for the war years. Only in 1935, however, was U.S. participation in the IPU first established by law. During the 1960s and 1970s the number of interparliamentary groups (IPGs), both multilateral and bilateral, increased dramatically, beginning with the establishment of the North Atlantic Assembly (then known as the NATO Parliamentary Conference) in 1955.

As will be recounted below, coordinating both of my groups was often interesting, always demanding, and sometimes comical—a mixed blessing. Appendix B alludes to the fundamental disparity between the outlooks and attitudes of U.S. members of Congress and their foreign counterparts that made my adventures on the interparliamentary circuit so challenging—and in the end rewarding.

In addition to exercising legislative power in a political system with separation of powers, our representatives needed to serve and visit their constituents regularly, sometimes at considerable distance, and raise funds and campaign for reelection. Contending with a skeptical and suspicious electorate, as well as critical and often hostile media, they were constantly on the defensive to justify their travel abroad. They had multiple competing demands on their time when Congress was in session, and left Washington after adjournment or during recess periods. All these factors made rounding up U.S. delegates for meetings abroad a constant problem.

Foreign parliamentarians, on the other hand, had less demanding legislative schedules and fewer constituent pressures to contend with at home. Exchanges with U.S. members of Congress were often a political *plus* for them. Widespread awareness abroad of the importance of influencing U.S. economic and foreign policies, recognition of the impact those policies had on domestic well-being, and the role of Congress in setting those policies lent stature to their contacts with U.S. legislators.

Mexican legislators operated in a presidential system like ours, but neither their country nor their legislative branch remotely approached ours in significance. European parliamentarians were part of a system in which their leaders had both executive and legislative power, but individual members of parliament played far less important roles in their countries' policies and politics than did our members.

Interparliamentary exchanges in themselves may have been less important for our representatives than the opportunity they provided, however fleeting, to become knowledgeable, however reluctantly, in foreign affairs. Not only the interparliamentary meetings themselves, but the visits to other countries that were often part of an interparliamentary itinerary, helped further the education process. These interesting, demanding and comical trips thus also served a serious purpose.

THE MEXICO–UNITED STATES INTERPARLIAMENTARY GROUP

A joint resolution (P.L. 86-420), approved April 9, 1960, authorized U.S. participation in annual parliamentary conferences with Mexico. The first conference took place in Guadalajara in the state of Jalisco, Mexico, in February 1961. Subsequent meetings have taken place in the United States in even-numbered years and Mexico in odd-numbered years.

P. L. 86-420 as amended stipulated that the House delegation consist of twelve members appointed by the Speaker, plus an equal number of senators appointed by the president *pro tempore* of that body. Traditionally, an equal number of majority and minority members were designated. The chairman or vice chairman was to be a member of the House Committee on Foreign Affairs (now called the Committee on International Relations),[1] and not less than four delegates were also to be members of that committee.

Meetings normally took place when Congress was in recess, namely, during the Presidents' Day break in February, the Easter recess, or the long Memorial Day weekend. By tradition, the delegations usually met with the host country's president.

Program and Agenda

Between the two opening and closing plenary sessions, dominated primarily by public speeches by the U.S. and Mexican leaders, the delegates participated in informal off-the-record "working sessions" to discuss problems of mutual interest. Originally there were two committees, political and economic. The idea was to provide an opportunity for frank discussion, a give-and-take "bull session" that would enable legislators from both countries to work out their differences in an environment free of press and public scrutiny. This format was only partially successful: Mexicans were not as accustomed to speaking off the cuff as were their American counterparts, and they tended to read verbatim from papers prepared and cleared by the Foreign Ministry. Now that the government party (the PRI) is being challenged, this monolithic approach to policy discussions may have opened up a bit. I hope so. But in my time the give-and-take was strictly on the U.S. side.

Initially the focus of the discussions was on bilateral border problems. Earlier deliberations (before my time) led to some notable achievements, such as the settlement on Chamizal (a disputed area near El Paso) and the Colorado River salinity agreement, both attributable to legislative initiatives resulting from the conference.

The agenda was subsequently broadened to include multilateral issues, such as those involving the Organization of American States, the United Nations, and the Law of the Sea. The topics of greatest interest to the Mexicans, however, were usually international trade and tourism. In the early days, Mexican sentiments were both strongly protectionist and interested in opening

U.S. markets to Mexican products. The modern, free-trade outlook of recent Mexican administrations is a new and almost unbelievable phenomenon. Tourism was Mexico's second largest foreign exchange earner after oil. On the U.S. side, the preoccupation was always with illegal aliens (listed on the agenda as "undocumented workers" in deference to Mexican sensitivities) and the traffic in narcotics.

The Mexicans traditionally assigned a high priority to the interparliamentary group as an institution and were extraordinarily hospitable. When the meetings were held in Mexico, the full resources of the Mexican government were placed at the group's disposal. Often entire communities were involved in preparations and welcoming functions. The more limited resources of the U.S. group and more demanding legislative schedule faced by U.S. members made it difficult to respond in kind. In 1976, when the delegations met in Atlanta and Denver during the bicentennial year, local groups made a major effort at hospitality. Generally, however, low attendance by U.S. delegates was a recurrent problem at meetings held in the United States.

My Rocky Road to "Leadership"
My Mexico duties began in 1975 when Marian Czarnecki, the Foreign Affairs Committee chief of staff at the time, telephoned me from home, where he had been laid up with the flu. He instructed me to pick up a memo he had written from his office, then stop by the office of the Hon. Robert N. C. Nix of Philadelphia (the House chairman of the IPG) to ask if he would like to accompany me to the inner sanctum office of Senate majority leader Mike Mansfield. Mr. Nix declined my invitation (as Marian anticipated), and so I proceeded to the Senate on my own. It only dawned on me after I entered the senator's office that I was to be the sole representative of the House of Representatives at what turned out to be a preparatory luncheon meeting to

discuss the dates, site, and agenda for the next interparliamentary "reunion."

Thus I became an instant "expert" on the Mexico–United States Interparliamentary Group. This was not unusual on Capitol Hill; a salient feature of life there is the ease with which a staff employee can take on such duties in a given field. (As noted in chapter 8, I once drafted a standard response—read "form letter"—to inquiries to Senator Joe Clark's office about the benefits provided by the Education Act, then recently passed by Congress, and soon became the recipient of all letters on education and the office "expert" on the subject. I was even called a few times for advice after I left the office.)

Similarly, with respect to Mexico, I attended one luncheon in the Senate majority leader's office and then ran the House section of the Mexico-U.S. IPG for the next eleven years. My qualifications included a smattering of high school Spanish and no experience whatsoever in Latin American affairs. In short, I was a natural for the job. Having served two years as the State Department desk officer for Canada and secretary of the U.S. Section of the Canada-U.S. Permanent Joint Board on Defense, I was clearly considerably more qualified to staff and support the Canadian-U.S. interparliamentary group. However, that group was a cinch to handle and essentially took care of itself. Troubleshooters like myself (even if involuntary) tend to go where the trouble is.

When I entered Senator Mansfield's office, he nodded to me politely, if not enthusiastically, and instructed me to sit at the far end of the table next to the Mexican ambassador. The latter informed me, among other things, who was going to win the forthcoming Mexican election. (In those days the PRI government party candidate, once nominated, always ran without opposition, which aided immeasurably in making electoral predictions.) After the meal and informal pleasantries, Senator Mansfield turned to his Mexican counterpart and said: "Well, Mr. Chairman, tell us what you have in mind."

The Mexican dignitary then proceeded to deliver a rapturous, fifteen-minute soliloquy about the proposed site of the next conference, Campeche, a "quaint, historic fishing village on the Gulf Coast," internationally famous for the largest and most succulent shrimp to be found anywhere in the world. The hotel we would be staying at was "first class" and was located on a beautiful sandy beach. "Of course," he emphasized, there would be a fishing boat at the disposal of all delegates at all times. After the closing plenary session, both delegations would fly (in Mexican aircraft) to the brand-new resort of Cancún, located on the Caribbean coast. President Echeverria would preside at an opening ceremony for the new airport there and then host a luncheon in our honor at one of the few hotels then in operation.

"Thank you, Mr. Chairman," Senator Mansfield responded without pausing for any other reaction. "That all meets with our approval. . . . Now what about the agenda?" I realized unhappily that the dates proposed were exactly the ones objected to (very emphatically) in Marian's memo, that the plans were a fait accompli, and that Marian's memo was in the D.O.A. (Dead on Arrival) category. Clearly, it was inappropriate for a staff man to object to an agreement already reached (long before the luncheon took place) between the Mexican delegation leadership and the majority leader of the U.S. Senate.

This entire scenario, I was to discover in due course, was the usual Senate-House arrangement—par for the course. The senator would work out all the arrangements with his Mexican colleagues, always to accommodate the *Senate* schedule, which he controlled anyway. House members were rarely consulted in advance, only notified when the plans had been firmed up. Despite a good deal of grumbling on the House side, in the last analysis no one felt strongly enough to do anything about the situation.

This Mexico-U.S. mechanism meant everything to Mansfield—his "pet project"—and not all that much to anyone else. Thus the senator became the absolute dictator of this particular exchange, even though he treated everyone, including staff members, with great outward courtesy. Everyone realized, however, that *he* was calling all the shots. Ironically, the media, which tended to criticize the senator, if at all, for being a "pushover" among his colleagues, never picked up this autocratic tendency. His accommodating style with his peers was always contrasted with LBJ's aggressiveness and strong "leadership." But popular perceptions are often deceiving.

After a number of years I discovered that the interparliamentary delegations actually fared better under one leader, rather than working at cross-purposes under several. Mansfield's leadership was clearly nurtured by the glaring weaknesses of the House delegation: the chairman, Representative Nix, was something of a loner, even among fellow members of the Black Caucus. Rumor had it that he was selected to head up the House section of the group by former Speaker John McCormack of Massachusetts, who was under the mistaken impression that the Mexicans would welcome an African-American in the U.S. leadership spot with open arms. On the very rare occasions when he had journeyed down to Mexico for the annual conferences, Nix had evidently felt distinctly uncomfortable and took out his frustrations in booze. (I was told that staff members had reportedly been obliged to help "prop him up" for public functions.)

Above all, Nix resented being relegated to a strictly secondary role to Senator Mansfield, and as a result he more or less retired from the fray altogether. "I don't want to be his 'nigger,'" he once confided to a thoroughly shocked Marian Czarnecki, who was totally unprepared for such blunt language from someone who normally presented a rather smooth and sophisticated exterior. (Whatever his shortcomings might have been, Mr. Nix did *not* strike a strident or militant pose and managed to get on quite well with his colleagues of all races.)

By the time I appeared on the scene, Nix had effectively removed himself from the de facto leadership of the House delegation, although he still retained the formal title of chairman. His usual strategy became entirely predictable: at the very last moment, he would call me in and announce that he would be unavailable to travel with the delegation because of overwhelming political commitments in his district. Jim Wright, long before he served as majority leader or Speaker, would end up as "acting" chairman. No one even hinted at the possibility that Mr. Nix might relinquish his title as chairman, as that would be considered an offense to the Black Caucus and definitely not "politically correct."

The Campeche-Cancún Caper

"Well," Marian said only half in jest, "you have managed to fail in your first mission to the *other body*. For that sin, you will have to do penance: you have now been appointed, with Chairman Nix's approval, the Number One staff member of the House section of the Mexican-U.S. Interparliamentary Exchange. Congratulations and good luck. You will need all the luck you can get." These words turned out to be prescient, to put it mildly.

Of all the annual conferences of the Mexico–United States Interparliamentary Group, the most memorable was my first, in the spring of 1975, in Campeche and Cancún. This exercise became the absolute embodiment of the principles underlying Murphy's Law: if something *can* go wrong, it *will*.

Indeed, we started off all wrong before we ever left Washington. Senator Mansfield, who had direct control over the Senate floor schedule, made certain that all debate on Friday afternoon was concluded in time for a

4:00 P.M. departure for the airport. The House had similar assurances from Speaker Carl Albert, but with less certainty. (The diminutive Oklahoman was highly popular on both sides of the aisle, but his control over that unruly body was not always complete.) The legislation being debated that afternoon was highly controversial, and opponents of the measure started to introduce a long series of amendments. I talked to Jim Wright, then the acting House delegation chairman, on several occasions throughout the afternoon and also kept my staff counterpart in the Senate, Bob Dockery, closely informed of developments. Wright kept hoping that the next vote would be the final one, but his optimism was not justified.

Finally at about 4:30 P.M. or thereabouts, Dockery called me with a strident edge to his voice: "Chips, meet us at the corner of South Capitol Street and Independence Avenue in fifteen minutes, with a copy of the draft opening plenary session remarks you prepared for Jim Wright. Senator Mansfield is going to deliver them tomorrow morning." "Are you telling me, Bob, that you are going to leave all of the House delegates behind? You can't do that, for God's sake," I replied in some consternation. "Chips, those are my orders . . . I only work here. . . ." and the phone went dead.

With great reluctance I did as I was told, and then returned to inform Jim Wright that the senators and their spouses had flown off to the Yucatán without any representation from the House of Representatives. Although Wright's reaction to this news is not printable, we both realized that, in the words of Grover Cleveland, a "condition, not a theory," confronted us. It was my unhappy duty to inform all the delegates' spouses, first and foremost, that the trip was off, at least for that day, and I would have to let them know as future arrangements were made.

The ladies, who had all gathered in front of the Rayburn House Office Building, with extensive luggage filled with finery for a number of ceremonial occasions, were even less sanguine about the situation than was Jim Wright, and they let me know it, since I was the only one around. Finally everyone left for home, and I went off to report what had happened to the chief of staff. (Spouses of delegates and principal staff members were authorized to accompany these interparliamentary delegations "for representational/ protocol reasons." Foreign delegates also brought their spouses. Travel was by military aircraft, not commercial carrier, so if there was room on the plane, the spouses did not constitute an additional cost.)

All in all, the beginning was hardly auspicious. As it turned out, Mansfield's actions, although highhanded, were perfectly proper. Despite Carl Albert's promises, the House debate continued until midnight, and if the plane had been delayed until then, it would not have been allowed to take off until the following morning. This way, at least a handful of senators were able to represent the United States at the opening session and avoid total embarrassment. Moreover, Senator Mansfield sent the plane back the same evening after his arrival in Mérida, the capital of Yucatán, so that the House members and staff could depart the following morning.

On the way south, there was a great deal of moaning and complaining about the way things had worked out so far. "Chips," one indignant House member told me over Bloody Marys, "I'm just going to tell Mike, and I'm not kidding: '*Mike, this sh-t's gotta cease.*' That's what I'm going to tell him, believe it or not." But believe it or not, when we arrived in Mérida the next day, a ten-piece band and a long line of dignitaries greeted us. The dignitaries included all the Mexican delegates, headed up by, you guessed it, Senator Mansfield. Everyone embraced like long-lost friends and the internecine war between House and Senate was put on hold, at least for the moment. (One of the great abilities of successful politicians, I have often found, is their uncanny ability to rise to all occasions.)

Campeche, alas, did not at all measure up to the Mexican's description in the majority leader's office. The town itself had very little to offer, except for three or four shops filled with tourist items. The hotel was seedy in the extreme, with sawdust on the floors and air-conditioning units that didn't work in the rooms. It was tremendously hot and humid, to such an extent that I had difficulty taking notes in the committee sessions as I dripped sweat on the paper. No air-conditioning there—not even a ceiling fan.

The "sandy beach" was nonexistent, just rocks that the waves washed over in front of the hotel. The hotel pool was filled with a kind of green slime and looked unusable. I was one of the few people who swam in it, for brief intervals. And no fishing boat could be discerned, far out onto the horizon. Instead, the Mexicans arranged for an eight-hour bus trip up and down the coast after the closing session. Mansfield pressured all of the senators and staff to accompany him, but fortunately Jim Wright had no interest in the proposal. As a result, all the House members and staff waited until the last bus left in the morning before coming downstairs for breakfast.

As is customary with such large groups, there were many disparate and some conflicting personalities. On the Senate side, both Vance Hartke and his wife were treated as virtual pariahs. The staff was instructed at the outset to refer any of their demands directly to Senator Mansfield. An old Capitol Hill joke had it that there were two senators from the state of Indiana: Bayh (Senator Birch Bayh) and "Bought," a reference to Hartke's labor backing. Mrs. Hartke chose the wrong person when she told my wife that the problem with the whole exchange was that "we have such inferior staff!" Senator Paul Laxalt of Nevada, who was to become a prominent Reagan supporter in future years, was then in his first term as a senator and very congenial and eager to please. One of the most lovable characters of all was Senator Jennings Randolph of West Virginia, a great bear of a man, who was a distinct pleasure to have around. Senator Stuart Symington, a longtime widower by that time, had arrived with a lady friend (whom he flew down and back at his own expense by commercial airline.) The lady, who was perfectly presentable in all respects, was for some reason very uncomfortable in her role as a congressional "guest" and more or less disappeared from sight. Suddenly the senator announced that he was driving his friend overland to Cancún, a route considered almost impassable by car. Somehow he made it.

On the House side, Charlie Wilson of Texas was perhaps the most glamorous personality, with his young and very attractive wife. They made the mistake of going on the bus trip, but at the first "pit stop" they grabbed a cab and came back to the hotel. Another prominent member was Hermann Badillo, a rising Puerto Rican politician from New York who later became a deputy mayor of New York City. He was a pain in the groin to the staff, as he demanded the delivery of the *New York Times* to his door every morning at 8:00, although there were only two planes a week that flew in to Mérida. Basically, we ignored him.

Perhaps one of the most unusual delegates was Representative Tennyson Guyer, a freshman Republican from Ohio. Tenny Guyer had been a clown in the circus, an accomplished magician (a student of Houdini), and a favorite speaker at Rotary and Lions Club luncheons. Finally, someone told him he ought to run for Congress, and he was elected easily. On the trip back to Washington on the Air Force plane, Senator Hartke was bothering everyone with a clumsy card trick: "Take any card," he would say, while everyone else was trying to eat lunch. Finally Guyer put him in his place: "Let me have those cards, Senator," he said and then threw the pack onto the floor, while the proper card flipped up by itself. It was a breathtaking moment and had the blessed result of shutting down the senator from Indiana for the remainder of the trip.

At one point during the trip Jim Wright took me aside and instructed me to ask Tenny Guyer to speak on a particular agenda topic (I forget which one). I remember telling him: "Mr. Guyer has been on our committee for over six months now, and I have never heard him utter a word or ask a single question. Are you sure you want him to speak?" "Believe me, Chips," our chairman responded, "He can give a hell of a speech!" Jim Wright was so right: the silent Tennyson Guyer delivered a totally spellbinding oration that managed to rivet everyone's attention, including the Mexicans. From that experience I learned that you never know what talent exists until you give it a chance.

About Jim Wright

I have always felt that Jim Wright, the Speaker of the House later forced to resign in disgrace, got a bum rap. Although his image became highly tarnished, I believe that the charges brought against him were really insubstantial. The "book deal" he was charged with may not have been greatly to his credit, but it did not seem illegal. (Perhaps the worst action he took was his attempt to influence a savings and loan regulator, but he was never charged with *that* offense, as he had so much company among his peers.) Some of his actions seemed extreme and even out of character, and they eventually destroyed him. He would extend the period for House votes, after time had expired, to enable him to round up additional votes to overcome an unfavorable outcome. But I have always believed he acted this way because he was essentially a loner and wanted to stay ahead of his troops, namely, the Young Turks on his left flank.

In the end, extreme partisanship—or its perception—did in both Wright and, to a lesser extent, Newt Gingrich, his main accuser. No one would have prevailed against such Speakers as John McCormack, Carl Albert, or even Tip O'Neill for the same alleged offenses. What happened to Jim Wright also happened to Gingrich some years later: both became extremely partisan in their actions, Gingrich before he became speaker and Wright after assuming the position.

In 1975, however, Wright projected an entirely different impression. He was the soul of bipartisanship, so much so that a Republican, Bob Lagomarsino of California, who had Reagan as a constituent and boasted one of the most conservative districts in the country, took to the House floor and commended "the gentleman from Texas for his outstanding leadership of the House delegation." This accolade appeared in the *Congressional Record* after that 1975 conference. Lagomarsino even added that that he felt a sense of pride for having been led by such a knowledgeable and effective chairman, who extended every possible courtesy to the minority members of the delegation. A decade or so later such rhetoric would have been unthinkable.

Jim Wright was reasonable in all respects and a pleasure to work with. It always pained me to see a man of such ability eventually brought down by his own excesses. At the conference he was an ideal chairman of the House section: he spoke fluent Spanish, had an instinctive understanding of Mexican sensibilities, and could use just the right language to make his point. Unlike his successor as chairman of the delegation, Kika de la Garza, he was in no way beholden to the Mexicans for anything and did not hesitate to promote the U. S. position vigorously on all issues before the conference, always in the right way. De la Garza himself often observed: "The Mexicans are really impressed when Jim Wright talks to them in Spanish. They merely *expect* it of me!"

On to Cancún

After the conclusion of the working sessions, the show moved to Cancún, then a newly developed resort on Mexico's Caribbean coast. Again, Murphy's Law dominated the arrangements. We flew in two separate Mexican propeller planes. The ladies were all assigned to the second plane. The first one landed just in time for the airport dedication ceremony, but the second one was kept aloft for security reasons until the ceremony was almost over. (Mexican regulations prohibited any planes from landing while "El Presidente" was in the area.) Apparently the air did not circulate properly in the second plane and the extended ride was hot, stuffy, and miserable. Consequently, the ladies deplaned in a rotten mood.

The airport dedication ceremony was a crashing bore and seemed to last interminably. Bob Dockery and I needed to get to the hotel as soon as possible to work on the joint statement. Bob, my wife, and I sneaked off early, hailed a cab and went directly to the hotel, to check in and go right to work. By the end of that day, I began to recall the advice given the delegations by Senator Laxalt during a discussion of the "tourism" item on the agenda. Recalling his experience with the opening of hotels and resorts in Las Vegas, he recommended above all else that you "do not open up to the public until you are fully prepared and ready to receive large numbers of guests. The *first impressions* you make are of maximum importance, as they are conveyed instantly to travel agencies around the world. If you open prematurely, your reputation will suffer and you will surely regret it." (Although not an exact quote, that is almost precisely what he said.)

Alas, the Mexicans did not heed this good advice. The hotel we stayed in was in no way prepared for an onslaught of tourists, not to mention some fifty delegates, their spouses and entourage, plus the Mexican presidential party. After Clara and I had checked in, we were escorted to our room by a pleasant young Mexican attendant with the key. When he opened the door, however, we found standing in front of us an entirely naked woman who had just emerged from the shower with water still running off her body. When she screamed loudly, the young man closed the door with dispatch. "Must be the wrong room," he concluded logically.

I did not have time to search for vacant rooms, so I left Clara in charge of that project and hastened to find Bob in the delegation's control room. We worked right up to lunch hour, until I had to return to our room to change for the presidential command performance. I jumped quickly into the shower and soaped up my entire body, at which point the water in the shower (and the sink as well) went off. I finally used a bottle of soda water to wash off as much soap as possible before dressing with some care.

The luncheon predictably dragged on forever, with an abundance of long-winded speeches. The president was no exception. By this time all of the Americans were anxious to get out on the "beautiful white sandy beach" on our last free afternoon in the Yucatán. At last the formalities were concluded, the president departed with his entourage, and the Americans hastened to return to their rooms. Clara and I shared an elevator with Senator and Mrs. Charles Percy (of Illinois). "You look worried, Senator," I remarked. "Is something wrong?"

"Well, I don't know," he responded. "I was told the water that went off before the luncheon came on again and flooded our room."

We accompanied the senator and his wife to their room and discovered to everyone's relief that all was well. False alarm, apparently. But when we opened the door to *our* room, we found our suitcases and most of our clothing floating on top of about a foot of water. Needless to say, the hotel was not at all prepared to cope with these problems.

My final trial by fire involved rubber rafts that had been rented for the afternoon by Charlie Wilson and his spouse. The rafts were fragile in composition and not at all suited for ocean surf; they were designed instead for the still-water lagoon located right next to the hotel. Guests never moved as they floated around the motionless lagoon. One trip on a breaker crashing on the beach destroyed these delicate rafts in short order. Since nobody had told the Wilsons what to expect, at the end of the afternoon they turned in barely recognizable pieces of equipment. The incensed manager of the surf shop followed me around for the next twelve hours trying to collect damages. I was willing to pay him something, but not the entire amount he demanded, as it was really partially his fault for not warning the Americans about the proper use of the equipment. Finally he made such a scene that Senator Mansfield instructed one of his aides to pay the amount in full to avoid further embarrassment. "The squeaky wheel gets the grease" is definitely the rule where Congress is concerned.

At this climactic moment, you could say one thing in favor of the Fifteenth Mexico–United States Interparliamentary Conference: it was over. According to my records, in February 1976 Jim Wright formally turned over the chairmanship of the House delegation to his Texas colleague, Representative Eligio (Kika) de la Garza, who served in this capacity until the House went Republican in 1994, long after my retirement in 1986.

Congressman Kika de la Garza

The House unquestionably had the upper hand in terms of U.S. participation in the conferences for those eighteen years under de la Garza (Senator Mansfield retired and went on to become ambassador to Japan). Kika's rhetoric was unquestionably effective, but his speeches, half in English and half in Spanish, with few full sentences in either language, were quite a problem for me in preparing the annual reports of the conferences.

Kika's greatest contribution to the annual exchanges was to abolish the joint statement issued after each meeting. Traditionally, the Mexicans would send us their version of what transpired at the conference and ask our members to sign on. Any American legislator who signed such a document could be defeated at the next election on that basis alone. In short, the text had to be completely rewritten and even then it was hard to get approval from the American side. It was just bad news for everyone!

De la Garza was a unique character among his House colleagues. Although there were numerous Hispanics in Congress, none looked quite as authentically Mexican as Kika. He just happened to have been born on the north side of the Rio Grande. This is not to say that he was or considered himself any less of an American patriot than any of his colleagues; rather, he had a special feel for, and a subtle understanding of, his primarily Mexican-American constituents. Kika was proud of his Mexican heritage and of being the only American legislator to receive the Aztec Eagle award from the Mexican government. He conceived of himself as a conciliator, called upon to smooth over rough edges and promote peace and harmony between the two national delegations. For this reason, he tried consistently—and usually successfully—to keep members off the House delegation who might be expected to rock the boat.

Delegates to these interparliamentary conferences were, by and large, knowledgeable about Mexican attitudes and had sizable Mexican-American constituencies. (For instance, Republican Rep. John Rousselot, a former official of the John Birch Society, and Senator Joseph Montoya, a New Mexico "leftist," were in full agreement on immigration policy.) Kika, however, was unenthusiastic about having other Hispanic members on his delegation. The wives allegedly did not get along, and he didn't want to share the Hispanic spotlight. One reason why he would wait until the last moment to recommend a slate of potential delegates to the Speaker may have been because he hoped that the Hispanic members would have other commitments by then. He was usually right about this, but then he had to round up senators. After Mansfield's departure, never more than three senators attended the conferences, mostly because their schedules were already full by the time they became aware of the meetings. De la Garza's inability to produce a sufficient number of senators eventually took away some of his luster in Mexican eyes.

De la Garza was also proud of his humble origin: he liked to remind his audiences that he rose from a "shoeshine boy" in McAllen, Texas, to become chairman of the full House Committee on Agriculture, a not insignificant achievement. He viewed the Senate as primarily a home for millionaires, and he distrusted both its membership and the institution. As a speaker to Mexican and Mexican-American audiences, he was without peer. Every year he would tell the same story about Lyndon Johnson interviewing Rio Grande flood victims: LBJ was confronted by an elderly Mexican lady, who stood her children up and told the president of the United States that if he ever came to visit her, he would find a "welcome and a humble home." The story brought tears to Mexican eyes.

Despite Kika's many sensitivities and hang-ups, his deviousness in dealing with his colleagues, and his resentment of his perceived detractors in "the other body," he had one overwhelmingly redeeming feature: an innate and incisive sense of humor. My favorite story is one he liked to tell on himself. At the twenty-first conference in Manzanillo in 1981, he was chatting amiably with his Senate counterpart, Senator Percy. At one point, Percy observed: "You know, Kika, after the flag-raising ceremony this morning, I was officially presented with the American flag; but then a fat little Mexican delegate came along and took it from me and I never saw it again." "That was *ME*, *Senador*," the House chairman responded, always to much laughter.

The Battle of Manzanillo Bay

The Manzanillo meeting was memorable to me for another reason: I almost drowned my chairman in Manzanillo Bay. After the working sessions, followed by the closing plenary, we had exactly one afternoon free before our scheduled departure the following morning. As a former sailor of sorts (on Wisconsin's inland lakes), I offered to take Kika and Shelly Livingston, the committee's budget and fiscal expert, on a sail in the blue waters of the bay. Several catamarans were available for rent and I asked the man in charge if I could take one of them on an outing.

"*Ay, caramba*," the man replied. "If you want that one, *señor*, you are welcome to it." I didn't realize at the time that he was telling me something important.

"Don't worry about me, honey," were Kika's last words to his wife. "Chips is an experienced sailor and will take good care of me."

Those words were to haunt me later in the day. While I had only sailed a catamaran once before, I did have a general knowledge of sailing principles: how to come about, tack, go before the wind, and turn into the wind if the craft were tipping too drastically. On this boat, however, the tiller did not respond very well to my "expert" touch. Only in the middle of the bay did I realize the two rudders were both broken off and unusable. By this time we were in a condition known as "in stays," which means pointed directly into the wind, with the sails flapping helplessly. I could not turn the craft in any direction, as the rudders did not work. Instead the wind blew us straight backward to the bay's far shore.

Kika and Shelly were laughing and telling jokes while sitting in the front of the boat, blithely unaware of impending doom. At one point I thought of jumping overboard to swim the boat around in another direction, but I soon rejected the idea: the wind might have been too strong and taken the craft away before I had a chance to reboard. I was the captain and had to stay with my ship. Always moving directly backwards, we made our way to the shore, where I noticed there were some fairly high waves breaking on the sand. Finally, I had no other choice but to order my passengers to jump, and I think I even resolved the chairman's indecision by pushing him into the sea. I regarded it as a lifesaving sort of move. Against my own wishes, I somehow felt obliged to stay with the ship, which crashed on the beach, with the mast breaking in two.

Fortunately, no one was injured, although the chairman lost his prescription glasses and his shoes. And we had to walk for miles over rocky cliffs to make our way back to the hotel. To say that I never lived this venture down is an understatement.

There follows my mock press release, followed by my bogus newspaper article describing the incident in full. The *Matamoros Mañana* newspaper did run a brief (mostly inaccurate) story on de la Garza's "swim." My *bogus* article (page 384) was quite different and was designed exclusively for humorous purposes.

COMMITTEE ON
FOREIGN AFFAIRS
HOUSE OF REPRESENTATIVES

COMMITTEE ON
FOREIGN RELATIONS
UNITED STATES SENATE

Mexico-United States Interparliamentary Group

United States Delegation

June 16, 1981

FOR IMMEDIATE RELEASE   MANZANILLO, MEXICO

NAVY ANNOUNCES SEAMANSHIP TROPHY WINNERS

The United States Navy is pleased to announce that this year's recipients of the Knapp Memorial Trophy for outstanding seamanship are messrs;

Ed Fox, Former Minority Consultant, and

J.C. Chester, Senior Consultant, Retired.

In his presentation address, Captain Knapp noted that among the criteria for this award are the skippers' ability to make key decisions under conditions of great external stress.

In the case of Mr. Fox, he noted, the ship's mast was placed in a downward vertical position in less than 60 seconds with the subsequent loss of only one relatively minor Subcommittee Staff Director.

Mr. Chester, however, was called upon to make a more critical command decision under severe emergency conditions when he pushed the distinguished Chairman of the House delegation and an unidentified, hysterical female companion into the open sea just prior to executing a forced crash landing on a deserted beach.

Although for this act of valor, Mr. Chester's services with the Mexico-U.S. Interparliamentary Delegation have been abruptly terminated, Captain Knapp observed that the only real loss accruing from this incident involved a pair of prescription glasses, a sail, and two smashed Rudders which were non-functional in the first place.

Both Skippers, Fox and Chester, have been transferred to the Armed Services Committee, where it is hoped that their expertise will be utilized by the U.S. Navy. Both have also been recommended for the Navy Cross.

"They are our cross to bear from now on...." Captain Knapp reluctantly concluded!

(*Note:* Captain Knapp was the ranking Navy escort officer who accompanied the delegation. Ed Fox was a Republican staffer who subsequently became assisant secretary of state for congressional relations. He managed to capsize his craft within minutes, with Victor Johnson, the ARA subcommittee staff director, on board.)

From the *MATAMOROS MAÑANA* (translated from the Spanish):

U.S. LEGISLATOR GOES OVERBOARD IN MEXICAN WATERS

Mexican authorities released this photograph today of a ship last seen in Manzanillo Bay last month, following the conclusion of the Twenty-First Mexico-United States "Reunion." According to unconfirmed reports, a prominent U.S. congressman and chairman of the U.S. delegation to the conference, together with two unidentified companions, were on board just before the craft capsized and crashed on a deserted beach across the bay from the luxurious Las Hadas Hotel.

The foreign ministry noted that among the topics discussed at the interparliamentary meeting were those relating to current multilateral negotiations on the Law of the Sea. Mexico has adopted a firm and consistent position with respect to exclusive fishing rights in areas of its jurisdiction. A ministry spokesman denied, however, that Chairman de la Garza had jumped overboard in search of tuna, shrimp or other species in defiance of Mexican law. Instead, it was alleged that he was trying to recover his prescription glasses and save the life of a female crew member. While some skepticism has been expressed over this explanation, no further comment was provided.

Final Thoughts on the Mexico-U.S. Interparliamentary Group

Many other stories could be recounted about this colorful interparliamentary exchange, but perhaps I have provided enough of the flavor. One of the last tasks I undertook for the committee before retiring in August 1986 was to draft a final House report on the Mexico-U.S. conference held in Colorado Springs. The Senate, as always, was months late in producing its input, so I handed the draft to a colleague who had been a participant in the last IPG trip; he placed it in a cardboard box next to his desk.

A year later, my successor, Gerry Pitchford, called me for assistance in putting together *last year's* report, in anticipation of the following year's conference. Since Gerry had not been on any of the previous conference trips, this was a rather challenging assignment for him. Fortunately, I was able to tell him to check Mark Tavlarides's box, where the draft still lay. This only reinforces my belief in a timeless principle: your value tends to increase when you are gone!

EUROPEAN PARLIAMENT— U.S. CONGRESS EXCHANGES

The semiannual European Parliament exchange came into being as a result of a personal feud within the Foreign Affairs Committee. Wayne Hays of Ohio could not tolerate Ben Rosenthal of New York, and the feeling was distinctly mutual. Hays became chairman of the U.S. House delegation to NATO (that is, the NATO Parliamentary Assembly) and effectively excluded Rosenthal from serving on his delegation, even though Ben was the newly elected chairman of the European subcommittee. While this was generally considered another highhanded and arbitrary action on Hays's part, as most of his actions were, I seriously question whether Ben Rosenthal ever had any real desire to serve under Hays's leadership.

Rosenthal decided to strike out on his own. He was aided and abetted by his close aide, Cliff Hackett, who made a career out of developing liberal alternatives to what he considered the committee's uninspired status quo. Together with Don Fraser of Minnesota, another prominent liberal and human rights advocate, and Floridian Sam Gibbons of the Ways and Means Committee, Rosenthal founded a new informal U. S.-European exchange. Although the membership of the U.S. delegation was always diversified politically, the leadership was strictly of a liberal cast. (Gibbons had moved closer to the center over the years, but he retained close links with the liberals. In fact, everyone liked Sam and especially his friendly wife, Martha, which accounts for the fact that he remained one of the three cochairmen long after the others dropped out.) Eventually Fraser left the House to run unsuccessfully for the Senate, and Rosenthal decided to resign as well. His long bout with cancer may have been a motivating factor.

In late 1977 or early 1978 I was drafted to take over the staffing of this exchange, with the primary—if unstated—objective of converting it from a Rosenthal-Fraser operation into a mainstream Zablocki institution. Zablocki agreed to be "interim" chairman of the U.S. group, at least for the January conference in Washington. He would later appoint someone else as de facto chairman of the U.S. delegation, eventually Rep. Leo Ryan of California. Ryan was anointed CEO of the group, a position he held when the delegations met in Sicily over the Easter recess in 1978.

The European Parliament

The European Parliament was one of four institutions which collectively ran the (originally) nine-nation European Community (EC), now called the European Union. (The nine nations have since been expanded to at least thirteen, although I am not certain any longer of the exact number; likewise many of the other specifics regarding the EP may have changed.) The other EC institutions were: the Commission, the Council of Ministers, and the Court of Justice

Parliament's headquarters was in Luxembourg, although plenary sessions were also held in Strasbourg. Committees of the Parliament met mostly in Brussels. An outgrowth of the Common Assembly of the three communities, Parliament originally consisted of 198 members, nominated by the parliaments of the nine

member countries and representing fifty-three national
parties. In June 1978, in the expanded Parliament's first
international elections, some 175 million European voters directly elected representatives. Just about every
conceivable segment of political opinion was represented in this body, including communists, who were
notably quiet and cooperative. The reason, I was told,
was that they were at the time seeking *respectability* above
all else.

Aside from serving as the forum of the European
Communities, in which policy issues affecting the Communities were discussed, Parliament had certain limited
powers, including especially the power to approve or
reject the EC budget. During my era, however, it func-
tioned largely as a mammoth debating society.

U.S. Participation

During my tenure with the U.S. delegation, no statutory authority existed for U.S. participation in the semiannual meetings of the US-EP delegations, held
alternately in the United States and abroad. Various attempts were made to "institutionalize" the mechanism
along the lines of the North Atlantic Assembly, the IPU,
and such groups as the Mexico-U.S. and Canada-U.S.
interparliamentary groups. The Foreign Affairs Committee usually opposed such moves, both on budgetary
grounds and because, as Congressman Ryan once argued in a Senate-House conference: "The informality
of the group is part of the reason why it works as well as
it does. It is the lack of institutionalization that I think
gives it some real value." The real reason, however,
was that the group's "informal" mode allowed the Foreign Affairs Committee to control every aspect of the
operation. Speaker Tip O'Neill had once appointed
Congressman Phil Burton of California to head up the
NATO group (discussed in greater detail in chapter 17).
That was a blunder no one on our committee wanted to
see repeated.

After Zablocki's interim chairmanship of the U.S. delegation, the first overall leader I served under was Congressman Ryan. Traditionally there had been three basically equal cochairmen, but in due course one emerged as more equal than the others. (At some point, Larry Winn, Jr., of Kansas, a Foreign Affairs Committee member, was named minority cochairman.) Leo Ryan represented the San Francisco Bay area and was evidently unrestrained in any fashion by political inhibitions. He had strong opinions on certain subjects like nuclear waste disposal, which, he warned the Europeans, was becoming a growing danger. Many of the European delegates were unhappy about this position, as they were interested in gaining U.S. technological assistance for construction of nuclear reactors. The 1979 Three-Mile Island incident eventually provided Leo with some vindication on this issue.

On to Europe

While Leo became a strong influence on the delegations, he was not exactly an "organization man." Instead he tended to go off on tangents, one of which proved extremely troublesome for me, in connection with the first meeting over which he presided, in Taormina, Sicily, in the shadow of the constantly (if moderately) erupting Mt. Etna.

The dates of the meeting were March 28 to April 3, 1978, during the Easter recess. As usual, we had a military plane assigned to us, and the U.S. members (not their spouses) were authorized per diem by their respective committee chairmen. This procedure saved the government money, compared with a separate appropriation for a "formalized" delegation. However, some chairmen of committees other than Foreign Affairs had misgivings about authorizing foreign travel for noncommittee business. I particularly recall Trent Lott of Mississippi, then a representative, telling me that if he had to explain this matter to Ray Madden, chairman of the Rules Committee and the oldest member of the House at the time, he "simply would not have gone." Fortunately, he had a more sympathetic chairman of another committee to help him out.

A Side Trip to Tunisia

We often had stopovers in other countries, scheduled either before or after the formal meetings with the Europeans. This time, at least part of the U.S. delegation was scheduled to join Leo Ryan after the conference on a brief side trip to Tunisia, just across the Mediterranean from Sicily. As it turned out, the U.S. ambassador to Tunisia, Edward Mulcahy, was another attractive and congenial Irishman whom Leo knew personally. The ambassador was enthusiastic about the proposed "study mission" to Tunisia and gave it his full backing in telegrams to the Department of State. Tunisia, which had traditionally displayed a pro-Western orientation under President Habib Bourguiba, had been rather neglected in recent years, in Mulcahy's opinion, and perhaps taken somewhat for granted. Bourguiba himself was both aging and ailing, and a succession problem loomed on the horizon. This was an ideal time to show the flag, so to speak, in the form of a full-fledged congressional visit, which the ambassador hoped would demonstrate renewed American interest in the country and a commitment to its future role as a moderate Arab state. Ambassador Mulcahy personally involved himself in all aspects of our impending visit, which was to include meetings with officials at the highest level and at least one dinner to be hosted by the Tunisian foreign minister.

What I did *not* realize until some time later was that all of these elaborate preparations in our behalf were actually a "cover" for a freewheeling secret mission planned by Leo Ryan and National Security Adviser Zbigniew Brzezinski. (One or two other executive branch officials may have been in on the scheme, but if so, I was not aware of them.) Leo planned, in fact, to meet secretly with Yasser Arafat at some undisclosed location in Tunis, and he planned to bring along any interested members. I was sworn to secrecy but had immediate misgivings. In those days, Arafat was generally regarded as a terrorist, not an international statesman, and just the act of meeting with him could cause some members with substantial Jewish constituencies a lot of political "heartburn." Even if they avoided the meeting itself, they might be tarred by an opponent merely for serving on the delegation. None of these inhibitions bothered Leo one iota. In California, evidently, one could meet with any rough character with impunity.

I specifically avoided telling any of this to either Clem Zablocki or his chief of staff, because the former already was perceived in some quarters as having a "Jewish problem." Clem had long believed that Israel was receiving an unjustified lion's share of U.S. grant aid, and that appropriations should reflect more balance in the amounts authorized. He was undoubtedly correct in that position, but about this time he had a Jewish primary opponent who was rumored to be receiving Israeli backing, although no one could prove such a charge. As it turned out, the challenge came to nothing. Several prominent Jewish leaders and old friends from his district came to his defense. Not even a slight implication of antisemitism would stick after that.

In any case, for all of these reasons I did not want to give anyone an opportunity to charge that the chairman had known and fully approved of this controversial meeting. I was, in fact, perfectly prepared to become the fall guy, but I wanted the chairman to be able to say with a straight face that he had *not* been in any way involved in this mission.

As our travels commenced, I became increasingly apprehensive on this score and tried to talk Ryan into at least informing the other delegates (confidentially if necessary) what he had in mind. Most of all, I feared a last minute blowup and perhaps a subsequent expose of the entire scheme. Leo was totally unperturbed, however. "They will all know in due time," he would say.

Finally, circumstance canceled the meeting: some Arab bomb throwers had committed an atrocity in northern Israel, blowing up a bus containing schoolchildren, and Arafat had to return to Lebanon, or Syria, to put his own house in order. The "secret meeting" was no longer a viable option, as we learned while we were still in Sicily. In typical mercurial fashion, Ryan decided to call off the entire Tunisian side trip. This would have been disastrous, of course, for our entire posture in Tunisia, and both the military control officer and I spent some time trying to talk him out of such a move. Finally, when I explained the extent of the embarrassment this would cause his friend, Ambassador Mulcahy, he agreed to go through with the Tunisian visit (which went off in low-key fashion), albeit without much enthusiasm.

I also had a secondary ulterior motive for wanting to go to Tunisia: a good friend of ours and a Smith College classmate of my wife's was married to a Tunisian and lived in a picturesque location just outside of town, where we stayed during the visit. We had an enjoyable evening, while the rest of the delegation attended a long drawn-out official dinner. The next day Clara and her friend spent a morning shopping for Tunisian carpets, which they had delivered in large bulk to our aircraft. But we had a different plane this time, *without* a storage hold, and all the rugs marked "Chester" were stored prominently in the main cabin of the plane, where they provided a kind of obstacle course for the passengers to climb around. I solved this problem somewhat by changing the tags to read "CODEL RYAN." There was nothing actually illegal about this procedure—just slightly embarrassing.

And there were also the birdcages. In Tunisia these artistic products are cherished by tourists. One did not even have to have birds to appreciate their attractiveness. Before our landing in Tunis, I polled all of the delegates and spouses as to whether they might want one of these creations. No one responded. But when they *saw* the finished product, as purchased by my wife, the sentiment changed dramatically. Leo Ryan, however, confronted me with an enormous personal dilemma at the end of the trip: he wanted a birdcage, even though he had not signed up in advance. My wife had *no* excess birdcages after those she had committed to her family, so I eventually had to turn my chairman down. "I really am sorry, Leo," I said with some discomfort, but I only *work* for you . . . I have to *live* with my family." He took the refusal with enormous good grace and understanding, for which I was eternally grateful.

The week after our return from Tunisia, the *Washington Post* ran a front-page series entitled "The Diary of a Junket," documenting the sins of the U.S. delegation to the Interparliamentary Union on what seemed like a sightseeing tour of little consequence. (That trip had coincided roughly with our US-EP mission.) A senator was even described as being unaware of the difference between the Red Sea and the Mediterranean. Leo immediately took the initiative and had me summarize all the discussions with the Europeans on the agenda topics. He then took to the House floor and spelled out the proceedings in detail, even challenging "our friends from the fourth estate, sitting up there in the (press) gallery," to find fault with what had occurred and to point out any error or inconsistencies in the U.S. position. The IPU continued to take it on the chin: some members stated for the record that they did not really want to go, but the Speaker had talked them into it! Our group, however, was totally exonerated.

This was, as it turned out, to be Leo's second-to-last foreign venture. He was assassinated in Jonestown, Guyana, in the fall of 1978, while on a mission investigating what became a mass suicide that included some of his constituents there.[2] Although some may have considered Leo Ryan essentially a "sensationalist," I always admired, above all, his ability to "lead" and not be intimidated, as many politicians tend to be, by the media. When Ryan went off to Jonestown, in fact, he took members of the press along (causing a few to be shot, as I recall, in the process). Leo had a "nose" for a good story; he was often on target, this time sadly.

More Interparliamentary Travel

Leo's successor as chairman was Don Pease, a Foreign Affairs Committee member from Ohio. Don proved to be an excellent choice and one of the most agreeable members I ever had to work with. Even-tempered and reasonable at all times, he ran a steady ship almost effortlessly. Although liberal in orientation, he was fair and balanced in all his dealings with both his American and European colleagues, gaining considerable respect in the process. The fact that our meetings were mainly uneventful during his tenure says a lot for his leadership. Much to my regret, we lost Don when he was favored with an opening on the Ways and Means Committee.

Don's successor was a most unusual member of Congress, the only one in my memory with a strong European (in this case Hungarian) accent. Tom Lantos and his wife, Annette, were both born and raised in Hungary and had the subsequent good fortune to have been saved from both the Nazis and the Communists, in that order. Both were from prominent Jewish families and destined for extinction, but they had been saved from deportation to a concentration camp by the famous Swedish diplomat Raoul Wallenberg. (Soon after his election to Congress, Tom introduced a bill, which eventually passed, conferring honorary U.S. citizenship on Wallenberg, who was presumed to have died in the Soviet Union either at the end of the war or soon thereafter.)

After the war, the Lantoses managed to escape to the West. Before running for Congress, Tom had been an economics professor at the University of California. He was very well informed about European historical and contemporary political and economic developments. There was no one quite like him, in fact: he could stand up and speak on just about any subject. Guy Van der

Jagt, one of our senior Republican delegates, told me on one occasion: "If I were Reagan, I'd send Tom Lantos on an extended speaking tour all over Europe."

Lantos was instrumental in arranging fact-finding missions to different regions of the world and would combine them with the formal interparliamentary meetings. He usually had a purpose in mind for his site selections. One year it was Morocco, the only Arab country that had permitted refueling stops for U.S. aircraft headed for Israel during the last Arab-Israeli conflict. Some AID funds, he discovered, had been "reprogrammed" to other priority areas of the world for emergency purposes. After our visit, the aid to Morocco was "reprogrammed back."

On that trip we met with the king of Morocco in his Casablanca palace while he was in mourning for his brother's death and had declined to meet with any foreign heads of state arriving for an Islamic summit conference. The king especially appreciated an opening comment by Texas Democratic representative J. J. Pickle: "Your Majesty, we don't have anything like this even in Texas!" (Harry Cromer, a former Foreign Affairs Committee staffer who was by then part of a Washington consulting firm, helped us set up that meeting, going personally to Rabat to smooth the way in advance).

The Soviet Union

The journey that will forever remain a vivid memory was our official visit to the Soviet Union and Eastern Europe, prior to our scheduled interparliamentary meeting with the Europeans in Athens. Lantos was particularly anxious to give the U.S. delegates a firsthand look at conditions in the Soviet bloc before discussing East-West relations with the Europeans. There was only one problem: the Soviets were not at all inclined to receive us in early January 1983, during the first Reagan administration, when Soviet-U.S. relations were at a low ebb.

Our visa requests were originally ignored until Representative Sam Gibbons went to the Soviet Embassy personally and refused to budge from his seat in the waiting room until Soviet ambassador Anatoly Dobrynin and his minions relented. Getting the visas, however, was only half the problem: the military plane we were to use on this mission had not been "cleared" by the proper authority in the Soviet Union. While visas were the responsibility of the foreign ministry, aircraft clearance had to come from the ministry of defense, and there was no apparent movement from that organization prior to our scheduled departure. (As a precaution, I picked up forty round-trip FINNAIR tickets between Helsinki and Leningrad, just in case we had to travel commercially. FINNAIR was not all that enthusiastic about refunding them after our trip was over!)

This forty-person CODEL thus took off from Andrews Air Force Base without knowing just exactly where we would be going. We knew we were heading for Helsinki, with a possible stop in Copenhagen en route, but that was about *it*. In mid-Atlantic, however, we received clearance for the Soviet Union, so we proceeded directly to Helsinki (overflying Copenhagen, where the U. S. ambassador had lined up a group of Danish officials to greet us). Helsinki had the last first-class (Hilton) hotel we were to see until our arrival in Athens.

Although our military escort officer normally handled most administrative matters, including paying bills (on a reimbursable basis), this time the colonel had talked me into putting all of the traveler's checks, representing the total authorized per diem, in my name, just in case he and his aircraft were denied entry into the Soviet Union at the last moment. High finance has never been my forte, but there seemed to be no viable alternative. I would later regret this action *exceedingly*.

Our first evening, in Leningrad, was most memorable. The consul general, Bill Shinn, a former Foreign Service colleague of mine, was hosting an evening jazz jam session bringing American musicians together with jazz buffs from across the expanse of Soviet territory, including Siberia. (The Soviet participants that evening traveled at considerable risk, as a KGB force stood at the gate to the residence, taking down names.) Although none of the Russians had played before with their U.S. counterparts, they certainly combined to make memorable music together. The entire evening was inspiring, as was a subsequent visit to the Hermitage Museum. When I paid the hotel bill just before our departure, however, I was shocked to discover that I had used up almost half of our per diem, and we still had three evenings to go in Moscow.

By the time we arrived at the Hotel Rossiya in downtown Moscow, a couple of blocks from Red Square, I was determined to husband my remaining resources with great care. I could not afford to give out any funds to any person for incidentals—like *food*. After checking in, we all assembled in the main dining room for a light supper.

"That's thirty dollars per person or sixty dollars per couple, the *maitre d'* informed me as soon as the guests were seated.

"O.K.," I said, "you can start serving (it was a fixed menu, as always) and we can work this out later."

"Nyet," was the reply. "First the dollars (and not rubles, please), and *then* we serve the vodka and caviar." I had no alternative but to collect the cash from each couple up front.

Some grumbled and said they were not going to eat in that dining room any more, but they did not have any choice. To compound the problem, we had not been given the right amount of per diem for Moscow, and I had to put in an emergency call to the committee. My colleague, Bob Boyer, answered the phone and said he could easily authorize an additional amount for members of *our* committee, but he might have difficulty getting funds from other chairmen, who were mostly out of town.

Everything finally evened out when we reached Athens, as we had more than enough per diem for Greece, but meanwhile there was a certain amount of "deficit financing." The military helped me out by covering the "control room" expenses (for delegation headquarters in the hotel), and we just managed to pay our collective bill on the morning of departure

Moscow, I discovered, had much less to offer than Leningrad. Once you had seen Red Square, St. Basil's Church, and the Kremlin, there wasn't much left, except perhaps the ballet and the circus. Moreover, most of the apartment buildings were modern, worn out, and ugly. The government stores, which had long lines in front of them, had almost no products on the shelf that anyone from a Western country would desire. Apparently anything of any value was sold on the black market. I was approached several times by teenagers who wanted jeans.

The embassy's main problem was what to do with evangelical Christians living in cramped and squalid conditions in the Embassy basement after crashing through the Embassy gate and seeking asylum. The Soviets had promised to let them leave the country if they could get foreign sponsors, and a German cult group had offered to help, but the two sides could not get together on an obscure interpretation of the Bible. Eventually the Soviets, who had not wanted to see us, relented and invited us into the Kremlin for a meeting with their official spokesman. Everything inside, I noted, was spotlessly clean and freshly painted, as contrasted with almost any other building or monument on the outside. At one point during our interview, Sam Gibbons spoke up and said: "You don't really want these Christians in our Embassy basement. Why don't you just let us take them with us on our plane?" (I'm not certain we had enough seats, but it was a generous offer nonetheless.) The spokesman gave us a look that said: "If only I could," but of course he was inhibited by official instructions. The families were released not long after our departure.

The final "scandal" I was involved in took place on the morning of our departure from the hotel. Having paid the bill with difficulty, I felt great relief and was in the process of getting everyone on the chartered bus and counting heads. Suddenly someone rushed up and told me several senior members of the Way and Means Committee were being held "hostage" on the third floor. There I found several of our dignitaries in serious discussion with the "floor manager." (This may not be the right term, but these were ladies large and brawny enough to serve as linebackers on an NFL football team who sat at desks on each floor, supposedly checking on the rooms and service. Actually, they were known to be KGB plants who checked on who was coming from or going in the rooms.)

Someone in room 303 went off with a hotel towel, she finally explained via an interpreter, and no one was allowed to leave the floor until it was returned. "Oh," I said, "that was my room," and I led the local floor leader into my bathroom. There, on the floor where it belonged, was the missing towel. Each room had only one towel, and this one, about the size of a small dish towel, was ripped. It was good for drying off one's face and little else after a shower. The Hotel Rossiya was billed as a top-flight international hostelry, but one must add "by Soviet standards." And we were inhabiting the first-class section of the hotel! How the Russian citizens fared is difficult to imagine.

From that moment on I was dubbed the "towel thief" and was the butt of a good deal of humor. One of the young Republican members from the House Agriculture Committee, Tom Coleman, had fun drafting daily press releases about my reported arrest, leading me to respond in kind. (As an experienced drafter of bogus press releases and the like, I take my hat off to him for his creative talents.) A sample of this exchange follows, just to provide some "flavor" of the continuing exercise.

MOSCOW—AP (ABSURD PRESS)
January 12, 1983

Tass reported today that an American congressional aide has been accused of appropriating state property at the Rossiya Hotel. The aide, John (Chips) Chester, was arrested in his hotel room. The specific charge in the indictment was towel stealing. Chester was reportedly living under the assumed name of Chester "Cannon." Witnesses reported that suitcases full of towels were found in Chester's luxurious hotel room. Chester, an aide to the Foreign Affairs Committee, was interrogated at length by the KGB at Lubyanka Prison. In a signed statement, he admitted taking the towels from the following sources: the Helsinki Inter-Continental Hotel sauna, the Leningrad Hotel, the Winter Palace, the American Consulate, and the men's room at the Moscow Circus. His arrest came after an in-depth investigation by the state police, who reportedly had Chester (Cannon) under tight surveillance. The case broke when Chester inadvertently mentioned the towel caper to a floor maid he had engaged in conversation during a wild vodka-drinking bout. Chester was reportedly despondent over having been $600 short on per diem expenses for an American congressional delegation and faced the prospect of having to work as a spittoon cleaner for six months to make up the difference. Close friends of the accused said that this was not his first brush with the authorities.

Coworker Elizabeth Daoust (a committee staffer) said Chester had undergone a remarkable personality change after visiting Turkey in 1975. It was there that he developed a close personal relationship with Turkish towels. "It started with little things. He would carry around an abundant supply of paper hand towels. I know for a fact he once stole a bath mat from the Hilton Hotel in Copenhagen in 1980. This is surely a human tragedy," Daoust said.

Chester has engaged the services of local Moscow attorney F. Lee Baileykov. Baileykov plans to call as a witness Dr. John Hutton (Air Force doctor for the U.S. delegation), who reportedly administered mind-altering sleeping pills to Chester the night before the arrest.

Congressman Tom Lantos (D-Calif), the chairman of the delegation, after visiting Chester in his cell, reported that the accused was resting well. "He's upset, of course, but coping with his situation. At the least the authorities have separated him from hardened criminals like bedspread thieves," Lantos said. Apparently the ordeal has taken a mental toll on Chester and further complicated matters. It seems as though he refuses to speak English and communicates only in the little-known language of Serbo-Croatian.

—MORE REPORTS TO FOLLOW—

This was my response:

For Immediate Release

PROMINENT MISSOURI CONGRESSMAN SENT ON FACT-FINDING MISSION IN ROMANIA

A United States Congressional delegation currently visiting a number of Eastern European countries announced today that the Honorable Tom Coleman of Missouri, a highly regarded member of the Agriculture Committee, would be assigned to a state farm approximately 200 miles north of Bucharest, Romania, for an indefinite period.

As explained by the chairman of the delegation, the Honorable Tom Lantos of California: "This is designed as a unique fact-finding mission to gain firsthand information about Romanian agricultural practices, which are in a highly depressed stage of development, even by European standards."

The farm in question has never before been visited by a Western official or journalist, since its work force consists almost entirely of dissidents, who are serving long terms of confinement for political offenses. Because Congressman Coleman will be provided with regular rations of bread and water twice daily, he will *not* require per diem (even at the old rate), and this entire experiment will be at no cost to the U.S. taxpayer.

In addition to acquiring a direct and valuable exposure to Romanian labor-intensive agricultural techniques, Congressman Coleman will also be afforded an opportunity to investigate the human rights situation in Romania and report to the Congress when and if he is released. (Apparently some minor confusion still exists over his eligibility for an exit visa, but he will be ably represented by a Soviet attorney, Comrade F. Lee Baileykov, who is quite experienced in handling such cases. Mr. Baileykov is presently seeking the release of another unidentified staff member of the CODEL from Lubyanka prison in Moscow, where he is serving an indeterminate term for petty larceny.)

The Romanian authorities have expressed full satisfaction over this entire program. The minister of agriculture, Mr. Popescu, commented: "We believe that we can inculcate in the congressman a more positive view of Socialist agriculture in a relatively brief period of time. We are, in fact, quite persuasive in this regard!"

Another advantage to life on the state farm is that Representative Coleman will not require a large quantity of drugs from Colonel Hutton to put him to sleep or to wake him up. The farm program will ensure that insomnia is no problem, and he will be awakened personally by the warden each day at 4:00 A.M.

In his final statement to reporters at the Bucharest airport, Chairman Lantos noted: "We will miss Tom Coleman very much from our delegation, but we will take good care of his wife and pray for his eventual safe return to his loved ones. Fortunately, Representative Don Bonker of Washington has promised to send him a Russian Bible, which will be comforting to him during the next Christmas holiday season."

On From Moscow

From Moscow we proceeded on to Budapest, where Tom Lantos was our Number One guide and seemed to get along famously with the local officials. (Most of the people we met were economically rather than politically oriented and they were clearly eager to establish closer ties with the United States. They tended to support U.S. positions in such organizations as GATT to a greater extent than did the West Europeans.)

From there we had some problems. The plane could not land in Bucharest because of a low cloud ceiling, and we detoured to the Black Sea port of Constanta instead. Finally, after two more abortive attempts, our leaders ordered the plane to proceed to Belgrade, one full day early. The embassy only had about an hour to prepare for our unscheduled arrival. Ambassador David Anderson, my former FSI fellow student in Serbo-Croatian, was suffering from the flu and had a temperature of over 102 degrees. When I got off the plane, he gave me a look of total disappointment, like someone betrayed by an old friend. The look signified: "How could you do this to me?" even though I had not in any way been consulted over the decision. Fortunately, the hotel was able to accommodate our large group, and after two nights and a day full of meetings, we finally made our way to Athens.

It so happened that another large CODEL, led by Clem Zablocki, arrived in Athens the same week, having covered Brazil and several African posts beforehand. The American Embassy really had its hands full that week. I sympathized with the ambassador, Monteagle Stearns, who went from briefing session to reception almost constantly. (Some years back, when I was en route to Malawi, he had taken me to luncheon at the Traveler's Club in London. It seemed to me that he had a better job then.)

After much persuasion, Lantos got Zablocki to authorize one plane to return to Bucharest for the missed meeting with President Nicolai Ceausescu. At the meeting, Bill Frenzel, the ranking Republican on the Ways and Means Committee, spent some time explaining to the president that unless he rescinded his recently imposed "tax on emigrants," Congress would never approve an extension of MFN (most favored nation) status for Romania. The president did not take kindly to these remarks and merely looked at a book about Washington he had been given by the U.S. delegates present. From time to time, he would grunt his disapproval. However, he never implemented the emigrant tax, so apparently he got the message. (Whatever one may think of interparliamentary travel, in this case a U.S. foreign policy objective was achieved.)

This was clearly the most eventful and colorful of all the European Parliament trips. The only exception might have been my midnight swim in the North Sea in January with Carol Vander Jagt (wife of Congressman Guy Vander Jagt of Michigan), the result of a late evening bet. The competition was supervised by a disapproving military doctor and the entire army escort team. But that is another story.

By now perhaps I have established the challenging nature of the interparliamentary delegation business. The rest can be written off as "classified" (even if it wasn't).

CHAPTER 17

Speechwriter and "Poet Laureate"

Starting in the early 1980s, some five years after Peter Frelinghuysen's retirement, I became Senior Consultant for Special Projects (a title I made up), a de facto public affairs adviser for the House Foreign Affairs Committee. I wrote speeches for the chairman, especially in his public appearances. I arranged committee meetings with governmental and public groups, including regular visits of State, CIA, and military officers to the committee under the auspices of the Foreign Service Institute's Interdepartmental Seminar. When committee members could not address the groups, I addressed them myself.

My new assignment was ambiguous. Originally recognized as a Republican appointee, albeit in a less-than-partisan capacity, I eventually evolved into an increasingly bipartisan figure following Peter Frelinghuysen's departure. I was to become, in fact, *the* "House Republican" on the Democratic payroll. Bob Boyer, unlike me, soon lost his original Republican identity altogether, mostly because his mentor, Bill Mailliard, did not use him very consistently for his own purposes. Bob ended up taking on mostly mainline legislative duties for the committee chairman and chief of staff.

During Clement Zablocki's tenure as chairman of the Foreign Affairs Committee, I left the mainstream of legislative work and moved into speechwriting as my main task. The process was gradual. Earlier chapters have demonstrated how even before coming to the Hill I seemed to have a knack for ghostwriting statements for other—sometimes mythical—people. I had then written many of Peter Frelinghuysen's speeches and newsletters and did the same for committee chairmen, preparing remarks for them in committee, on the House floor, and in public forums.

I suddenly found myself with unaccustomed seniority. The chief of staff, Jack Brady, informed me that I was entitled to have my name appear on the committee roster immediately under his. I preferred to recede in favor of Bob Boyer, who had the same seniority I did and who had spent much more of his time on regular committee legislation. Instead, the title Senior Consultant for Special Projects provided me with suitable ambiguity and "cover." The title must have sounded mysterious. I later found out that in early CIA days, the clandestine service was briefly named the Office of Special Projects, then quickly renamed—even more innocuously—the Office of Policy Coordination.[1]

From that moment on, no one knew exactly what my main function was, which suited me perfectly. That way I could freewheel with "special assignments," while not being chained to the committee's relentless legislative schedule. As the last chapter explained, my availability for freewheeling also led to assignments like staffing interparliamentary groups, which proved to be my "penance."

I soon became the chairman's main speechwriter, especially before public audiences. I no longer was called upon to draft "introductory remarks" to specific pieces of legislation, although I did continue to provide an abundance of material for the *Congressional Record*, in the form of eulogies for departing or departed members; National Day speeches for Lithuania, Latvia, and Estonia, not to mention Poland and the remainder of Eastern Europe; and general policy statements not tied directly to legislation.

A less popular duty was to edit, which often meant rewrite, the remarks drafted by other staff members—a good way to make enemies in a hurry. That is where my bipartisan image and "Special Projects" title helped: most people recognized that I had no political agenda of my own and was hardly an "empire builder." Quite the contrary, I was always resisting excess assignments. Anything I did was under orders, either from the chairman or the chief of staff. A number of my colleagues even took the precaution of bringing me drafts to look over before submitting them to Jack Brady. Eventually, reviewing controversial manuscripts of one kind or another became a principal responsibility.

SPEECHWRITING FOR CHAIRMEN ZABLOCKI AND FASCELL

This posture was put to a severe test when Lewis Gulick and I were assigned the unenviable task of editing the text of a staff report on the infamous tragedy of Jonestown, Guyana, where a member of the committee, Leo Ryan of California, had been slain. Gulick was a highly respected professional journalist for much of his adult life and enjoyed a less-than-partisan image. The staff team had been carefully selected and balanced between majority and minority staffers and every attempt had been made to keep the findings as objective and nonpolitical as possible. The study of the facts in the case had been quite thorough and the conclusions were persuasive. The only problem, as our perceptive chief of staff was quick to recognize, was that the report just did not hold together properly and had to be completely overhauled. It was not so much a question of writing as of organizing the material in some coherent form.

It is *not* a comfortable assignment to remake in twenty-four hours what a highly regarded staff team has produced over a period of some weeks or even months, but I think we came up with a much improved product without changing any of the substance of the report. Best of all, there were no adverse repercussions.

Clem Zablocki, one of the most astute politicians and able statesmen I have ever known, was *not* an accomplished speaker. He was very much in the Doc Morgan tradition and, like Doc, tended to stumble over words and break the "cadence" of his speechwriter's inspired oratory. (He was, however, a considerable improvement over Doc in pronouncing Polish surnames.) Nevertheless, he liked most of what I wrote and would read my texts verbatim. Once I provided him with some draft remarks to use before the Rotary Club of Milwaukee only to discover that he was scheduled to visit Australia and other countries in East Asia beforehand. I am told that on his way home from that excursion he addressed the Rotary Club as follows: "This speech was written by Verne Read's brother-in-law (Verne was the only member of my family who was then a Rotarian); it was very appropriate some three weeks ago, but now is somewhat out of date." He then read it word for word anyway. Again, in very *un*congressional fashion, he was delighted to assign credit elsewhere (and blame, if it backfired).

As much as I valued and appreciated the chairman's confidence, at times his faith in my abilities—and particularly my *knowledge*—made me uneasy. As a *generalist* veteran of the foreign policy process, I was reasonably aware of worldwide developments, especially the Zablocki outlook toward most of them. I was not, however, an area specialist who understood all the subtleties and intricate "buzzwords" that American diplomats, in particular, learned to avoid. This was especially true of Latin America, where innuendo and style rarely reflected the realities of a given situation.

A case in point was the Falkland Islands–Malvinas crisis in the spring of 1982. The islands were called the Falklands in the English-speaking world, and the Malvinas in Argentina and much of South America. In fact, just using one or another of the terms tended to identify one's position on the issue. Hence many speakers would refer to "Falklands-Malvinas" to avoid such a perception. While the islands were inhabited by people of British descent, Argentina had a longtime historic claim to them which, valid or not, carried a strong emotional appeal to the Argentine body politic. The floundering military government of Argentina, unable to resist the temptation of exploiting this issue to distract the public from its failures at home, finally launched an invasion, which Great Britain successfully resisted.

Like most Foreign Affairs Committee members of both parties, Zablocki considered this initially as *one* international dispute in which the United States should stay neutral or at least unengaged. This view was strongly supported by the Latin America Bureau at State (ARA), which feared adverse repercussions throughout the region if the United States came down hard on the side of its NATO ally.

If this seemingly minor (to Americans) crisis evoked patriotic fervor on the part of Argentines, however, it also had the same effect in the United Kingdom, and not just among those aging Tories still nostalgic over the loss of empire. An overwhelming majority of the British electorate strongly supported Margaret Thatcher's military mission to "liberate" the islands and its residents from what was perceived to be clear aggression. The luxury liner *Queen Elizabeth II* was transformed into a troop ship and sent into battle. Prince Andrew, the Duke of York, participated as a Royal Navy officer in the rescue exercise—possibly the *last* action by a member of the royal family that received universal acclaim. I happened to know this bit of trivia because my son John had been booked for passage on the QE II when the ship was requisitioned for war. (He ended up taking it to England on the first cruise following the cessation of hostilities.)

Against this background, the British ambassador paid an urgent call on the chairman of the House Foreign Affairs Committee. Like many of his Washington colleagues, he had begun to learn that it was not enough to rely upon one's State Department contacts to carry one's message to Congress. Direct appeals were clearly a necessity. As it turned out, the two gentlemen were locked up in the chairman's office for the better part of the day. When the meeting was finally concluded, I received an urgent call from Zablocki. With some reluctance, he told me, he had agreed to make a floor statement on the Falklands-Malvinas crisis; he did not wish to take sides in the dispute, but he would support the principle that old established borders, however unjustified historically, should not be altered by force of arms. I had the rest of the evening to draft appropriate remarks and bring them to the floor the following morning, when the House happened to be scheduled for a rare Saturday morning session. No member of Congress had issued a policy pronouncement on the matter, perhaps in deference to the Foreign Affairs Committee chairman (and also, perhaps, because it was not an issue of compelling concern to most Americans).

It was too late to contact anyone at State for guidance. I needed all the time it would have taken me to locate the appropriate official (either in the office or at home) to work on a preliminary draft. Essentially, I was on my own to guess *what* Clem wanted to say and *how* to say it without causing a major diplomatic faux pas.

The following morning, April 6, 1982, I met the chairman in the Speaker's lobby just off the House floor. "I hope I have this right," I told him, "but you better look over the text pretty carefully. I'm not certain of the emphasis."

"I am sure it is just fine," Zablocki responded, "but come and sit with me on the floor and I'll go over the text in detail. I am not due to speak for another half hour."

Or so we thought. Evidently the originally scheduled speakers had not yet arrived, so the Speaker of the House immediately recognized "the Gentleman from Wisconsin, the very distinguished chairman of the Foreign Affairs Committee." Too late for review, and once again the chairman read my text into the *Record*, word for word:

The Falkland Islands–Malvinas Crisis: A Question of Principle

Mr. Speaker: The sudden confrontation between the United Kingdom and Argentina, which is less than a week old, is a matter of serious concern and intense disappointment to the United States. However bizarre and unlikely the circumstances, it represents a crisis between two countries with which the United States not only maintains normal and friendly relations, but also important treaty commitments.

The United Kingdom, our staunch and traditional ally during two world wars in this century, is a bulwark of NATO, to which this administration and all previous postwar administrations have assigned the highest priority. In the affairs of this hemisphere, Argentina is expected to play a highly significant role, which can become crucial to the fulfillment of long-standing U.S. foreign policy objectives.

Because of the gravity—and indeed, delicacy—of the current, still-unresolved situation, this would not appear to be an appropriate time for inflammatory rhetoric. It is, on the contrary, a time for some circumspection and restraint.

There is, however, an overriding principle at stake here, which transcends all other considerations. It involves the forcible, unprovoked invasion of the territory of one nation by the armed forces of another. It involves a serious matter of precedent: If the United States or the world community condones the forcible acquisition of territory—the boundaries of which *may*, and I stress the word *may*, be based on historical injustice—there is no telling where this process may lead.

If we wish to maintain some semblance of international order, we cannot afford to acquiesce in the blatant invasion and occupation of one state by another on the basis of an historic claim.

In one respect, at least, the Falkland Islands—or Malvinas—crisis is virtually unique in terms of contemporary history, that is, since the founding of the United Nations: We are not confronting here a local insurrection which is being assisted by outside forces. There are no "oppressed" Argentine minorities on these islands calling for "liberation" and a change of the status quo. Instead we are talking about naked aggression by the armed forces of one country over the unwilling inhabitants of another. There is no conceivable issue of self-determination at stake in this region.

Mr. Speaker, the United States does not—and should not—involve itself in the substance of this dispute. The question of sovereignty of these islands is beyond the purview of our competence. We fervently hope that this dispute may be resolved peacefully. Our only role, if we have a role, is to offer our good offices for mediation, as President Reagan has just announced his willingness to do.

Our government, and I believe a majority of the Congress, supports the text of the resolution adopted by the United Nations Security Council on April 3rd—by a vote of ten to one. It is a short and simple resolution which calls for a "diplomatic solution" to differences, but it also embodies the principles of the United Nations Charter, which we will ignore at our peril.

I looked up at the visitors' gallery and saw that it was filled with representatives of the British embassy, many of whom *seemed* to be pleased with the wording, as far as I could tell. They should have been, as I gave the British the benefit of the doubt. That being the case, however, I wondered what kind of flap these remarks might cause south of the border. I am certain the speech was not exactly welcomed in Latin America. Fortunately, it was ignored, as all rhetoric on the subject was soon overtaken by events. End of crisis, at least for me.

On another—this time internal—contretemps during the Zablocki era, I really believe, with all appropriate

modesty, that I helped to resolve a nagging and ener-
vating personality conflict. In December 1976 Jim Wright
of Texas had beaten the late Phil Burton of California
for majority leader by one vote. It was a real cliffhanger,
and something of a surprise, because no member of the
House was a better vote-counter (or district gerry-
manderer) than Phil Burton. Evidently someone had
double-crossed him in a secret ballot, as he had been
confident of victory.

Speaker Tip O'Neill had remained publicly neutral
on this matter, although it was generally assumed that
Jim Wright was his actual preference. (Burton was a
power broker like Wayne Hays who liked to throw his
weight around and would not really be anyone's choice
for a deputy.) However, when the vote was over, Tip
wanted to make amends and do something to assuage
the wounded Burton ego. A grand gesture, it seemed,
was needed, and Tip discovered that he had a few perks
to dispense under current regulations. He could and did
appoint Burton chairman of the House delegation to the
NATO Assembly. To Tip this merely represented a symbolic action of no special significance to the operation
of the House. Zablocki, however, was furious; he had
not been consulted about the appointment and would
definitely *not* have approved, as the NATO chairman
had always been (by tradition and precedent, if not by
law) a member of the Foreign Affairs Committee.

Quite predictably, Burton turned out to be a dreadful
chairman, as his mind was elsewhere, and he treated
the NATO assignment as a strictly honorific title without substance. He also managed to alienate most of his
European colleagues, several of whom wrote Zablocki
bitter letters of protest about the "Burton problem."
Tip had clearly blundered, but there wasn't much he
could do after the fact. A "cold war" atmosphere began
to permeate relations between the Foreign Affairs Committee and the Speaker's Office.

Until this unfortunate development occurred, we had
enjoyed quite good relations with the Speaker, espe-

cially with his staff, who recognized our committee as among the most prestigious and effective organizations on the Hill. From a purely practical standpoint, the erection of a "Berlin Wall" (my favorite image) between the two offices was a no-win situation for everyone concerned. It was not a question of politics, but of personality and/or protocol, which in Congress is of infinitely greater sensitivity.

Finally I was given a small opportunity to put things right. Chairman Zablocki was hosting an afternoon tea meeting for the prime minister of Ireland in the main committee room in the Rayburn building. As usual, the House majority and minority leadership, various full committee chairmen, and specially interested members of Congress from outside the committee, were also invited to attend. I was asked to write a few introductory remarks for the chairman to make when introducing the various House dignitaries.

It goes without saying that Speaker O'Neill was not only invited, but was a certain attendee. Nothing meant more to Tip than his historic ties with the Irish homeland. I decided that this was a chance to lay it on thick. I not only reminded everyone (needlessly) about the Speaker's Irish heritage, but mentioned how much he was admired as an Irish politician who had worked his way up through the ranks to become the leader of "this body," a renowned statesman, and a role model for future generations, and so forth and so on. Zablocki looked at my draft rather quizzically: "You don't actually expect me to *SAY* all this bulls—t," he remonstrated. "Well," I said, "Mr. Chairman, you always used to say, if it doesn't *cost* anything, go ahead and do it. This seems like the right occasion."

"Well," he shook his head: "This is just too much." When the time came for Zablocki to introduce the Speaker, however, he read my remarks verbatim. Tip O'Neill beamed and looked exceedingly relieved. As he rose to speak, he enveloped the diminutive Zablocki in a bear hug. The "kill-'em-with-kindness" Zablocki strategy, so effective with Ben Rosenthal, had been invoked again. The wall fell—and the cold war was over.

When Dante Fascell succeeded Clem Zablocki as committee chairman, I continued my role in the writing department even though Dante, unlike Doc Morgan or Clem, was an inveterate ad libber. He liked to have my text along even if he did not use it. Because he was a voluble talker, he tended to be interviewed constantly by the press and the broadcast media, including World Net, a USIA TV program distributed to USIS posts abroad for local use. Finally, to meet the demand, I devised something called the State of the World speech, which summarized the chairman's policy pronouncements on key foreign policy issues around the world. This time I sought input from the relevant subcommittees, which I then rewrote, edited, or updated as necessary. It became a useful reference, even though Fascell liked to carry it more than to use it.

In addition to Cubans in his home district, pro-Israeli groups, especially the Washington lobbying group American Israel Public Affairs Committee (AIPAC), severely pressured Fascell. He claimed to have the right ancestry for ethnic politics: an Italian father and a Jewish mother, or so it was said. (I later learned that the Italian side of the family was *Protestant*, of all things, although Dante didn't feel obliged to publicize the fact.) As a result, he was always being asked to address a Jewish school, old folks' home, or synagogue, and he was always as responsive as possible. Once he suggested that I call AIPAC headquarters in Washington to get some "feel" for the audience he was asked to address and the issues of greatest interest to the group as a whole. The man I talked to then began to dictate word for word what he wanted Fascell to say, and I finally cut him off in disgust. The AIPAC folks were undeniably efficient and politically effective, but they could also be, putting it mildly, a collective "pain in the ass." I avoided them thereafter to the extent possible.

In time my direct speechwriting for Fascell became less and less original and more editing the input of others. Finally, as recounted in chapter 16, I became preoccupied with two interparliamentary groups, which took up most of my time.

To his *great credit*, however, I should add that Dante Fascell probably listened to more of my "poems" than any other member of the House and for that I owe him a debt of gratitude. And that leads me to another subject.

POET LAUREATE AND OTHER "SPECIAL PROJECTS"

Throughout this journal I have attempted to maintain a degree of modesty about my accomplishments, so as to keep all past events in a minimally proper perspective. Some of my colleagues have even claimed that I had a lot to be modest *about!* However, in one respect I feel justified in claiming I was indeed irreplaceable, namely, as Foreign Affairs Committee "poet laureate." After my departure there was no replacement laureate, and I had to be recalled from retirement from time to time for ceremonial occasions.

Like many assignments on Capitol Hill, this one began harmlessly enough and then managed to develop its own momentum. It all started in Peter Frelinghuysen's office, carried over to the Committee on Foreign Affairs, and eventually escalated into a major commitment. Originally I was "volunteered" by Bill Kendall, Peter's chief of staff, to compose a few lines of doggerel verse to highlight the most notable characteristics of a departing staff member. This would be read at the farewell party for the individual in question and was designed to portray the person's known strengths and weaknesses in a humorous vein. If you kept it light and laughable, I soon discovered, no one could object. Quite the contrary. Soon everyone whose birthday or departure was being celebrated (and most left the office voluntarily for varying career reasons) came to expect the same treatment. For purposes of staff morale, my role became increasingly essential.

When I moved to the Foreign Affairs Committee, my reputation had managed to precede me. Before long, I became the "poet laureate" at all retirement parties, which tended to be more gala occasions than the semi-private functions in the Frelinghuysen office. Again, the focus was on the staff, but often many of the retirees were quite senior, with many years of experience behind them. Consequently a number of the committee members began to attend these functions as well. Doc Morgan and Dante Fascell were the most faithful attendees, the former at least initially out of a sense of duty, and the latter because he never wanted to miss a party where a diverse assortment of ladies might be present.

It was only a matter of time before I was reciting poems for departing members, or at birthday parties for the chairman and/or the chief of staff. The practice took on political overtones: If I wrote a poem for a Republican, I had to do the same for a Democrat, and if for some reason I was out of the country or otherwise unavailable, the party would be postponed. In any case, the rule became that the poet laureate could say *anything* as long as it rhymed.

At one point during my tenure, the real "poet laureate" of the state of Maryland received a great deal of unwanted publicity, as he was discovered to be on the state payroll for approximately $1,000 per annum. The Maryland taxpayers were outraged and wrote many hostile letters to both the *Washington Post* and the *Baltimore Sun* until the infamous employee was removed from office and his position abolished. The wags in the Foreign Affairs Committee liked to point out that "our poet laureate is clearly worth $1,000; it's just the *rest* of his salary that is questionable!"

In terms of volume of honorees in one poem, "Of Ashes and Embers" and "Losing Five Members" probably represented the record. "If you can get Shirley Pettis and Mike Harrington in the same poem," Zablocki observed, "you're a genius!"

Shirley Pettis was the attractive and popular widow of a Republican member from California who was killed in an air crash, leaving her to take over his congressional seat for a few years. Michael Harrington was another story: a far-left member from Boston, he was essentially a publicity hound who managed to leak some material from a classified Defense Department briefing to the press and then blamed staff for the infraction. He had been transferred to Foreign Affairs from the Armed Services Committee and proved equally unpopular in both places. Finally, he took the hint and opted *not* to run for another term. He was on his way to Boston when the farewell party took place. Tip O'Neill delivered the "eulogy" for his defecting Boston colleague. He managed to skip all references to Harrington personally while lauding the character and accomplishments of Mike's *father*. That, one might conclude, was a way of damning a man with faint praise! (I ran into Mike in the mid-1990s in Woodstock, Vermont, and found him a most congenial ex-colleague. He had become more centrist and more rational and persuasive in his thinking.)

I did manage to include Representatives Harrington, Pettis, Nix of Pennsylvania, and Don Fraser of Minnesota in one poem, but only by setting aside one or two stanzas for each individual and *not* trying to establish any specific connection between these disparate personalities. On rereading the text of this poem, I find I have forgotten the meaning of a number of the references, although they were certainly poignant and clear to the audience of the day.

With respect to Don Fraser, the Hubert Humphrey–type liberal from Minnesota, who established a national (if controversial) reputation for hearings in his subcommittee on human rights, I included one stanza as follows:

In human rights
Who emotes for our sakes?
Or carries the fights
Over boats on the lakes?

This was a reference to Fraser's abortive run for the Senate with the support of all the Humphrey-Mondale forces in Minnesota. Despite his national and even international reputation in foreign affairs, he lost the Democratic primary on a strictly local issue—whether motor boats of a certain size or velocity should be allowed on Minnesota freshwater lakes. Apparently he took the wrong side and was badly beaten by a probusiness Democrat, who subsequently lost to a Republican in the general election. Instead Fraser became mayor of Minneapolis. He also became somewhat more conservative in his old age, lately critical of welfare abuse.

My Finest Hour

Two occasions in my "poet laureate" phase were for me the pinnacle of success. The first was Peter Frelinghuysen's valedictory address to the House on foreign aid, when, for the first time, he did not change a word of my original draft. Every committee staff member who had ever tried to write for Peter recognized the extent of this accomplishment.

The second was Doc Morgan's *committee* retirement party, one of numerous functions held in his honor over an entire week that also included a dinner hosted by the Pennsylvania House delegation; a party given by his grateful district supporters; and a ceremony in the main committee hearing room, where his former medical school alma mater, Wayne State University, conferred an honorary doctorate on him. That hearing room, Room 2172 of the Rayburn Building, was christened the "Doc Morgan Room" in honor of the committee's longest-serving chairman.

Our party was to be a kind of "family affair," an in-house evening where all members and staff of the committee, plus a few selected outside guests, could enjoy a few informal hours with our beloved leader. Doc's anointed successor, Clem Zablocki, was particularly anxious to make this occasion a memorable one, especially since Doc had been most supportive of Clem's succession as chairman. "Stop whatever you are doing," he advised me, "and make this your best effort. Doc has come to appreciate your poems, and it is high time he received one of his own." Indeed!

As usual, I had very little time to prepare this piece, as we only organized our party at the last minute. I thought that a few light comparisons between Doc and Henry Kissinger, then the highly publicized secretary of state engaged in "shuttle diplomacy" in the Middle East, seemed particularly appropriate, especially at Henry's expense. The references were relatively harmless but clearly rather flippant to an outside observer.

The party began quietly enough but then unexpectedly shifted into high gear: a horde of dignitaries suddenly appeared, including the Speaker, majority and minority leaders of the House, and numerous committee chairmen, who commandeered the upper tier of the congressional seats in the main hearing room. Moreover, visitors suddenly jammed the room, some even backing up into the hallway. Clearly, this was no longer a family affair, and I was becoming apprehensive.

After a few opening remarks by the various dignitaries, Secretary of State Kissinger suddenly and unexpectedly appeared with a large entourage of aides and security types, en route to an embassy dinner. I assumed he would make a few laudatory remarks and then excuse himself and go off to his dinner, as was his custom. Instead, he took a seat on the upper podium and announced in a stentorian voice: "Because of my *great* respect and affection for Chairman Morgan, I am going to stay here through the entire program. I wouldn't miss a word that is spoken about this great patriot, and the

embassy will just have to wait." With that pronouncement he then sat down heavily amid loud applause.

I was next on the program and it was too late to improvise. I considered changing one of the stanzas for a
brief moment, but then decided against it: I would just
mess up the language as well as the meter. Better to
swallow hard and go through with the original text as
written. "When I wrote this poem," I started to explain,
"I did not realize that we would have the pleasure of
the Secretary's company. However, I am told that he is
a very tolerant individual" (this was a patent misrepre-
sentation of fact). "*DUNNN'T COUNT ON IT*," came
the booming response, amidst laughter.

At that moment of truth, what I was really counting
on was definitely *not* his tolerance, as I had heard all of
the stories about his treatment of staff, but on his sense
of humor and the fact that he did not have any choice
but to laugh uproariously, which he did. "Ve should haf
this man vorking on the seventh floor (at State); ve need
some laffs," the secretary announced obligingly, and
then posed with me for some photo ops. Under the circumstances, I had escaped unscathed.

As I walked off stage center, Dante Fascell made the
memorable comment: "That was OK, Chips, you did
fine. I have listened to a lot of your crazy poems," he
added, "but this was the first time you used a senior
cabinet officer for your straight man." Indeed, I reflected
later that evening, for a poet on the public payroll, that
may well have represented my finest hour. The text of
the poem was as follows (with "genre" in the third stanza
pronounced "gen-ree"):

> *On Trying to Smile-It*
> *While Losing our Pilot*

A man revered—of great renown,
A man endeared to Fredericktown,
A man who's being shown this blast
Is now returning home—at last.

His patients and his friends rejoice
To hear that he has made that choice.
For those described as "on the Hill"
He has prescribed a bitter pill!

When we are gauche, he can berate,
But *man* can he *ne-go-she-ate!*
To keep the peace and lead rebuttal
He doesn't even need to shuttle.
Oh, we of every caste or gen-re
Know he could even outlast Henry.

What fate we reap we cannot know,
For who will keep the troops in tow?
How can as leader, seer, and proctor
He leave us *here* without a doctor?

For on the floor and in debate
This much we know and have to state:
"The way is paved around the blocks;
The bill is saved because it's *Doc's!*"

But if we cannot change his course,
And must accept it with remorse,
Then toast we *must*—his wife and fame—
And know life *just* won't be the same!

Beyond Poet Laureate

As it turned out, my social responsibilities were not confined exclusively to poetry. On two occasions—for the birthdays of one administrative assistant, Bill Kendall, and one chief of staff, Jack Brady—I emerged in drag (dress, wig, and fur coat) from a *papier maché* cake and sang "Take Back Your Mink" while performing respectable stripteases. Both times I was selected by acclamation, for a simple reason: no one else in the Frelinghuysen office or on the committee had the chutzpah to undertake such an assignment.

By the time we celebrated Jack Brady's sixtieth birthday the following year, I had turned respectable and served as master of ceremonies in top hat and tails. I

421

introduced all of the speakers, including House members and staff from both bodies, who roasted our chief in turn. Then came a female chorus line staffed by the women of the committee, all duly immortalized in *Roll Call*, the newspaper of capitol Hill.

A couple of months later it was Zablocki's turn to have his seventieth birthday celebrated, a year late. Jack was determined that *this* presentation should surpass his own celebration, if at all possible. The only option which had not already been *tried*, it seemed, was an all-male chorus line, a la the Princeton Triangle Club. Again, I organized a high-kick rendition of "A Pretty Girl is like a Melody." While the quality of this effort left much to be desired, Clem clearly relished every moment. As he died only a couple of weeks afterwards, it is well that we did not postpone the event, as we at one point contemplated because of the press of late evening legislative sessions.

Life on the Foreign Affairs Committee may sound like an extended party, but such an impression would not be accurate. We worked long hours in those days, and, more important, we worked cooperatively and effectively. No operation, I firmly believe, works as smoothly and efficiently as when the staff at the working level is having a good time. Call this the "Chester Rule," which some may consider frivolous (like the "Chester Amendment" in its time), but it works.

Roll Call, Washington,DC
September 22, 1983

CAN-CAN girls surround honoree John Brady

Party a Foreign Affair

All that was missing was Toulouse Lautrec, as staffers of the House Foreign Affairs Committee staged a Gaiite Parisien roast honoring the 60th birthday of popular Chief of Staff John Brady, Jr. Sept. 13.

Garbed in top hat and tails, Senior Staff Consultant John Chapman "Chip" Chester mc'd the show which included roasts and toasts by such luminaries as Committee Chairman Clement Zablocki, former Rep. Ed De-

rwinski, now Counselor to the State Dept., and Reps. Dante Fascell and Stephen Solarz.

Highlights of the evening was the appearance of the Can Can chorus line—composed entirely of committee staff members wearing glamorous French costumes. The line consisted of Julie Ilsely, Roxanne Peragino, Connie Yesh, Shelly Livingston, Margaret Goodman, Marian Chambers, Elizabeth Daoust, Carol Glassman, and Jennifer Fohl.

MC "Chip" Chester elegantly garbed, presides

The Last Word: A Good Life

As I look back upon my fifteen years on the Hill, with the benefit of hindsight I sometimes think that I should have retired after one of my two finest hours (recounted in the previous chapter), which for me were the pinnacle of success.

But then again, on the Hill or in Foggy Bottom, in my early life or as a GI, I consider most of the hours of my life good ones. In fact, this book could have been entitled "A Good Life," if Ben Bradlee, former executive editor of the Washington Post (whom I have been told I resemble slightly), had not already expropriated that title for his own memoirs. While my professional life has not been as illustrious as his, in many respects it has been just as "good."

In the last chapter I referred to the "Chester Rule," which proclaims that a man does his best work when he is having a good time. (This may also apply to women, but I have learned over time never to presume anything on their behalf.) But I also made the point that on the Hill we worked long hours, and we worked hard, cooperatively, and effectively. My period in Congress has led me to reflect on the characteristics of the "ideal member of Congress" and the "ideal congressional staffer," neither of whom exists. Nevertheless, let me try to define these impossible standards.

THE IDEAL MEMBER OF CONGRESS

The ideal member of Congress should:

- Be entrenched. If not, he or she should work hard to achieve such status. Only members who have seniority and relatively safe districts have the opportunity to accomplish something constructive. (Clearly, then, I disapprove of term limits.)
- Be a good listener, not only to your constituents, but also to your staff.
- Be appreciative of your staff and do not blame them publicly whenever something goes wrong. Unloading your frustration on a staff member in private is normal and legitimate. An example of the right attitude is reflected in the personality and behavior of Peter Frelinghuysen and H. R. Gross. The egregious exception is the late Wayne Hays—and look what happened to *him!*
- Be a good negotiator, and recognize the value of a judicious compromise. Members of Congress need negotiating skills as much as do diplomats, and in both instances the negotiating process has to be carried out behind closed doors to be successful. Open mark-up sessions are a joke, as the real hard bargaining has always been done beforehand and in private.
- Be at least reasonably knowledgeable in international affairs. This means congressional travel, even if the media give you a hard time. In today's interdependent world (forgive the cliché), you cannot help your constituents in the long run if you are ignorant about what is happening abroad.
- Be always cognizant of the national as opposed to the parochial interest in legislative proposals. However, "political courage" can be overdone. One must be selective in supporting unpopular causes. A member of Congress must remain in office to be effective.

THE IDEAL CONGRESSIONAL STAFFER

The ideal congressional staffer should:

- Recognize, above all, that your principal responsibility is to serve your particular member or chairman, not to use one or the other to pursue your own agenda.
- Seek anonymity, not public recognition. The confidence of your member or chairman is your reward.
- Be "up front" with both members and staff colleagues. Devious deal-making can result in short-term success but will inevitably weaken your ultimate position. Trust is the name of the game.
- As a corollary, do not leak to your media contacts information received on a privileged basis. The staff gets blame enough for leaks by members. If you get a reputation for leaking, you will not be told anything of value.
- Keep secrets or confidences. Above all, never expose information received in confidence for monetary gain—that is the lowest form of life.
- Be willing to tell your chairman or member what he or she ought to hear, not necessarily what he or she wants to hear. If the above rules are adhered to, the advice will be accepted, if not always followed.
- Retain a sense of humor. Without it, a staffer is lost from the start.

I will leave the quality of my work to the judgment of others. I can only attest to the fact that in my thirty-one years of service to Uncle Sam, I have mostly had a hell of a good time. I could not ask for more.

APPENDICES

Appendix A

LETTERS FROM MALAWI ON
IN-COUNTRY TRAVEL, 1969

July 1969 Trip to Nsanje in the South

Dear Family,

I have just returned from a three-day trip to Nsanje (called "Port Herold" on many of the old maps of Nyasaland), and I thought I would record some of my impressions while they are still fresh in mind. Nsanje is located on the Shire River (pronounced shee-ree) at the very southernmost tip of Malawi, bordering on Mozambique. In fact, Mt. Chipperone (which gives its name to the chill rain and wind which sweeps over most of Malawi about once a month during the winter season) is located just across the Mozambique border and is clearly visible from Nsanje.

Driving to Nsanje from Blantyre is all downhill, beginning at about 3,500 feet (Blantyre) and ending up at approximately 100 feet above sea level (Nsanje). I departed Wednesday at 6:00 A.M. with my neighbor, Ted Shawley, who is the police commissioner for the entire Southern Region of Malawi, which includes Blantyre and Zomba and extends all the way down to Mozambique. He is a classic Kiplingesque type of colonial administrator who has some forty years of experience as a servant of the crown in such places as

India and Malaya. Sporting a large handlebar mustache, neatly pressed khaki uniform with shorts and high socks, he appears almost as an anachronism in the independent black Africa of the sixties. Nevertheless, his no-nonsense approach to his work and his subordinates has much to recommend it: During the course of one brief inspection stopover, I watched him fire one man for (admitted) petty larceny and drunkenness, promote two others and send a third officer on emergency leave to visit his sick wife. It was an impressive performance and struck me as eminently fair in every respect. So far, my impression is that the so-called "ex-pats" in both police and army enjoy the absolute loyalty and respect of their subordinates (in striking contrast to the ex-colonials who staff the middle echelon of many of the ministries—where there is considerable discontent—especially among the educated civil servants who have returned from several years of study in the U. K. and the U. S.)

At any rate, the trip down the "escarpment" into the lower Shire River valley was a memorable experience. The scenery is magnificent under any circumstances and it is especially impressive at sunrise. The green lush valley seems to extend indefinitely to the mountains on the distant horizon, and as one descends, it seems that all of Africa is visible below. We arrived in Nsanje at 9:30 A.M., at which point Ted reviewed his "troops," already standing at parade rest awaiting inspection, while I paid a call on the district commissioner.

From this moment on, my itinerary was effectively controlled by the D. C., the member of parliament for Nsanje South, and the district chairman of the MCP (Malawi Congress Party). Apparently this part of the country is rarely visited by dignitaries from Blantyre. During the rainy season, from December until May, the roads become flooded and impassable, and the climate and mosquitoes make life very unpleasant indeed. The President made a fence-mending tour of the area last June, but on the whole the region is left very much to its own devices. Although rich in agricultural resources (cotton, maize, sugar cane, cattle and some rice), the standard of living is primitive beyond belief.

One of the Peace Corps volunteers took me on a walking tour of the "bush" villages, where life has not progressed much further than in the days of David Livingstone. Clothing is minimal; mud huts are everywhere in evidence, and they can't be any different than those which were seen by the first European explorers—no windows, dirt floors, and straw roofs. In fact, the most vivid impression is the almost complete lack of movement. The men sit in a kind of stupor while the women sit for the most part nursing their babies. Otherwise life appears to be at a complete standstill. The reception one gets, on the other hand, is very cordial. The villagers line up in droves to shake your hand and exchange "zikomos." In Chichewa or Chisena, which most of the people speak in Nsanje, this is the all-important word, which has every possible meaning: thank you, you're welcome, hello, goodbye, excuse me, come again.

Although no one seems to be starving, there is strong evidence of malnutrition: many children with extended pot-bellied stomachs, probably the result of a thoroughly monotonous diet consisting of a corn meal mush called "encima." Although some profess to find this particular dish appetizing, if dipped in a spicy sauce, it seems to me like a combination of raw flour, toothpaste and soap, except that it is absolutely tasteless. The great deficiency is protein, as Africans count their wealth in the number of cattle, goats and/or pigs they own, which means none or very few ever get slaughtered. Then there are the polluted streams the people bathe in from time to time, infecting themselves with a parasite called bilharzia, which if untreated eventually attacks the liver and is fatal. It is a depressing picture, to say the least, but in many respects a curiously fascinating one: life is reduced to the very basic elements: birth, food (such as it is), reproduction and death. It is small wonder that those who manage to escape the village rarely seem to return.

Despite the bleak picture described above, there has evidently been progress, particularly in Nsanje proper (as opposed to the outlying areas). The district commissioner impressed me as a highly intelligent, hardworking young (in his late twenties) African who is doing everything in his power to improve the lot of his people. There are several good schools by African standards, and I attended several "ceremonial" dedications of those portions of the construction which were financed by U.S. AID funds. In all cases this involved so-called "self-help" projects which required the local people to build the facilities themselves, with modest financing of the materials by AID. If U.S. aid is unappreciated in many parts of the world, this was certainly not the case in Nsanje: the most elaborate preparations were made in our behalf, including traditional dances and endless speeches by the local politicians. As the ranking U.S. official, I was practically mobbed by well-wishers, including chiefs, school committeemen and district officials at every turn. One evening a special dance was staged in our honor—an exhausting affair which lasted well into the night and required all of the vigor and stamina I could muster.

Yesterday we returned to Blantyre, stopping off to visit two other AID projects in the remote villages of Chiromo and Makwira. On this part of the trip, incidentally, I was accompanied by the AID representative for Malawi and another embassy officer, whom I joined at Nsanje on Wednesday P.M. (Ted Shawley returned to Blantyre the same evening.) We were all put up at a government rest house situated on a mountain overlooking the valley. The house was comfortable except for the lack of electricity and water. One evening we returned some of the hospitality we received by slaughtering a ram (presented to the AID man by one of the communities he visited en route to Nsanje), roasting it on an outdoor spit, and then inviting the local officials and Peace Corps volunteers to celebrate the Apollo 11 crew splashdown, which we listened to on the radio the same evening. The ram was not the tastiest of animals (I think he was a bit old and underfed), but the party was a success.

There is more to tell, but these are the highlights.

October–November 1969 Trip to the Northern Region

Dear Family,

Clara and I have just returned from an official trip throughout the Northern Region—which explains, in part at least, why we have been such poor correspondents of late. Our entire journey lasted a week and took us from Mzuzu (the administrative capital of the North) to Nkhata Bay, Chinteche, and Bandawa on the Lake and thence to Chitipa, the northernmost village of Malawi. It was quite an extensive excursion and we covered a great deal of territory—traversing most of the country north of Blantyre via long, dusty and unpaved roads. I am enclosing a road map which may assist you in tracing our route.

The main purpose of this travel was to provide Embassy representation at official "opening ceremonies" of two recently completed U.S. AID-assisted "self-help" projects at Bandawa and Chitipa. Although the bilateral AID program for Malawi has terminated, we still receive a modest allotment of funds to support the self-help program in Malawi. Under this scheme the people of a community actually do the construction work themselves, while we contribute something towards the building materials, such as brick, cement, etc. At the moment I am serving as chairman of the embassy's Self-Help Committee, which attempts to screen the various proposals submitted by the district development committees throughout the country and select the most worthy causes.

In both instances the projects we visited were school (classroom) buildings: the one at Bandawe was particularly impressive and had been completed in less than three months, whereas the one at Chitipa (Kapoka Primary School) had been under construction for over three *years*. The difference apparently stemmed from the fact that the Bandawe builder was a professional artisan who had been trained in South Africa for approximately fifteen years, while the expertise in Chitipa is somewhat limited. Also Chitipa is so remote, it is hard to get the necessary materials. Both projects filled a very real need, however, and had considerable local impact.

Clara and I sat with the VIPs at both ceremonies, including such dignitaries as the district commissioner, the members of Parliament for the districts concerned, the local party chairman, representatives of the Women's League of Malawi and (in Bandawe) the Minister for the Northern Region. There were the usual long speeches, the exhortation to work harder in the future, and the colorful traditional dances. Although the government likes to take as much credit as possible for these projects, all of these officials were generous in their praise of the U.S. contribution, and I had no cause for complaint. These ceremonies generate great local enthusiasm and are invariably well-attended by tribal chiefs and village headmen, as well as the populace at large.

We left Blantyre on Wednesday, October 29, at 7:00 A.M., by air, arriving at 10:00 in Mzuzu, where we were met by two Peace Corps community development workers who have been very much involved in the self-help program in the North. Later in the day Duncan, the embassy driver, arrived in the embassy jeep station wagon (having departed the day before) and drove us during the remainder of our journey.

Our first stop was Nkhata Bay, where we spent the afternoon swimming in the beautiful clear blue water of Lake Malawi. In this area the water is very similar to that off the Dalmatian coast, although it is considerably warmer and of course free of salt. That evening we dined at the humble quarters of one of the Peace Corps couples, albeit rather elegantly in comparison with subsequent meals, which were mostly from tins—a monotonous diet, to say the least. The next day we spent at Bandawe (just south of Nkhata Bay) and again returned to Mzuzu for the night.

Friday morning we set off at 6:00 A.M. for Chitipa, traveling a good deal of the way on a road which passed through neighboring Zambia and arriving in time for the 1:30 P.M. opening ceremony. Since there is no place to stay in Chitipa, we had to return to Chisenga, about twenty-six miles away, where the government maintains a "rest house." The district commissioner had even sent his car down with supplies of food, including some inedible meats and a package of rice which was not much better—even the Peace Corps volunteer who accompanied us on this stage of our journey couldn't get it down, but nevertheless it *was* a thoughtful gesture which was greatly appreciated.

Saturday we departed early in the morning for the Nyika Plateau (8,000 feet) and government game reserve, which is one of the famous sights of Malawi. (Mt. Mlanje, Malawi's highest peak, is at 10,000 feet.) The air is clear and brisk and a welcome relief from the heat which is prevalent at most other locations at this time of year. Although the plateau is somewhat barren, except for certain areas which are covered with pine trees (planted in the early 1950s), the vast expanse, as far as the eye can see, has a peculiar charm which grows on one after a few hours on the summit. We had a chalet to ourselves, a cook, although nothing much in the way of food as we were running a bit short by that time, and a guide to take us through the park. Most of our time Saturday afternoon and Sunday morning was spent in search of animals, primarily various forms of deer (reedbuck, "duiker," bushbuck, etc.) and zebras, plus several families of warthogs. It was a restful interlude after all of the driving of the past few days.

Sunday P.M. we returned to Mzuzu, where we again spent the night at the government rest house. Alas, this was our *least* successful night, as we both were devoured by some kind of bedbug, which left us covered with red welts. Clara was the major victim, but after two days the situation began to ease up a bit. On Monday we were scheduled to fly back to Blantyre, but it turned out that Air Malawi had inadvertently canceled our reservations and we were forced to return by jeep, inching most of the way over the Vipya Plateau (at 7,000 feet between Mzuzu and Mzimba, which unlike the Nyika is covered with thick forest) and then to Kasungu (where the President was born), and finally Lilongwe, where we spent the night, returning to Blantyre the following morning. As a result of this journey, I have now traveled from Nsanje in the south (last July) to Chitipa in the north, and have already covered most of the country.

Appendix B

REPORT ON
INTERPARLIAMENTARY ACTIVITIES,
FEBRUARY 1978

House of Representatives
Committee on International Relations

February 3, 1978

To: Honorable Clement J. Zablocki, Chairman
From: John Chapman Chester, Staff Consultant
Subject: *House Participation in Interparliamentary Activities*

The following two-part report, prepared at the initial suggestion of Honorable Lee H. Hamilton and pursuant to instructions from the Chief of Staff, attempts:

In *Part I*, to provide members of the committee with updated summary descriptions of interparliamentary group activities. It focuses specifically on the role which

Note: Appendix B consists of a rather technical report on a somewhat obscure subject. Thus, even members of my immediate family are excused from reading the full text.

To the best of my knowledge, however, this is the only comprehensive report on all interparliamentary groups that existed up to February 1978, and publishing it now may be helpful to future researchers interested in the topic. (It has already been cited extensively in one master's thesis that I know of.) The report is thus included here for the possible benefit of future generations.

has accrued both by law and tradition to the Committee on International Relations.

In *Part II*, to identify emerging problems and priorities and suggest possible procedural improvements in the overall IPG process. It contains staff conclusions and suggestions which you may wish to consider, among many others, in evaluating current interparliamentary group policies and procedures.

Part I — INTERPARLIAMENTARY GROUP ACTIVITIES

The participation of Members of Congress in interparliamentary group activities, both multilateral and bilateral in nature, has increased dramatically over the past two decades, beginning with the establishment of the North Atlantic Assembly (then known as the NATO Parliamentary Conference) in 1955.

While the precedent for such participation dates back to the last century, the number of such groups has proliferated in the past decade, leading to increased demands on the time of individual member-delegates, on the committee's financial resources (for those groups not funded under specific House resolutions), and on staff support, traditionally provided by this committee.

In preparing this report, I have consulted with all staff members who have been directly involved in IPG activities, and I have received considerable input from each of them. Particular attention has been devoted to the committee's obligations and responsibilities (both legal and traditional) vis-à-vis the House as a whole. The emphasis is on organization and procedure—not substance.

Many of the interparliamentary groups meet increasingly outside capitals, to help focus members' attention on formal discussions and scheduled IPG activities. This practice has become more widespread because two factors make it difficult to round up delegates for interparliamentary meetings, particularly for the U.S.:

a) competing demands on a legislator's time when Congress or Parliament is in session.

b) a general *exodus* from the capital cities after adjournment or during recess periods.

This report deals separately with 1) Statutory Interparliamentary Groups and 2) "Informal" Interparliamentary Groups, those which function on a regular basis but without specific legal authority. Except for financing, the two categories differ little; once an "informal" IPG becomes operational, member countries—normally the home country delegations—assume on a rotating basis certain de facto obligations and responsibilities: organization, administrative preparations, staffing, and hospitality.

For statutory IPGs, the recently-enacted provisions of P. L. 95-45, enacted on June 15, 1977, prescribe that: a) the chairman or vice chairman of each delegation be a member of the Committeeon International Relations; and b) a specified number of delegates—indicated below on a case-by-case basis—also be members of that committee.

A. Statutory Interparliamentary Groups

1. The North Atlantic Assembly

The largest of the interparliamentary groups, the North Atlantic Assembly, is also the most active in terms of meetings held throughout the year, and most demanding on the time of member-delegates.

The Assembly was created in 1955 against the background of cold war and a growing conviction that member countries of the North Atlantic Alliance should be encouraged to cooperate more actively in political, economic and parliamentary—as well as military—activities. In response to a 1953 proposal of the North Atlantic Council, delegates from all Alliance parliaments met in Paris for the first time in July 1955, and established an ad hoc committee to organize future meetings. This committee, redesignated the following year as the

Standing Committee, emerged as the governing body of the newly formed institution.

In 1957 the Assembly became NATO Parliamentarians' Conference, and in 1958 committees were established to handle the preparatory work of the conference, as set forth below. In 1966 the name of the organization was changed to North Atlantic Assembly. In 1968 headquarters was transferred from Paris to Brussels and the Secretariat was completely reorganized.

In effect, therefore, a loosely organized conference has been transformed over the years into an institutionalized framework in which parliamentary delegations from North America and Europe can discuss subjects of wide-ranging interest, and develop a full and frank interchange of ideas on the major problems facing the Atlantic Alliance. In the intervening years the Assembly's deliberations have had considerable impact on the decision-making process of the North Atlantic Council itself.

The Assembly consists of parliamentarians from the fifteen NATO member countries appointed by their respective parliaments. Of a total membership of 172 delegates, the United States is allotted thirty-six; the United Kingdom, France, Germany and Italy eighteen each; and other NATO member nations a lesser number each.[1]

Officers consist of a president, three vice presidents (of different nationalities) and a treasurer. North America (the United States or Canada) must be represented among the officers. The Standing Committee, the Assembly's governing body, has overall responsibility for directing activities between sessions, preparing the budget and agenda, and ensuring implementation of Assembly recommendations and resolutions. The Standing Committee has one member and alternate from each delegation, each with one vote, except for weighted votes on additional expenditures. The Standing Committee appoints the Secretary General and determines the size and functions of the Secretariat.

Five committees, with national representation in the same proportion as the membership of the Assembly itself, carry out the major work of the Assembly, and make proposals to annual plenary sessions. They are the *Economic Committee* (thirty-six members); the *Educational, Cultural Affairs and Information Committee* (twenty-two members); the *Military Committee* (forty members); the *Political Committee* (forty-six members) and the *Scientific and Technical Committee* (twenty-eight members). Committee sessions are closed to the public, except for—on occasion—the *Educational, Cultural Affairs and Information Committee.*

P. L. 84-689 (July 11, 1956) as amended by P. L. 95-45 (June 15, 1977) provides the basic authority for continuing United States participation in the North Atlantic Assembly. House delegates shall not exceed twelve, appointed by the Speaker of the House; at least four are to be from the Committee on International Relations. The chairman or vice chairman of the House delegation shall be from the Committee on International Relations, also designated by the Speaker. A continuing annual appropriation of $25,000 is authorized for expenses.

Unlike the other parliamentary groups discussed in this paper, which normally meet at most once or twice annually, the Assembly and its constituent bodies meet numerous times during the year. Typically, the plenary session is held for one full week in the autumn, in a different member country capital each year. The Standing Committee meets at least three times a year, in the early spring prior to the spring committee meetings, during the fall autumn plenary session, and at other times "according to prevailing circumstances." Each of the five committees meets twice a year, once during the spring and again prior to the autumn plenary session. Subcommittees meet at irregular intervals on an ad hoc basis.

Other special activities and events include study tours for parliamentarians of member countries, held each year alternatively in Europe and North America; Atlantic "congresses," like the one in 1959 to mark the Tenth Anniversary of NATO and in 1962 to discuss the future of the Alliance; seminars in 1969 and 1970 on public administration at the initiative of the Committee on Education, Cultural Affairs and Information; and a study conducted over a two-year period by a "Committee of Nine" on the future of the Alliance and the most appropriate role to be played by the Assembly.

U.S. participation in Assembly activities is the dominating theme in planning meetings, briefings, and study tours. Europeans regard the size and quality of the American delegation as a litmus test of congressional support for NATO. Committee and subcommittee meetings are generally scheduled to facilitate the attendance of American delegates. The topic of conversation in the weeks before every spring and fall session is the size and makeup of the American delegation. Low U.S. attendance in recent years, especially by the Senate, has provoked frequent queries and comments about American intentions toward Western Europe.[2]

2. Interparliamentary Union

The Interparliamentary Union (IPU) is the oldest of the interparliamentary institutions, with a membership that varies but currently includes seventy-five national groups. It promotes personal contacts between members of parliaments, provides for better understanding of national attitudes, supports development of representative institutions, and helps advance international peace and cooperation. With broad participation from so-called North/South and East/West countries, the IPU provides a forum for debate and negotiation similar to the UN. Participants represent parliaments and not governments; thus, the views and voting behavior of IPU participants does not necessarily correlate one-to-one with their governments' official policies.

Western European and Third World participants, as well as those of the Soviet Union and Eastern Europe,

444

treat the IPU very seriously. Traditional friends and allies of the United States look on it as an opportunity to explore U.S. congressional and governmental opinion. The IPU provides a vehicle for the industrialized and nonindustrialized countries to relate their sometimes divergent policies and interests, and for examining some of the details of East-West détente.

While U.S. participation was first established by law in 1935, members of Congress attended the first meeting in 1889, and have done so almost consistently, except for wartime, ever since. Three conferences of the IPU have met in the U.S.: in 1904 in St. Louis in conjunction with the World's Fair; and in 1925 and 1953 in Washington.

Every senator and representative is automatically a member of the U.S. Group. Delegations are chosen for each IPU conference in accordance with U.S. law. Under current law, the Speaker appoints no more than twelve delegates from the House, at least four of them from the HIRC. The chairman or vice chairman is also to be a member of that committee.

The U.S. contributes 13.61 per cent of the IPU budget annually—subject to approval of the American Group—toward maintaining the Bureau of the Interparliamentary Union, for purposes of promoting international arbitration, and up to $45,000 a year for expenses of the U.S. delegation. The U.S. Group elects a president, three vice presidents, a secretary, a treasurer, an executive committee of nine, and two council members. The permanent executive secretary of the U.S. Group is chosen by the executive committee annually. For the last seven years Mr. Darrell St. Claire, Assistant Secretary of the Senate, has held this position. HIRC staff members have notbeen involved in carrying out these responsibilities. Under P. L. 95-45, however, after December 31, 1977 the executive secretary is to be an officer or employee of the Senate or House, appointed by the chairman of the Senate delegation during odd-numbered Congresses, and by the chairman of the House delegation in even-numbered Congresses.

IPU conferences are held once a year. The Council normally meets twice a year. The Council's spring meeting is usually held during Easter Week, and the Council's fall meeting and the conference are usually in late September. In 1978 a spring meeting was scheduled for Lisbon, a fall meeting in Bonn, and a special IPU-sponsored session on Security and Cooperation in Europe for Vienna in May.

Because of the length of the sessions. attendance at regularly scheduled IPU sessions by a full delegation of twelve appointed House delegates has been a serious problem. For instance, at the plenary meeting in Sofia, Bulgaria, in September 1977, only one delegate attended the first week, and only seven others the second week. Both at that meeting and generally, foreign participants look on U.S. participation as a major example of U.S. leadership or lack of leadership in world affairs generally. U.S. participation is important to balance some of the more strident rhetoric and actions which the meetings produce. Thus, in the Sofia meeting the U.S. delegation helped negotiate a compromise resolution on Israeli settlements that did not force an IPU investigative team on Israel.

3. Canada-United States Interparliamentary Group

The Canada-U.S. Interparliamentary Group was established in 1959. It meets annually, alternating each year between Canada and the United States. Because of the difficulty in getting host-member participation during meetings held in the respective capital cities, the Group no longer holds the meeting in Ottawa or Washington. The first meeting was in Washington, D.C., in 1959. The last meeting was in Victoria, British Columbia, in May 1977. Meetings are normally held in the first part of the calendar year, in Canada usually in the spring, and in the U.S. usually in the late winter.

The Nineteenth Meeting is scheduled for February 9-13, 1978, in New Orleans.

The Group is staffed on the Canadian side by the Interparliamentary Relations Branch (which staffs most interparliamentary meetings for the Canadian Parliament) and on the U.S. side by Senate Foreign Relations Committee and House International Relations Committee staff. In recent years the agenda has covered various bilateral economic and environmental issues and a few international issues. Most of the discussion focused on bilateral issues, particularly energy, pollution and broadcasting.

U.S. participation in the annual meetings is authorized by P. L. 86-42, passed on June 11, 1959. The annual authorization for each house of $15,000 was increased to $25,000 beginning with calendar year 1978. That sum covers all official delegation expenses, except for transportation to the meeting, which is by military plane. The host country delegation provides all internal transportation and covers expenses for meals and other representational costs, but each delegation pays for the costs of its hotel rooms.

P. L. 86-42 stipulates that twenty-four members of Congress, half from the Senate and half from the House, shall be appointed to attend the annual meeting. The House members are appointed by the Speaker, and at least four must be from the House International Relations Committee. Those four members serve for an entire Congress; the other eight House members serve for only one session. The House chairman is traditionally from the Committee on International Relations, although the law merely prescribes that *either* chairman *or* vice chairman be from that committee.

Traditionally the Canadians have been better prepared than the U.S. delegates. The Canadian Group is structured so that participation in briefings is mandatory for attendance at the annual meeting. In the last few years U.S. participation has improved, with U.S. members taking a more active part in preparing for the meeting. Improvement still needs to be made in the briefing books, which have tended to be too lengthy and not very useful.

4.Mexico-United States Interparliamentary Group

The only other bilateral group established and funded by specific House resolution is the Mexico-United States Interparliamentary Group, which has been in existence since 1960. The first conference was held in Guadalajara, Jalisco, in February 1961, and following the tradition set by the Canadian-U.S. Group, subsequent meetings have been held in the United States in even-numbered years and in Mexico in odd-numbered years. The most recent meeting was held over the Memorial Day recess last May in Hermosillo, Sonora.

The initial focus of these sessions was on bilateral border problems, in an effort to ease long-standing tensions between Mexico and the United States. Early deliberations led to some notable achievements, such as the Chamizal settlement and the Colorado Salinity Agreement, both attributable to legislative initiatives resulting from the conferences.

The agenda was later broadened to include multilateral issues such as the Organization of American States, the United Nations, and the International Law of the Sea. During the past two years the IPG has proven to be a particularly useful mechanism for discussion of priority issues involving traffic in weapons and narcotics, the increasing influx of "undocumented workers"(illegal aliens) into the United States, and the prisoner exchange treaty.

Meetings normally take place during periods when the House is in recess, namely, in February (during the Lincoln-Washington break), during the Easter recess, or over the long Memorial Day weekend. Plans for the 1978 conference call once again for scheduling during the Memorial Day period so as not to conflict with the Canadian-U.S. Interparliamentary Conference to be held in February. For logistical reasons, it is preferable not to have the conferences of these two groups scheduled at the same time, as occurred in May 1977.

U.S. participation in annual parliamentary conferences with Mexico was authorized by a joint resolution (P. L. 86-420), approved April 9, 1960. A continuing annual authorization of $15,000, increased to $25,000 beginning in calendar year 1978, for each delegation (House and Senate) wasalso provided for to cover official delegation expenses. By tradition, the host country delegation provides internal transportation in the country where the meeting is held, and covers certain representational costs (not including hotels rooms and food) of delegates and staff.

P. L. 86-420 as amended by P. L. 95-45 stipulates that the House delegation shall consist of twelve members of Congress, appointed by the Speaker. Traditionally, an equal number of majority and minority members have been designated. The chairman or vice chairman is to be a member of the Committee on International Relations, and not less than four delegates are also to be members of that committee. While the four HIRC members are to serve for the duration of each Congress, other delegates are appointed and serve on an annual basis.

Special factors or problems include:

a. Hospitality. The Mexicans assign a high priority to the IPG as an institution and are extraordinarily hospitable. When the meetings are held in Mexico, the full resources of the Mexican Government, not just the Congress, are placed at the group's disposal and often entire communities are involved in preparations and welcoming functions. Owing to the more limited resources of the U.S. group and a more demanding legislative schedule faced by U.S. members, it has proven difficult to reciprocate in kind. A major effort was made in 1976 when the delegations met in Atlanta and Denver during the bicentennial year, which was facilitated by the participation of local groups in the activities. Attendance by U.S. delegates when meetings are held in the United States, however, has become a recurrent problem. This is especially true of conferences held in Washington, as the Canadian Group has also discovered.

b. Presidential Meetings. By tradition, the delegations have usually met with the presidents of Mexico and/or the United States, depending on the conference site. The White House has consistently cooperated in scheduling informal receptions with the President when the U.S. Group hosts the conference.

c. Turnover among Mexican Delegates. Mexican legislators are prohibited by law from being reelected after their initial terms have expired (that is, until they have been out of office for the same period of time as they served in Congress). A deputy can move directly to the Senate, and vice versa, but this rarely happens. The practice affords large numbers of Mexican legislators the opportunity to participate in the IPG process, but the almost complete turnover in membership of the Mexican delegation, and usually staff as well, puts an increased burden on the U.S. delegation to provide continuity.

B. Informal Interparliamentary Groups

Although the groups described below under this heading are not specifically authorized by House resolution, they tend over time to become "institutionalized" by tradition. Some, like the European Parliament and the British/French-U.S. bilateral groups, meet regularly under continuing and established procedures. Others are still in the category of ad hoc parliamentary "visits" which in varying degrees have become (or could become) self-perpetuating institutions.

1. European Parliament

The European Parliament, one of four institutions which run the nine-nation European Community, is located in

Luxembourg, where it holds about half its weeklong monthly sessions. It has 198 members, nominated by the parliaments of member countries, and represents fifty-three national parties. It will expand to 410 members in its first international elections, scheduled for June 1978 or 1979. Parliament can only give "opinions" to the European Commission and Council of Ministers, which run the EC; however, it has an influence on decisions through consultation, and is of growing importance.

Parliament has been meeting with the U.S. Congress informally since 1972, most recently in July 1977 in London, and in November in Washington. It is to meet in March 1978 in Palermo, Sicily. Only House members have attended so far. The HIRC has taken the initiative in organizing and participating in such meetings.

The fiscal year 1978 Foreign Relations authorization bill contained a Senate-sponsored amendment to provide statutory authority for US-European Parliament meetings, along lines of those with the North Atlantic Assembly and the IPU. A Senate-House conference deleted the amendment, primarily because of House reservations that the meetings had worked well because of their informality, and because the parliament had some delicate membership problems of its own, which a unilateral U.S. change could complicate. The conferees, however, recommended that "appropriate committees" (that is, the HIRC) provide adequate funding for continued U.S. participation.

At the November 1977 Washington meeting, loosely organized on a crash basis, congressional attendance was poor, and staff members had to fill in. To avoid a repeat, and to implement the conferees' recommendations, the HIRC will take on the main financial and logistical burden in planning for meetings. A House member will be chairman of the U.S. delegation, and another House staff member and myself will provide staffing for the upcoming Palermo meeting.

2. British-American
Interparliamentary Group

While its membership often overlaps with that of the North Atlantic Assembly, the British-American Interparliamentary Group is an entirely separate body, and in the "informal category." It met for the first time in Bermuda in 1961. It was designed essentially as a mechanism for in-depth discussions, primarily of bilateral issues, which were less appropriate for a multilateral forum. Meetings have been informal, off the record, and unstructured, without formal rules of procedure, interpreters, verbatim reports, and the like. No reports have been published except a financial one for the U.S. Group.

U.S. participation and interest in the 1961 Bermuda meeting were high. U.S. delegates were Senators J. W. Fulbright, Hubert Humphrey, Wayne Morse and John Sherman Cooper, and Representatives Thomas E. Morgan, Wayne L. Hays, Omar Burleson and Frances P. Bolton. Former president Harry S. Truman, who was vacationing in Bermuda, attended some of the sessions.

Until 1970, joint Senate-House delegations met on an annual basis with their British counterparts. Thereafter House and Senate delegations attended IPG meetings separately in alternate years. In 1976 the meeting with House delegates was canceled owing to scheduling complications arising from the U.S. bicentennial.

The 1977 meeting had to be canceled, causing considerable embarrassment to all concerned. Because that year was the Queen's Silver Jubilee, the British made extensive preparations for a parliamentary conference to be held in Edinburgh, Scotland, October 20-23. For the first time since 1970, a *joint* House-Senate delegation was invited to participate. The British delegates, under the leadership of the Rt. Hon. Merlyn Rees, the Home Secretary, attached considerable importance to the proceedings. As it turned out, the meeting had to be canceled just two days before it was to have convened.

This unfortunate episode once again points up the difficulties often encountered by House delegation leaders in recruiting U.S. participants to attend many such interparliamentary conferences when the House is in session, especially during the last weeks of a busy legislative session. In this case, Congressman Burton, chairman of the House delegation to the North Atlantic Assembly, had acquired—by virtue of that position—de facto responsibility for House participation. He had initially agreed to the October dates on the assumption that Congress would have adjourned by then, and had warned the British that complications would arise if Congress were still in session. However, plans of host country delegations tend to generate a momentum of their own, leading to rising expectations, administrative commitments, and—inevitably—disappointment when fall-outs occur.

3. France–United States Friendship Society

According to a comment by General Pierre Billotte, the France-U.S. Friendship Society has been in existence for about twenty-five years. The group has met irregularly. In 1971, for instance, the Group met in France in April and in Washington from 30 September to 7 October. The last meeting took place in France in 1975; the most recent Washington meeting was held October 3-8, 1977.

The French members of the group take the meetings very seriously. They generally look forward to a full day's meeting with U.S. members. The second day is used for appointments with officials from the executive departments who can authoritatively discuss subjects of current interest to the French. Over the years, the custom has developed of concluding the meeting with a three-five day tour of the host country, with the host paying for all expenses. At the last meeting the staffs agreed informally that the next meeting in France would not take place before spring 1979. U.S. and French elections preclude a 1978 meeting.

The Secretary of the House delegation has advised Robert Moinet, Director of Parliamentary Relations for the French National Assembly, that new House rulings may prevent U.S. members from accepting payment of hotel and meal expenses during future conferences.

4. German-American Conferences

The most recent meeting of the German-American Conference took place November 14-16, 1971 in Washington. While the meeting is referred to as the Seventh American-German Conference, there are no records on hand of previous meetings of this group. In 1974 former Speaker Carl Albert invited the President of the German Bundestag, Mrs. Annemarie Renger, and a delegation from the Bundestag to a meeting in the Capitol on April 8 and 9. At the Speaker's request, the meting was handled by the then-chairman of the House delegation to the North Atlantic Assembly, Wayne L. Hays.

During the past two years, individual German parliamentarians have informally inquired about inviting a U.S. delegation to Germany. Nothing has developed out of these inquiries, but the Germans clearly are interested in instituting a regular system of exchange.

5. Norwegian Parliamentary Visit

In 1975 the Department of State contacted former HIRC chairman Morgan about the impending visit of a group of Norwegian parliamentarians. The committee staff director referred the inquiry to the Secretary of the House delegation to the North Atlantic Assembly, and the meeting was hosted by Mr. Hays. While no subsequent meetings have been scheduled, a follow-up invitation by the Norwegians (with potential precedent-setting implications) is an ever-present prospect.

6. Soviet-U. S. Parliamentary Exchanges

Soviet-U.S. parliamentary exchange visits began in 1974, when a group of Soviet parliamentarians and accompanying officials, under the leadership of Boris Ponomarev (member of the Politburo and Secretary of the Central Committee) met with designated House members in Washington, at the invitation of then-Speaker Carl Albert. A return House-Senate visit to the Soviet Union followed in 1975. Albert and the then-ranking HIRC Democrat Zablocki headed the House delegation, while Senator Humphrey led the Senate group.

In 1977 Speaker O'Neill and Senate Majority Leader Byrd extended a joint invitation to the Soviet Union for a U.S. visit in January 1978. The Soviet delegation, again led by Boris Ponomarev, visited Washington for four days beginning January 22, and then embarked on a seven-day tour of the United States. At the Speaker's request, Majority Whip Brademas was assigned overall responsibility for the House proceedings, functions, and welcoming activities planned for the delegation.

While these exchange visits have not yet been institutionalized on the House side, the Senate has passed an authorizing and funding resolution with precedent-setting ramifications. In any case,whether or not the Soviet-U.S. exchanges remain on an informal basis, the tradition may be expected to continue into the future, depending perhaps on the overall climate of Soviet-U.S. relations

7. Yugoslav-U. S. Parliamentary Visits

At the Speaker's invitation, approximately eight-ten members of the Federal Assembly of Yugoslavia had originally planned to visit the House in February 1978, to be followed by five days of travel within the United States. However, in light of President Tito's impending visit to the U.S. in March, the parliamentary trip was canceled and will be rescheduled for July 1978.

This represents a further follow-up to the visit of former Speaker Albert and approximately seventeen House members to Yugoslavia in 1975 as guests of the Federal Assembly. While such exchanges have not been formalized in any specific manner, the pattern has been set for future visits on a periodic (perhaps biannual) basis.

8. Commonwealth Parliamentary Association

The Commonwealth Parliamentary Association (CPA) is an association of Commonwealth parliamentarians who are "united to the Commonwealth by community of interests, respect for the rule of law and the rights of the individual citizen, and the pursuit of positive ideals of parliamentary democracy." Founded in 1911 as the "Empire Parliamentary Association," it has pursued these objectives since 1945 by organizing annual Commonwealth and regional conferences and the interchange of parliamentary delegations.

Although the United States is not a member of the association, members of both Houses have been invited to attend its conferences since at least 1950. In 1969 one such observer delegation, led by former HIRC member Leonard Farbstein and Senator J. William Fulbright, participated in the Fifteenth CPA conference, held in Port-of-Spain, Trinidad and Tobago, October 13–17. A report of the proceedings and activities of this group was issued on November 7, 1969 as a committee print (see Vol. 5, Committee on Foreign Affairs, "Miscellaneous Documents and Staff Memorandum," 91st Congress, 1st Session.)

While the committee's records do not indicate that any subsequent House delegations were appointed for this purpose, future invitations may be anticipated.

9. Western European Union

From time to time the Assembly of the Western European Union travels to the United States as a guest of either the State Department or the Department of Defense. The most recent visit took place March 28–April 1, 1977. Members of the House delegation to the North Atlantic Assembly were invited to a lunch offered by the Department of Defense and to a reception hosted by the Minister of the United Kingdom Embassy. Both events took place on March 28.

While members of the Western European Union seek to meet with American congressmen when the opportunity arises, there does not appear to be a desire to establish a more structured relationship.

Part II— CONCLUSIONS AND SUGGESTIONS

A basic difference in outlook between U.S. legislators and their foreign counterparts needs to be addressed in any meaningful discussion of the U.S. role in interparliamentary institutions:

For foreign participants, on the one hand, parliamentary exchanges with U.S. members of Congress are generally regarded as a political *plus*. This results largely from a widespread public awareness abroad of the importance of influencing (or attempting to influence) U.S. economic and foreign policies, recognition of the impact those policies have on domestic well-being, and the role of Congress in setting those policies. Parliamentarians from other countries, therefore, tend to gain stature and political prestige from meetings with their U.S. colleagues and have every incentive to promote an expansion of the interparliamentary process. Foreign parliamentarians also have less demanding legislative schedules to contend with at home and fewer constituent pressures.

On the other hand, the position of U.S. participants in IPG conferences obviously presents a striking contrast. Confronted by a skeptical and suspicious electorate, aided and abetted by a critical—often hostile—communications media, even the most conscientious member of a U.S. interparliamentary delegation is constantly on the defensive to justify and explain why "this trip (or meeting) is necessary."

These problems arise from the institutional nature of most IPG activities, and will simply have to be lived with. Other problems, however, may be amenable to some form of improvement through better organization, advance planning, and liaison with the Speaker's office where applicable.

From the staff viewpoint, the major complications in the IPG process are summarized below. Suggestions are made for their amelioration wherever possible. These suggestions, it should be emphasized, are merely "factors" which the Chairman may wish to consider, among many others, in evaluating current IPG policies and procedures. At best, they are offered as *guidelines*, other things being equal (which they rarely are!).

1. Establishment of Additional Groups: Anti-Proliferation Policy Needed

The record of House participation in bilateral interparliamentary meetings and conferences clearly leaves much to be desired. The unavoidable conclusion is that the number of such mechanisms presently in existence, both formal and informal, has already reached the saturation point.

Nevertheless, pressure for establishment of *new* bilateral groups is relentless and difficult to resist. Members who are approached on the subject by foreign officials are understandably reluctant to appear unresponsive and uninterested in the suggestion. Initial favorable reactions tend to be regarded abroad as signals of approval.

At the moment the Germans, the Italians, the Indonesians and the Japanese are pressing for regular bilateral exchanges with U.S. legislators, and additional approaches along this line are sure to follow. The hard reality, however, is that one precedent inevitably leads to another and the extent and *quality* of House participation in all of these fora will suffer in almost direct proportion to the increase in the number of groups so established.

SUGGESTION: To the extent feasible, the institutionalized framework should be avoided in favor of the ad hoc "study mission" type of approach, allowing us maximum flexibility on timing and especially on follow-up visits. The normal pattern, for instance, is for the initial bilateral meeting to be well attended and successful, while subsequent meetings are characterized by substantial fallout on the U.S. side. The British-American Group is a classic example of that scenario.

Valid and persuasive reasons exist for parliamentary exchanges between members of Congress and their counterparts in such countries as Japan, our second largest trading partner, Germany, a vital NATO ally, and Italy, a traditional friend in economic and political trouble. Similar arguments could be made with respect to other countries (Israel, for example).

The point might be made, however, with the foreign promoters of such exchanges that U. S. interest and participation would be greatly enhanced by the ad hoc arrangement, which would actually transform each exchange visit into a "special occasion" rather than a routine obligation which the Congress is often unable to fulfill. Adherence to such a line would perhaps be more defensible than outright rejection of foreign overtures, which could have adverse repercussions.

2. Selection of U.S. Members

Despite the best of intentions and periodic attempts at long-range planning, selection of U.S. delegates for participation in interparliamentary conferences often ends up being a last-minute crash procedure (the "scramble for bodies," as one member has described it).

Although, to ensure political, regional and professional balance, delegations are appointed in many instances only after extensive consultation, dropouts frequently occur as the deadline for a specific meeting approaches. It is not uncommon for a delegation chairman to spend the last few days before a scheduled conference recruiting substitute delegates—on and off the floor—in an air of quiet desperation.

Clearly this is a situation which will always be with us and which the Committee on International Relations has only limited ability to control. To the extent possible, however, increased weight might be given to the following factors in the selection/recommendation process:

A. Delegates appointed to the North Atlantic Assembly should be confined to this one interparliamentary activity, which, as noted above, involves extensive year-round commitments. Ideally, the same rule should apply to such multilateral groups as the IPU and the European Parliament, which is becoming increasingly active and requires more extensive preparation than in the past.

B. Delegation chairmen should warn delegates in advance of the precise nature and extent of their prospective IPG responsibilities (how many committee meetings and plenary sessions per year, etc.) and especially of the reciprocal obligations which accrue to the United States when the U.S. delegation acts as host, and when fallout is normally at its peak.[3]

C. A schedule of upcoming activities and events of each parliamentary group (as they are known and/or revised to meet changing circumstances) should be circulated to appointed delegates at regular intervals. There is no substitute for the personal touch, preferably by a delegation leader rather than a staff member.[4]

3. Timing of Meetings

Again, this is an institutional problem which lends itself only to marginal stopgap remedies. As pointed out in Part I, the North Atlantic Assembly has made a conscious effort to schedule committee and subcommittee meetings to facilitate the attendance of American delegates. Also, in even-numbered years, the plenary session takes place in November after the U.S. election, another concession to the Americans. However, the very number of such meetings, and the fact that the scheduling of legislative business on the House floor is not always predictable in advance, remain formidable obstacles.

For the two statutory bilateral groups, limited scheduling changes have already been put into effect: in 1978, the meeting with Canadians will take place in February so as not to conflict with the Mexico-U.S. conference, scheduled over the Memorial Day recess.

By contrast, the U.S. delegation to the IPU has virtually no control over the timing of that institution's annual meeting—which lasts three full weeks—or the spring and fall council meetings. Aside from encouraging appointed delegates to attend, possibly in "shifts" during the annual conference, little can be done to alter this situation.

SUGGESTION: There is no evident solution for the timing problem. Staff members should, of course, be alert to announced changes in the House legislative schedule and bring potential conflicts to the attention of delegation chairmen and/or de facto leaders. Only those chairmen and leaders, however, can make the necessary decisions, which need to be communicated immediately to foreign delegations, and which are too often deferred until the last moment for a variety of perfectly legitimate and understandable reasons. This is essentially a "live-with-it" situation.

4. Public/Media Attitudes toward IPGs: Can Substance Improve Image?

Conventional wisdom has been that media coverage of IPG proceedings and events constitutes a political liability and should be downgraded to the extent possible. Past variations from thistraditional outlook, however, are worth considering: several members of the Mexico-U.S. IPG have discovered in recent years that a number of agenda topics, such as international traffic in arms and narcotics, the illegal alien ("undocumented worker") problem, and an exchange of prisoners treaty, are of major concern at home. Papers which have been presented to the IPG by U.S. delegates have, in fact, been reprinted and summarized in the form of press releases and apparently have been well received in the members' congressional districts.

SUGGESTION: More positive initiatives, with increased emphasis on substance, could undoubtedly be made along these lines. A particularly useful device for stimulating U.S. delegate participation would be to assign individual members specific topics prior to the IPG meetings. Thus, at the recent Washington-based conference with members of the European Parliament, Representatives Fithian, Findley and Fraser, and Senator Sarbanes, respectively, presented papers on such topics as trade and protectionism (focusing on steel imports), nuclear proliferation, human rights, and the IMF Witteveen facility. In addition, Congressman Fascell reported to the group on recent CSCE developments at Belgrade, and Mr. Solarz led off the discussion on the Middle East. Had there been more extensive press coverage of these (open) proceedings and the vigorous—at times heated—rebuttal statements made by the Europeans, some of the distorted characterization of the IPG as an exercise in ceremonial rites and frivolity might have been dispelled.

While media criticism and sensationalism are an ever-pressing reality to be dealt with, in the last analysis the best defense may be an effective offense, in the form of: (1) adequate preparation on the part of U. S. delegates, and (2) the articulate presentation of U.S. positions in IPG fora. To some degree, at least, substance can affect image, provided, of course, that U.S. spokesmen have something timely and significant to contribute.

5. Delegation Travel Costs—Reporting Requirements

As noted above, press and public scrutiny of interparliamentary activities has tended to focus in recent years on the travel expenses incurred by individual members rather than on the purpose of such travel or on matters of substance. Under the Freedom of Information Act, all official travel costs are readily available to media representatives in one form or another, while the *way* such information is reported—and presented to the public—varies widely, depending on an individual agency's or reporter's interpretation.

Under current bookkeeping procedures, Congress has little or no control over expenses incurred and reported by the Department of Defense with respect to travel by interparliamentary delegations on military aircraft. Often the entire cost of moving such aircraft from point A to point B and back is included in lump-sum fashion, possibly including not only food and fuel, but maintenance, salaries of pilot and crew, and related costs which would accrue to the Pentagon in any event. This total is then divided up by the number of delegates who happened to travel on the aircraft at a given time, and reported as if they were individual expenses. The political vulnerability of members of Congress under this system is obviously enormous, and could easily become an effective bar to active participation by House members in future IPG meetings.

The "Obey" Commission. Procedural changes might alleviate this problem significantly. The commission on Administrative Review of the House of Representatives, commonly referred to as the "Obey Commission" (after Congressman David Obey of Wisconsin), specifically recognized this problem, and suggested improvements in a relatively little-known section of its report on "reorganization of the administrative system of the House."

At the suggestion of Hon. Lee Hamilton, Joyce Raupe and I met with the Commission's retiring staff director, Mr. Joseph Cooper, and its General Counsel, Mr. Allen J. Katz, just prior to the expiration of the Commission on December 31, 1977. Two general issues emerged from that discussion:

a. Reimbursement to Defense Department for use of military aircraft. Heretofore the Defense Department has paid for all transportation costs when military aircraft have been used for official congressional travel. This practice has left the record-keeping and reporting in the hands of the Pentagon and has caused considerable embarrassment to members traveling on legitimate business when the Defense-supplied data, as interpreted by Defense, has been publicized.

The Obey Commission recommended that the House reimburse executive agencies for *actual incremental expenses* incurred, namely for food and fuel, *not* for maintenance and operation of aircraft which "would be in use, even if Congress were not using them." In this connection, the Commission points out:

> ... the House can better control how money is spent if the House repays funds spent on behalf of members. It is assumed that departments and agencies will still provide certain routine services for traveling congressional delegations, and that they will only bill Congress for expenses over and above those normally incurred.

Under this procedure, Congress would have an opportunity (presently denied it) to review Defense bills *before* making reimbursement, to ensure that they are accurate and reasonable. Moreover, the *reporting* of such expenditures should accrue to Congress exclusively, and not be left to the accounting "whims" of other departments or agencies.

b. Individual vs. Group Reporting Procedures. The Commission has recommended that members and staff report the money received to defer their official expenses and that committees report the expenses incurred by entire delegations. "Individuals," the report states, "should be held accountable for their own official expenses" (which would include room and board or per diem and any individually authorized in-country transportation). *But,* the Commission concludes:

> ... it does not follow logically that expenses incurred by an entire delegation should be divided equally among those in the delegation and reported as if they were individual expenses. Rather, these expenses are for services which accrue to the entire delegation and frequently serve to benefit the committee authorizing the trip. There are group gains as well as individual gains from committee travel. Thus the Commission feels that expenses attributable to an entire

delegation should be billed to the authorizing committee, accurately reflecting that they are group expenses.[5]

c. In-Country Transportation. Another issue mentioned by the Obey Commission concerned the adverse publicity surrounding congressional travel. Much of that publicity has centered around the relatively high costs of local or "in-country" transportation, which accounts for a high proportion of the expenses incurred by American embassies abroad. While abuses have occurred, in most instances members need local transportation to meet their scheduled commitments in a very limited time. The Commission recommended:

> ... Local transportation for delegations visiting foreign countries has accounted for an extremely high proportion of the expenses associated with congressional travel incurred by local embassies. Local embassies have the ability to handle the travel needs of a small number of visitors, but it is necessary for them to incur extra expenses when large delegations visit. ...

> On occasion it is necessary for members and staff to have rented cars or chauffeurs available for use during official visits. However, frequently these arrangements are made by local embassies without consulting visiting members. Rental and chauffeured cars are extremely expensive in most foreign countries; a significant savings in local transportation costs could be achieved if members and local embassies kept the use of these vehicles to a minimum. Under the provisions of this recommendation, traveling members of Congress must take direct responsibility for these extra expenses by approving rental or chauffeured cars. Moreover, when arrangements such as these are made, the Congress will be billed by the State Department.

COMMENT: The entire question of congressional travel, including accounting and reporting requirements, is evidently a highly technical one, requiring additional study and perhaps debate. The Obey Commission recommendations merely represent one possible approach to the problem, which the committee, and the House as a whole, may wish eventually to consider.

If the committee's consensus is that adoption of some or all of the Commission's foreign travel proposals would be desirable (as distinct from other elements in the report which were rejected), Mr. Katz suggested that the simplest and most expedient procedure might be to have them brought before the organizing caucus in December 1978, following the November elections.

6. Coordination with Speaker's Office

Preliminary discussions with a member of the Speaker's staff have elicited the following suggestions for improved coordination between the committee and the Speaker's office:

a. Press Release and Background Material. Numerous press inquiries are received by that office regarding IPG delegations appointed by the Speaker. Since press releases on specific conferences often are not available until a day or two before the delegates are scheduled to depart, the timely receipt of appropriate background material on the group's activities would be helpful. The emphasis should be on *substance* (issues to be discussed and in what context). Because many agenda items tend to recur, copies of past IPG reports would also be useful.

b. Staff Contact. The Speaker's staff has requested (and received) a list of names and telephone numbers of HIRC staff members involved in various IPG functions. The Speaker's officefrequently needs to consult such individuals, especially at the working level, on *details*, to ensure that statements emanating from that office are consistent with the information being provided by the committee. A system of regular consultation on these matters at the staff level would be mutually beneficial.

c. Follow-up Reports. The Speaker is interested in receiving informal reports from delegation chairmen about members' interest and participation in IPG affairs. Those members who have contributed most to IPG deliberations should, in the Speaker's judgment, be given priority consideration for continuing service as delegates. The minority leader's office has followed this practice in recent years with generally good results.

7. Staff

Most other countries maintain sizable centralized staffs whose duties are *confined* to interparliamentary affairs, both substantive and administrative. For instance, the twenty European parliamentarians who arrived in Washington on November 1 of this year were accompanied by no less than ten staff members, none of whom has any responsibilities for national legislation.

While the establishment of such an operation within the committee is neither practical nor desirable, the staff issue sooner or later will have to be faced. All the interparliamentary groups described in this paper are staffed almost exclusively by the Committee on International Relations. If the present trend toward *more and more* IPGs—with *more and more* meetings and obligations—continues, our present staff resources will not be sufficient to meet the demands placed on them.

SUGGESTION: The above considerations are in the long-range category. For the time being I would merely submit that:

a. No staff member who is involved in the regular legislative work of the committee should be assigned primary responsibility for more than one of the four statutory IPGs and/or the European Parliament. This means that the IPG burden will have to be shared by staff members already on the committee's rolls, and leaves open the question of whether additional staff may eventually be required for a specific group. As noted under c) below, assignments have already been made by the Chief of Staff in accordance with this general principle.

b. The North Atlantic Assembly continues to be a full-time job, requiring the services of at least one staff member, unencumbered by other duties, with the possible exception of informal bilateral groups. This designation is essential, I believe, to very minimal standards of performance which should be met by the U.S. delegation to the assembly.

c. Full committee and subcommittee staff members should become increasingly involved in the substantive preparatory work of the IPGs in their respective areas of expertise. This procedure was adopted on an emergency basis before the November meetings with the European parliamentarians in Washington and worked quite well.

Each IPG has been assigned one staff member with primary direct responsibility for overall coordination, administrative planning and arrangements. It is important, I believe, to have *one* person serve as the focal "clearance" point for all such staff activities, while substantive contributions can—and should—come from a variety of sources.

FINAL COMMENT: Only those who have worked with IPG delegations in the past can really appreciate what the assignment entails. Their collective advice, I have found, is worth listening to.

Notes

3. VICE CONSUL IN GERMANY

1. Some might say John Hemenway lacked finesse and intellectual sophistication. Certainly in his later years he became the quintessential advocate of the confrontational approach against the entire State Department hierarchy, from Rusk and Kissinger on down. His brief tenure as president of the American Foreign Service Association (AFSA) was tumultuous, to say the least. (I am told that at one meeting of the executive committee someone threw a pitcher of water at him, but that has never been officially confirmed.)

   Although I testified in his behalf at the grievance hearing, I have long believed that the real tragedy of the John Hemenway saga was that his considerable executive and conceptual talents were wasted over a period of many years in essentially negative pursuits. So much of value was lost in the process. It all began, however, when John became convinced—not without justification—that he had been "sandbagged" by those very superiors to whom he had provided loyal and devoted service.

5. THE PEACE CORPS—"PRESENT AT THE CREATION"

1. Gerard T. Rice, *The Bold Experiment: JFK's Peace Corps* (Notre Dame, Ind.: University of Notre Dame Press, 1985), 64–66.
2. The emphasis on youth has changed considerably over the years. Retirees from business and the professions are now well represented in the ranks.
3. After Lyndon Johnson took the oath of office as president, it was only a matter of time before Bill Moyers was recalled from Peace Corps headquarters to the White House. There he played several roles, including eventually the most visible one as White

House spokesman (press secretary). The only Kennedy relative whom LBJ appointed to high office was Sargent Shriver, as head of the Office of Economic Opportunity and ambassador to France, among others. I always believed that the early Moyers Peace Corps connection remained a strong motivating factor years later.

Predictably, Bill Moyers did well in all his assignments, evoking criticism only from his puritanical, fussbudget Baptist Church for doing the "frug" at local charity balls. It must have been a great relief when he was finally replaced by George Christian. One could only work for LBJ for so long, unless you were Jack Valenti. (A memorable LBJ quote: "We are replacing a good Baptist like Bill with a Christian like George.")

6. CONSUL IN CROATIA

1. Yugoslavia in my day consisted of six republics, Bosnia-Herzegovina, Croatia, Macedonia, Montenegro, Serbia, and Slovenia, and two "semiautonomous regions," Kosovo (with a 90 percent Albanian majority), and Vojvodina (with a large Hungarian minority).

2. Slivovitz or plum brandy was the universally favored national product. Among foreigners, it was sometimes called "liquid halitosis." One of the local sayings had it that Slivovitz never produced a hangover; you just woke up still drunk! In any case, it was virtually impossible to conduct any business with a Croatian official without first accepting a small shot glass of "sljivo," washed down with Turkish coffee—the "heartburn special," as it was termed. It was not always a welcome experience at 9:00 A.M., but I learned over time that it was best to "get it over with" fast and then state your case!

3. One form that UDBA provocations took were well-dressed young (supposed) "students" requesting help in "escaping" the country. They did not seem overly distressed when I turned them down for visas. Their attire was a giveaway that they were on the UDBA payroll.

4. Krajina was held in the 1990s by Serbian irregular forces, which—with regular Yugoslav army support—effectively expelled all Croat residents from the territory. The Serb objective was to unite this entire border area with Serbia proper. Eventually, in 1995, Croatian forces retook Krajina in a forty-eight-hour invasion, which Yugoslav Prime Minister Slobodan Milošević, desperately trying to get UN sanctions lifted, declined to oppose militarily. Many Croatian Serbs consider him a traitor for this "sin." In 1998, UN troops were still monitoring a tenuous cease-fire.

9. MALAWI MEMORABILIA

1. Bilharzia (also known as liver fluke or schistosomiasis) is spread by a snail in stagnant water and attacks the vital organs, especially the liver, in humans. If untreated, the disease is fatal, although it may be cured completely if caught in its early stages. Most of the streams and small lakes in Malawi were poisoned by bilharzia. By 1969, however, most (but not all) of Lake Malawi was uncontaminated and safe for swimming.

2. Thomas Tull, the British high commissioner, even consulted Marshall regarding personnel problems in his own mission—an unheard-of move by a British diplomat. Tull was a classic stuffed shirt, cordially disliked by the entire British community, including (rumor had it) by his own DCM and staff. On one occasion, His Excellency complained to Ambassador Jones that he was running into a lot of red tape getting the "Thomas Tull trophy" accepted for presentation at the Malawi national soccer championship match. "Try calling it the H. Kamuzu Banda trophy," Marshall suggested. The idea was brilliant—and it worked!

3. The Malawi flag never made it to the moon, because Malawi's ambassador to the United Nations, Mbekeani, was late submitting it to Washington for inclusion in the Apollo capsule along with miniature flags from other UN member states. The Ngwasi was never informed of this lapse, however, so nothing was lost in the long run. The particles from the moon's surface were genuine.

4. Malawi reporters who covered VIPs arriving at the airport were not abrasive or intrusive, but shy, retiring, and gentle. One had to encourage them to speak, in fact, and Marshall Jones made a habit of taking them off in a corner where they were less rattled by public exposure. Later in the same day, however, their editor would call to "clarify" the situation!

5. Lt. Col. Willie Haywood was a highly professional black American officer who had served in Vietnam with distinction. Dr. Banda at first viewed him with suspicion: "Don't send me any more of your 'front-office' niggers," he once told the shocked Marshall Jones. "I don't like to be patronized." Willie was not fully accepted by the president until a British brigadier, the top adviser to the minuscule Malawi army, certified Willie's professional credentials to the Ngwasi. Shades of the attitude Banda displayed in the meeting with Congressman Diggs, reported earlier!

10. STARTING OUT ON THE HILL

1. This outlook is very different from that in a parliamentary form of government. British Foreign Office professionals, the equivalent of our FSOs, for instance, are deeply involved in parliamentary affairs from day one, as their ultimate boss, the foreign

secretary, is a member of Parliament. The latter is not only deeply immersed in day-to-day legislative matters but is also periodically subjected to "question period" in the House of Commons. Foreign Office staff members must thus be as familiar as their ministers with the inner workings of the national legislature.

2. A recent newsletter sent out by Rodney Frelinghuysen (Peter's son who now holds his father's seat) indicates that as of May 1998 the congressman representing New Jersey's Fifth District has successfully kept the arsenal open.

11. THE INFLUENTIAL HOUSE FOREIGN AFFAIRS COMMITTEE

1. Peter Frelinghuysen and William S. Mailliard of California were equally senior and politically compatible, representing the "international" wing of the party in foreign affairs.

2. David McCullough, *Truman* (New York: Simon and Schuster, 1992), p. 404.

12 AN ECLECTIC COMMITTEE STAFF

1. Chief of staff, staff administrator, and staff director were interchangeable terms for the top staff members of the committee. The incumbents themselves chose their preferred term, often for personal reasons. Boyd Crawford called himself "staff administrator" as an act of deliberate modesty, since he once shared the staff leadership with a Harvard professor. Boyd's successor, Roy Bullock (who also ruled the staff with an iron hand) used the same title. Marian Czarnecki later changed the designation to chief of staff—perhaps to emphasize his preeminent role when subcommittee staffs were proliferating. His successor, Jack Brady, kept that term, probably also because he had once been an army colonel. Technical or legislatively, however, we were all "clerks."

2. The term "clerk" enjoyed a much higher status historically than is generally understood today. In the early days of the republic, the third-ranking officer in the Department of State was the clerk, and he enjoyed almost unlimited institutional power. In Congress, the term "clerk" was evidently incorporated into the original law providing for committee staff. To the best of my knowledge, that provision was never changed. Hence, we were all "clerks," despite our grandiose titles on official committee lists. When the chairman calls for a vote in committee, in fact, he always says: "The Clerk will call the roll."

3. An administrative assistant (AA) is the chief of staff in a congressman's office. There are no AAs on committees.

4. The staff worked in partitioned-off areas, slightly larger than a cubicle or carrel but smaller than a normal-sized room. A desk, several chairs, one or two filing cabinets, and perhaps a side

table filled with books, publications, and miscellaneous papers, but not much else, filled up the space. Even the staff administrator occupied one of these half-rooms at the front end of the corridor. Eventually, Roy Bullock's successor moved to an actual room (albeit a windowless one) just off the front reception area.

13 THE COMMITTEE'S LEGISLATIVE ACTIVITIES

1. U.S. Congress, House of Representatives, 92d Congress, 1st Session, *Staff Memorandum on Treasury Borrowing and Foreign Aid—A Recapitulation*, printed for the use of the Committee on Foreign Affairs (Washington: U.S. Government Printing Office, 1971).

14 AROUND THE WORLD WITH CONGRESSMAN FRELINGHUYSEN

1. Tikki Kaul was subsequently to become India's ambassador to the United States. During his Washington tour, a large brouhaha took place over India's testing and explosion of a nuclear bomb. The ambassador appeared on numerous television news broadcasts, defending the Indian decision in his usual sarcastic and abrasive manner. In the traditional Krishna Menon modus operandi, he managed to exacerbate the problem in the court of U.S. public opinion. His performance was totally in character.
2. George Warren later joined the Foreign Affairs Committee staff after my retirement. He died of a heart attack while seated in a chair next to *my* old desk!
3. U.S. Congress, House of Representatives, 93d Congress, 2nd Session, *Old Problems—New Relationships*, Report of a Study Mission to the Middle East and South Asia, to the Committee on Foreign Affairs (Washington: U.S. Government Printing Office, 1974).
4. U.S. Congress, House of Representatives, 93d Congress, 2nd Session, *Vietnam—A Changing Crucible*, Report of a Study Mission to South Vietnam, to the Committee on Foreign Affairs (Washington: U S. Government Printing Office, 1974).

15. STAFF STUDY MISSIONS TO ASIA, AFRICA, AND LATIN AMERICA

1. U.S. Congress, House of Representatives, 93d Congress, 1st Session, *Report of a Staff Survey Team to the Committee on Foreign Affairs, The Peace Corps in the 1970s* (Washington: U.S. Government Printing Office, 1973).
2. Kevin Lowther and C. Payne Lucas, *Keeping Kennedy's Promise: The Peace Corps, Unmet Hope of the New Frontier* (Boulder, Colo.: Westview Press, 1978), chap. 2, "The Numbers Game."
3. TEFL is the same as TESOL, but for some reason the nomenclature was different in Thailand.

4. U.S. Congress, House of Representatives, 94th Congress, 2nd Session, *Report of a Staff Survey Team to the Committee on International Relations, The Peace Corps in West Africa* (Washington: U.S. Government Printing Office, 1976).

5. U.S. Congress, House of Representatives, 95th Congress, 1st Session, *Report of a Staff Survey Team to the Committee on International Relations, U.S. Information and Cultural Programs: Focus on Latin America, 1976* (Washington: U.S. Government Printing Office, 1977).

6. In the mid-1990s Senator Jesse Helms, chairman of the Foreign Relations Committee, made a serious and effective attempt to abolish USIA and return its functions to State. The Clinton administration was ambivalent. Helms said Secretary of State Warren Christopher favored the idea, while other administration officials disagreed. An amended version of Helms's views finally won out.

16 THE INTERPARLIAMENTARY CIRCUIT

1. The committee was known as the Committee on International Relations from January 1975 until December 1978 (94th to 95th Congresses), when it was changed back to Foreign Affairs. After the Republicans took over the House in 1995, it was changed back to International Relations again.

2. He had asked me to accompany him, but I had the good fortune to be involved with another project at the time. Jim Scholbert, a relatively new staff member eventually assigned to this mission, was left behind in Georgetown, Guyana, to make room for a media staffer. Had I been along, I probably would have insisted on going to Jonestown, as Zablocki's chief representative. My good luck!

17. SPEECHWRITER AND "POET LAUREATE"

1. Evan Thomas, *The Very Best Men* (New York: Simon and Schuster, 1995), p. 29.

APPENDIX B: HOUSE PARTICIPATION IN INTERPARLIAMENTARY ACTIVITIES

1. Although the Assembly has allotted the United States a total of thirty-six delegate positions (or eighteen from each House), the legislation enacted by Congress provides for the appointment of only twelve U.S. delegates (or six from each House). The number of delegates was increased from nine to twelve by P. L. 95–45, which did not go into effect until June 15, 1977.

2. The following schedule for 1978 is a typical Assembly schedule after a major session:

23–25 Jan.	Meeting of Joint Subcommittee on Defense Cooperation in Washington, D. C.
25–27 Jan.	Meeting of Economic Committee at OECD — Paris
27 Feb.–2 Mar.	Subcommittee on Northern Region — Oslo and Copenhagen
2 Mar.	Subcommittee on Defense — Washington, D.C.
20–21 Mar.	Standing Committee — Washington, D.C.
22–24 Mar.	Joint Subcommittee on Energy Policy — Washington, D.C.
25–28 May	Spring Committee Meetings — Brussels
24–28 July	Subcommittee on Northern Region — London and Reykjavik
1–14 Aug.	Study Tour of Northern Region — starts at SHAPE, Brussels
25 Nov.–1 Dec.	1978 Plenary session — Lisbon

3. In terms of member participation, in most cases Washington has proven to be the least desirable site for interparliamentary meetings held in the United States. Just too many other crises and distractions exist here. When the House is in session, however, especially toward the close of a busy legislative year, Washington has emerged as the only practical alternative, as proved to be the case with the fall 1977 meeting of the European Parliament.

4. Papers distributed to members' offices frequently get lost or are not brought to members' attention in a timely fashion. Example: prior to the January 1978 meeting of the European Parliament here, three separate memoranda, including two with program schedules attached, were sent to all HIRC members, all members of the Ways and Means Committee, and to the offices of all known past participants in these conferences. As the conference convened, however, or after it was over, the committee received numerous telephone calls from members and staff claiming total ignorance of the proceedings.

5. The term "delegation" refers to CODELS involved in study missions under the authority of the "authorizing committees." In the case of the statutory interparliamentary groups, which are funded by special House resolution, delegation expenses would be paid from official delegation funds, since there is no "authorizing committee" as such.

Index